ProgressionSeries

Law

For entry to university and college in 2010

PUBLISHED BY: UCAS ROSEHILL NEW BARN LANE CHELTENHAM GL52 3LZ

PRODUCED IN CONJUNCTION WITH GTI SPECIALIST PUBLISHERS

© UCAS 2009

UCAS REGISTERED IN ENGLAND NUMBER: 2839815
REGISTERED CHARITY NUMBER IN ENGLAND AND WALES: 1024741
REGISTERED CHARITY NUMBER IN SCOTLAND: SC038598

ISBN: 978-1-84361-108-0

UCAS REFERENCE NUMBER: PU035010
PUBLICATION REFERENCE: 09_026

UCAS ACCEPTS ADVERTISING FOR PUBLICATION THAT PROMOTES PRODUCTS AND SERVICES RELATING TO HIGHER EDUCATION AND CAREER PROGRESSION. REVENUE GENERATED BY ADVERTISING IS INVESTED BY UCAS IN ORDER TO ENHANCE OUR APPLICATIONS SERVICES AND TO KEEP THE COST TO APPLICANTS AS LOW AS POSSIBLE.

UCAS DOES NOT ENDORSE THE PRODUCTS AND SERVICES OF OTHER ORGANISATIONS THAT APPEAR IN THIS PUBLICATION.

FURTHER COPIES AVAILABLE FROM WWW.UCASBOOKS.COM

POST: UCAS MEDIA PO BOX 130 CHELTENHAM GL52 3ZF
E: publicationservices@ucas.ac.uk F: +44 (0)1242 544 806

FURTHER INFORMATION ABOUT THE UCAS APPLICATION PROCESS
T: +44 (0)871 468 0 468 F: +44 (0)1242 544 961

CALLS TO THE 0871 NUMBER QUOTED ABOVE FROM BT LANDLINES WITHIN THE UK WILL COST NO MORE THAN £0.09 PER MINUTE. CALLS FROM MOBILES AND OTHER NETWORKS MAY VARY.

UCAS QUALITY AWARDS

Contents

UCAS gti

Foreword

THINKING ABOUT LAW?

Researching the type of course you would like to study at higher education level means that you are halfway towards choosing the right qualification for you. Knowing which subject or subjects you would enjoy is a distinct advantage, but each course can vary depending on the specific areas covered and the university or college you choose to attend. Even if the course title is the same at a number of institutions, it does not mean that the content or teaching methods will be the same. Finding a university or college which will suit you academically and personally can take time.

Throughout the year there are opportunities to visit the different universities and colleges, where advisers can tell you about the courses in detail and you can see where you will be living and studying for the next few years of your life.

Speaking to former students of the course you would like to study is extremely useful – they can give you an insider's view of university life and of the teaching standards that you could not find anywhere else.

We at UCAS have teamed up with GTI Specialist Publishers to provide careers advice and real-life case studies in *Progression to Law*. You will find information on careers in this subject area, entry routes and advice on applying through UCAS, and course listings. We hope you find this publication helps you to choose a course and university that is right for you.

Applying for higher education through **www.ucas.com** has never been easier: the UCAS website has everything you need to know, from a Course Search with entry requirements, short videos to help you choose your courses and make your application. Plus lots more! The online application is clear and

simple to use; with help at hand online and from our
team of telephone advisers should you need them.

On behalf of UCAS and GTI Specialist Publishers, I
wish you every success in your research.

Anthony McClaran, Chief Executive, UCAS

Introducing law

ProgressionSeries

It could be you…

… prosecuting a careless hit-and-run driver	– criminal law
… drafting a sponsorship deal for premier-league football	– sport law
… bringing an employment tribunal case for unfair dismissal	– employment law
… negotiating terms on a commercial lease for a retail chain	– real estate law
… drawing up a finance deal for a film production company	– media law
… conducting 'due diligence' on a large corporate merger	– corporate law
… fighting a newspaper's claim on freedom of expression	– human rights law
… arranging paperwork on foster care or adoption	– family law
… registering a patent on an entrepreneur's new invention	– intellectual property law

… and lots more besides. Could a career in the legal profession be for you? The aim of this guide is to help you decide.

A CAREER IN LAW?

Here are a few facts you should know if you want to work in the legal profession.

- You don't need to take a law degree to become a lawyer – see **Entry routes** on page 51
- Admissions tutors and legal recruiters look at your grades, and at your communication and problem-solving ability – see **Is law for you?** on page 30
- Qualifying as a solicitor or barrister takes five to eight years' full-time study – see **Entry routes** on page 51
- 78% of solicitors work in private practice – see **A career as a solicitor** on page 17
- Most barristers are self-employed – see **A career as a barrister** on page 19

THE LAW IN CONTEXT

From birth to death, aspects of legislation and the legal system help shape the framework within which we live our lives: from the age at which you can take your driving test, to the speed at which you can drive when you pass it; from the minimum wage you can expect to earn in a new job, to the rights to which you're entitled should you lose it. Such laws are:

- initially brought into being by the governing authorities, ie Parliament and the European Union, on behalf of the society that they represent
- overwhelmingly designed to bring order to or 'regulate' society
- hopefully adhered to by that society's citizens
- ultimately upheld by the courts and the legal system.

THE ENGLISH LEGAL SYSTEM

At the heart of the English legal system is a hierarchical court structure, split into civil and criminal courts. In civil courts, organisations and individuals may bring cases against each other for a whole range of 'civil' law issues, eg breach of contract, discrimination, unfair dismissal, human rights, and data protection. In criminal courts, eg dealing with cases of murder, manslaughter, domestic violence and child abuse, the 'Crown' always prosecutes the accused.

Minor criminal cases, and some licensing applications, are normally heard in the **magistrates' courts.** There is no jury; instead a bench of elected magistrates (also known as justices of the peace) hear each case and decide on a suitable sentence.

County courts are where civil cases are heard. Again, no jury is usually involved. Instead, judge will preside over hearings on their own, dealing with such cases as divorce hearings, private family issues, and care and adoption proceedings.

The **highest court** for the whole of the UK is the **House of Lords**, which only considers appeals on points of law, heard by five Law Lords.

However, if the point at issue is from **European Community law**, the case may be referred to the **European Court of Justice** for a guide on interpretation.

Solicitors and barristers

Advising on, and ultimately enforcing, the law falls to two main groups of legal professionals – barristers and solicitors. Although recent rules have blurred the lines between the two roles, they remain two distinct professions with two distinct training and career structures.

If you're interested in a possible career in law, then this guide can help point you further in the right direction.

Read on to discover:

- the main roles on offer
- the skills and educational grades legal recruiters look for
- how to get into university or college and the routes to qualification as a professional lawyer
- advice from young lawyers in different areas of practice.

Why law?

Choose a career that is...

VARIED

The two branches of the profession – the Bar and the solicitors' profession – offer very different careers. Intending barristers are often motivated by the advocacy opportunities and the freedom that comes with essentially working for yourself. Solicitors, on the other hand, may be driven by increased client contact, teamwork and the security of a regular pay cheque. Either way, if you want to experience working with different people on a variety of projects, a career in law is the way to do it.

AT THE CENTRE OF THINGS

A career in law affords the opportunity to work with interesting people and businesses on projects vital to everyday existence. Lawyers are often at the centre of a web of other professionals, such as bankers, accountants and investors. Working with leaders in industry and business can definitely be a big attraction of the job.

RISK RESISTANT

When other professions, such as banking and IT, ease off on recruitment during an economic downturn, law stays largely cheerful. The profession is, on the whole, less vulnerable to market highs and lows. True, certain practice areas thrive during boom times, but others, such as family law, insolvency and litigation, do well no matter how the City is faring.

(LARGELY) WELL PAID

Average starting salaries for trainee solicitors vary enormously depending on the type of firm you go to. Those heading for firms with large corporate clients can expect to be paid well from day one, whereas those who take on legally aided work will take home a much more modest salary. Life at the commercial and chancery Bar offers lucrative work and large pupillage awards, whereas criminal barristers need to get three or four years' experience under their belt before matching their counterparts in solicitors' firms.

OPEN TO LAW AND NON-LAW GRADUATES ALIKE

You don't need a law degree to be a lawyer and your degree subject will not be at the top of many recruiters' wish lists. Some of the skills needed to become a good lawyer – analytical, research and teamwork skills – are often developed during non-law degrees. In fact, non-law graduates can bring a different perspective to their work and the legal profession likes to recruit people from a variety of backgrounds.

WHAT DO LAWYERS SAY?

"Every day is different: as a trainee solicitor you are given exposure to as many matters as possible. I have spent some days on conference calls, attending meetings and taking notes, and other days doing legal research or drafting letters, court documents and defences."
Anand Gangadia, trainee solicitor, Herbert Smith

"Being self-employed is great but the camaraderie and support of being in chambers with other barristers is wonderful too."
Elizabeth Searley, tenant, 6 King's Bench Walk

"I'm given a great deal of responsibility, ranging from drafting and negotiating documents directly with other solicitors and serving papers in Court right through to managing whole cases from start to finish."
Alistair Rattray, trainee solicitor, Burges Salmon LLP

"I work with several different people at different levels of their career on a daily basis, both within the firm's London office and from other locations as far flung as Sydney, New York, Bangkok and Beijing."
Sarah Cramp, trainee solicitor, Baker & McKenzie LLP

a parent?

get the facts about higher education

Exclusive parents' website

To find out all about higher education and the application process, log on to our new website, exclusively for parents.

Free guide for parents

For a wealth of information about finance, student welfare and selecting the right course and university or college, register online and receive your free copy of the Parent Guide and bi-monthly email bulletins.

Register today at www.ucas.com/parents

Your career should be your choice

Which is why we give you so many.

TARGETjobs *City & Finance*, TARGETjobs *Civil & Structural Engineering*, TARGETjobs *Construction (School Leaver edition)*, TARGETjobs *Construction & Building Services Engineering*, TARGETjobs *Engineering*, TARGETjobs *Finance & Law Channel Islands*, TARGETjobs *IT*, TARGETjobs *Law*, TARGETjobs *Law Scotland*, TARGETjobs *Management Consulting*, TARGETjobs *Property*, TARGETjobs *Public Service*, TARGETjobs *Quantity Surveying & Building Surveying*, TARGETjobs *Retail Management & Sales*, TARGETjobs *Teaching*, TARGETjobs *Work Experience*, TARGETjobs *Work Experience Law*, TARGETjobs *Europe*, TARGETjobs *Magazine*, TARGETjobs *Diversity*, TARGETjobs *First*, GET directory, *The Careers Centre Guide Aston, The Careers Centre Guide Birmingham, The Bristol Guide to Career Planning, The Cambridge Careers Guide, The Careers Service Guide Cardiff, The Durham Guide to Career Planning, The Careers Service Guide Edinburgh, The Exeter Careers Service Guide, The Careers Service Guide Glasgow, The Imperial College London Careers Advisory Service Guide, The Leeds Guide to Career Planning, The Careers Service Guide Leicester, The Careers Service Guide London, The Careers Guide Loughborough, The Manchester Careers Guide, The Careers Service Guide Newcastle, Guide to Career Development Nottingham, The Careers Guide - (Oxford's edition), The Careers Guide Queen's University Belfast, The Careers Service Guide Sheffield, The Career Planning Guide Southampton, The Careers Centre Guide St Andrews, The Trinity Careers Service Guide, The Warwick Careers Guide, The Cambridge Guide to Careers in Asia, The Imperial College London Guide to Careers in Asia, The LSE Guide to Careers in Asia, The Asia Careers Guide — (Oxford's edition), London Business School Guide to Career Services, INSEAD Alumni Speak,* TARGETcourses *Conversion & Vocational Law, Pupillages Handbook,* TARGETjobs *Engineering Design & Construction*

Pick up a free copy of one of our publications from your careers service or academic department.

TARGETjobs

more **graduate jobs** and **careers intelligence**

Solicitor
or barrister?

ProgressionSeries

Solicitor or barrister?

SOLICITOR	BARRISTER
Mostly employed in private law firms, so receives regular monthly salary	Mostly self-employed, so receives irregular (but often substantial) fees
Deals more with the public	Deals more with solicitors and other barristers
Office-based	Chambers and court-based
Engages more in ongoing advisory and one-to-one client work	Engages more in one-off advocacy, ie court cases
Aspires to 'partner', ie part ownership of the firm, and entitled to a percentage of its profits	Aspires to 'silk', ie to becoming Queen's Counsel (QC)

A career as a solicitor

There are currently more than 130,000 practising solicitors in the UK. Solicitors are the first point of contact for the 'client', ie an organisation or member of the public.

SOLICITORS

As a solicitor, you'll provide clients with expert legal advice and assistance. In 'contentious' cases, ie where there is a dispute, the solicitor then contacts a barrister's office, called 'chambers', and 'instructs' a barrister to act as advocate on their client's behalf. The barrister then has two clients – the solicitor and the organisation or individual they represent. The barrister will deal primarily with the solicitor rather than the solicitor's client.

Role

For many solicitors, much of the day-to-day work involves 'non-contentious' work, such as drawing up contracts, negotiating terms on behalf of clients and advising on policy. The precise work solicitors perform will depend largely on the type of firm for which they work.

- **High-street firms:** These mostly advise individual clients on a range of legal issues, such as buying or selling a house, divorce papers, personal injury claims, drawing up wills.
- **Large firms:** These are usually based in large cities, and many have offices in different countries. They will mostly advise corporate clients on topics such as banking, employment law, mergers and acquisitions, defending personal injury claims from customers, corporate taxation.
- **Niche firms:** These firms are mostly in the corporate field and will specialise in a particular aspect of corporate or commercial law, eg media, shipping, construction.

SOLICITOR STATS

- **Around 76%** of solicitors in England and Wales work in private practice.
- **Women** now make up over 40% of the profession.
- **At least 10%** of those qualifying into the profession are from ethnic minority backgrounds.

- **Public sector:** Central government solicitors are employed to draft and advise government on public legislation. Local government solicitors may find themselves working in child welfare, local employment, housing issues.

Pay

Salaries vary from the Law Society's £16,790 recommended starting salary for trainee solicitors outside London (£18,870 in London) to average salaries of £44,000 for an associate solicitor and £64,051 for an equity partner in private practice (Law Society solicitor salaries 2008).

Working conditions

It is hard to generalise, but for the most part, solicitors are more likely than barristers to work a regular, though often long, 'office' day. Extra long hours and even 'all-nighters' are to be expected, especially in commercial or corporate law when working on completing a deal, or prior to a tribunal or court case in other areas of law, when preparing a client and a case.

The long-term career path

There is no typical timeline, and different firms may operate different structures with more levels in between. According to the Law Society, the best solicitors combine expert legal knowledge with people skills to help their clients cope. The typical career path is **trainee – assistant/associate solicitor – partner.**

SOLICITOR ADVOCATES

Since July 2000, solicitors have had the right to appear as 'solicitor advocates' in some courts, blurring the line between solicitors' and barristers' roles. If they obtain further advocacy training and qualification, solicitors may even appear before the higher courts (eg Crown Court), but without the traditional wig and gown worn by barristers.

A career as a barrister

There are currently more than 14,000 practising barristers in the UK; opportunities are much more limited in this branch of the legal profession.

BARRISTERS

Barristers are specialist legal advisers and courtroom advocates. They are independent and objective and trained to advise clients on the strengths as well as the weaknesses of their case.

Role

Their principal role is to represent their clients in court. However, the amount of time they spend in court depends on the area of law in which they specialise and the complexity of the case. A criminal barrister will spend more time in court, while a civil law barrister involved in a complex case based on contract law, for example, will spend more time on advisory work, writing opinions in chambers, ie barristers' offices.

BARRISTERS IN BRIEF

- As of December 2007, there were over 12,000 self-employed barristers (Bar Council).
- Around 66.6% of barristers work in London-based chambers.
- **Women** now make up 50% of those called to the Bar and in pupillage.

Pay

It is hard to provide a typical salary for barristers; it's the classic 'how long is a piece of string?' question. Dozens of QCs (top barristers called Queen's Counsel or 'silks') earn more than £1 million per year, while many barristers earn £250,000+, yet new barristers may earn as little as £25,000 per year in their first few years. Trainee or 'pupil' barristers are only guaranteed £10,000 in their training or 'pupillage' year, although many chambers now pay them much more, sometimes up to £45,000. The general rule of thumb when it comes to solicitor vs barrister pay, however, is that solicitors earn more early on while barristers are building their reputations, a gap which many barristers more than make up for later on in their careers.

Most barristers are **self-employed**, working out of chambers, with only 2,972 at the 'Employed Bar', ie as employees of either the government or industry. Being self-employed means barristers can, in theory, set their own hours when they are not appearing in court. On court days, their time is set for them by the court system, which is more concerned about maximising a judge's time, so delays and adjournments are not uncommon. Their self-employed status also means they have to contribute a share to the running costs of their chambers.

Working conditions

Stories of afternoon tea at 3pm in chambers, and the splendour (in London, where most chambers are based) of the physical environment in which barristers work, help create a sense of a very civilised, genteel profession. However, this belies the intense competition, the analytical and legal rigour, and the irregular pace of a barrister's work. It is just as possible to find a barrister sitting at Euston station, en route to a regional circuit court, eating a shrink-wrapped sandwich and reading a dossier on a case, while waiting for a train.

The long-term career path

There is no specific timeline laid down for progression, since barristers' reputations and fee-earning capacity depend as much on the cases they win as the length of time they've been practising at the Bar. The long-term career path is **pupil – barrister – Queen's Counsel**.

QUEEN'S COUNSEL (QC)

- Being appointed Queen's Counsel (QC) is a mark of outstanding ability. QCs are normally instructed in very serious or complex cases. Most senior judges once practised as QCs.

Which area?

Only those outside the profession see 'law' as one profession or general career path. Those inside the profession know that there is a whole range of options and career choices once you've made your solicitor vs barrister decision. This section outlines some of the main areas of practice in which you can specialise.

COMMON LAW

The work

General common law encompasses a wide range of claims based on contract law and tort, such as personal injury, clinical negligence, product liability, professional negligence, contractual disputes, nuisance, fires, floods and property damage. Solicitors' firms usually specialise in one or two of these areas of practice, eg personal injury, while barristers have conventionally handled a broader range of work.

The conditions

Trainee solicitors normally work (nearly) conventional office hours and spend a lot of time liaising with clients. Barristers often draft pleadings or advise on a number of different cases at a time. In recent years, conditional fee agreements (CFAs), which effectively allow people to bring claims at no financial risk to themselves, have led to a growth in the number, but not the quality, of claims. Many barristers report an increase in their earnings as a result of the fees they can earn in successful cases, but there is a risk they can end up with no fee at all if they lose.

The upside

There is a great deal of variety and the prospect of lots of advocacy. It's usual for less experienced barristers to cut their teeth on low-value personal injury claims.

The downside

Losing a case while on a conditional fee agreement, thereby earning nothing for all your hard work. A large number of cases also settle, so you can miss out on a deliciously exciting trial if a worried claimant loses their nerve as the prospect of a few hours in the witness box approaches.

CORPORATE/COMMERCIAL

The work

As a solicitor, you could be working on the 'deal' side, which includes mergers and acquisitions, and IPOs (initial public offerings), ie stock market flotations for companies. The commercial side involves drafting and negotiating contracts for corporate clients, and advising them on issues such as tax, data protection, competition law and regulatory issues. Clients range from international businesses to small start-ups. As a barrister, practising commercial law generally involves helping to resolve disputes between businesses, from takeovers that have gone wrong to disagreements involving small businesses.

The conditions

Weekend work and all-nighters are not unheard of. You may work late (for example, drafting urgent contracts) but this is balanced by quieter periods.

The upside

The pay (corporate lawyers are among the most highly paid, whether solicitor or barrister) and, for solicitors, international travel.

The downside

Having to cancel social engagements because you're working on a deal. Occasionally you'll also need to make important decisions under pressure and on the basis of limited information.

CRIME

The work

Criminal lawyers find themselves advising, and, if they're barristers, prosecuting or defending, people involved in incidents ranging from muggings to murder. A guilty plea can be dealt with in a couple of days or less, but a more complex case can take months just to come to trial.

The conditions

Solicitors in this field will be called upon to represent clients at police stations during out-of-office hours on a rota system. On non-rota days, you can expect to work a more regular nine-to-five schedule.

The upside

The unpredictability of what case you'll have next.

The downside

For solicitors, not being appreciated by the general public; for barristers, being given very short notice to prepare a case.

EMPLOYMENT

The work

As a solicitor in this field, you'll be working on 'contentious' work, ie employment tribunal or high court litigation, and 'non-contentious' work, eg drafting contracts of employment, advising on dispute resolution, working hours, family-friendly policies, such as maternity leave, child care schemes etc. Your client could be the employer or the employee. As a barrister, you'll be appearing on behalf of the employee or employer in (mostly) a tribunal or court.

The conditions

This is a growing field, thanks to all the new EU employment legislation. Occasional late nights preparing a tribunal case are to be expected. For barristers, tribunals are held all over the country, so a fair bit of travelling is involved. 'Instructions' can also come in quite late, so it may require late nights or early mornings to prepare for the case.

The upside

The human element to all your work.

The downside

People are relying on your success, which can lead to tremendous lows if things go against you in court.

EUROPEAN

The work

Many aspects of day-to-day life and work are affected not just by English law, but also by the rulings of the European Court of Justice and EU legislation. The areas covered can range from environment to taxation, employment to finance and competition to contract. This area of practice is fast-changing. Recently, for example, as national courts have been given more authority, uncertainty has arisen as decisions vary between member states.

The conditions

Clients include the government, individuals and companies, both large and small. Company cases can include competition complaints, fines, issues about tax and VAT, and public procurement. Lawyers in this field work hard, but are unlikely to work through the night on a regular basis. Tasks include looking at new areas, researching points of law, drafting, making small applications, participating in case management hearings before national courts and tribunals,

occasional trips to Luxembourg, Strasbourg or Brussels and assisting more senior lawyers.

The upside

This area of practice is very buoyant, due to the growth of European legislation, and the work is intellectually challenging and varied.

The downside

Constant changes to EU law mean you have to work hard to stay up to date with developments, especially as cases sometimes take years to reach a conclusion. Corporate clients can also be very demanding.

FAMILY

The work

Broadly speaking, family lawyers are split into two categories: those dealing with financial settlements on divorce and child-related issues, and those dealing with children, including care work, local authorities and adoption. Solicitors' clients are often families going through painful processes, but they may also be local authorities.

The conditions

This area is relatively recession-proof, so it is one of the more stable fields for lawyers. The post-holiday months of January and September are reputedly the busiest times for new clients. Family solicitors don't tend to burn the midnight oil, but work intensely during office hours. Regular client contact is common. For barristers, most of the emphasis is on negotiation, especially in child contact cases, so it should involve fewer court appearances and more in-chambers conferences.

The upside

The relationships and trust that you can build with clients.

The downside

The sometimes unreasonable demands of clients. For barristers, the low rates of pay for publicly funded work.

HUMAN RIGHTS

The work

This field of law is wide-ranging and includes immigration or asylum cases; privacy cases affecting celebrities; and news organisations seeking to protect their freedom of expression. The solicitor's client base will be equally wide-ranging, from a low-income refugee being advised by a *pro bono* lawyer, to a large news organisation or a government department.

The conditions

This area of work is extremely buoyant, as more and more cases are brought under the Human Rights Act. Cases vary in length, from an injunction in privacy obtained within two hours of taking instructions, to a fully contested case that can last up to two years. Human rights lawyers may occasionally work unpredictable hours in short sharp bursts – for example, injunctions can happen outside working hours.

The upside

Your success can make a huge difference to a whole section of society.

The downside

Trying to persuade clients that not every wrong perpetrated on them is a breach of their 'human rights'.

INSOLVENCY

The work

Insolvency law demands both technical knowledge and commercial awareness, and is a very buoyant area of practice. Insolvency lawyers are involved in restructuring companies in financial difficulties or, where a company cannot be rescued, ensuring the proper distribution of assets of the insolvent company among its creditors. Typical clients are restructuring teams at accountancy firms, banks, bond-holders and licensed insolvency practitioners.

The conditions

For solicitors, formal insolvency procedures may involve a court order that outlines a plan for creditors to be paid in a way that best suits the client. The most commonly used procedure is known as 'administration'. Actual cases vary a great deal in size and complexity. A junior barrister will work alone on smaller cases, where they may receive papers a week or so in advance. Larger cases can last for anything up to five years and will involve at least one senior barrister.

The upside

Being able to apply the law to a set of facts and arrive at a solution that will benefit as many different parties as possible. There is also a very strong sense of camaraderie between insolvency professionals.

The downside

As service providers, insolvency lawyers have to be accessible to their clients – this can result in a few late nights, although all-nighters are rare.

INTELLECTUAL PROPERTY

The work

This involves protecting the exploitation of intellectual ideas. For example, it may range from securing copyright in a hit single, to contesting a 'copycat' logo, to registering a patent for a new pharmaceutical formula in different jurisdictions. Some cases can take a year or more to get to court, and involve numerous appeals. This is a very technical field, and one in which there is seldom a black and white answer, so it would suit lawyers who enjoy ferreting around in legal documents for minute points of law on which to build cases. There is no such thing as a 'typical' client. They range from entrepreneurs about to launch their first product to established multinationals, and every variation in between.

The conditions

An IP lawyer's workload will fluctuate. A big transaction or the run-up to a court hearing can be all-consuming, so IP lawyers may need to work through the night to meet a deadline or prepare complex court cases.

The upside

Growing with your client; for example, you could act for a fledgling company of two science researchers and then help them develop into an organisation with a significant number of staff and a portfolio of patents.

The downside

Copyright can be fiendishly complicated and the legal cases very protracted.

MEDIA

The work

This is a mix of IP law (especially copyright) and more general commercial law. Copyright is a broad field affecting many aspects of media law, such as protection of a footballer's image, or the use of a painting on a DVD cover. Media lawyers represent bands, celebrities, film and TV producers, broadcasters, distributors and lenders, among others.

The conditions

As a result of the recent development of digital TV channels, this field is very buoyant. It involves peaks and troughs of workload, and lawyers' hours are affected by the end of the tax or financial year.

The upside

Even a potentially dull sub-licensing agreement takes on a whole new level of interest when one of the contracting parties did the song that was on the radio when you were dressing for work.

The downside

Disputes are often factually complex, and nobody in the media ever seems to write anything down, so piecing together what may actually have happened is often difficult!

PRIVATE CLIENT

The work

Private client lawyers advise on all aspects of the financial affairs of clients who are 'high-net worth' individuals, but the core work involves advising on capital gains tax, setting up lifetime trusts and preparing wills. Some clients have more specialist needs – for example, landed clients might include farmers with thousands of acres seeking advice on how to structure their business or owners of historic estates open to the public who need advice on protecting their heritage assets. Wealthy philanthropists also normally seek advice on ways to donate to charities that are tax-efficient both for them and for the receiving organisation.

The conditions

Increasing numbers of people fall above the inheritance tax threshold, so there is a greater need for individual 'lifetime planning'. Busy periods arise around the time of the Budget and the end of the financial year but, by nature, this work does not carry the same time pressures associated with commercial law, and therefore late nights are relatively unusual.

The upside

Getting to know clients well, and becoming a vital support to them and their families.

The downside

This area of law is extremely complex, and can be a little daunting when starting out. Also, the more sedate pace may disappoint those seeking the fast pace of, say, commercial law.

PROPERTY AND REAL ESTATE

The work

Essentially this covers all matters to do with property, particularly transactions and the relationship between landlord and tenant – especially disputes. Your first taste of property law will most probably be signing a tenancy agreement if you're renting a room at university. Clients can range from squatters to a major retailer planning to open 100 new stores.

The conditions

Property and real estate lawyers are often specialists. Transactions are usually dealt with by solicitors, and take eight to 12 weeks. They involve property searches and enquiries to check there is nothing that may adversely affect the use of the property, checking legal title, negotiating and exchanging agreements and dealing with the Land Registry. Property barristers tend to focus on legal disputes. A lot of their work takes place outside court, advising clients on points of law, and even once inside court, a typical case can be over very quickly.

The upside

You get to work closely with clients on major transactions, and it's very enjoyable and fulfilling to negotiate and close deals. The working hours are mostly pretty 'civilised' too.

The downside

You have to love the detail and be prepared to complete lots of official documentation. As a property barrister, you may well find yourself spending a lot of time in county court waiting rooms.

TAX

The work

Tax lawyers advise companies and personal clients on their tax affairs. This might involve working on a corporate deal, like a merger, taking anything from two to six months. The duration isn't necessarily a sign of the size of the company involved – for example, if a company is up for sale and several parties are interested in buying it, this can draw the process out. For barristers, issues may include how to remunerate high-earning City employees without paying National Insurance, or how to avoid paying 4% stamp duty land tax on a large building development. Tax lawyers are responsible for small, discrete pieces of work for a lot of different transactions, whereas in other areas of law you may do a lot of work on one deal at a time.

The conditions

Tax lawyers are less affected by market conditions than, say, corporate lawyers as they have a broader range of work. Nevertheless, a large proportion of this is transactional and so the level of work will follow the level of market activity, which is currently buoyant.

The upside

The academic nature of the area – you will spend a lot of your time conducting legal research and considering what words mean. And the pay, of course.

The downside

The work is rather dry – there are always new rules introduced that you need to be aware of, and there's no interesting gossip to tell your colleagues at the end of the working day!

Confused about courses?
Indecisive about institutions?
Stressed about student life?
Unsure about UCAS?
Frowning over finance?

Help is available.

Visit www.ucasbooks.com to view our range
of over 75 books covering all aspects
of entry into higher education.

www.ucasbooks.com

The career for you?

Is law for you?

Being a successful solicitor or barrister calls for more than an in-depth understanding of relevant legislation. It also requires certain skills and personal qualities or 'attributes'.

To help you decide if a career in the legal profession is for you, consider the following questions:

- What do you want from your future work?
- What does a law course typically involve?
- Which skills and qualities do legal recruiters look for?

WHAT DO YOU WANT FROM YOUR FUTURE WORK?

You may not have an instant answer for this now, but your current studies, work experience and even your hobbies can help give you clues about the kind of work you enjoy and the skills you have already started to develop. Start with a blank sheet of paper and note down your answers to the questions opposite to help get you thinking. Be as brutally honest with yourself as you can – don't write what you think will impress your teachers or parents. Write what really matters to you and you'll start to see a pattern emerging.

QUESTIONS TO ASK YOURSELF BEFORE DECIDING ON A CAREER IN LAW

- When you think of your future, in what kind of environment do you see yourself working? For example, office, outdoor, 9am to 5pm, high-pressure, regular routine?
- What are your favourite hobbies?
- What is it about them that you enjoy? For example, working with people, working out how things work?
- What are your favourite subjects?
- What is it about them that you enjoy most? For example, being able to create something, debating, problem solving, practical hands-on work?
- What do you dislike about the other subjects you're studying?
- Which aspects of your work experience have you most enjoyed?

WHAT DOES A LAW COURSE TYPICALLY INVOLVE?

Unsurprisingly, all the skills required for a career as a solicitor or barrister will also be required at various stages of your law studies. It's important to understand, however, that the first part of your studies – known as the 'academic' stage – will involve a great deal of legal research and essay writing, since most of the coursework during your law degree or conversion course will be assessed by means of essays. The good news for trainee barristers is that, once you reach the 'vocational' stage of your studies (ie after your law degree), you'll move on to developing the professional skills needed through 'mooting' (mock trials in which two law students argue a case), drafting legal opinions and (video-recorded) role playing. For trainee solicitors, the professional law course is still rather dry, but your in-company training will bring it to life.

WHICH SKILLS AND QUALITIES DO LEGAL RECRUITERS LOOK FOR?

Without doubt, recruiters for both of the main branches in law (barristers and solicitors) look for strong academic ability, plus clear evidence of either a commitment to the Bar or interest in the work of a solicitor (which can usually be demonstrated through work-experience placements). Beyond this, the key skills required of any potential law student are:

- excellent written and oral communication skills
- in the case of barristers, strong presentation skills for effective advocacy in court
- strong 'people' skills to build rapport and relationships with individual clients
- commercial awareness (ie an appreciation of issues that affect clients)
- client handling skills, and credibility in the eyes of individual, corporate or legal clients as required
- problem-solving ability, eg the ability to think laterally, and to cut to the core of issues quickly and incisively
- attention to detail – it is crucial for legal professionals not to miss the finer points of law.

WHAT RECRUITERS SAY...

Graduate recruitment teams at leading firms and chambers share their insights into what makes a good candidate. The following list are the skills and abilities they think are important:

- the ability to work as part of a team
- academic ability
- attention to detail
- enthusiasm and energy
- flexibility
- a genuine interest in a legal career
- good judgement
- precise written and oral communication skills, including accurate grammar and punctuation
- self-motivation
- self-confidence.

Alternative careers

You don't have to be a solicitor or barrister to work in the legal profession.

The great news for anyone studying law is that the skills you'll develop on your course are prized by employers in many sectors outside the legal profession, as well as inside it. Such 'transferable' skills include your communication skills (think of all those essays!), your ability to process complex information quickly and your attention to detail. If you think that a career as a barrister or solicitor may not be for you, but you would still like to work in the legal field, then the following roles may be of interest.

IF YOU DON'T WANT TO TAKE A LAW DEGREE...

Legal executive lawyers

Under the Legal Services Act 2007, legal executive lawyers are classed as authorised persons undertaking reserved legal activities, alongside solicitors and barristers.

Their daily work is similar to solicitors. Legal executive lawyers are Commissioners of Oaths; give advice on compromise agreements; and can instruct barristers directly without going through a solicitor. They can also become advocates after taking an additional qualification.

The changing legal landscape means there are now opportunities for legal executive lawyers to run departments; manage other legal executives, solicitors and administrative staff; become partners in legal disciplinary partnership firms; and to be judges and tribunal chairs. Looking ahead, legal executive lawyers can set up their own practices when the relevant sections of the 2007 Act come into force.

Most legal executives combine a day job with studying through distance learning or night school spread over four years' of part-time study. Study, exam and registration fees cost around £3,500 – £6000.

If you hold a qualifying law degree then you should be eligible for exemptions: from September 2009 an ILEX graduate fast-track diploma qualification is available, which will only cost around £1500 in fees. Non-qualifying law degrees or other degrees with legal content are assessed by ILEX before exemptions are granted. Those holding a BVC or LPC are exempt from the ILEX qualifications.

To be a legal executive lawyer you won't need a training contract or pupillage, but you have to work under the supervision of a solicitor or qualified lawyer for five years (two of which must be after completing your ILEX qualifications).

Qualified legal executives can continue their studies to become a solicitor, and if you are a qualified legal executive before you complete the Legal Practice Course (LPC) you should be exempt from the SRA's two-year training contract.

Entry to be a legal executive lawyer is open to those holding a variety of qualifications. See **www.ilexcareers.org.uk.**

Barristers' clerk

A clerk performs a key support and admin role within barristers' chambers. The work ranges from preparing papers and issuing invoices as a junior clerk to managing a master diary; winning, negotiating fees for and allocating barristers' work; and liaising between solicitors, clients and barristers as a senior clerk. There are no formal entry requirements, and some barristers' clerks now start with A levels and even degrees,

although minimum standards are typically four GCSEs at grades A–C, including English and maths. Vacancies are typically advertised on the Institute of Barristers' Clerks' website. See **www.ibc.org.uk**.

IF YOU DON'T QUITE MAKE THE GRADE ON YOUR LAW DEGREE...

Paralegals

For would-be solicitors who leave university with a 2:2 and have difficulty securing a training contract with a firm of solicitors, working as a paralegal can provide useful experience that will be of great help in your application to become a solicitor. A US import, the role of paralegal is becoming more accepted in the UK, where paralegals sometimes carry out solicitor-level work: a good route to follow if you still want to be a solicitor. Some firms offer training contracts to their paralegals, while others even reduce the length of the training contract for staff with paralegal experience. Alternatively, you may decide that this level and kind of work suits you, and can begin to forge a career as a paralegal. See the Institute of Paralegals website: **www.instituteofparalegals.org**.

IF YOU'VE DONE A LAW DEGREE, BUT DON'T WANT TO BECOME A LAWYER...

Careers outside the legal profession

For those with an interest in statutes, **tax consultancy** within accountancy firms is a popular and highly lucrative route. The field of arbitration and dispute resolution is also a growing field within **personnel consultancy** for those with a particular interest in employment law. For those wishing to combine legal expertise and business knowledge in a corporate environment, the route of **company secretary** also offers great responsibility and reward.

Graduate destinations

Law
HESA Destination of Leavers of Higher Education Survey

Each year, comprehensive statistics are collected on what graduates are doing six months after they complete their course. The survey is co-ordinated by the Higher Education Statistics Agency (HESA) and provides information about how many graduates move into employment (and what type of career) or further study and how many are believed to be unemployed.

The full results across all subject areas are published by the Higher Education Careers Service Unit (HECSU) and the Association of Graduate Careers Advisory Services (AGCAS) in *What Do Graduates Do?*, which is available from **www.ucasbooks.com.**

	Law
In UK employment	34.7%
In overseas employment	0.9%
Working and studying	10.9%
Studying in the UK for a higher degree	5.8%
Studying in the UK for a teaching qualification	0.6%
Undertaking other further study or training in the UK	34.8%
Studying overseas	0.5%
Not available for employment, study or training	4.3%
Assumed to be unemployed	3.7%
Other	3.9%

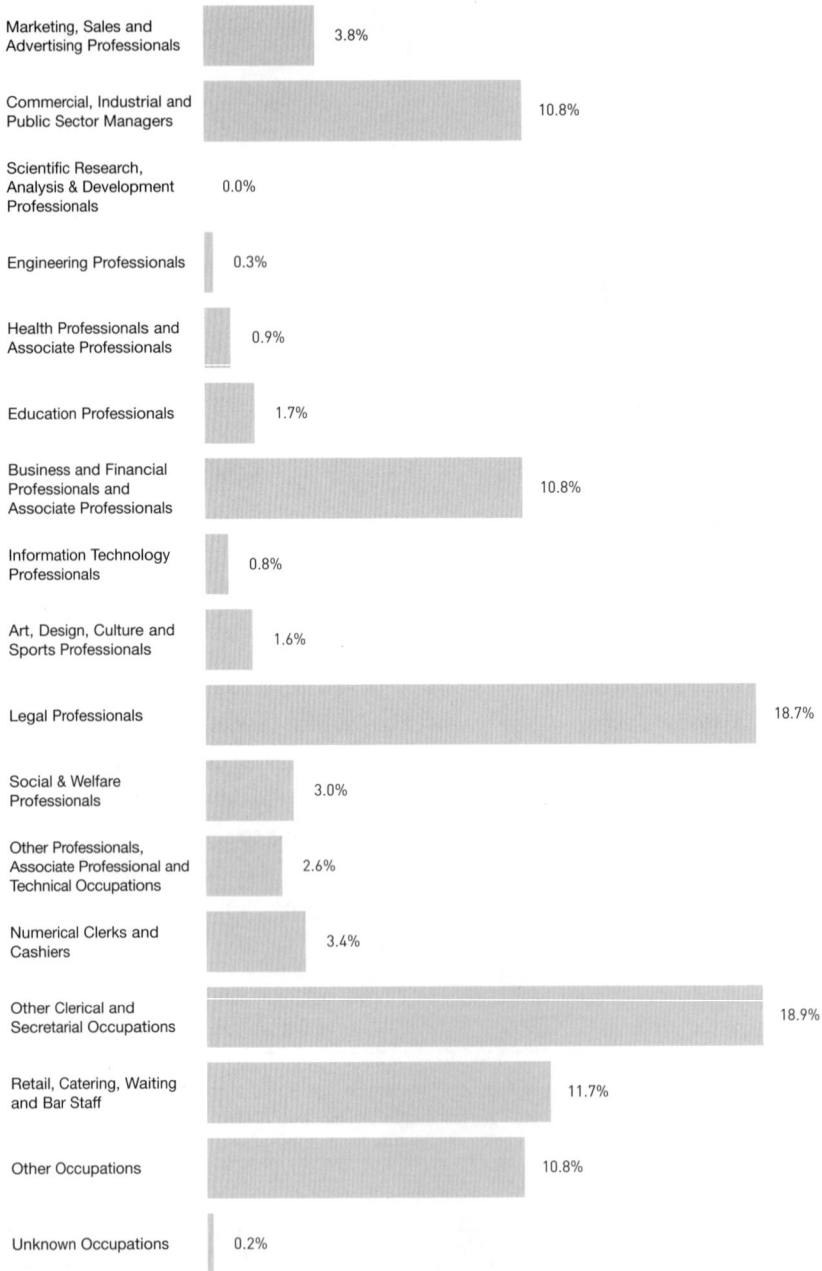

Occupation	Percentage
Marketing, Sales and Advertising Professionals	3.8%
Commercial, Industrial and Public Sector Managers	10.8%
Scientific Research, Analysis & Development Professionals	0.0%
Engineering Professionals	0.3%
Health Professionals and Associate Professionals	0.9%
Education Professionals	1.7%
Business and Financial Professionals and Associate Professionals	10.8%
Information Technology Professionals	0.8%
Art, Design, Culture and Sports Professionals	1.6%
Legal Professionals	18.7%
Social & Welfare Professionals	3.0%
Other Professionals, Associate Professional and Technical Occupations	2.6%
Numerical Clerks and Cashiers	3.4%
Other Clerical and Secretarial Occupations	18.9%
Retail, Catering, Waiting and Bar Staff	11.7%
Other Occupations	10.8%
Unknown Occupations	0.2%

Case studies

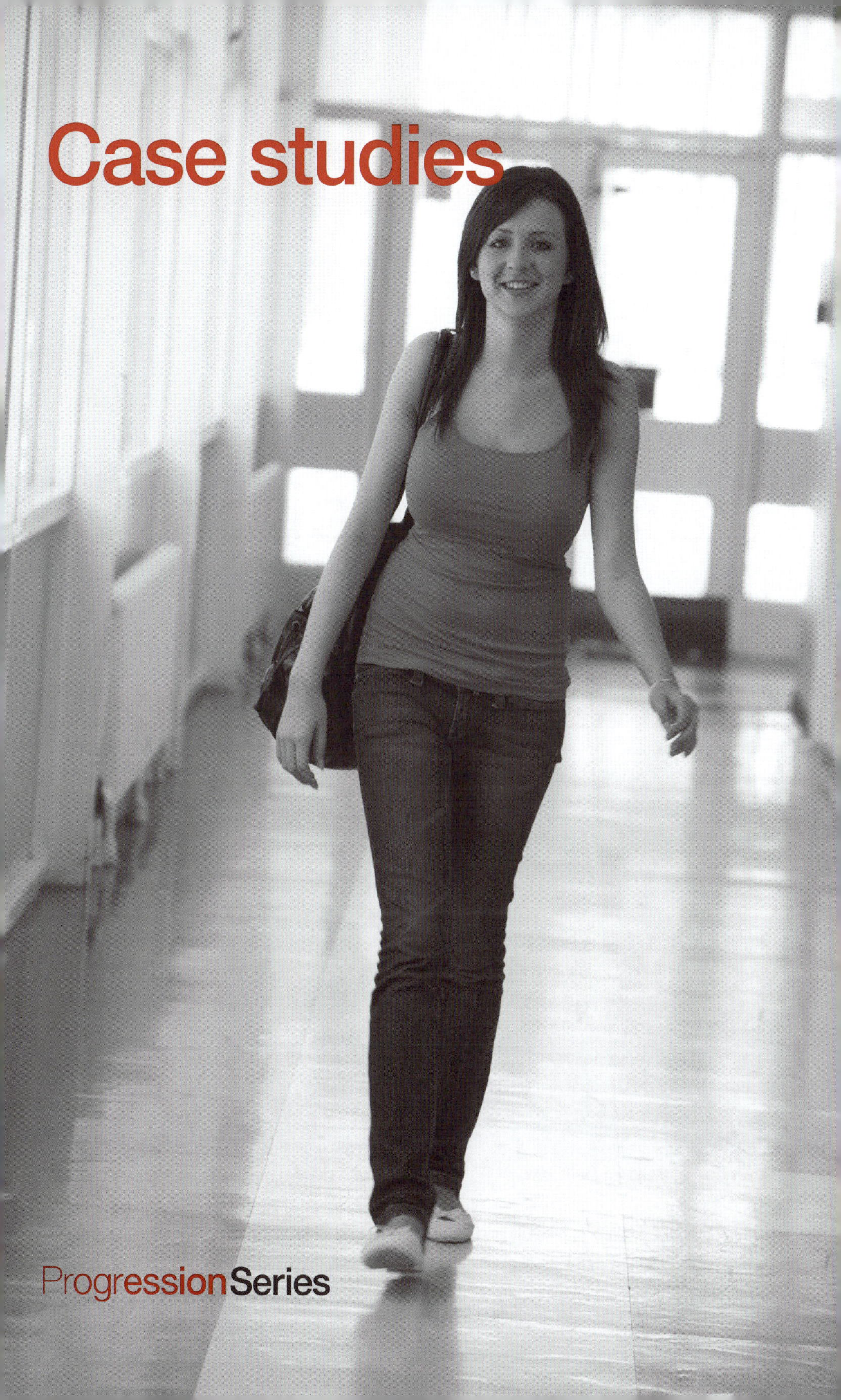

ProgressionSeries

A WORLD OF LAWYERS

Still not sure whether you want to work in law? Perhaps you don't know if being a barrister is your cup of tea or whether life as a solicitor takes your fancy. Read the following profiles to see where the world of work has taken recent graduates in the legal profession and beyond.

Trainee solicitor

Herbert Smith

ANAND GANGADIA

Route into law:
A levels – biology, economics and history; AS level – chemistry and general studies; LLB law, University College London (2007); LPC, BPP Law School, London (2008)

WHY LAW?

I wanted to apply my interest in business and economics to the law and provide legal advice in a way that illustrates an understanding of the wider economy and the individual client's needs (the company or individual) in both a dispute and general business context. I therefore chose to obtain a training contract within a corporate City law firm.

HOW I GOT TO WHERE I AM TODAY

I undertook vacation schemes at three City law firms in the summer of my second year, which helped me decide which law firm I wanted to further my career

with, and accepted Herbert Smith's offer of a training contract starting in August 2008. After graduating, I began my LPC, and my employer paid the fees. At the end of the LPC, I began work as a trainee solicitor. My first seat was in the litigation and arbitration division.

WHAT MY CURRENT ROLE INVOLVES

Every day is different: as a trainee solicitor you are given exposure to as many matters as possible. I have spent some days on conference calls, attending meetings and taking notes, and other days doing legal research or drafting letters, court documents and defences.

I am also responsible for keeping the matters I'm working on in an organised and structured format, keeping an accurate record of notes taken during meetings and conference calls, and supporting my supervisor in drafting complex defences, legal submissions, instructions to counsel and letters. Liaising with clients and conducting accurate and important legal research are also part of the job.

So far, my hours have been quite reasonable; I usually work from 9.30am until 6.30 or 7pm and have not had any very late nights or weekends. However, this really depends on the type of group you work in and the level of work in the department. Although we are very busy there isn't the need to be working all the hours into the night, and this is common within litigation, as opposed to the corporate department.

MY BIGGEST CHALLENGE TO DATE

When I started my first seat I was given quite a complex piece of legal research and a drafting exercise to do. The latter consisted of drafting full instructions to counsel on a matter that looked as if it would go to court. I not only had to read up on the last few months of correspondence and legal argument but also to assimilate all of that information into a coherent and logical document for counsel. This was quite challenging but obtaining help from other associates and the training provided as part of the induction process helped.

AND THE BEST BITS?

- Meeting clients/counsel (attending court), discussing the practical implications of the law and thus obtaining what the client wants: a commercially practical solution.
- Drafting interesting and complex defences on high-profile disputes and individuals.
- Experiencing the variety of work the litigation division carries out, particularly with the type of work created by the 'credit crunch', and the atmosphere created within a team when you are working on large, high-profile and high-value cases.

ANAND'S TOP TIPS

Working hard at sixth form and university, and achieving good grades, will undoubtedly help you secure a training contract with a firm you want to work for. Demonstrating enthusiasm, individuality and commercial awareness, as well as an appreciation and interest in the law, will most definitely help you.

Tenant, criminal law

6 King's Bench Walk, Chambers of Roy Amlot QC

ELEANOR SEARLEY

Route into law:

A levels – music, English literature, ancient history, general studies; BA music, York (2003); CPE, College of Law Birmingham (2005); BVC, College of Law London (2006)

WHY LAW?

What I enjoyed most about music was performing: being in the spotlight and under pressure to perform. Jury trials provide the same level of adrenaline and excitement. I also really enjoyed the musical analysis part of my degree, but that wouldn't really be a large part of a career as a professional musician. Criminal law, on the other hand, involves daily legal and factual analysis so I felt that being a barrister combined the best bits of performance and analysis in one career. I decided on criminal law because I wanted to do as much advocacy as possible and jury trials really appealed. I also wanted to work in an area that was client focused because I enjoy the human interest.

HOW DID YOU GET TO WHERE YOU ARE TODAY?

I did several weeks of mini-pupillages in several different sets in order to see which areas of law interested me the most, and applied by sending in my CV with a covering letter. I was offered and completed a 12-month pupillage at 6 King's Bench Walk and was offered my tenancy at the end.

WHAT DOES YOUR JOB INVOLVE?

I work about 60 hours a week and tend to have about fifteen cases on the go at one time. In general, I spend several hours a day in court, then go back to chambers. I regularly get briefs for the next day the night before and may suddenly find myself with a lot of preparation to do.

I both prosecute and defend, working on trials in the magistrates' and Crown Courts, alongside sentencing hearings, plea and case management hearings and mentions. Additionally, I write advices on evidence and see clients in conference. The types of cases I deal with range from road traffic offences through to robberies, assaults and sexual offences.

I tend to be the only barrister working on my cases. Defending usually involves advising the client as to their plea, trial venue and potential sentence, and then representing them in court. When prosecuting, I liaise with the CPS and the police. I have also been led by a more senior barrister in an attempted murder case and an armed robbery case.

WHAT HAS BEEN YOUR BIGGEST CHALLENGE?

Helping to prosecute in an attempted murder case – a gang shooting – in London. It involved lots of behind-the-scenes work with the police to make sure the evidence was presented at its best to the jury, and much hard work during the trial itself. When the jury returned a guilty verdict it was fantastic to feel that all of our hard work had paid off and we'd helped get the correct verdict, especially as the defendant ultimately admitted his guilt at the sentencing hearing.

AND THE BEST BITS?

- The variety – every day is different, with different challenges, so you never get bored or stuck in a rut.
- The responsibility – the decisions you take or the performance you give matters.
- The independence – being self-employed is great but the camaraderie and support of being in chambers with other barristers is wonderful too.

ELEANOR'S TOP TIPS

Anyone wanting to go to the criminal bar needs to recognise very early on that they will need to take every opportunity to make their application stand out. This includes not only excellent academic results but also examples where they can show they have used their own initiative or stood on their own two feet: for example, working abroad for a year between school and university.

Trainee solicitor, regional firm

Burges Salmon LLP

ALISTAIR RATTRAY

Route into law:

A levels – computing, physics and maths; MSc computer science, Manchester (2005); CPE and LPC, University of the West of England.

WHY LAW?

Although I qualified into IT, I soon discovered that it wasn't for me. Working in industry helped me realise this, while giving me a chance to see the legal aspects of business, which greatly interested me. I discussed the various options with solicitors and barristers and, although it was hard choosing between them, I decided that the type of work and the teamwork opportunities available to solicitors were more appealing.

DESCRIBE YOUR CAREER PATH TO DATE

I took the one-year conversion course (CPE) followed by the LPC and, while studying, I applied to a number of firms for a training contract. I am currently nearing the end of this process and have completed four 'seats', the latest of which was banking.

WHAT DOES YOUR JOB INVOLVE?

My work varies from department to department, and even during the course of sitting within one department, depending on what is going on in the market. The work is always changing and there's inevitably something new to get involved in. I'm given a great deal of responsibility, ranging from drafting and negotiating documents directly with other solicitors and serving papers in Court right through to managing whole cases from start to finish. However, I am always supervised and there is a team of solicitors around me who are always keen to help.

From week to week my role is different and my working hours reflect this, although on average I work from 8.30am until 6pm.

WHAT HAS BEEN YOUR BIGGEST CHALLENGE TO DATE?

One of the primary functions of a solicitor is problem-solving and I enjoy helping our clients face and overcome the various challenges that they meet.

However, one of the biggest challenges is actually gaining a training contract. The choices of firm are endless, with different types of work, different environments and different approaches to that work.

Moreover, the competition for jobs is intense and learning to accept rejection is part of the process. However, by thinking long and hard about the firms I wanted to work for, targeting my applications, and persevering, I succeeded.

AND THE BEST BITS?

- The variety of the work. With the trends and demands of business constantly changing, the types of client and the nature of the work is always evolving, with opportunities to learn something new or become involved in developing areas of law.
- The importance of the work. Law affects each and every one of us, from the rights of individuals to the intricacies of business. As such, our work is always relevant and the results are visible, even if only in the shape of news headlines.
- The people. I work with a wide selection of people within various teams, both within the firm and with our clients.

ALISTAIR'S TOP TIPS

Although working towards any successful career requires a lot of hard work, you really do need to know what is out there and be prepared if you want to be a solicitor. A bit of research into the different areas of law and the types of firm and what they do can make all the difference.

Trainee solicitor, US law firm

Baker & McKenzie LLP

SARAH CRAMP

Route into law:

A levels – French, German, English literature, general studies; BA modern and medieval languages (French and German), Clare College, Cambridge (2005)

WHY LAW?

My interest in law was initially sparked by a school careers talk. However, to know for sure, I subsequently undertook various work experience placements, which confirmed for me that a career as a solicitor would provide interesting and academically challenging work, an opportunity to develop my commercial awareness, and a chance to learn more about the business world through advising a wide range of clients from different industries, and potentially a chance to travel and work abroad.

HOW DID YOU GET TO WHERE YOU ARE TODAY?

I spent three weeks in the summer of my penultimate year at university working for Baker & McKenzie as one of their vacation scheme students, after which I was offered a training contract. After graduating, I moved to Nottingham to study for the Graduate Diploma in Law (GDL) and the Legal Practice Course (or LPC) at Nottingham Law School. In September 2007 I started my training contract: my first two seats were in the Corporate and Private Banking departments. I am currently sitting in the Employment department and hope to spend part of my fourth seat on secondment to the firm's Paris office.

WHAT DOES YOUR JOB INVOLVE?

Every day is different, depending on the matters I am working on at the time. For example, I might be researching and writing a memo on an aspect of employment law (eg age discrimination, managing sickness absence or redundancy); preparing for or attending a hearing at the Employment Tribunal; or contacting colleagues in the firm's other offices around the world to ask for their advice on behalf of a client. I usually work from 9am to 6.30pm, but when we are busy I sometimes have to work later. (The free dinner from the office restaurant helps to make up for it!) I work with several different people at different levels of their career on a daily basis, both within the firm's London office and from locations as far flung as Sydney, New York, Bangkok and Beijing.

WHAT HAS BEEN YOUR BIGGEST CHALLENGE?

In the Corporate department I worked on a deal with a very tight timescale and pressured deadlines, which meant very long hours every day for a couple of weeks.

I had been here at work for only two months and found this a shock after the student lifestyle! However, the whole team was very supportive and made an effort to let me know that my hard work was appreciated. The most rewarding part was when the deal closed and we were taken out for a delicious meal with plenty of champagne to celebrate!

AND THE BEST BITS?

- The work I do is interesting, challenging and varied.
- Trainees are given plenty of responsibility, but also lots of guidance and excellent training.
- I really enjoy the international aspect to the work and very much hope that I can gain some practical experience of this by undertaking a secondment abroad.

SARAH'S TOP TIPS

Vacation or summer schemes are excellent for gaining an insight into the work of a firm of solicitors and can be really helpful in getting a training contract. However, competition for places can be intense so be prepared and organised from an early stage, as application deadlines crop up surprisingly early in the academic year. Try to get as much legal work experience as possible, even if it's just helping out at a local firm during the holidays. Finally, open days and talking to trainees, associates and partners about their experiences are great ways to find out more about a career as a solicitor.

Tenant, Commercial and Chancery law

4 Stone Buildings

DONALD LILLY

Route into law:

International Baccalaureate (Higher subjects: English, European history and biology; standard subjects: economics, German and maths); BA law, Wadham College, Oxford (2004); BCL, Wadham College, Oxford (2005)

WHY LAW?

I chose to study law at the last moment. I'd always intended to study history, but as I approached the UCAS deadline I wanted to try something different and law seemed a natural choice, especially as it provides a clear career path.

I chose the Bar as I wanted more independence in the way that I worked: being self-employed was a major advantage for me. You also have more control at the Bar over the areas in which you wish to practise. While firms (especially the large ones) have highly specialised

practice groups, you can only join one if there's a vacancy. At the bar, most chambers specialise as a whole, so once you've got your pupillage within a particular set, you are pretty much ensured work in that area.

HOW DID YOU GET TO WHERE YOU ARE TODAY?

After I graduated, I took the BCL (a taught master's degree in law) before taking the BVC. I then spent a year in Canada working for a property development company before returning to England for my pupillage year at 4 Stone Buildings. I am now a few months into my tenancy.

WHAT DOES YOUR JOB INVOLVE?

At the junior bar the work is quite varied. Generally, most of it is paper based, with glamorous jobs such as disclosure (reading documents to determine relevancy to the proceedings) and drafting advice on litigation matters. I spend at least one day a week in court, usually on small insolvency matters or minor corporate/commercial disputes.

Levels of responsibility depend on whether you are working on your own or are being 'led'. Around half of my work is led, which means I work alongside a more senior barrister or barristers, undertaking such jobs as legal research and document management on their behalf. When I work on my own, I read the documents, prepare the advice, draft the documents to push the matter forward and finally appear in court to obtain the order sought by my client.

There are no set hours. If my desk is clear then I can take the day off work; on the other hand, if something must be done by the next morning I could easily be working until late (or early in the morning)! Because barristers are self-employed, they can choose the amount of work they wish to undertake (of course, the less you take on, the less you tend to earn since most work is paid on an hourly rate).

WHAT HAS BEEN YOUR BIGGEST CHALLENGE?

Having an answer for everything! Barristers are expected to know the answer to legal problems, even when caught off guard – whether by a judge in court asking a tricky question or a solicitor calling requiring immediate advice. Being able to give quick and robust advice off the cuff is something that requires a great deal of experience.

AND THE BEST BITS?

- Starting a case from inception and seeing it the whole way through to a court order in your favour. (Of course, that is in contrast to the worst bit, which is putting huge effort into a case that falters and fails at the last moment!)
- The sense of achievement when something goes as planned, from a well-drafted letter to a major trial. It's great to be able to say: "I did that".
- The variety. At the junior end there is something new almost every day.

DONALD'S TOP TIPS

Be methodical. Within the time constraints, make sure you have done everything you can to see the problem from every angle. That way, you will be less surprised.

Criminal barrister

Garden Court Chambers

TOM WAINWRIGHT

Route into law:
A levels – English literature, mathematics, history; MA jurisprudence, Exeter College, Oxford (2002);
BVC, The College of Law, London (2003)

WHY LAW?

I don't remember what initially attracted me to law: I just always knew it was what I wanted to do. As I looked into it more, the fact that it has the potential to affect the lives of so many people for better (or for worse) interested me: I wanted to try and ensure it was the former as far as possible.

As a barrister you are at the cutting edge, having to think on your feet and make important decisions. I always enjoyed public speaking and debating, and wanted to use these in a job where I got to work closely with people on important issues.

HOW DID YOU GET TO WHERE YOU ARE TODAY?

After graduation I took the BVC and began applying for pupillage. Not having secured one by the end of my BVC, I started working as a paralegal at an East London criminal solicitors firm in order to gain some more practical experience. While there, I became an accredited police station representative, which involved advising clients who had been charged with a wide range of offences, including murder, aggravated burglary and drugs importation. After a further two years I started pupillage at a chambers and eventually got taken on after that. I was called to the Bar in 2003.

WHAT DOES YOUR JOB INVOLVE?

Every day I attend court and then work from home or in chambers, preparing papers for upcoming cases. My main responsibilities include representing my clients and putting their case forward as powerfully as possible. The working hours vary – as a barrister I'm self-employed and hearings can take between five minutes and a full court day (10am to 4pm). Often there will be work to do in the evening to prepare for the following day's hearing or a large case coming up in the future.

I am based in chambers, where I can access legal resources, store case papers and seek advice from more experienced barristers when faced with difficult questions. Other preparation is often carried out at home. Otherwise I attend courts all over the country for hearings and occasionally have to attend prisons for conferences with clients. I work with lots of different people: judges, juries, defendants, their families, other barristers, solicitors. A very wide spectrum!

I have acted as junior counsel in some serious cases but normally I appear in court on my own. My clients tend to be young or vulnerable and I have also represented some who were judged not fit to plead. The sorts of cases I deal with include those involving violence, dishonesty, drugs and sexual offences.

WHAT HAS BEEN YOUR BIGGEST CHALLENGE?

The biggest challenge I've faced to date has to have been obtaining a tenancy. The competition has always been tough and, with current legal-aid cutbacks, it's getting tougher; the fear at the Bar is that this will put off those who are the most talented but least able to afford it. I worked to support myself while studying and applying for pupillages, and was also lucky enough to be granted a scholarship and get a loan specially designed for prospective barristers from my bank.

AND THE BEST BITS?

- Getting the right verdict.
- Having the opportunity to argue, define and change the law.
- Meeting and working with a variety of people.

TOM'S TOP TIPS

Think carefully, find out as much as you can about the job and, if your heart is set on it, then stick with it and persevere.

www.ucas.com

helping students into higher education

Entry routes

Routes to qualification

There are clearly defined routes to professional qualification as a solicitor or barrister.

Qualifying as a solicitor or barrister involves three stages:
1 academic stage + 2 vocational stage +
3 practical stage.

Stage 1 is the same for both barristers and solicitors. The main differences come at stages 2 and 3.

Solicitor and barrister

1 ACADEMIC STAGE

Through one of two routes:

a The quickest way is to take a 'qualifying law degree' in the UK, ie an undergraduate law degree that contains the seven core legal subjects (see 'The seven core law subjects' on the next page). Nearly all law degrees in England, Wales and Northern Ireland meet this requirement, as does the English law course at the University of Dundee in Scotland. This route gives you more time to go into subjects in greater depth and to fit in more substantial work experience.

or

b Take a non-law degree followed by a one-year full-time (two-year part-time) conversion course in law, the CPE or GDL. This route gives you the chance to take a different degree that might help you to stand out from other law students later on, and to be seen as more 'rounded'. It is, however, more intensive and more expensive – typical fees for the one-year, full-time CPE course currently range from £2,900 to £8,100, depending on location.

CPE COMMON PROFESSIONAL EXAMINATION (CPE): A ONE-YEAR COURSE FOR GRADUATES WHOSE FIRST DEGREE ISN'T IN LAW.

GDL GRADUATE DIPLOMA IN LAW: A ONE-YEAR COURSE FOR GRADUATES WHOSE FIRST DEGREE ISN'T IN LAW.

THE SEVEN CORE LAW SUBJECTS

To count as a 'qualifying law degree' the course must cover:

1. constitutional and administrative law
2. criminal law
3. law of contract
4. law of tort
5. land law
6. equity and trusts
7. EU law.

Solicitors only

2 VOCATIONAL STAGE = A ONE-YEAR FULL-TIME, OR TWO-YEAR PART-TIME, LEGAL PRACTICE COURSE (LPC)

There are currently some 29 institutions validated by the Law Society to run the full-time LPC in England and Wales, offering around 10,675 full-time places. Currently, all LPC courses cover the same six skills – practical legal research, writing and drafting, interviewing, advising and advocacy. There are also three compulsory subjects – business law and practice, conveyancing, and litigation. However, by September 2010, all LPC providers will be able to offer more flexibility in their training programmes, and the LPC will be split into two stages: the first comprising the three essential practice areas, as well as the core subjects; and the second will be made up of three vocational elective modules. See **www.sra.org.uk/students/lpc/lpc-update.page**.

It is worth noting that some law firms – particularly City ones – state a preference for LPC provider, so do check this out on their website.

Assessment is normally a combination of exams and coursework. Course fees vary from £6,710 to £11,500, full time, depending on location. The Central Applications Board provides application forms and

HELP WITH FEES

Some (large) law firms are prepared to sponsor students through the vocational stage of their training – ie pay all or part of their LPC training. Check out what each firm offers on their website, and get your application in early.

guidance notes for full-time courses. More info is available at **www.lawcabs.ac.uk**.

3 PRACTICAL STAGE = 'TRAINING CONTRACT'

Content

This is normally a two-year period with a firm of solicitors, made up of several 'seats', ie periods of a few months spent in different departments to give trainees the most comprehensive grounding. As a result, work is very varied, ranging from attending client conferences to research to drafting legal papers. You'll also have to attend a short professional skills course during your training, covering interviewing skills, drafting, negotiation etc. Securing a training contract is often seen as the most difficult part of qualifying as a solicitor due to increasing competition.

Competition

Competition for places is not as intense as the barrister route, but still stiff nonetheless. According to the Law Society's *Annual Statistical Report 2007*, the number of trainee solicitors commencing contracts in 2007 was 6,012.

Remuneration

Good news for trainee solicitors – you will be paid a salary during your training contract, ranging from the Law Society's recommended rates of £16,790 for trainees outside London, and £18,870 for central London trainees, to £40,000+ from the more generous (usually large, London) firms, who are prepared to offer more for the best trainees.

Post-training employment

To keep the pressure on, most firms won't let you know until near the end of your training contract if they would like to keep you on. Not all trainees want to stay with the same firm after qualifying, though most do.

Qualifying as a solicitor

3-4 years		1 year		2 years		
LLB	+	LPC	+	TRAINING	=	SOLICITOR

or

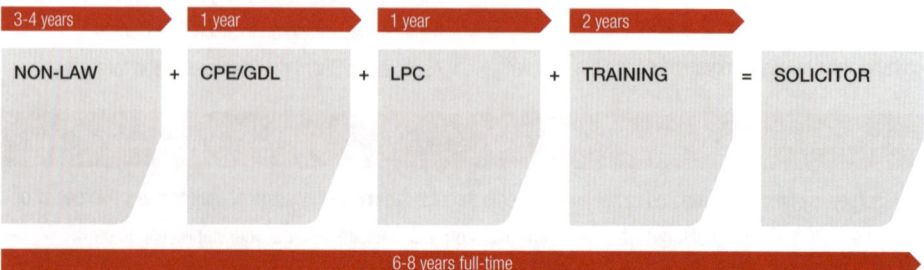

3-4 years		1 year		1 year		2 years		
NON-LAW	+	CPE/GDL	+	LPC	+	TRAINING	=	SOLICITOR

6-8 years full-time

Solicitor – how to apply

APPLYING FOR	APPLY THROUGH	APPLY BY
Undergraduate law degree	UCAS Apply online – see **www.ucas.com** and click on Apply	mid-October for Oxford University and University of Cambridge; mid-January for other universities and colleges
CPE or GDL	The Central Applications Board for full-time courses. Online applications preferred See **www.lawcabs.ac.uk** For part-time courses, apply direct to institutions	late January/early February
LPC	For full-time courses, apply through the Central Applications Board. Online applications preferred See **www.lawcabs.ac.uk** For part-time courses, apply direct to institutions	late November for 1 December
Training contract	Directly to individual firms of solicitors Check out their websites, online recruitment sites and TARGETjobs *Law* for advertisements	deadlines vary from firm to firm

Barristers only

2 VOCATIONAL STAGE = A ONE-YEAR FULL-TIME, TWO-YEAR PART-TIME, BAR VOCATIONAL COURSE (BVC)

Before you start the BVC, you have to join one of the four 'Inns of Court' (all based in London): Lincoln's Inn, Inner Temple, Middle Temple or Gray's Inn. All Inns offer students the same kinds of support – eg access to a library and to members of staff and 'mentors' to provide guidance and advice. During your BVC year you will be required to attend at least 12 'qualifying sessions' with your Inn in order to be eligible to be called to the Bar: these may include lectures, dinners, advocacy courses, moots and residential weekends. Choosing an Inn should be based on a combination of personal criteria (eg how do you find the atmosphere?) and practical considerations (eg how many scholarships does the Inn offer for BVC students?).

There are currently eight institutions in the UK offering more than 2,000 BVC places between them. (For the full list of courses see page 125.) Course fees range from approximately £8,950 to £14,150 for the one-year course, but some barristers' chambers offer candidates selected for pupillage an advance on their pupillage fees to help cover the cost. The course covers the skills required for practice at the Bar, and typical exercises include:

- drafting written opinions – and case preparation
- advocacy – based on briefs similar to those that junior barristers receive
- enacting court procedures – typically video-recorded role plays of mock court trials.

Changes to the BVC

Changes to the Bar vocational course are under consultation. The course will be renamed as the Bar Professional Training Course (BPTC) and applicants will have to complete an aptitude test before being accepted. These changes are due to come into effect at the start of the 2010–2011 academic year – see **www.barstandardsboard.org.uk** for the most up-to-date information.

3 PRACTICAL STAGE = 'PUPILLAGE'

Content

This is a one-year period of in-chambers training (sometimes extended by six months) for trainee barristers, split into two 'sixes' – a first non-practising six, when you'll literally sit in the same office as your 'pupil supervisor' and shadow him or her, plus a second 'practising' six, when you may get to supply legal services in your own right, though under supervision. How soon you are able to act on your own depends as much on the field of law in which you're working as it does on your ability – for example, barristers specialising in criminal and family law are likely to spend most of their second six in court on their own cases; others, for example in the complex intellectual property field, are more likely to spend their second six 'led' by their seniors, ie assisting them in large, complex cases away from court.

Competition

Competition for pupillage places is VERY intense, as there are more applicants than there are pupillage places. Of the 1,500 or so students who start the BVC each year only about 500 will eventually find tenancies. Selection for pupillage places is rigorous – with recruiters looking for evidence of commitment to the Bar (which is where work experience comes in), as well as legal knowledge (assessed, for example, by a mini-case-based test) and presentation skills. Their advice to prospective pupils is to gain as much work experience as you can at both university and on the BVC by participating in 'mooting' activities or debating, and attending your Inn's advocacy weekends and mock trials.

Remuneration

The good news for trainee barristers is that all pupillages must now offer minimum funding of £10,000 for the year, with several (especially London-based) chambers offering considerably more (as much as £45,000) for the year.

Tenancy

The not-so-good news for trainee barristers is that, after pupillage, you have one more hurdle to negotiate – securing 'tenancy' or a permanent place in chambers. Some chambers try not to take on more pupils than they are likely to want as tenants. Others make pupils compete throughout their pupillage year for a limited number of tenancies at the end.

Qualifying as a barrister

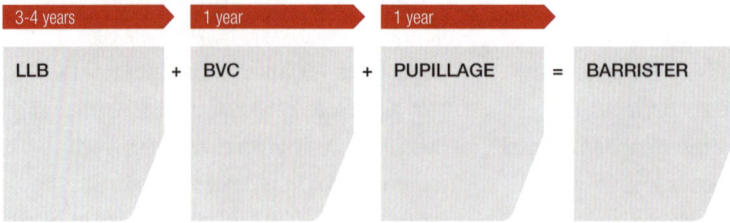

3-4 years		1 year		1 year		
LLB	+	BVC	+	PUPILLAGE	=	BARRISTER

or

3-4 years		1 year		1 year		1 year		
NON-LAW	+	CPE/GDL	+	BVC	+	PUPILLAGE	=	BARRISTER

5-7 years full-time

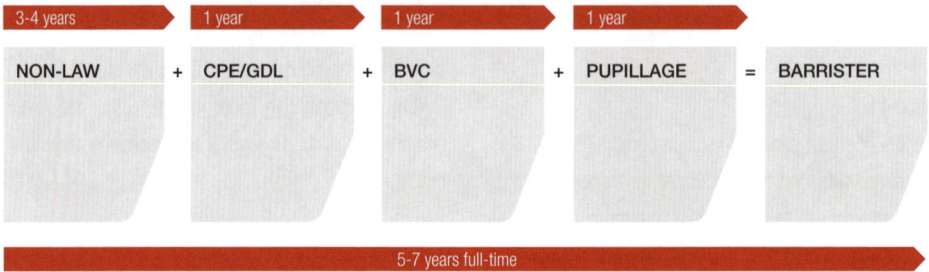

Barrister – how to apply

APPLYING FOR	APPLY THROUGH	APPLY BY
Undergraduate law degree	UCAS Apply online – see www.ucas.com and click on Apply	mid-October for Oxford University and University of Cambridge; mid-January for other universities and colleges
CPE or GDL	The Central Applications Board for full-time courses. Online applications preferred See www.lawcabs.ac.uk For part-time courses, apply direct to institutions	late January/early February
BVC	www.bvconline.co.uk Online applications only	beginning or mid-January
Pupillage	Either through the Pupillage Portal (the online pupillage application system) at www.pupillages.com for two-thirds of chambers, or directly to the remaining third of chambers, who don't recruit through the Pupillage Portal. ALL pupillage vacancies are advertised on the the Pupillage Portal site	end April for summer season pupillages; end September for autumn season pupillages

Northern Ireland and Scotland

The UK legal system has different routes to qualification in Northern Ireland and Scotland.

NORTHERN IRELAND

1 law degree or equivalent + 2 vocational stage + 3 training period

The key difference is that both barristers and solicitors must take the same one-year postgraduate course leading to the Certificate in Professional Legal Studies. The third stage, the training period, is different for solicitors and barristers.

Solicitors

Training is through a 'split' apprenticeship, which lasts for two years and is done under the supervision of a 'master'. Trainees spend four months in a solicitor's office, followed by one year at the Institute of Professional Legal Studies, and a further eight months in a solicitor's office. Solicitors have an initial further restriction placed on them when they start practising, in the shape of a restricted practising certificate, which allows them to act as an assistant solicitor in a firm, but does not allow them to practise on their own or in partnership for three years (reducible to two with attendance at a continuing legal education programme).

More info at **www.lawsoc-ni.org**.

Barristers

Trainees spend four weeks in a citizens' advice bureau or law centre followed by a week shadowing a practising barrister immediately prior to commencing their course. This is then followed by a 12-month pupillage on graduation from the Institute of Professional Legal Studies.

SCOTLAND

1 law degree or equivalent + 2 vocational stage + 3 training period.

Both barristers and solicitors have to take a (seven-month) postgraduate Diploma in Legal Practice.

Solicitors

After the diploma, solicitors undertake two years' further practical training in a solicitor's office in the form of a training contract. This training period normally pays at least the salary recommended by the Law Society of Scotland – £15,500 for the first year and £18,550 for a second-year trainee, based on 2008 figures. Trainees must complete detailed logbooks of their work and, after six months, must attend a professional competence course. After satisfactorily completing one year of training, a trainee can apply to be admitted as a solicitor in order to gain experience of appearing in court. At the end of the two-year training period, the training contract must be formally 'discharged' in order for the trainee to gain a full practising certificate.

More info at **www.lawscot.org.uk**.

Advocates (Barristers)

After the diploma, barristers – called 'advocates' in Scotland – have to spend approximately 21 months of their training period in a solicitor's office before going to the Bar. They then spend approximately nine months 'devilling', ie working for an experienced advocate. Barristers must also become a member of the Faculty of Advocates, and pass the Faculty's exam in evidence, practice and procedure.

More info at **www.advocates.org.uk**.

Applicant journey

SIX EASY STEPS TO UNIVERSITY AND COLLEGE

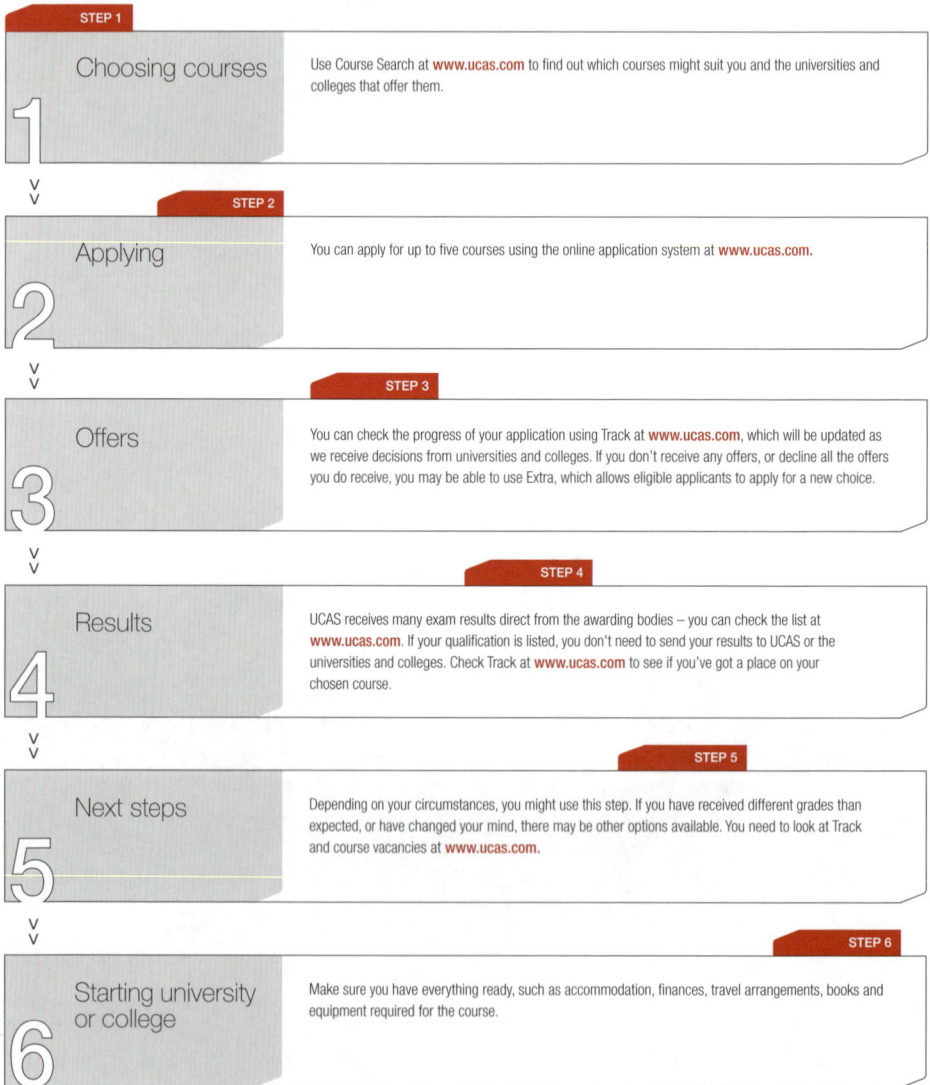

STEP 1

1

Choosing courses

Use Course Search at **www.ucas.com** to find out which courses might suit you and the universities and colleges that offer them.

STEP 2

2

Applying

You can apply for up to five courses using the online application system at **www.ucas.com.**

STEP 3

3

Offers

You can check the progress of your application using Track at **www.ucas.com**, which will be updated as we receive decisions from universities and colleges. If you don't receive any offers, or decline all the offers you do receive, you may be able to use Extra, which allows eligible applicants to apply for a new choice.

STEP 4

4

Results

UCAS receives many exam results direct from the awarding bodies – you can check the list at **www.ucas.com**. If your qualification is listed, you don't need to send your results to UCAS or the universities and colleges. Check Track at **www.ucas.com** to see if you've got a place on your chosen course.

STEP 5

5

Next steps

Depending on your circumstances, you might use this step. If you have received different grades than expected, or have changed your mind, there may be other options available. You need to look at Track and course vacancies at **www.ucas.com.**

STEP 6

6

Starting university or college

Make sure you have everything ready, such as accommodation, finances, travel arrangements, books and equipment required for the course.

Choosing courses

1

Step 1 – Planning your application for law

Planning your application is the start of your journey to finding a place at a university or college.

This section will help you decide what course to study and how to choose a university or college where you'll enjoy living and studying. Find out about qualifications, degree options, how they'll assess you, and coping with the costs of higher education.

ENTRY REQUIREMENTS

NB: This section covers routes into law from A levels. (An additional, longer route to becoming a solicitor is available through the Institute of Legal Executives (ILEX), which is not covered here. See **www.ilex.org.uk**.)

Which subjects?

Newsflash – you **don't** have to study law at A level (A2 level) or even at undergraduate level to become a solicitor or barrister. In fact, some law courses positively prefer students not to have studied law at A level, as they find they have to get students to 'unlearn' what they think they already know!

Similarly, almost all law recruiters – both chambers and firms of solicitors – welcome recruits who have taken a non-law degree, especially if the first degree is in a subject of interest, eg modern languages for EU or corporate solicitors. Gap years are also of interest, as legal recruiters want to hire 'rounded' people who can relate to the world in which they'll be working.

However, although they don't require law at A level, most university law departments will look for subjects that reflect the rigour and skills required on a law degree. This means they're mostly looking for academic subjects, for example English or history, which will provide evidence of making logical arguments and strong written communication skills so essential to a career in law. The only subject not accepted as a valid A level by most law schools is general studies.

Which grades?

While the subject you've studied may not be quite so important, grades most certainly are. Competition for places in the top law schools is becoming more intense each year, so AAB at A level is a common entry grade requirement for the leading law schools today.

REMEMBER

You don't have to study law at university to become a lawyer, but this book focuses on studying a law degree. You can study a non-law degree of your choosing and then take a postgraduate course.

1 Choosing courses

Choosing courses

USE COURSE SEARCH AT WWW.UCAS.COM TO FIND OUT WHICH COURSES MIGHT SUIT YOU, AND THE UNIVERSITIES AND COLLEGES THAT OFFER THEM.

Start thinking about what you want to study and where you want to go. Read the section on 'Finding a course' (page 70), and see what courses are available where in the chapter on 'Courses' (page 125). Check the entry requirements required for each course meet your academic expectations.

Use the UCAS website – www.ucas.com has lots of advice on how to find a course. Go to the students' section of the website for the best advice or go straight to Course Search to see all the courses available through UCAS. See the section on Entry Profiles on page 72 which explains what they are and how to find them on our website.

Watch UCAStv – at **www.ucas.tv** there are videos on 'how to choose your course', 'attending events' as well as case studies and video diaries from students talking about their experience of finding a course at university or college.

Attend UCAS conventions – UCAS conventions are held throughout the country. Universities and colleges have exhibition stands where their staff offer information about their courses and institutions. Details of when the conventions are happening are shown at **www.ucas.com/students/exhibitions.**

Look at the prospectuses – Universities and colleges have prospectuses and course-specific leaflets on their undergraduate courses. Your school or college library may have copies or go to the university's website to download a copy or you can ask them to send one to you.

Go to university open days – most institutions offer open days to anyone who wants to attend. See the institution information pages on Course Search and the UCAS/COA Open Days publication for information on when they are taking place.

League tables – these can be helpful but bear in mind that they attempt to rank institutions in an overall order reflecting the views of those that produce them. They may not reflect your views and needs.

Do your research – speak and refer to as many trusted sources as you can find. The section on 'Which area?' on page 21 will help you identify the different areas of law you might want to enter.

Finding a course

Through UCAS you can apply to five courses in total. How do you find out more information to make an informed decision?

How do you narrow down your courses to five? First of all, look up course details in this book or online on **www.ucas.com.** This will give you an idea of the full range of courses and topics on offer. You may want to study law by itself, but there are also many courses which also include study of different legal systems, or with additional options, such as a modern language (check out the degree subjects studied by our lawyer case studies). You'll quickly be able to eliminate institutions that don't offer the right course, or you can choose a 'hit list' of institutions first, and then see what they have to offer.

Once you've made a short(er) list, read the university and college Entry Profiles (see page 72) to find out what particular courses offer. You can then follow this up by looking at university or college websites, and generally finding out as much as you can about the course, department and institution. Don't be afraid to contact them to ask for more information, request their prospectus or arrange an open day visit.

UCAS WEBSITE – www.ucas.com

Whether you want advice about applying to higher education, to check out what courses are available, to find out what qualifications you need, or to monitor the status of your application, **www.ucas.com** is a great place to start. The UCAS website is one of the most popular websites in the UK and the most heavily used educational one, with over 1.5 million unique users a month. It is popular for good reason. From it, you can use Course Search as a quick and easy way to find out more about the courses you are interested in, including the vital code information you will need to include in your application later on. From Course Search, you can link to the websites of the universities and colleges in the UCAS system. Once you've applied through UCAS, you can use Track to check the progress of your application, including any decisions from universities or colleges, and you can make replies to your offers online.

Choosing courses

1

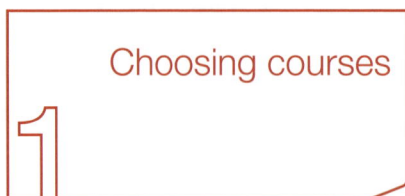

Entry Profiles

WHAT ARE THEY?

Entry Profiles give potential applicants to higher education specific information to help them make informed decisions about the courses they apply for. Detailed knowledge about the course, formal entry requirements and the qualities and experiences institutions are looking for in their applicants can help ensure that every applicant finds their way onto the right course. Entry Profiles are published on the UCAS website and can be reached using Course Search. They are available for all potential applicants and their advisers to see as they start making important decisions about where to apply. All course providers are asked to contribute Entry Profiles for the UCAS Course Search facility.

WHY USE THEM?

Courses can vary at different universities and colleges, even though they have the same name. Differences in course content, structure, optional modules, and the department's approach to teaching and learning can make the experience of studying any subject very different for students at different institutions, even before the size and location of the institution are taken into account.

It is important that you are fully informed about the courses and the institutions offering them before you apply, and that you know what academic qualifications and personal qualities are being sought in an applicant. Then you can avoid mistakes and make fully informed choices.

HOW DO I USE THE ENTRY PROFILES?

- When you find courses that interest you, search for the Entry Profile through the Course Search at www.ucas.com. Look for the symbol EP after the course title on the results page. This tells you that it has a complete Entry Profile.
- Courses without the EP symbol have academic entry requirements only.

TOP TIP

Don't be afraid to pick up the phone – university and college admissions officers welcome enquiries directly from students, rather than careers officers phoning on your behalf. It shows you're genuinely interested and committed to your own career early on.

Choosing courses

1

Choosing your institution

Different people look for different things from their university or college course, but the checklist on the next page sets out the kinds of factors all prospective students should consider when choosing their university. Keep this list in mind on open days, when talking to friends about their experiences at various universities and colleges, or while reading prospectuses and websites.

WHAT TO CONSIDER WHEN CHOOSING YOUR LAW COURSE

Location	Do you want to stay close to home? Would you prefer to study at a city or campus university or college?
Grades required	Use the Course Search facility on the UCAS website, www.ucas.com, to view entry requirements for courses you are interested in. Also, check out the university or college website or call up the admissions office. Some institutions specify 'grades' required, eg AAB, while others specify 'points' required, eg 340. If they ask for points, it means they're using the UCAS Tariff system, which basically awards points to different types and levels of qualification. For example, an A grade at A level = 120 points; a B grade at A level = 100 points. The full Tariff tables are available on pages 104-109 and at www.ucas.com.
Employer links	Ask the course tutor or department about links with employers, especially for placements or work experience.
Graduate prospects	Ask the careers office for their list of graduate 'destinations'.
Cost	Ask the law admissions office about variable tuition fees and financial assistance, especially at the 'top' university law departments.
Law or non-law degree?	Is there another subject that you enjoy, that you could study first, that might actually help give you an edge in employers' eyes?
Degree type	Do you want to study law on its own ('single' honours degree) or 50/50 with another subject ('joint') or as one of a few subjects ('combined' degree)? If you opt for a joint or combined course, check that it's still a qualifying law degree, ie that you won't need to do a conversion course.
Teaching style	How many lectures per week, amount of tutorial or one-to-one work, etc?
Course assessment	Can you see yourself writing endless essays and doing filmed mock trials?
Facilities for students	Check out the law library and computing facilities, and find out if there is a careers adviser dedicated to law.
'Fit'	Even if all the above criteria stack up, this one relies on gut feel – go and visit the institution if you can and see if it's 'you'.

1 Choosing courses

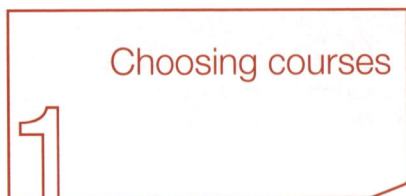

How will they choose you?

ADMISSIONS TESTS

Students applying to some courses are required to sit an admissions test as part of the application process. The tables on page 78-79 give details of some of the law courses that use admissions tests as part of their selection criteria. This is not a definitive list, so check the Entry Profile for your chosen course(s) on Course Search on the UCAS website, or contact the university or college for the most up-to-date information on their admissions tests. An up-to-date list of tests can be found on **www.ucas.com/students/beforeyouapply/admissions/index.html**.

Admissions tests are a way to manage application numbers for high-demand courses by helping to differentiate fairly between well-qualified applicants. They can widen access and participation in higher education as they measure academic potential without being influenced by educational background.

Admissions tests broaden and complement other selection criteria as they often assess aptitude and reasoning rather than achievement and recall.

Admissions tests do not generally require additional teaching, although applicants should familiarise themselves with a specimen paper beforehand. Check with the test centre about what type of preparation is required. It is usually the applicant's own responsibility to ensure they are entered for a test by the closing date. Some tests are taken at the applicant's school or college, others require applicants to sit the test at a test centre or at the university or college as part of an interview day. Overseas applicants may not be required to sit an admissions test – check with the course provider.

LNAT

Such is the level of competition for places on some law courses that a number of university law departments now require applicants to sit a standardised entry test as part of their selection criteria. Why? The test helps universities to make fairer choices among the many highly qualified applicants who want to join their undergraduate law programmes, and is also a possible aid to widening participation by helping to identify academic potential.

NATIONAL ADMISSIONS TEST FOR LAW (LNAT)	
Which universities require it?	University of Birmingham University of Bristol Durham University University of Glasgow King's College London (University of London) The National University of Ireland, Maynooth (mature candidates only) University of Nottingham University of Oxford University College London (University of London) Check the LNAT website for the latest information.
What does it involve?	An on-screen written test under exam conditions, comprising two sections: 80 minutes – 30 multiple-choice questions to assess your 'critical reasoning' and how well you analyse and interpret data and make logical deductions from passages 40 minutes – essay (on a choice of subjects)
Where is the test held?	In one of a global network of test centres operated by test provider, Pearson VUE. See the LNAT website – **www.lnat.ac.uk**.
How much does it cost	For UK and EU centres £40. For centres outside EU £60 (as of 2008–09).
How can I prepare?	This test does NOT test your legal knowledge, so swotting up on the law of tort won't get you very far. Instead, it aims to assess your 'aptitude for law', by testing your written communication and logical thinking, so any practice you can get writing essays to weigh up pros and cons of issues and come to a logical conclusion is useful. You can also check out the 'sample test', (which is available as an executable test or as a document that can be printed out) with answer key and commentary, and the advice given in the Preparation section on the LNAT website..
Where can I get more info?	**www.lnat.ac.uk**

LNAT course details

UNIVERSITY/COLLEGE	COURSE	CODE	DATE OF TEST
University of Birmingham (B32)	Law	M100	
	Law with Business Studies	M1N1	
	Law with French (4 years)	MR11	
	Law with German (4 years)	MR12	
University of Bristol (B78)	Law	M100	
	Law and French (4 years)	MR11	
	Law and German (4 years)	MR12	
	Law with Chemistry	M1F1	
Durham University (D86)	Law	M101	
	Law with Foundation (international students only)	M102	
University of Glasgow (G28)	Law	M114	
	Law with Czech Language	M1R7	
	Law with French Language	M1R1	
	Law with French Legal Studies	M121	
	Law with German Language	M1R2	
	Law with German Legal Studies	M122	
	Law with Italian Language	M1R3	
	Law with Italian Legal Studies	M1M9	
	Law with Polish Language	M1RR	
	Law with Spanish Language	M1R4	
	Law with Spanish Legal Studies	M123	
	Law/Business Economics	MN11	
	Law/Business Management	MN12	
	Law/Economic and Social History	MV13	
	Law/Economics	ML11	
	Law/English Literature	MQ13	
	Law/Gaelic Language	MQ15	
	Law/Geography	ML17	
	Law/History	MV11	
	Law/Philosophy	MV15	
	Law/Politics	ML12	
	Law/Slavonic Studies	MR17	

UNIVERSITY/COLLEGE	COURSE	CODE	DATE OF TEST
King's College London (University of London) (K60)	Law	M100	
	Law with German Law	M122	
	English and French Law (LBB Honours)	M121	
National University of Ireland, Maynooth†	Law and Arts	MH115 BCL*	
	Business and Law	MH406 BBL*	
The University of Nottingham (N84)	Law	M100	
	Law with German	M1R2	
	Law with French	M1R1	
University of Oxford (O33)	Law	M100	Candidates for the University of Oxford are required to register and book a test slot by 15 October 2009 and to sit the LNAT by 1 November 2009
	Law with Spanish Law	M194	
	Law with Italian Law	M193	
	Law with French Law	M191	
	Law with German Law	M192	
	Law with European Law	M190	
University College London (University of London) (U80)	English and German Law LLB and Baccalaureus Legum (4 years)	M146	November
	Law	M100	November
	Law with Advanced Studies (4 years)	M101	November
	Law with Another Legal System	M102	November
	Law with French Law (4 years)	M141	November
	Law with German Law (4 years)	M142	November
	Law with Hispanic Law (4 years)	M144	November
	Law with Italian Law (4 years)	M143	November

Further information can be found on the LNAT website, **www.lnat.ac.uk.** Candidates are advised to check the 2009 LNAT website (which will be launched in summer 2009) for up to date information on courses, deadlines etc. For entry in 2009/10 or deferred entry in 2011 LNAT registration begins on 1 August 2009, and LNAT testing starts on 1 September 2009.

†This is not a UCAS member institution. Check **www.nuim.ie** for information on how to apply.
*Mature candidates only. Candidates should consult the LNAT website for deadlines.

Cambridge Law Test

Until last year, Cambridge participated in the National Admissions Test for Law (LNAT). However, from 2010 entry, the LNAT will not play any part in the Cambridge admissions process. Instead, most colleges will require applicants for Law to take the Cambridge Law Test.

The Cambridge Law Test is designed to provide an assessment of your potential for our Law course. In most cases applicants will take the test when they are in Cambridge for interview. The college dealing with your application will contact you about the arrangements if they are using it. There is no need for you to register for this test.

Further information about the test, including specimen questions and answers, will be available from 1 May 2009 on the Faculty of Law website: **www.law.cam.ac.uk/admissions/.**

Choosing courses

1

The cost of higher education

As a student, you will have to pay for two things:

- tuition fees for your course
- living costs, such as rent, food, books, transport and entertainment.

If that sounds expensive, don't worry. You can get financial help from the Government in the form of loans and grants.

FEES

The amount of tuition fees you have to pay, and the financial assistance you may be entitled to, depends on:

- where you live
- where you want to study
- what you want to study
- your financial circumstances.

STUDENT LOANS, GRANTS AND BURSARIES

The purpose of a student loan is to help cover the costs of your tuition fees and basic living (rent, bills, food etc). Many other kinds of loan are available to students while they are studying at university or college. Depending on the source of the loan, the interest rate can have a severe impact upon the overall debt at the end of your degree. However, a student loan (or student maintenance loan as it is sometimes known) only takes inflation into account, so the overall amount will only be slightly higher than the figure borrowed. Maintenance loans are available to all citizens who satisfy UK residency requirements.

Remember that a student loan is not a grant: you do have to pay it back once you have left university and are earning over £15,000 a year.

In addition, there are non-repayable grants and bursaries available, depending on your circumstances and the courses and institutions to which you are applying.

USEFUL WEBSITES

There is lots of information available about student finance. Listed below are some websites you may find useful:

UCAS
www.ucas.com/students/studentfinance

National Union of Students
www.nus.org.uk/money

If your family lives in England, you should visit
www.direct.gov.uk/studentfinance.

If your family lives in Wales, you should visit
www.studentfinancewales.co.uk
www.cyllidmyfyrwyrcymru.co.uk.

If your family lives in Northern Ireland, you should visit
www.studentfinanceni.co.uk.

If your family lives in Scotland, you should visit
www.saas.gov.uk.

Disabled Students' Allowance

If you have a disablilty or specific learning difficulty you may be able to apply for a Disabled Students' Allowance. To find out more go to the websites above and search on Disabled Student.

Childcare Grant

This is available to students who have dependent children and a low household income. This includes students who are lone parents and students who are married to, or the partners of, other students.

TOP TIP

Before you choose your institution, make sure you find out about the bursaries they offer. Some are likely to be more generous than others, and this may make the difference between a financially comfortable or uncomfortable time.

1 Choosing courses

International students

APPLYING TO STUDY IN THE UK

Deciding to go to university or college in the UK is very exciting. You need to think about what course to do, where to study, and how much it will cost. The decisions you make can have a huge effect on your future but UCAS is here to help.

What is UCAS?

UCAS is the organisation that manages applications to full-time undergraduate courses in the UK. All the UK universities and many colleges use us. We are respected around the world and you can access our website 24 hours a day, seven days a week at **www.ucas.com**.

Whatever your age or qualifications, if you want to apply for any of the 50,000 courses listed at over 300 universities and colleges on the UCAS website, you must apply through UCAS at **www.ucas.com**. If you

are unsure, your school, college, adviser, or local British Council office will be able to help. Further advice and a video guide for international students can be found on the non-UK section of the UCAS website at **www.ucas.com/students/nonukstudents**.

If you already have a degree from your own country, you will probably have to take a conversion course in English law. Most British Council offices will have information and advice about entry to UK law schools.

What is Apply?

Apply is our secure online application system that you can use anytime and anywhere, giving you the flexibility to fill in your application when it suits you. Each time you log in, you can enter more information and take as long as you wish to change and complete it. Using Apply is the fastest and most efficient method of applying, but students with limited or no internet access should contact the UCAS Customer Service Unit on +44 (0)870 11 222 11 for advice on what to do. By applying through UCAS, you are able to use the one application for up to five choices.

Students may apply on their own or through their school, college, adviser, or local British Council if they are registered with UCAS to use Apply. If you choose to use an education agent's services, check with the British Council to see if they hold a list of certificated or registered agents in your country. Check also on any charges you may need to pay. UCAS charges only the application fee (see below) but agents may charge for additional services.

How much will my application cost?

If you choose to apply to more than one course, university or college you need to pay UCAS £19 GBP when you apply. If you only apply to one course at one university or college, you pay UCAS £9 GBP.

WHAT LEVEL OF ENGLISH?

UCAS provides a list of English language qualifications and grades that are acceptable to most UK universities and colleges, however you are advised to contact the institutions directly as each have their own entry requirement in English. For more information go to **www.ucas.com/students/nonukstudents/englangprof**.

INTERNATIONAL STUDENT FEES

If you study in the UK, your fee status (whether you pay full-cost fees or a subsidised fee rate) will be decided by the UK university or college you plan to attend. Before you decide which university or college to attend, you need to be absolutely certain that you can pay the full cost of:

- your tuition fees (the amount is set by universities and colleges, so contact them for more information – visit their websites where many list their fees)
- the everyday living expenses for you and your family for the whole time that you are in the UK, including accommodation, food, heat, light, clothes, travel
- books and equipment for your course
- travel to and from your country.

You must include everything when you work out how much it will cost. You can get information to help you do this accurately from the international offices at universities and colleges, UKCISA (UK Council for International Student Affairs) and the British Council. There is a useful website tool to help you manage your money at university – **www.studentcalculator.org.uk.**

Scholarships and bursaries are offered at some universities and colleges and you should contact them for more information. In addition, you should check with your local British Council for additional scholarships available to students from your country who want to study in the UK.

LEGAL DOCUMENTS YOU WILL NEED

As you prepare to study in the UK, it is very important to think about the legal documents you will need to enter the country.

Everyone who comes to study in the UK needs a valid passport. If you do not have one, you should apply for one as soon as possible. People from certain countries also need visas before they come into the UK. They are known as 'visa nationals'. You can check if you require a visa to travel to the UK by visiting the UK Border Agency website and selecting "Studying in the UK". So, please check the UK Border Agency website at **www.ukba.homeoffice.gov.uk** for the most up-to-date guidance and information about the United Kingdom's visa requirements.

When you apply for your visa you need to make sure you have the following documents:

- A visa letter from the university or college where you are going to study or a Confirmation of Acceptance for Study (CAS) number. The university or college must be on the UKBA Register of Sponsors.
- A valid passport.
- Evidence that you have enough money to pay for your course and living costs.
- Certificates for all qualifications you have that are relevant to the course you have been accepted for and for any English language qualifications.

You will also have to give your biometric data.

Do check for further information from your local British Embassy or High Commission. Guidance information for international students is also available from UKCISA and from UKBA.

ADDITIONAL RESOURCES

There are a number of organisations that can provide further guidance and information to you as you prepare to study in the UK:

- British Council
  www.britishcouncil.org
- Education UK (British Council website dealing with educational matters)
  www.educationuk.org
- English UK (British Council accredited website listing English language courses in the UK)
  www.englishuk.com
- UK Border Agency (provides information on visa requirements and applications)
  www.ukba.homeoffice.gov.uk
- UKCISA (UK Council for International Student Affairs)
  www.ukcisa.org.uk
- BUILA (British Universities, International Liaison Association)
  www.buila.ac.uk
- DIUS (Department for Innovation, Universities and Skills)
  www.dius.gov.uk

Applying

2

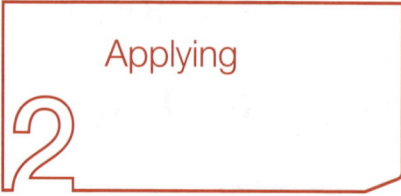

Step 2 – Applying

Apply for up to five courses using the UCAS online application system at **www.ucas.com.**

WHEN TO APPLY

Make a note of these important dates for your diary.

- **Early September 2009**
  Opening date for receiving applications.
- **15 October 2009**
  Application deadline for the receipt at UCAS of applications for all medicine, dentistry, veterinary medicine and veterinary science courses and for all courses at the universities of Oxford and Cambridge.
- **15 January 2010**
  Application deadline for the receipt at UCAS of applications for all courses except those listed above with a 15 October deadline.

- **25 February 2010**
  Start of Extra.
- **30 June 2010**
  Final deadline for all applications, including those from outside the UK and EU. Any applications we receive after this date go directly into Clearing.
- **20 September 2010**
  Last date for Clearing applications.

Don't forget…

Universities and colleges guarantee to consider your application if we receive it by the appropriate deadline. If you send it in after the deadline, but by 30 June 2010, universities and colleges will consider it if they want to make more offers.

Applying

2

How to apply

You apply online at **www.ucas.com** through Apply – a secure, web-based application service that is designed for all our applicants, whether they are applying through a UCAS-registered centre or as an individual, anywhere in the world. Apply is:

- easy to access – all you need is an internet connection
- easy to use – you don't have to complete your application all in one go: you can save the sections as you complete them and come back to it later
- easy to monitor – once you've applied, you can use Track to check the progress of your application, including any decisions from universities or colleges. You can also reply to your offers using Track
- watch the UCAStv guide to applying through UCAS at **www.ucas.tv.**

DEFERRED ENTRY

If you want to apply for deferred entry in 2011, perhaps because you want to take a year out between school or college and higher education, you should check that the university or college will accept a deferred entry application. Occasionally, tutors are not happy to accept students who take a gap year, because it interrupts the flow of their learning. If you apply for deferred entry, you must meet the conditions of any offers by 31 August 2010. If you accept a place for 2011 entry and then change your mind, you cannot reapply through us in the 2011 entry cycle unless you withdraw your original application.

INVISIBILITY OF CHOICES

Universities and colleges cannot see details of the other choices on your application until you reply to any offers or you have not been successful at any of your choices.

You can only submit one UCAS application in each year's application cycle.

APPLYING THROUGH YOUR SCHOOL OR COLLEGE

1 GET SCHOOL OR COLLEGE 'BUZZWORD'

Ask your UCAS application coordinator (may be your sixth form tutor) for your school or college UCAS 'buzzword'. This is a password for the school or college.

2 REGISTER

Go to **www.ucas.com/students/apply** and click on **Register/Log in** to use **Apply** and then **Register**. After you have entered your registration details, the online system will automatically generate a username for you, but you'll have to come up with a password and answers to security questions.

3 COMPLETE SIX SECTIONS

Complete the sections of the application. To access any section, click on the section name at the top of the screen and follow the instructions. The sections are:

Personal details – contact details, residential status, disability status

Additional information – only UK applicants need to complete this section

Choices – which courses you'd like to apply for

Education – your education to date

Employment – for example, work experience, holiday jobs

Personal statement – page 92.

4 PASS TO REFEREE

Once you've completed all the sections, send your application electronically to your referee (normally your form tutor). They'll check it, approve it and add their reference to it, and will then send it to UCAS on your behalf.

USEFUL INFORMATION ABOUT APPLY

- Important details like date of birth and course codes will be checked by Apply. It will alert you if they are not valid.
- The text for your personal statement and reference can be copied and pasted into your application.
- You can change your application at any time before it is completed and sent to UCAS.
- You can print and preview your application at any time.
- Your application will normally be processed at UCAS within one working day.
- Your school, college or centre can choose different payment methods. For example, they may want us to bill them, or you may be able to pay online by debit or credit card.

NOT APPLYING THROUGH A SCHOOL OR COLLEGE

For example, if you are not currently studying – you can follow the same steps, but, as you can't supply a 'buzzword', you'll just be asked a few extra questions to check you are eligible to apply, and you'll have to supply a reference from someone who knows you well enough to comment on your suitability for higher education. Guidance on choosing a suitable referee is available in Apply and on the UCAS website. If you are not applying through a school, college or other UCAS-registered centre, you should apply online and pay by debit or credit card.

If you have recently left school or college you can ask them to supply your reference online.

Applying

2

Making
your application

We want this to run smoothly for you and we also want to process your application as quickly as possible. You can help us to do this by remembering to do the following:

- check the closing dates for applications – see page 88
- start early and allow plenty of time for completing your application – including enough time for your referee to complete the reference section
- read the instructions carefully before you start
- consider what each question is actually asking for
- ask a teacher, parent, friend or careers adviser to review your draft application – particularly the personal statement
- pay special attention to questions that ask you about your interests and experience
- if you have extra information that will not fit on your application, send it direct to your chosen universities or colleges after we have sent you your Welcome letter with your Personal ID – don't send it to us
- keep a copy of the final version of your application, in case you are asked questions on it at an interview.

Applying

2

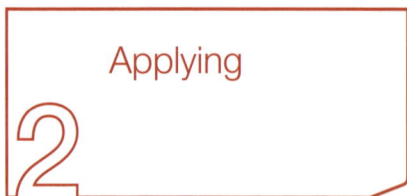

The personal statement

Next to choosing your courses, this section of your application will take up most of your time. It is of immense importance as many colleges and universities rely solely on the information in the UCAS application, rather than interviews and admissions tests, when selecting students. The personal statement can be the deciding factor in whether or not they offer you a place. If it is an institution that interviews, it could be the deciding factor in whether you get called for interview.

Keep a copy of your personal statement – if you are called for interview, you will almost certainly be asked questions based on it.

Tutors will look carefully at your exam results, actual and predicted, your referee's statement and your own personal statement. Remember, they are looking for reasons to offer you a place – try to give them every opportunity to do so!

A SALES DOCUMENT

The personal statement is your opportunity to sell yourself, so do so. The university or college admissions tutor who reads your personal statement wants to get a rounded picture of you to decide whether you will make an interesting member of the university or college both academically and socially. They want to know more about you than the subjects you are studying at school.

HOW TO IMPRESS

Don't be put off by the blank space. The secret is to cover key areas that admissions tutors always look for. Include things like hobbies and work experience, especially if they are linked in some way to the type of course you are applying for. You could talk about your career plans and interesting things you might have done outside the classroom. Have you belonged to sports teams or orchestras or held positions of responsibility? Maybe you've been a school play stalwart or been involved in community activities. If you left full-time education a while ago, talk about the work you have done and the skills you have gathered or how you have juggled bringing up a family – that is evidence of time management skills. Whoever you are, make sure you explain what appeals to you about the course you are applying for.

WHAT ADMISSIONS TUTORS LOOK FOR	WHAT TO TELL THEM
• Your reasons for wanting to take this course. • Your communication skills – how you express yourself in the personal statement. • Relevant experience – experience that's related to your choice of course. • Evidence of your interest in this field. • Evidence of your teamwork. • Evidence of your skills, for example, IT skills, people skills, debating and public speaking. • Other activities that show your dedication and ability to apply yourself.	• Why you want to do this subject. • What experience you already have in this field – for example work experience, school projects, hobbies, voluntary work. • The skills and qualities you have as a person that would make you a good student, for example anything that shows your dedication, communication ability, academic achievement, initiative. • Anything that shows you can knuckle down and apply yourself, for example running a marathon, raising money for charity. • If you're taking a gap year, why and (if possible) what you're going to do during it. • About your other interests and activities away from studying – to show you're a 'rounded' person.

WORK EXPERIENCE

How much does it count? Ask any law admissions tutor or legal recruiter about the importance of work experience on a candidate's application and they'll all agree – work experience shows a real, rather than theoretical, interest in the legal profession. An absence of work experience suggests questionable commitment to your choice of career.

Work experience will not only give you a real insight into the work of a solicitor or barrister, it will also give you valuable examples of the skills you have to offer. As part of the application process, you'll be asked to write a personal statement setting out which subject you'd like to study, why you'd like to study it, and what skills and experience you bring that would make you a great student for the course. This is where your work experience will help you stand out.

Unfortunately for sixth formers, most of the formal work experience schemes offered by chambers and firms of solicitors are aimed at undergraduates (see the table on the next page). However, there are still some alternative work experience routes for the dedicated A-level student, including taster days and introductory courses offered by universities and colleges, volunteering at your local Citizens' Advice Bureau or community advice centre, or work placements in a firm of solicitors organised by your school or college.

WORK EXPERIENCE SCHEMES FOR LAW UNDERGRADUATES

	BARRISTERS	SOLICITORS
Scheme	Mini-pupillages	Vacation placements
Typical tasks	Attending court Drafting legal opinions Researching litigation Sitting in on client conferences	Shadowing a solicitor Researching legal points Drafting letters Attending client meetings
Duration	Typically 3–5 days in barristers' chambers; it's now the norm for law students to do several mini-pupillages in different chambers and sectors	1–4 weeks in a firm of solicitors; most common are summer vacation schemes
How to apply	www.pupillages.com offers a list of organisations that operate mini-pupillages, but you'll still have to apply to chambers directly	Check out the individual law firms' websites and write directly to them
Note	Some chambers now operate assessed mini-pupillages, in which participants are given a task, eg drafting an opinion, which is formally assessed, and which may be used as part of their assessment for a full pupillage at a later date.	Firms are not obliged to pay trainees on vacation placements, though most now do. Rates range from around £165–£300 per week (of those firms that pay!).

If you have only non-legal work experience, it will still be useful to include it in any applications you make. The trick is to pull out the professional and personal skills you have developed of relevance to the work of a barrister or solicitor.

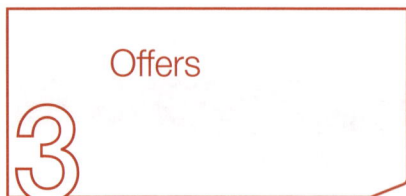

Offers

3

Step 3 – Offers

Once we have sent your application to your chosen universities and colleges, they will all consider it independently and tell us whether or not they can offer you a place. Some universities and colleges will take longer to make decisions than others. You may be asked to attend an interview, sit an additional test or provide a piece of work such as an essay before a decision can be made.

You may or may not be called for an interview as part of the selection process. Many institutions prefer not to interview people, as it's a very subjective and time-consuming process. However, some interview candidates as a matter of process, and others interview to clarify some aspect of a candidate's application – for example, if you're an international student in the UK, to check your communication skills, or if your grades are borderline.

If you are called for interview, the key areas they are likely to cover will be:

- evidence of your academic ability
- your capacity to study hard
- your commitment to a law career, best shown by work experience
- your awareness of current issues in the news that may have an impact on your chosen field of study, for example, new Acts of Parliament or EU Directives
- your logic and reasoning ability.

- How would you feel about defending a known criminal or dealing with a conflict of interest? (To explore your approach to 'ethical' issues.)
- Do you enjoy public speaking or debating? (One for the would-be barristers.)
- What do you think of the changes to employment law, etc? (To test your awareness of what's going on in your chosen field.)

A lot of the interview will be based on information supplied on your application – especially your **personal statement** – see pages 92 and 93 for tips about the personal statement.

Each time a university or college makes a decision about your application we record it and let you know. You can check the progress of your application using Track at www.ucas.com. This is our secure online service which gives you access to your application using the same username and password you used when you applied. You can use it to find out if you have been invited for interview or need to provide an additional piece of work, as well as check to see if you have received any offers.

Find out more about how to use Track in the UCAStv video guide at www.ucas.tv.

Types of offer

Universities and colleges can make two types of offer: conditional or unconditional. If they want you to pass your exams before they can accept you, they will make a conditional offer. The conditions of the offer may specify the number of UCAS Tariff points, for example 340 points from three A levels, or the grades for your A levels, such as B in English and A in history.

If they want to offer you a place and you already have all the necessary qualifications, they will make you an unconditional offer. This means that if you accept this offer you have a definite place.

However, for either type of offer there may be some non-academic requirements:

- For courses that involve contact with children and vulnerable adults you may need to have criminal record checks and ISA registration before you can start the course.
- For students who are not resident in either the UK or the EU, there may be some financial conditions to meet.

Offers

3

Replying to offers

When you have received decisions for all your choices, you must decide what you want to accept and you do this by using Track. You will be given a deadline by which to decide what to accept.

You can accept up to two offers. If you accept a conditional offer as your firm or preferred choice, you may accept another offer as an insurance or back-up choice. You may accept an unconditional or conditional offer as your insurance choice. If you accept an unconditional offer as your firm or preferred choice, you cannot accept another offer and you will go straight to step 6 on your applicant journey.

When you accept your firm and, if permitted, insurance choice, you must turn down all your other offers.

If you turn down all your offers, you may be able to apply for further courses using Extra (page 100). If you are not eligible to use Extra, you can contact universities and colleges with vacancies in Clearing (page 112). For more information and advice about replying to your offers, watch the UCAStv video guide at **www.ucas.tv.**

What if you have no offers?

If you have applied through UCAS and are not holding any offers, you may be able to add more choices, if you have not used all five choices, or apply through Extra for another course.

If you are not eligible for Extra, you can contact universities and colleges with vacancies in Clearing from mid-July 2010 (page 112).

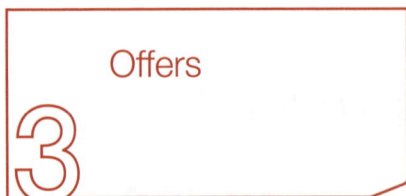

Offers

3

Extra

Extra allows you to make additional choices, one at a time, without having to wait for Clearing in July. It is completely optional and free, and is designed to encourage you to continue researching and choosing courses if you need to. The courses available through Extra will be highlighted on Course Search, at **www.ucas.com**.

Who is eligible?

You will be eligible for Extra if you have already made five choices and:

- you have had unsuccessful or withdrawal decisions from all five of your choices, or
- you have cancelled your outstanding choices and hold no offers, or
- you have received decisions from all five choices and have declined all offers made to you.

How does it work?

We contact you and explain what to do if you are eligible for Extra. If you are eligible you should:

- see a special Extra button on your Track screen
- check on Course Search for courses that are available through Extra; they are shown by the symbol X after the course title.
- choose one that you would like to apply for and enter the details on your Track screen.

When you have chosen a course, a copy of your application will be sent to the university or college.

What happens next?

We give universities and colleges 21 days to consider your Extra application. During this time, you cannot be considered by another university or college. After 21 days you can refer yourself to a different university or college if you wish, but it is a good idea to ring the one currently considering you before doing so. If you are made an offer, you can choose whether or not to accept it.

If you are currently studying for examinations, any offer that you receive is likely to be an offer conditional on exam grades. If you decide to accept a conditional offer, you will not be able to take any further part in Extra.

If you already have your examination results, it is possible that a university or college may make an unconditional offer.

If you accept an unconditional offer, you will be placed. You cannot then apply to any other universities or colleges in Extra.

If you decide to decline the offer, or the university or college decides they cannot make you an offer, you will be given another opportunity to use Extra, time permitting. Your Extra button on Track will be reactivated.

Once you have accepted an offer in Extra, you are committed to it in the same way as you would be with an offer through the main UCAS system. Conditional offers made through Extra will be treated in the same way as other conditional offers, when your examination results become available.

If your results do not meet the conditions and the university or college decides that they cannot confirm your Extra offer, you will automatically become eligible for Clearing if it is too late for you to be considered by another university or college in Extra.

If you are unsuccessful, decline an offer, or do not receive an offer, or 21 days has elapsed since choosing a course through Extra, you can use Extra to apply for another course.

From 1 October – 30 June

Applicants informed as they become eligible for Extra.

From 25 February – early July

The Extra service is available to eligible applicants through Track at **www.ucas.com**.

Advice

Do some careful research and seek guidance on your Extra choice of university or college and course. If you applied to high-demand courses and institutions in your original application and were unsuccessful, you could consider related or alternative subjects or perhaps apply for the subject you want in combination with another. Your teachers or careers advisers or the universities and colleges themselves can provide useful guidance. Entry Profiles, which appear with most courses listed on Course Search, are another important source of information. Be flexible, that is the key to success. But you are the only one who knows how flexible you are prepared to be. Remember that even if you decide to take a degree course other than law, you can take the postgraduate route into the profession.

Visit **www.ucas.tv** to watch the video guide on how to use Extra.

> Offers

3

The Tariff

Admission to higher education courses is generally dependent upon an individual's achievement in level 3 qualifications, such as GCE A levels. Did you know that there are currently over 3,000 level 3 qualifications available in the UK alone?

As if the number of qualifications available was not confusing enough, different qualifications can have different grading structures (alphabetical, numerical or a mixture of both). Finding out what qualifications are needed for different higher education courses can be very confusing.

The UCAS Tariff is the system for allocating points to qualifications used for entry to HE. It allows students to use a range of different qualifications to help secure a place on an undergraduate course.

Universities and colleges use the UCAS Tariff to make comparisons between applicants with different

qualifications. Tariff points are often used in entry requirements, although other factors are often taken into account. Entry Profiles provide a fuller picture of what admissions tutors are seeking.

The tables on the following pages show the qualifications covered by the UCAS Tariff. There may have been changes to these tables since this book was printed. You should visit **www.ucas.com** to view the most up-to-date tables.

FURTHER INFORMATION?

Although Tariff points can be accumulated in a variety of ways, not all of these will necessarily be acceptable for entry to a particular HE course. The achievement of a points score therefore does not give an automatic entitlement to entry, and many other factors are taken into account in the admissions process.

The Course Search facility at **www.ucas.com** is the best source of reference to find out what qualifications are acceptable for entry to specific courses. Updates to the Tariff, including details on how new qualifications are added, can be found at **www.ucas.com/students/ucas_tariff/.**

HOW DOES THE TARIFF WORK?

- Students can collect Tariff points from a range of different qualifications, eg GCE A level with BTEC Nationals.
- There is no ceiling to the number of points that can be accumulated.
- There is no double counting. Certain qualifications within the Tariff build on qualifications in the same subject. In these cases only the qualification with the higher Tariff score will be counted. This principle applies to:
    - GCE Advanced Subsidiary level and GCE Advanced level
    - Scottish Highers and Advanced Highers
    - Key Skills at level 2, 3 and 4
    - Speech, drama and music awards at grades 6, 7 and 8.
- Tariff points for the Advanced Diploma come from the Progression Diploma score plus the relevant Additional and Specialist Learning (ASL) Tariff points. Please see the appropriate qualification in the Tariff tables to calculate the ASL score.
- The Extended Project Tariff points are included within the Tariff points for Progression and Advanced Diplomas. Extended Project points represented in the Tariff only count when the qualification is taken outside of these Diplomas.
- Where the Tariff tables refer to specific awarding bodies, only qualifications from these awarding bodies attract Tariff points. Qualifications with a similar title, but from a different qualification awarding body do not attract Tariff points.

HOW DO UNIVERSITIES AND COLLEGES USE THE TARIFF?

The Tariff provides a facility to help universities and colleges when expressing entrance requirements and when making conditional offers. Entry requirements and conditional offers expressed as Tariff points will often require a minimum level of achievement in a specified subject (for example '300 points to include grade A at A level chemistry', or '260 points including SQA Higher grade B in mathematics').

Use of the Tariff may also vary from department to department at any one institution, and may in some cases be dependent on the programme being offered.

WHAT QUALIFICATIONS ARE INCLUDED IN THE TARIFF?

The following qualifications are included in the UCAS Tariff. See the number on the qualification title to find the relevant section of the Tariff table.

1   AAT NVQ level 3 in Accounting
2   Advanced Diploma
3   Advanced Extension Awards
4   Advanced Placement Programme
5   Asset Languages Advanced Stage (from 2010 entry onwards)
6   British Horse Society Stage 3 Horse Knowledge & Care, Stage 3 Riding and Preliminary Teacher's Certificate
7   BTEC Early Years
8   BTEC National Award, National Certificate and National Diploma
9   CACHE Diploma in Child Care and Education
10 Cambridge Pre-U
11 Certificate of Personal Effectiveness (COPE)
12 Diploma in Fashion Retail
13 Diploma in Foundation Studies (Art & Design; Art, Design & Media)
14 EDI Level 3 Certificate in Accounting, Certificate in Accounting (IAS)
15 Extended Project
16 Free-standing Mathematics qualifications
17 GCE AS, AS Double Award, A level, A level Double Award and A level with additional AS
18 Higher Sports Leader Award
19 Institute of Financial Services, Certificate and Diploma in Financial Studies
20 International Baccalaureate Diploma
21 International Baccalaureate Certificate
22 iMedia Users (iMedia) Certificate and Diploma
23 IT for Professionals (iPRO) Certificate and Diploma
24 Irish Leaving Certificate - Higher and Ordinary levels
25 Key Skills at levels 2, 3 and 4
26 Music examinations at grades 6, 7 and 8
27 OCR National Certificate, National Diploma and National Extended Diploma
28 Progression Diploma (from 2010 entry onwards)
29 Scottish Higher and Advanced Higher, Skills for Work Higher, and National Progression Awards
30 Speech and Drama examinations at grades 6, 7 and 8 Performance Studies
31 Welsh Baccalaureate Advanced Diploma

Updates on the Tariff, including details on the incorporation of any new qualifications, are posted on www.ucas.com.

UCAS TARIFF TABLES

1

AAT NVQ LEVEL 3 IN ACCOUNTING	
GRADE	TARIFF POINTS
PASS	160

2

ADVANCED DIPLOMA

Advanced Diploma = Progression Diploma plus Additional & Specialist Learning (ASL). Please see the appropriate qualification to calculate the ASL score. ASL has a maximum Tariff score of 140. Please see the Progression Diploma (Table 28) for Tariff scores

3

ADVANCED EXTENSION AWARDS	
GRADE	TARIFF POINTS
DISTINCTION	40
MERIT	20

Points for Advanced Extension Awards are over and above those gained form the A level grade

4

ADVANCED PLACEMENT PROGRAMME (US & CANADA)	
GRADE	TARIFF POINTS
Group A	
5	120
4	90
3	60
Group B	
5	50
4	35
3	20

5

ASSET LANGUAGES ADVANCED STAGE			
GRADE	TARIFF POINTS	GRADE	TARIFF POINTS
Speaking		Listening	
GRADE 12	28	GRADE 12	25
GRADE 11	20	GRADE 11	18
GRADE 10	12	GRADE 10	11
Reading		Writing	
GRADE 12	25	GRADE 12	25
GRADE 11	18	GRADE 11	18
GRADE 10	11	GRADE 10	11

Points for Asset Languages come into effect for entry into higher education from 2010 onwards

6

BRITISH HORSE SOCIETY	
GRADE	TARIFF POINTS
Stage 3 Horse Knowledge & Care	
PASS	35
Stage 3 Riding	
PASS	35
Preliminary Teacher's Certificate	
PASS	35

Awarded by Equestrian Qualifications (GB) Ltd (EQL) on behalf of British Horse Society

7

BTEC EARLY YEARS					
GRADE	TARIFF POINTS	GRADE	TARIFF POINTS	GRADE	TARIFF POINTS
Theory				Practical	
Diploma		Certificate		D	120
DDD	320	DD	200	M	80
DDM	280	DM	160	P	40
DMM	240	MM	120		
MMM	220	MP	80		
MMP	160	PP	40		
MPP	120				
PPP	80				

8

BTEC NATIONALS					
GRADE	TARIFF POINTS	GRADE	TARIFF POINTS	GRADE	TARIFF POINTS
National Diploma		National Certificate		National Award	
DDD	360	DD	240	D	120
DDM	320	DM	200	M	80
DMM	280	MM	160	P	40
MMM	240	MP	120		
MMP	200	PP	80		
MPP	160				
PPP	120				

UCAS TARIFF TABLES

9

CACHE DIPLOMA IN CHILD CARE & EDUCATION

GRADE	TARIFF POINTS	GRADE	TARIFF POINTS
Theory		Practical	
AA	240	A	120
BB	200	B	100
CC	160	C	80
DD	120	D	60
EE	80	E	40

10

CAMBRIDGE PRE-U

GRADE	TARIFF POINTS	GRADE	TARIFF POINTS	GRADE	TARIFF POINTS
Principal Subject		Global Perspectives and Research		Short Course	
D1	TBC	D1	TBC	D1	TBC
D2	145	D2	140	D2	TBC
D3	130	D3	126	D3	60
M1	115	M1	112	M1	53
M2	101	M2	98	M2	46
M3	87	M3	84	M3	39
P1	73	P1	70	P1	32
P2	59	P2	56	P2	26
P3	46	P3	42	P3	20

Points for PRE-U come into effect for entry into higher education from 2010 onwards

11

CERTIFICATE OF PERSONAL EFFECTIVENESS (COPE)

GRADE	TARIFF POINTS
PASS	70

Points are awarded for the Certificate of Personal Effectiveness (COPE) awarded by ASDAN and CCEA

12

DIPLOMA IN FASHION RETAIL

GRADE	TARIFF POINTS
DISTINCTION	160
MERIT	120
PASS	80

Awarded by ABC Awards

13

DIPLOMA IN FOUNDATION STUDIES (ART & DESIGN, AND ART, DESIGN & MEDIA)

GRADE	TARIFF POINTS
DISTINCTION	285
MERIT	225
PASS	165

Points are awarded for Edexcel Level 3 BTEC Diploma in Foundation Studies (Art & Design) and Level 3 Diploma in Foundation Studies (Art, Design & Media) awarded by ABC Awards and WJEC

14

EDI LEVEL 3 CERTIFICATE IN ACCOUNTING AND CERTIFICATE IN ACCOUNTING (IAS)

GRADE	TARIFF POINTS
DISTINCTION	120
MERIT	90
PASS	70

15

EXTENDED PROJECT (STAND ALONE)

GRADE	TARIFF POINTS
A*	70
A	60
B	50
C	40
D	30
E	20

Points for the Extended Project cannot be counted if taken as part of Progression/Advanced Diploma

16

FREE-STANDING MATHEMATICS

GRADE	TARIFF POINTS
A	20
B	17
C	13
D	10
E	7

Covers free-standing Mathematics - Additional Maths, Using and Applying Statistics, Working with Algebraic and Graphical Techniques, Modelling with Calculus

17

GCE

GRADE	TARIFF POINTS	GRADE	TARIFF POINTS	GRADE	TARIFF POINTS	GRADE	TARIFF POINTS	GRADE	TARIFF POINTS
GCE Double Award		A level with additional AS (9 units)		GCE A level		GCE AS		GCE AS Double Award	
A*A*	280	A*A	200	A*	140	A	60	AA	120
A*A	260	AA	180	A	120	B	50	AB	110
AA	240	AB	170	B	100	C	40	BB	100
AB	220	BB	150	C	80	D	30	BC	90
BB	200	BC	140	D	60	E	20	CC	80
BC	180	CC	120	E	40			CD	70
CC	160	CD	110					DD	60
CD	140	DD	90					DE	50
DD	120	DE	80					EE	40
DE	100	EE	60						
EE	80								

18

HIGHER SPORTS LEADER AWARD

GRADE	TARIFF POINTS
PASS	30

19

INSTITUTE OF FINANCIAL SERVICES

GRADE	TARIFF POINTS	GRADE	TARIFF POINTS
Certificate in Financial Studies (CeFS)		Diploma in Financial Studies (DipFS)	
A	60	A	60
B	50	B	50
C	40	C	40
D	30	D	30
E	20	E	20

Completion of both qualifications will result in a maximum of 120 UCAS Tariff points

20

INTERNATIONAL BACCALAUREATE (IB) DIPLOMA

GRADE	TARIFF POINTS	GRADE	TARIFF POINTS
45	768	34	512
44	744	33	489
43	722	32	466
42	698	31	422
41	675	30	419
40	652	29	396
39	628	28	373
38	605	27	350
37	582	26	326
36	559	25	303
35	535	24	280

INTERNATIONAL BACCALAUREATE (IB) DIPLOMA (REVISED FOR 2010 ENTRY ONWARDS)

GRADE	TARIFF POINTS	GRADE	TARIFF POINTS
45	720	34	479
44	698	33	457
43	676	32	435
42	654	31	413
41	632	30	392
40	611	29	370
39	589	28	348
38	567	27	326
37	545	26	304
36	523	25	282
35	501	24	260

UCAS TARIFF TABLES

21

INTERNATIONAL BACCALAUREATE (IB) CERTIFICATE

GRADE	TARIFF POINTS	GRADE	TARIFF POINTS	GRADE	TARIFF POINTS
Higher Level		Standard Level		Core	
7	130	7	70	3	120
6	110	6	59	2	80
5	80	5	43	1	40
4	50	4	27	0	10
3	20	3	11		

Points for the IB Certificate come into effect for entry into higher education from 2010 onwards

22

iMEDIA USERS (iMEDIA)

GRADE	TARIFF POINTS
DIPLOMA	66
CERTIFICATE	40

Awarded by OCR

23

IT PROFESSIONALS (iPRO)

GRADE	TARIFF POINTS
DIPLOMA	100
CERTIFICATE	80

Awarded by OCR

24

IRISH LEAVING CERTIFICATE

GRADE	TARIFF POINTS	GRADE	TARIFF POINTS
Higher		Ordinary	
A1	90	A1	39
A2	77	A2	26
B1	71	B1	20
B2	64	B2	14
B3	58	B3	7
C1	52		
C2	45		
C3	39		
D1	33		
D2	26		
D3	20		

25

KEY SKILLS

GRADE	TARIFF POINTS
LEVEL 4	30
LEVEL 3	20
LEVEL 2	10

26

MUSIC EXAMINATIONS

GRADE	TARIFF POINTS	GRADE	TARIFF POINTS	GRADE	TARIFF POINTS
Practical					
Grade 8		Grade 7		Grade 6	
DISTINCTION	75	DISTINCTION	60	DISTINCTION	45
MERIT	70	MERIT	55	MERIT	40
PASS	55	PASS	40	PASS	25
Theory					
Grade 8		Grade 7		Grade 6	
DISTINCTION	30	DISTINCTION	20	DISTINCTION	15
MERIT	25	MERIT	15	MERIT	10
PASS	20	PASS	10	PASS	5

Points shown are for the ABRSM, Guildhall, LCMM, Rockschool and Trinity College London Advanced level music examinations

UCAS TARIFF TABLES

27

	OCR NATIONALS				
GRADE	TARIFF POINTS	GRADE	TARIFF POINTS	GRADE	TARIFF POINTS
National Extended Diploma		National Diploma		National Certificate	
D1	360	D	240	D	120
D2/M1	320	M1	200	M	80
M2	280	M2/P1	160	P	40
M3	240	P2	120		
P1	200	P3	80		
P2	160				
P3	120				

28

PROGRESSION DIPLOMA	
GRADE	TARIFF POINTS
A*	350
A	300
B	250
C	200
D	150
E	100

Points for the Progression Diploma come into effect for entry to higher education from 2010 onwards.

Advanced Diploma = Progression Diploma plus Additional & Specialist Learning (ASL). Please see the appropriate qualification to calculate the ASL score. ASL has a maximum Tariff score of 140

29

	SCOTTISH QUALIFICATIONS				SCOTTISH QUALIFICATIONS (REVISED FOR 2010 ENTRY ONWARDS)		
GRADE	TARIFF POINTS	GRADE	TARIFF POINTS	GRADE	TARIFF POINTS	GRADE	TARIFF POINTS
Advanced Higher		Higher		Advanced Higher		Higher	
A	120	A	72	A	130	A	80
B	100	B	60	B	110	B	65
C	80	C	48	C	90	C	50
D	72	D	42	D	72	D	36
				Ungraded Higher		NPA PC Passport	
				PASS	45	PASS	45

30

	SPEECH & DRAMA EXAMINATIONS						
GRADE	TARIFF POINTS	GRADE	TARIFF POINTS	GRADE	TARIFF POINTS	GRADE	TARIFF POINTS
PCertLAM**		Grade 8		Grade 7		Grade 6	
DISTINCTION	90	DISTINCTION	65	DISTINCTION	55	DISTINCTION	40
MERIT	80	MERIT	60	MERIT	50	MERIT	35
PASS	60	PASS	45	PASS	35	PASS	20

Points shown are for ESB, LAMDA, LCMM and Trinity Guildhall Advanced level speech and drama examinations accredited in the National Qualifications Framework. A full list of the subjects covered is available on the UCAS website.

31

WELSH BACCALAUREATE CORE	
GRADE	TARIFF POINTS
PASS	120

These points are for the Core and are awarded only when a candidate achieves the Welsh Baccalaureate Advanced Diploma

Results

4

Step 4 – Results

We receive many exam results direct from the exam boards – check the list at **www.ucas.com**. If your qualification is listed, you don't need to send your results to us or the universities and colleges. Check Track at **www.ucas.com** to see if you've got a place on your chosen course.

If your qualification is listed, we send your results to the universities and colleges that you have accepted as your firm and insurance choices. If your qualification is not listed, you must send your exam results to the universities and colleges where you are holding offers.

You should arrange your holidays so that you are at home when your exam results are published because, if there are any issues to discuss, admissions tutors will want to speak to you in person.

After you have received your exam results check Track to find out if you have a place on your chosen course.

If you have met all the conditions for your firm choice, the university or college will confirm that you have a place. Sometimes, they may still confirm you have a place even if you have not quite met all the offer conditions; or they may offer you a place on a similar course.

If you have not met the conditions of your firm choice and the university or college has not confirmed your place, but you have met all the conditions of your insurance offer, the university or college will confirm that you have a place.

When a university or college tells us that you have a place, we send you confirmation by letter.

WHAT IF YOU DON'T HAVE A PLACE?

If you have not met the conditions of either your firm or insurance choice, and your chosen universities or colleges have not confirmed your place, you are eligible for Clearing. In Clearing you can apply for courses that still have vacancies. Clearing operates from mid-July to late September 2010 (page 112).

BETTER RESULTS THAN EXPECTED?

If you obtain exam results that meet and exceed the conditions of the offer for your firm choice, you can for a short period look for an alternative place, whilst still keeping your original firm choice (page 113).

Next steps

5

Step 5 – Next steps

IF YOU FIND YOURSELF IN CLEARING, YOU WILL NEED TO

Find a course you like – do your research thoroughly and quickly. You could consider related or alternative subjects or perhaps apply for the subject you want in combination with another. Your teachers or careers advisers or the universities and colleges themselves can provide useful guidance. If your results are reasonable, and you are flexible about where and what you want to study, you have every chance of finding a place on a suitable course.

Talk to the institutions – don't be afraid to call them. Prepare a list of what you will say to them about:

- why you want to study the course
- why you want to study at their institution
- what relevant employment or activities you have done that relate to the course
- your grades

and have ready your:

- Personal ID
- Clearing number.

Getting an offer – don't be pressured into doing something you don't like but once you find a course you will enjoy, stick with it.

IF YOUR RESULTS MEET AND EXCEED YOUR CONDITIONAL FIRM OFFER, YOU CAN ADJUST YOUR PLACE

You may decide to research alternative institutions and courses. Talk to your school or college adviser first. If you find a course that you think you may be qualified for and which has places available, you need to talk to the new institution to adjust your place.

There are no published vacancies in Adjustment so you'll need to talk to the institutions – have all your information ready before you call:

- full details of your exam results
- why you want to change your course
- why you want to study at their institution
- what relevant employment or activities you have done that relate to the course
- your Personal ID.

You may be able to adjust to a deferred entry place if there are no places left and if your results meet the course entry requirements – you do not need to withdraw and reapply. Be aware that you have only five calendar days (including weekends) to consider changing your course in these circumstances – you must complete both your research and your negotiation within this time.

IF YOU ARE STILL WITHOUT A PLACE TO STUDY:

You could re-sit your exams and try again next year, find employment, decide to do a further education course or apply for a part-time course and a part-time job. Seek advice from your school or college or careers office.

> 6

Starting university
or college

Step 6 – Starting university or college

Make sure you have everything ready, such as accommodation, finances, travel arrangements, books and equipment required for the course.

Congratulations! Now you have your place at university or college you will need to make plans on how to get there, where to live and how to finance it.

Where to live - Unless you are planning to live at home, your university or college will usually provide you with guidance on how to find somewhere to live. The earlier you contact them the better your chance of finding a suitable range of options to choose from.

Student finance – You will need to budget for living costs, accommodation, travel, books and tuition fees. Tuition fees vary depending on the course and university you choose, and are shown on Course Search at **www.ucas.com**. Help is available from some

universities and colleges in the form of bursaries and scholarships. Details of these bursaries and scholarships can also be found on Course Search.

Yougofurther.co.uk – You might have already registered for **www.yougofurther.co.uk**, the social community website brought to you by UCAS that is exclusively for students. The site allows you to make friends with other applicants who are going to the same university or college and/or who are going to be on the same course, or who live in your area. It has all the essential information you need for life at university. Whether it's jobs, money, travel, housing or healthy living – yougo's got it covered.

Useful contacts

For information relating to the UCAS application process, please contact the UCAS Customer Service Unit on 0871 468 0 468. Calls from BT landlines within the UK will cost no more than 9p per minute. The cost of calls from mobiles and other networks may vary.

If you have hearing difficulties, you can call the RNID typetalk service on 18001 0871 468 0 468 (outside the UK +44 151 494 1260). Calls are charged at normal rates.

CAREERS ADVICE

Connexions is for you if you live in England, are aged 13 to 19 and want advice on getting to where you want to be in life.

Connexions personal advisers can give you information, advice and practical help with all sorts of things, like choosing subjects at school or mapping out your future career options. They can help you with anything that might be affecting you at school, college, work or in your personal or family life.

For where to find your local office, look at **www.connexions.gov.uk**.

Careers Scotland provides a starting point for anyone looking for careers information, advice or guidance. **www.careers-scotland.org.uk**.

Careers Wales – Wales' national all-age careers guidance service. **www.careerswales.com**.

Northern Ireland Careers Service website for the new, all-age careers guidance service in Northern Ireland. **www.careersserviceni.com**.

Learndirect – Not sure what job you want? Need help to decide which course to do? Give learndirect a call on 0800 101 901 or, for Scotland, 0808 100 9000. **www.learndirect.co.uk**. **www.learndirectscotland.com**.

YEAR OUT

For useful information on taking a year out, see **www.gap-year.com**.

The Year Out Group website is packed with information and guidance for young people and their parents and advisers. **www.yearoutgroup.org**.

STUDENT SUPPORT

Each country in the UK has its own rules and procedures, and you should check the websites for the country where you normally live for more information. The following websites should give you information about what grants and loans you may be eligible to apply for and how you can apply.

If your family lives in England, you should visit, **www.direct.gov.uk/studentfinance.**

If your family lives in Wales, you should visit **www.studentfinancewales.co.uk** or **www.cyllidmyfyrwyrcymru.co.uk.**

If your family lives in Scotland, you should visit **www.saas.gov.uk.**

If your family lives in Northern Ireland, you should visit **www.studentfinanceni.co.uk.**

If your family lives in Guernsey, Jersey or the Isle of Man, you should visit **www.gov.gg/, www.gov.je/** or **www.gov.im/.**

Disabled Students' Allowance
If you have a disability or specific learning difficulty, you may be able to apply for a Disabled Students' Allowance. To find out more you should visit the websites listed above and search on Disabled Student.

Essential reading

UCAS has brought together the best books and resources you need to make the important decisions regarding entry to higher education. With guidance on choosing courses, finding the right institution, information about student finance, admissions tests, gap years and lots more, you can find the most trusted guides at **www.ucasbooks.com**.

The publications listed on the following pages are available through **www.ucasbooks.com** or from UCAS Publication Services unless otherwise stated. Postage and packing charges are not included in the price. You will be advised of the postage and packing charge when placing your order.

UCAS Publication Services

UCAS Publication Services
PO Box 130
Cheltenham
Gloucestershire   GL52 3ZF

f: 01242 544 806
e: publicationservices@ucas.ac.uk
// **www.ucas.com**
// **www.ucasbooks.com**

NEED HELP COMPLETING YOUR APPLICATION?

How to Complete your UCAS Application 2010
A must for anyone applying through UCAS. Contains advice on the preparation needed, a step-by-step guide to filling out the UCAS application, information on the UCAS process and useful tips for completing the personal statement.
Published by Trotman
Price £12.99

Insider's Guide to Applying to University
Full of honest insights, this is a thorough guide to the application process. It reveals advice from careers advisers and current students, guidance on making sense of university information and choosing courses. Also includes tips for the personal statement, interviews, admissions tests, UCAS Extra and Clearing.
Published by Trotman
Price £12.99

How to Write a Winning UCAS Personal Statement
The personal statement is your chance to stand out from the crowd. Based on information from admissions tutors, this book will help you sell yourself. It includes specific guidance for over 30 popular subjects, common mistakes to avoid, information on what admissions tutors look for, and much more.
Published by Trotman
Price £12.99

CHOOSING COURSES

Progression Series 2010 entry
UCAS, in conjunction with GTI Specialist Publishers, has produced a series of ten titles for 2010 entry. The 'Progression to...' titles are designed to help you access good quality, useful information on some of the most competitive subject areas. The books cover advice on applying through UCAS, routes to qualifications, course details, job prospects, case studies and career advice.

Progression to...
Art and Design
Economics, Finance and Accountancy
Engineering and Mathematics
Health and Social Care
Law
Media and Performing Arts
Medicine, Dentistry and Optometry
Psychology
Sports Science and Physiotherapy
Teaching and Education
Published by UCAS
Price £15.99 each

UCAS Parent Guide
Free of charge.
Order online at **www.ucas.com/parents**
or call 0845 468 0 468.

Open Days 2009
Attending open days, taster courses and higher education conventions is an important part of the application process. This publication makes planning attendance at these events quick and easy.
Published annually by UCAS in association with Cambridge Occupational Analysts.
Price £3.50

Getting in, Getting on 2010

Conventions have become a central part of the post-16 careers education and guidance programme. This publication has been designed to be used before, during and after the event. It can make a difference.
Published by UCAS
Price £16

'Getting into…' guides

Clear and concise guides to help applicants secure places. They include qualifications required, advice on applying, tests, interviews and case studies. The guides give an honest view and discuss current issues and careers.

Getting into Business and Management Courses
Getting into Oxford and Cambridge
Getting into US and Canadian Universities
Getting into Veterinary School
Published by Trotman
Price £12.99 each

Choosing Your Degree Course & University

With so many universities and courses to choose from, it is not an easy decision for students embarking on their journey to higher education. This guide will offer expert guidance on the questions students need to ask when considering the opportunities available.
Published by Trotman 11th Edition
Price £22.99

Degree Course Descriptions

Providing details of the nature of degree courses, the descriptions in this book are written by heads of departments and senior lecturers at major universities. Each description contains an overview of the course area, details of course structures, career opportunities and more.
Published by COA
Price £12.99

Insider's Guide to Applying to University

Full of honest insights, this is a thorough guide to the application process. It reveals advice from careers advisers and current students, guidance on making sense of university information and choosing courses. Also includes tips for the personal statement, interviews, admissions tests, UCAS Extra and Clearing.
Published by Trotman
Price £12.99

CHOOSING WHERE TO STUDY

The Virgin 2010 Guide to British Universities

An insider's guide to choosing a university or college. Written by students and using independent statistics, this guide evaluates what you get from a higher education institution.
Published by Virgin
Price £15.99

Times Good University Guide 2010

How do you find the best university for the subject you wish to study? You need a guide that evaluates the quality of what is available, giving facts, figures and comparative assessments of universities. The rankings provide hard data, analysed, interpreted and presented by a team of experts.
Published by The Times
Price £15.99

Guardian University Guide 2010

Packed with no-nonsense advice, this book takes prospective students through every process they will encounter: from applications to interviews, accommodation to finances. The Guardian subject ratings are based on the UCAS entry Tariffs so that students can judge for themselves which are the best universities available to them.
Published by The Guardian
Price £15.99

The Daily Telegraph Guide to UK Universities 2010

Includes profiles of all institutions offering higher education courses, with information from current students providing a unique, independent insight into what each institution is really like. Included are details of the location, housing, cost of living, sports, nightlife, information on fees and bursaries and more.
Published by Trotman
Price £17.99

Getting into the UK's Best Universities and Courses

This book is for those who set their goals high and dream of studying on a highly regarded course at a good university. It provides information on selecting the best courses for a subject, the application and personal statement, interviews, results day, timescales for applications and much more.
Published by Trotman
Price £12.99

FINANCIAL INFORMATION

Students' Money Matters 2010

With graduate debt increasing, this guide provides invaluable information for students about loans, overdrafts, work experience, jobs and accommodation. Also includes advice on budgeting, borrowing and top-up fees.
Published by Trotman
Price £16.99

University Scholarships, Awards & Bursaries

Students embarking on HE courses face an increasingly challenging financial situation. This book enables applicants and current students to find the support that may help them make ends meet. Packed with information on virtually all awards available.
Published by Trotman 7th Edition
Price £22.99

CAREERS PLANNING

What Do Graduates Do?

A comprehensive look at graduate employment. Providing data detailing the first destinations of first-degree and HND graduates, this guide profiles how many leavers enter employment or further study and how many are unemployed. To complement the data, there are articles and editorial for each subject area.
Published by Graduate Prospects
Price £14.95

The Careers Directory

An indispensable resource for anyone seeking careers information, covering over 350 careers. It presents up-to-date information in an innovative double-page format. Ideal for students in years 10 to 13 who are considering their futures and for other careers professionals.
Published by COA
Price £15.99

DEFERRING ENTRY

Your Gap Year

The essential book for all young people planning a gap year before continuing with their education. This up-to-date guide provides essential information on specialist gap year programes, as well as the vast range of jobs and voluntary opportunities available to young people around the world.
Published by Crimson Publishing
Price £12.99

Summer Jobs Worldwide 2009

This unique and specialist guide contains over 40,000 jobs for all ages. No other book includes such a variety and wealth of summer work opportunities in Britain and aboard. Anything from horse trainer in Iceland, to a guide for nature walks in Peru, to a yoga centre helper in Greece, to an animal keeper for London Zoo, can be found.
Published by Crimson Publishing
Price £12.99

Teaching English Abroad

The definitive and acclaimed guide to opportunities for trained and untrained teachers across the world. With the field of teaching English as a foreign language booming, this guide offers extensive information for anyone wishing to teach English abroad. Including listings of recruitment organisations, a directory of more than 380 courses, and 1,150 language school addresses to contact for jobs.
Published by Crimson Publishing
Price £14.99

Please note all publications incur a postage and packing charge. All information was correct at the time of printing.

For a full list of publications, please visit
www.ucasbooks.com.

wondering how much higher education costs?

need information about variable fees, grants and student loans?

Visit www.ucas.com/studentfinance and discover everything you need to know about student money matters.

With access to up-to-date information on bursaries, scholarships and variable fees, plus our online budget calculator. Visit us today and get the full picture.

Courses

Courses

Keen to get started on your law career? This section contains details of the various degree courses available at UK institutions.

EXPLAINING THE LIST OF COURSES

We list the universities and colleges by their UCAS institution codes. Within each institution, courses are listed first by award type (such as BA, BSc, FdA, HND, MA and many others), then alphabetically by course title.

You might find some courses showing an award type '(Mod)', which indicates a combined degree that might be modular in design. A small number of courses have award type '(FYr)'. This indicates a 12-month foundation course, after which students can choose to apply for a degree course. In either case, you should contact the university or college for further details.

Generally speaking, when a course comprises two or more subjects, the word used to connect the subjects indicates the make-up of the award: 'Subject A and Subject B' is a joint award, where both subjects carry equal weight; 'Subject A with Subject B' is a major/minor award, where Subject A accounts for at least 60% of your study. If the title shows 'Subject A/Subject B', it may indicate that students can decide on the weighting of the subjects at the end of the first year. You should check with the university or college for full details.

Each entry in the UCAS sections shows the UCAS course code and the duration of the course. Where known, the entry contains details of the minimum qualification requirements for the course, as supplied to UCAS by the universities and colleges. Bear in mind that possessing the minimum qualifications does not guarantee acceptance to the course: there may be far more applicants than places. You may be asked to attend an interview, present a portfolio or sit an admissions test.

Before applying for any course, you are advised to contact the university or college to check any changes in entry requirements and to see if any new courses have come on stream since the lists were approved for publication. To make this easy, each institution's entry starts with their address, email, phone and fax details, as well as their website address. You will also find it useful to check the Entry Profiles section of Course Search at **www.ucas.com**.

> Unlock your potential
It's as easy as 1, 2, 3.

1 Search

Use Course Search to look for courses in your subject; find out about your chosen universities and colleges and lots more.

2 Apply

Use our online system Apply to make your application to higher education.

3 Track

Then use Track to monitor the progress of your application.

UCAS   helping students into higher education   www.ucas.com

A20 THE UNIVERSITY OF ABERDEEN

UNIVERSITY OFFICE
KING'S COLLEGE
ABERDEEN AB24 3FX

t: +44 (0) 1224 273504 f: +44 (0) 1224 272034
e: sras@abdn.ac.uk

// www.abdn.ac.uk/sras

M1N2 LLB Law with options in Management Studies

Duration: 3FT/4FT Ord/Hon

Entry Requirements: *GCE:* BBB. *SQAH:* ABBBB-AABB. *SQAAH:* BBB. *IB:* 34.

A40 ABERYSTWYTH UNIVERSITY

WELCOME CENTRE, ABERYSTWYTH UNIVERSITY
PENGLAIS CAMPUS
ABERYSTWYTH
CEREDIGION SY23 3FB

t: 01970 622021 f: 01970 627410
e: ug-admissions@aber.ac.uk

// www.aber.ac.uk

M1N1 BA Law with Business & Management

Duration: 3FT Hon

Entry Requirements: *GCE:* 280. *IB:* 27.

N1M1 BScEcon Business & Management with Law

Duration: 3FT Hon

Entry Requirements: *GCE:* 260. *IB:* 27.

A60 ANGLIA RUSKIN UNIVERSITY

BISHOP HALL LANE
CHELMSFORD
ESSEX CM1 1SQ

t: 0845 271 3333 f: 01245 251789
e: answers@anglia.ac.uk

// www.anglia.ac.uk

NM11 BA Business and Law

Duration: 3FT Hon

Entry Requirements: *GCE:* 220-260. *SQAH:* AABC. *SQAAH:* AB. *IB:* 30.

A80 ASTON UNIVERSITY, BIRMINGHAM

ASTON TRIANGLE
BIRMINGHAM B4 7ET

t: 0121 204 4444 f: 0121 204 3696
e: admissions@aston.ac.uk

// www.aston.ac.uk

M1N2 LLB Law with Management

Duration: 4SW Hon

Entry Requirements: *GCE:* 320-340. *SQAH:* AAABB-AAAAB. *SQAAH:* ABB-AAB. *IB:* 34. *BTEC ND:* DDM. *OCR NED:* Distinction.

B06 BANGOR UNIVERSITY

BANGOR
GWYNEDD LL57 2DG

t: 01248 382016/2017 f: 01248 370451
e: admissions@bangor.ac.uk

// www.bangor.ac.uk

M1N1 LLB Law with Business Studies

Duration: 3FT Hon

Entry Requirements: *GCE:* 280. *IB:* 28.

B25 BIRMINGHAM CITY UNIVERSITY

PERRY BARR
BIRMINGHAM B42 2SU

t: 0121 331 5595 f: 0121 331 7994
e: choices@bcu.ac.uk

// www.bcu.ac.uk

MN21 BA Business and Business Law

Duration: 3FT/4SW Hon

Entry Requirements: *GCE:* 240. *IB:* 24. *BTEC NC:* DM. *BTEC ND:* MMP.

NM22 BA Management and Business Law

Duration: 3FT/4SW Hon

Entry Requirements: *GCE:* 240. *IB:* 24. *BTEC NC:* DM. *BTEC ND:* MMP.

B32 THE UNIVERSITY OF BIRMINGHAM

EDGBASTON
BIRMINGHAM B15 2TT

t: 0121 415 8900 f: 0121 414 7159
e: admissions@bham.ac.uk

// www.bham.ac.uk

M1N1 LLB Law with Business Studies

Duration: 3FT Hon

Entry Requirements: *GCE:* AAA. *SQAAH:* AAA. *IB:* 36. *BTEC NC:* DD. *BTEC ND:* DDD. Admissions Test required.

B44 THE UNIVERSITY OF BOLTON
DEANE ROAD
BOLTON BL3 5AB
t: 01204 900600 f: 01204 399074
e: enquiries@bolton.ac.uk
// www.bolton.ac.uk

NM11 BA Business Management and Law
Duration: 3FT Hon

Entry Requirements: *GCE:* 220. *IB:* 20. *BTEC NC:* DD. *BTEC ND:* MMM.

GM51 BSc Business Information Systems and Law
Duration: 3FT Hon

Entry Requirements: *GCE:* 220. *IB:* 20. *BTEC NC:* DD. *BTEC ND:* MMM.

B56 THE UNIVERSITY OF BRADFORD
RICHMOND ROAD
BRADFORD
WEST YORKSHIRE BD7 1DP
t: 0800 073 1225 f: 01274 235585
e: course-enquiries@bradford.ac.uk
// www.bradford.ac.uk

NM11 BA Business Studies and Law
Duration: 3FT Hon

Entry Requirements: *GCE:* 240. *IB:* 24.

NM21 BA Business Studies and Law (4 years)
Duration: 4SW Hon

Entry Requirements: *GCE:* 240. *IB:* 24.

B72 UNIVERSITY OF BRIGHTON
MITHRAS HOUSE
LEWES ROAD
BRIGHTON BN2 4AT
t: 01273 644644 f: 01273 642607
e: admissions@brighton.ac.uk
// www.brighton.ac.uk

M1NC LLB Law with Business
Duration: 3FT/4SW Hon

Entry Requirements: *GCE:* BBC. *IB:* 30.

B80 UNIVERSITY OF THE WEST OF ENGLAND, BRISTOL
FRENCHAY CAMPUS
COLDHARBOUR LANE
BRISTOL BS16 1QY
t: +44 (0)117 32 83333 f: +44 (0)117 32 82810
e: admissions@uwe.ac.uk
// www.uwe.ac.uk

NM11 BA Business and Law
Duration: 3FT Hon

Entry Requirements: *GCE:* 240-300.

B90 THE UNIVERSITY OF BUCKINGHAM
YEOMANRY HOUSE
HUNTER STREET
BUCKINGHAM MK18 1EG
t: 01280 820313 f: 01280 822245
e: info@buckingham.ac.uk
// www.buckingham.ac.uk

M1N2 LLB Law with Management Studies
Duration: 2FT Hon

Entry Requirements: *GCE:* 300. *IB:* 28. *BTEC NC:* DD. *BTEC ND:* DMM.

C30 UNIVERSITY OF CENTRAL LANCASHIRE
PRESTON
LANCS PR1 2HE
t: 01772 201201 f: 01772 894954
e: uadmissions@uclan.ac.uk
// www.uclan.ac.uk

MN11 BA Law and Business
Duration: 3FT Hon

Entry Requirements: *GCE:* 220. *IB:* 26. *BTEC NC:* DM. *BTEC ND:* MMP.

C55 UNIVERSITY OF CHESTER
PARKGATE ROAD
CHESTER CH1 4BJ
t: 01244 511000 f: 01244 511300
e: enquiries@chester.ac.uk
// www.chester.ac.uk

N1M1 BA Business with Law
Duration: 3FT Hon

Entry Requirements: *GCE:* 240. *SQAH:* BBBB. *IB:* 24. *BTEC NC:* DM. *BTEC ND:* MMM.

MN11 BA Law and Business
Duration: 3FT Hon

Entry Requirements: *GCE:* 240. *SQAH:* BBBB. *IB:* 24. *BTEC NC:* DM. *BTEC ND:* MMM.

M1N1 BA Law with Business

Duration: 3FT Hon

Entry Requirements: *GCE:* 240. *SQAH:* BBBB. *IB:* 24. *BTEC NC:* DM. *BTEC ND:* MMM.

M1N2 BA Law with Management

Duration: 3FT Hon

Entry Requirements: *GCE:* 240. *SQAH:* BBBB. *IB:* 24. *BTEC NC:* DM. *BTEC ND:* MMM.

NM21 BA Management and Law

Duration: 3FT Hon

Entry Requirements: *GCE:* 240. *SQAH:* BBBB. *IB:* 24. *BTEC NC:* DM. *BTEC ND:* MMM.

N2M1 BA Management with Law

Duration: 3FT Hon

Entry Requirements: *GCE:* 240. *SQAH:* BBBB. *IB:* 24. *BTEC NC:* DM. *BTEC ND:* MMM.

C85 COVENTRY UNIVERSITY

THE STUDENT CENTRE
COVENTRY UNIVERSITY
1 GULSON RD
COVENTRY CV1 2JH

t: 024 7615 2222 f: 024 7615 2223
e: studentenquiries@coventry.ac.uk

// www.coventry.ac.uk

MN11 LLB Law and Business

Duration: 3FT Hon

Entry Requirements: *GCE:* 300. *BTEC ND:* DDM.

D26 DE MONTFORT UNIVERSITY

THE GATEWAY
LEICESTER LE1 9BH

t: 0116 255 1551 f: 0116 250 6204
e: enquiries@dmu.ac.uk

// www.dmu.ac.uk

MN11 BA Business and Law

Duration: 3FT/4SW Hon

Entry Requirements: *GCE:* 240. *IB:* 28. *BTEC NC:* DD. *BTEC ND:* MMM. Interview required.

D39 UNIVERSITY OF DERBY

KEDLESTON ROAD
DERBY DE22 1GB

t: 08701 202330 f: 01332 597724
e: askadmissions@derby.ac.uk

// www.derby.ac.uk

NM21 BA Business Management and Law

Duration: 3FT Hon

Entry Requirements: *Foundation:* Merit. *GCE:* 180-240. *IB:* 26. *BTEC NC:* DM. *BTEC ND:* MMP.

D58 DUDLEY COLLEGE OF TECHNOLOGY

THE BROADWAY
DUDLEY DY1 4AS

t: 01384 363277/6 f: 01384 363311
e: admissions@dudleycol.ac.uk

// www.dudleycol.ac.uk

11MN HND Business and Law

Duration: 2FT HND

Entry Requirements: *GCE:* 40-80.

E25 EAST LANCASHIRE INSTITUTE OF HIGHER EDUCATION AT BLACKBURN COLLEGE

DUKE STREET
BLACKBURN BB2 1LH

t: 01254 292594 f: 01254 260749
e: he-admissions@blackburn.ac.uk

// www.elihe.ac.uk

11MN HND Business and Law

Duration: 2FT HND

Entry Requirements: *GCE:* 40.

E28 UNIVERSITY OF EAST LONDON

DOCKLANDS CAMPUS
UNIVERSITY WAY
LONDON E16 2RD

t: 020 8223 2835 f: 020 8223 2978
e: admiss@uel.ac.uk

// www.uel.ac.uk

NM11 BA Business Studies & Law (Extended)

Duration: 4FT Hon

Entry Requirements: *GCE:* 80.

MN11 BA Business Studies/Law

Duration: 3FT Hon

Entry Requirements: *GCE:* 240. *IB:* 28. *BTEC NC:* DD. *BTEC ND:* MMM.

M1N1 BA Law with Business Studies

Duration: 3FT Hon

Entry Requirements: *GCE:* 240. *IB:* 28. *BTEC NC:* DD. *BTEC ND:* MMM.

N1M1 BSc Business Studies with Law

Duration: 3FT Hon

Entry Requirements: *GCE:* 200. *IB:* 28.

E42 EDGE HILL UNIVERSITY

ORMSKIRK
LANCASHIRE L39 4QP

t: 0800 195 5063 f: 01695 584355
e: enquiries@edgehill.ac.uk
// www.edgehill.ac.uk

M1N2 LLB Law with Management

Duration: 3FT Hon

Entry Requirements: *GCE:* 260. *IB:* 28. *BTEC NC:* DD. *BTEC ND:* MMM.

E56 THE UNIVERSITY OF EDINBURGH

STUDENT RECRUITMENT & ADMISSIONS
57 GEORGE SQUARE
EDINBURGH EH8 9JU

t: 0131 650 4360 f: 0131 651 1236
e: sra.enquiries@ed.ac.uk
// www.ed.ac.uk/studying/undergraduate/

MN11 LLB Law and Business Studies

Duration: 4FT Hon

Entry Requirements: *GCE:* BBB. *SQAH:* BBBB. *IB:* 34.

NM11 MA Business Studies and Law

Duration: 4FT Hon

Entry Requirements: *GCE:* BBB. *SQAH:* BBBB. *IB:* 34.

E77 EUROPEAN BUSINESS SCHOOL, LONDON

INNER CIRCLE
REGENT'S PARK
LONDON NW1 4NS

t: +44 (0)20 7487 7505 f: +44 (0)20 7487 7425
e: ebsl@regents.ac.uk
// www.ebslondon.ac.uk

N1MC BA International Business with Law and two languages

Duration: 3FT/4FT Hon

Entry Requirements: *SQAH:* BBCC. *SQAAH:* CC. *IB:* 28.

G14 UNIVERSITY OF GLAMORGAN, CARDIFF AND PONTYPRIDD

ENQUIRIES AND ADMISSIONS UNIT
PONTYPRIDD CF37 1DL

t: 0800 716925 f: 01443 654050
e: enquiries@glam.ac.uk
// www.glam.ac.uk

M1N1 LLB Law with Business

Duration: 3FT Hon

Entry Requirements: *GCE:* 280-320. *IB:* 30. *BTEC NC:* DD. *BTEC ND:* DMM.

NM11 BA Business and Law

Duration: 3FT Hon

Entry Requirements: *GCE:* 280-320. *IB:* 30. *BTEC NC:* DD. *BTEC ND:* DMM.

N1M1 BA Business with Law

Duration: 3FT Hon

Entry Requirements: *GCE:* 240-280. *IB:* 30. *BTEC NC:* DD. *BTEC ND:* DMM.

G28 UNIVERSITY OF GLASGOW

THE UNIVERSITY OF GLASGOW
THE FRASER BUILDING
65 HILLHEAD STREET
GLASGOW G12 8QF

t: 0141 330 6062 f: 0141 330 2961
e: ugenquiries@gla.ac.uk (UK/EU undergrad enquiries only)
// www.glasgow.ac.uk

MN12 LLB Law/Business Management

Duration: 4FT Hon

Entry Requirements: *GCE:* AAB. *SQAH:* AAAAB. *IB:* 34. Admissions Test required.

G53 GLYNDWR UNIVERSITY

PLAS COCH
MOLD ROAD
WREXHAM LL11 2AW

t: 01978 293439 f: 01978 290008
e: SID@glyndwr.ac.uk
// www.glyndwr.ac.uk

N1M1 BA Business Management with Law in Business

Duration: 3FT Hon

Entry Requirements: *GCE:* 200.

G70 UNIVERSITY OF GREENWICH

GREENWICH CAMPUS
OLD ROYAL NAVAL COLLEGE
PARK ROW
LONDON SE10 9LS

t: 0800 005 006 f: 020 8331 8145
e: courseinfo@gre.ac.uk

// www.gre.ac.uk

N1MD BA Business Administration with Law
Duration: 3FT Hon

Entry Requirements: *GCE:* 180. *IB:* 24.

N1M9 BA Business Administration with Law (Extended)
Duration: 4FT Hon

Entry Requirements: *GCE:* 160. *SQAH:* CCC. *SQAAH:* BC. *IB:* 24.

MN11 BA Law and Business
Duration: 3FT Hon

Entry Requirements: *GCE:* 180. *IB:* 24.

1M1N HND Business Studies with Law
Duration: 2FT HND

Entry Requirements: *GCE:* 100. *IB:* 16.

H36 UNIVERSITY OF HERTFORDSHIRE

UNIVERSITY ADMISSIONS SERVICE
COLLEGE LANE
HATFIELD
HERTS AL10 9AB

t: 01707 284800 f: 01707 284870

// www.herts.ac.uk

N1M1 BSc Business/Law
Duration: 3FT/4SW Hon

Entry Requirements: *GCE:* 260.

M1N1 BSc Law/Business
Duration: 3FT Hon

Entry Requirements: *GCE:* 260.

H50 HOLBORN COLLEGE

WOOLWICH ROAD
LONDON SE7 8LN

t: 020 8317 6000 f: 020 8317 6001
e: admissions@holborncollege.ac.uk

// www.holborncollege.ac.uk

N7M1 BA Business Administration with Law
Duration: 3FT Hon

Entry Requirements: Contact the institution for details.

H60 THE UNIVERSITY OF HUDDERSFIELD

QUEENSGATE
HUDDERSFIELD HD1 3DH

t: 01484 473969 f: 01484 472765
e: admissionsandrecords@hud.ac.uk

// www.hud.ac.uk

MN11 BA Law and Business
Duration: 3FT/4SW Hon

Entry Requirements: *GCE:* 240. *SQAH:* BBCC. *IB:* 28.

H72 THE UNIVERSITY OF HULL

THE UNIVERSITY OF HULL
COTTINGHAM ROAD
HULL HU6 7RX

t: 01482 466100 f: 01482 442290
e: admissions@hull.ac.uk

// www.hull.ac.uk

M1N1 LLB Law with Business
Duration: 3FT Hon

Entry Requirements: *GCE:* 320. *IB:* 28.

K12 KEELE UNIVERSITY

STAFFS ST5 5BG

t: 01782 734005 f: 01782 632343
e: undergraduate@keele.ac.uk

// www.keele.ac.uk

MN19 BA Business Management and Law
Duration: 3FT Hon

Entry Requirements: *GCE:* 300-320.

K24 THE UNIVERSITY OF KENT

INFORMATION, RECRUITMENT & ADMISSIONS REGISTRY
UNIVERSITY OF KENT
CANTERBURY. KENT CT2 7NZ

t: 01227 827272 f: 01227 827077
e: information@kent.ac.uk

// www.kent.ac.uk

MN12 BA Law and Business Administration
Duration: 3FT Hon

Entry Requirements: *GCE:* 320. *SQAH:* AAAAA. *IB:* 34. *BTEC NC:* DD. *BTEC ND:* DDM.

K84 KINGSTON UNIVERSITY

STUDENT INFORMATION & ADVICE CENTRE
COOPER HOUSE
40-46 SURBITON ROAD
KINGSTON UPON THAMES KT1 2HX

t: 020 8547 7053 f: 020 8547 7080
e: aps@kingston.ac.uk
// www.kingston.ac.uk

M1N1 LLB Law with Business

Duration: 3FT Hon

Entry Requirements: *GCE:* 320. *IB:* 26. *BTEC ND:* DDM.

N1M1 BA Business with Law

Duration: 3FT Hon

Entry Requirements: *GCE:* 280. *IB:* 31. *BTEC ND:* DMM.

N1MC BA Business with Law with industrial placement (4 years)

Duration: 4FT Hon

Entry Requirements: *GCE:* 140.

N1MD BA Business with Law with year abroad (4 years)

Duration: 4FT Hon

Entry Requirements: *GCE:* 140.

N1MA BA International Business with Law

Duration: 3FT Hon

Entry Requirements: *GCE:* 280-320. *BTEC ND:* DMM.

L23 UNIVERSITY OF LEEDS

THE UNIVERSITY OF LEEDS
LEEDS LS2 9JT

t: 0113 343 3999
e: admissions@adm.leeds.ac.uk
// www.leeds.ac.uk

MN12 BA Management and Law

Duration: 4FT Hon

Entry Requirements: *GCE:* AAA. *SQAAH:* AAA. *IB:* 37.

L24 LEEDS TRINITY & ALL SAINTS (ACCREDITED COLLEGE OF THE UNIVERSITY OF LEEDS)

BROWNBERRIE LANE
HORSFORTH
LEEDS LS18 5HD

t: 0113 283 7150 f: 0113 283 7222
e: enquiries@leedstrinity.ac.uk
// www.leedstrinity.ac.uk

N1M1 BA Business with Law

Duration: 3FT Hon

Entry Requirements: *GCE:* 200. *IB:* 24. *BTEC NC:* PP. *BTEC ND:* PPP.

L39 UNIVERSITY OF LINCOLN

ADMISSIONS
BRAYFORD POOL
LINCOLN LN6 7TS

t: 01522 886097 f: 01522 886146
e: admissions@lincoln.ac.uk
// www.lincoln.ac.uk

NM11 LLB Law and Business

Duration: 3FT Hon

Entry Requirements: *GCE:* 260.

L41 THE UNIVERSITY OF LIVERPOOL

THE FOUNDATION BUILDING
BROWNLOW HILL
LIVERPOOL L69 7ZX

t: 0151 794 2000 f: 0151 708 6502
e: ugrecruitment@liv.ac.uk
// www.liv.ac.uk

MN11 BA Law and Business

Duration: 3FT Hon

Entry Requirements: *GCE:* ABB-BBB. *SQAH:* BBBB. *IB:* 32. *BTEC ND:* DDD.

L46 LIVERPOOL HOPE UNIVERSITY

HOPE PARK
LIVERPOOL L16 9JD

t: 0151 291 3295 f: 0151 291 2050
e: admission@hope.ac.uk
// www.hope.ac.uk

MN11 BA Business and Law

Duration: 3FT Hon

Entry Requirements: *GCE:* 240. *IB:* 25.

L68 LONDON METROPOLITAN UNIVERSITY

166-220 HOLLOWAY ROAD
LONDON N7 8DB

t: 020 7133 4200
e: admissions@londonmet.ac.uk

// www.londonmet.ac.uk

MN11 BA Business and Law

Duration: 3FT Hon

Entry Requirements: *GCE:* 240. *IB:* 28.

NM11 BA International Business and Law

Duration: 3FT Hon

Entry Requirements: *GCE:* 240. *IB:* 28.

L75 LONDON SOUTH BANK UNIVERSITY

103 BOROUGH ROAD
LONDON SE1 0AA

t: 020 7815 7815 f: 020 7815 8273
e: enquiry@lsbu.ac.uk

// www.lsbu.ac.uk

M1N2 LLB Law with Management

Duration: 3FT Hon

Entry Requirements: *GCE:* 240. *IB:* 24.

N6M1 BA Human Resource Management with Law

Duration: 3FT Hon

Entry Requirements: *GCE:* 240. *IB:* 24.

N2M1 BA Management with Law

Duration: 3FT Hon

Entry Requirements: *GCE:* 240. *IB:* 24.

G5M1 BSc Business Information Technology with Law

Duration: 3FT Hon

Entry Requirements: *GCE:* 240. *IB:* 24.

M40 THE MANCHESTER METROPOLITAN UNIVERSITY

ADMISSIONS OFFICE
ALL SAINTS (GMS)
ALL SAINTS
MANCHESTER M15 6BH

t: 0161 247 2000

// www.mmu.ac.uk

N2M2 BA Business Management with Legal Studies

Duration: 3FT Hon

Entry Requirements: Contact the institution for details.

M80 MIDDLESEX UNIVERSITY

MIDDLESEX UNIVERSITY
THE BURROUGHS
LONDON NW4 4BT

t: 020 8411 5555 f: 020 8411 5649
e: enquiries@mdx.ac.uk

// www.mdx.ac.uk

MN21 BA Law and Business

Duration: 3FT Hon

Entry Requirements: *GCE:* 200-300. *IB:* 28.

N37 UNIVERSITY OF WALES, NEWPORT

CAERLEON CAMPUS
PO BOX 101
NEWPORT
SOUTH WALES NP18 3YH

t: 01633 432030 f: 01633 432850
e: admissions@newport.ac.uk

// www.newport.ac.uk

NM11 BA Business and Law

Duration: 3FT Hon

Entry Requirements: *GCE:* 240. *IB:* 24.

N38 UNIVERSITY OF NORTHAMPTON

PARK CAMPUS
BOUGHTON GREEN ROAD
NORTHAMPTON NN2 7AL

t: 0800 358 2232 f: 01604 722083
e: admissions@northampton.ac.uk

// www.northampton.ac.uk

N1MC BA Business Entrepreneurship/Law

Duration: 3FT Hon

Entry Requirements: *GCE:* 220-260. *SQAH:* AAB-BBBB. *IB:* 24.

N1M1 BA Business/Law

Duration: 3FT Hon

Entry Requirements: *GCE:* 220-260. *SQAH:* AAB-BBBB. *IB:* 24.

M1NG BA Law with Applied Management

Duration: 3FT Hon

Entry Requirements: *GCE:* 220-260. *SQAH:* AAB-BBBB. *IB:* 24.

M1N1 BA Law/Business

Duration: 3FT Hon

Entry Requirements: *GCE:* 220-260. *SQAH:* AAB-BBBB. *IB:* 24.

M1NF BA Law/Business Entrepreneurship

Duration: 3FT Hon

Entry Requirements: *GCE:* 220-260. *SQAH:* AAB-BBBB. *IB:* 24.

M1N2 BA Law/Management

Duration: 3FT Hon

Entry Requirements: *GCE:* 220-260. *SQAH:* AAB-BBBB. *IB:* 24.

N2M1 BA Management/Law

Duration: 3FT Hon

Entry Requirements: *GCE:* 220-260. *SQAH:* AAB-BBBB. *IB:* 24.

N91 NOTTINGHAM TRENT UNIVERSITY

DRYDEN CENTRE
BURTON STREET
NOTTINGHAM NG1 4BU
t: +44 (0) 115 941 8418 **f:** +44 (0) 115 848 6063
e: admissions@ntu.ac.uk
// www.ntu.ac.uk/

M1N1 LLB Law with Business

Duration: 3FT Hon

Entry Requirements: *Foundation:* Pass. *GCE:* 280. *SQAH:* BBBBC. *SQAAH:* BBC. *IB:* 24. *BTEC NC:* DM. *BTEC ND:* DMM. *OCR ND:* Merit. *OCR NED:* Merit.

O66 OXFORD BROOKES UNIVERSITY

ADMISSIONS OFFICE
HEADINGTON CAMPUS
GIPSY LANE
OXFORD OX3 0BP
t: 01865 483040 **f:** 01865 483983
e: admissions@brookes.ac.uk
// www.brookes.ac.uk

NM21 BA/BSc Business Management/Law

Duration: 3FT Hon

Entry Requirements: *GCE:* BBC.

P55 PETERBOROUGH REGIONAL COLLEGE

PARK CRESCENT
PETERBOROUGH PE1 4DZ
t: 0845 8728722 **f:** 01733 767986
e: info@peterborough.ac.uk
// www.peterborough.ac.uk

MN11 BA Business and Law

Duration: 3FT Deg

Entry Requirements: *GCE:* 120. Interview required.

P60 UNIVERSITY OF PLYMOUTH

DRAKE CIRCUS
PLYMOUTH PL4 8AA
t: 01752 588037 **f:** 01752 588050
e: admissions@plymouth.ac.uk
// www.plymouth.ac.uk

M2N1 BSc Law with Business

Duration: 3FT Hon

Entry Requirements: *GCE:* 300. *IB:* 32.

P80 UNIVERSITY OF PORTSMOUTH

ACADEMIC REGISTRY
UNIVERSITY HOUSE
WINSTON CHURCHILL AVENUE
PORTSMOUTH PO1 2UP
t: 023 9284 8484 **f:** 023 9284 3082
e: admissions@port.ac.uk
// www.port.ac.uk

M1NC LLB Law with Business

Duration: 3FT/4SW Hon

Entry Requirements: *GCE:* 280.

M1Q3 BA Law with Business English

Duration: 2FT Hon

Entry Requirements: Contact the institution for details.

R36 THE ROBERT GORDON UNIVERSITY

ROBERT GORDON UNIVERSITY
SCHOOLHILL
ABERDEEN
SCOTLAND AB10 1FR
t: 01224 26 27 28 **f:** 01224 262147
e: admissions@rgu.ac.uk
// www.rgu.ac.uk

M990 BA Law and Management

Duration: 4FT Hon

Entry Requirements: *GCE:* 240. *SQAH:* BBB-BBCC. *IB:* 26.

S03 THE UNIVERSITY OF SALFORD

SALFORD M5 4WT
t: 0161 295 4545 **f:** 0161 295 3126
e: ugadmissions-exrel@salford.ac.uk
// www.salford.ac.uk

N1M1 BSc Business and Management Studies with Law

Duration: 3FT Hon

Entry Requirements: *GCE:* 240-260. *IB:* 28. *BTEC NC:* DD. *BTEC ND:* MMM. *OCR ND:* Distinction. *OCR NED:* Merit.

S30 SOUTHAMPTON SOLENT UNIVERSITY

EAST PARK TERRACE
SOUTHAMPTON
HAMPSHIRE SO14 0RT

t: +44 (0) 23 8031 9039 **f:** + 44 (0)23 8022 2259
e: admissions@solent.ac.uk or ask@solent.ac.uk

// www.solent.ac.uk/

M1NF LLB LLB (Hons) with Business Management

Duration: 3FT Hon

Entry Requirements: *GCE:* 220. *BTEC NC:* MM. *BTEC ND:* PPP.

N2M2 BA Business Management with Commercial Law (with Business Foundn Year)

Duration: 4FT Hon

Entry Requirements: *GCE:* 40.

S72 STAFFORDSHIRE UNIVERSITY

COLLEGE ROAD
STOKE ON TRENT ST4 2DE

t: 01782 292753 **f:** 01782 292740
e: admissions@staffs.ac.uk

// www.staffs.ac.uk

MN11 LLB LLB with Business Studies

Duration: 3FT Hon

Entry Requirements: *GCE:* BB-ABB. *SQAAH:* BB-ABB. *IB:* 26. *BTEC NC:* DM. *BTEC ND:* DDM. *OCR ND:* Distinction.

S75 THE UNIVERSITY OF STIRLING

STIRLING FK9 4LA

t: 01786 467044 **f:** 01786 466800
e: admissions@stir.ac.uk

// www.stir.ac.uk

MN11 BA Business Studies and Law

Duration: 4FT Hon

Entry Requirements: *GCE:* CCC. *SQAH:* BBBB. *SQAAH:* AAA-CCC. *BTEC ND:* DMM.

S84 UNIVERSITY OF SUNDERLAND

STUDENT HELPLINE
THE STUDENT GATEWAY
CHESTER ROAD
SUNDERLAND SR1 3SD

t: 0191 515 3000 **f:** 0191 515 3805
e: student-helpline@sunderland.ac.uk

// www.sunderland.ac.uk

NM21 BA Business Management and Law

Duration: 3FT Hon

Entry Requirements: *GCE:* 220-360. *BTEC NC:* DM. *BTEC ND:* MMM. *OCR ND:* Distinction. *OCR NED:* Merit.

NM61 BA Human Resource Management and Law

Duration: 3FT Hon

Entry Requirements: *GCE:* 220-360. *BTEC NC:* DM. *BTEC ND:* MMM. *OCR ND:* Distinction. *OCR NED:* Merit.

N6M1 BA Human Resource Management with Law

Duration: 3FT Hon

Entry Requirements: *GCE:* 220-360. *BTEC NC:* DM. *BTEC ND:* MMM. *OCR ND:* Distinction. *OCR NED:* Merit.

M1N1 BA Law with Business Management

Duration: 3FT Hon

Entry Requirements: *GCE:* 220-360. *BTEC NC:* DM. *BTEC ND:* MMM. *OCR ND:* Distinction. *OCR NED:* Merit.

M1N6 BA Law with Human Resource Management

Duration: 3FT Hon

Entry Requirements: *GCE:* 220-360. *BTEC NC:* DM. *BTEC ND:* MMM. *OCR ND:* Distinction. *OCR NED:* Merit.

NM51 BA Marketing Management and Law

Duration: 3FT Hon

Entry Requirements: *GCE:* 220-360. *BTEC NC:* DM. *BTEC ND:* MMM. *OCR ND:* Distinction. *OCR NED:* Merit.

N5M1 BA Marketing Management with Law

Duration: 3FT Hon

Entry Requirements: *GCE:* 220-360. *BTEC NC:* DM. *BTEC ND:* MMM. *OCR ND:* Distinction. *OCR NED:* Merit.

S93 SWANSEA UNIVERSITY
SINGLETON PARK
SWANSEA SA2 8PP
t: 01792 295111 f: 01792 295110
e: admissions@swansea.ac.uk
// www.swansea.ac.uk

N2M1 BA Business Management with Law
Duration: 3FT Hon

Entry Requirements: *GCE:* 280.

T20 UNIVERSITY OF TEESSIDE
MIDDLESBROUGH TS1 3BA
t: 01642 218121 f: 01642 384201
e: registry@tees.ac.uk
// www.tees.ac.uk

N1M1 BA Business with Law
Duration: 3FT/4SW Hon

Entry Requirements: *IB:* 24. *BTEC NC:* MM. *BTEC ND:* MMP.
Interview required.

W20 THE UNIVERSITY OF WARWICK
COVENTRY CV4 8UW
t: 024 7652 3723 f: 024 7652 4649
e: ugadmissions@warwick.ac.uk
// www.warwick.ac.uk

MN11 BA Law and Business Studies (3/4 years)
Duration: 3FT Hon

Entry Requirements: *GCE:* AABc. *SQAAH:* AAB. *BTEC NC:* DD. *OCR ND:* Distinction.

W75 UNIVERSITY OF WOLVERHAMPTON
ADMISSIONS UNIT
MX207, CAMP STREET
WOLVERHAMPTON
WEST MIDLANDS WV1 1AD
t: 01902 321000 f: 01902 321896
e: admissions@wlv.ac.uk
// www.wlv.ac.uk

NM11 BA Business and Law
Duration: 3FT Hon

Entry Requirements: *GCE:* 160-220. *IB:* 28.

W76 UNIVERSITY OF WINCHESTER
WINCHESTER
HANTS SO22 4NR
t: 01962 827234 f: 01962 827288
e: course.enquiries@winchester.ac.uk
// www.winchester.ac.uk

MN12 BA Law and Business Management
Duration: 3FT Hon

Entry Requirements: *Foundation:* Pass. *GCE:* 220-260. *IB:* 26. *BTEC NC:* DD. *BTEC ND:* MMP. *OCR ND:* Distinction.

NM21 DipHE Business Management and Law
Duration: 2FT Dip

Entry Requirements: *Foundation:* Pass. *GCE:* 120. *IB:* 20. *BTEC NC:* MP. *BTEC ND:* PPP.

BUSINESS LAW

A40 ABERYSTWYTH UNIVERSITY
WELCOME CENTRE, ABERYSTWYTH UNIVERSITY
PENGLAIS CAMPUS
ABERYSTWYTH
CEREDIGION SY23 3FB
t: 01970 622021 f: 01970 627410
e: ug-admissions@aber.ac.uk
// www.aber.ac.uk

M140 LLB Business Law
Duration: 3FT Hon

Entry Requirements: *GCE:* 280. *IB:* 27.

B06 BANGOR UNIVERSITY
BANGOR
GWYNEDD LL57 2DG
t: 01248 382016/2017 f: 01248 370451
e: admissions@bangor.ac.uk
// www.bangor.ac.uk

HM62 BSc Electronics for Business (Business Law)
Duration: 3FT Hon

Entry Requirements: *GCE:* 220-260. *IB:* 28.

B25 BIRMINGHAM CITY UNIVERSITY
PERRY BARR
BIRMINGHAM B42 2SU
t: 0121 331 5595 f: 0121 331 7994
e: choices@bcu.ac.uk
// www.bcu.ac.uk

M221 LLB Business Law
Duration: 3FT Hon

Entry Requirements: *GCE:* 280.

MN25 BA Advertising and Business Law
Duration: 3FT/4SW Hon

Entry Requirements: *GCE:* 240. *IB:* 24. *BTEC NC:* DM. *BTEC ND:* MMP.

MN23 BA Business Law and Finance
Duration: 3FT/4SW Hon

Entry Requirements: *GCE:* 240. *IB:* 24. *BTEC NC:* DM. *BTEC ND:* MMP.

MN26 BA Business Law and Human Resource Management
Duration: 3FT/4SW Hon

Entry Requirements: *GCE:* 240. *IB:* 24. *BTEC NC:* DM. *BTEC ND:* MMP.

NM52 BA Marketing and Business Law
Duration: 3FT/4SW Hon

Entry Requirements: *GCE:* 240. *IB:* 24. *BTEC NC:* DM. *BTEC ND:* MMP.

MP22 BA Public Relations and Business Law
Duration: 3FT/4SW Hon

Entry Requirements: *GCE:* 240. *IB:* 24. *BTEC NC:* DM. *BTEC ND:* MMP.

B94 BUCKINGHAMSHIRE NEW UNIVERSITY
QUEEN ALEXANDRA ROAD
HIGH WYCOMBE
BUCKS HP11 2JZ

t: 0800 0565 660 f: 01494 605023
e: admissions@bucks.ac.uk
// www.bucks.ac.uk

M221 LLB Business Law
Duration: 3FT Hon

Entry Requirements: Interview required.

D26 DE MONTFORT UNIVERSITY
THE GATEWAY
LEICESTER LE1 9BH
t: 0116 255 1551 f: 0116 250 6204
e: enquiries@dmu.ac.uk
// www.dmu.ac.uk

M221 LLB Business Law
Duration: 3FT/3FT Hon/Ord

Entry Requirements: Contact the institution for details.

G42 GLASGOW CALEDONIAN UNIVERSITY
CITY CAMPUS
COWCADDENS ROAD
GLASGOW G4 0BA

t: 0141 331 3000 f: 0141 331 3449
e: admissions@gcal.ac.uk
// www.gcal.ac.uk

M221 BA Business Law
Duration: 4FT Hon

Entry Requirements: *GCE:* BC. *SQAH:* BBBC. *IB:* 28.

G53 GLYNDWR UNIVERSITY
PLAS COCH
MOLD ROAD
WREXHAM LL11 2AW

t: 01978 293439 f: 01978 290008
e: SID@glyndwr.ac.uk
// www.glyndwr.ac.uk

MN11 BA Law in Business
Duration: 3FT Hon

Entry Requirements: *GCE:* 200.

G70 UNIVERSITY OF GREENWICH
GREENWICH CAMPUS
OLD ROYAL NAVAL COLLEGE
PARK ROW
LONDON SE10 9LS

t: 0800 005 006 f: 020 8331 8145
e: courseinfo@gre.ac.uk
// www.gre.ac.uk

M221 BA Business Law
Duration: 3FT Hon

Entry Requirements: Contact the institution for details.

N1M1 BA Business with Law
Duration: 3FT Hon

Entry Requirements: Contact the institution for details.

H24 HERIOT-WATT UNIVERSITY, EDINBURGH
EDINBURGH CAMPUS
EDINBURGH EH14 4AS
t: 0131 449 5111 f: 0131 451 3630
e: ugadmissions@hw.ac.uk
// www.hw.ac.uk

NM32 MA Accountancy and Business Law
Duration: 4FT Hon

Entry Requirements: *GCE:* BCC. *SQAH:* BBBB. *SQAAH:* BC. *IB:* 29.

N2M2 MA Management with Business Law
Duration: 4FT Hon

Entry Requirements: *GCE:* BCC. *SQAH:* BBBB. *SQAAH:* BC. *IB:* 29.

H60 THE UNIVERSITY OF HUDDERSFIELD
QUEENSGATE
HUDDERSFIELD HD1 3DH

t: 01484 473969 f: 01484 472765
e: admissionsandrecords@hud.ac.uk
// www.hud.ac.uk

M221 LLB LLB Business Law
Duration: 3FT Hon

Entry Requirements: HND required.

K24 THE UNIVERSITY OF KENT
INFORMATION, RECRUITMENT & ADMISSIONS
REGISTRY
UNIVERSITY OF KENT
CANTERBURY. KENT CT2 7NZ

t: 01227 827272 f: 01227 827077
e: information@kent.ac.uk
// www.kent.ac.uk

1M1N HND Business (Law)
Duration: 2FT HND

Entry Requirements: HND required.

L62 THE LONDON COLLEGE, UCK
VICTORIA GARDENS
NOTTING HILL GATE
LONDON W11 3PE

t: 020 7243 4000 f: 020 7243 1484
e: admissions@lcuck.ac.uk
// www.lcuck.ac.uk

122M HND Business Law
Duration: 2FT/3SW HND

Entry Requirements: *BTEC NC:* PP. *BTEC ND:* PPP.

522M HNC Business Law
Duration: 1FT/2SW HNC

Entry Requirements: *BTEC NC:* PP. *BTEC ND:* PPP.

L68 LONDON METROPOLITAN UNIVERSITY
166-220 HOLLOWAY ROAD
LONDON N7 8DB

t: 020 7133 4200
e: admissions@londonmet.ac.uk
// www.londonmet.ac.uk

M221 LLB LLB (Business Law)
Duration: 3FT Hon

Entry Requirements: *GCE:* 320. *IB:* 28.

MN21 BA Business Law and Business
Duration: 3FT Hon

Entry Requirements: *GCE:* 220. *IB:* 28.

MNF1 BA Business Law and International Business
Duration: 3FT Hon

Entry Requirements: *GCE:* 220. *IB:* 28.

MN25 BA Business Law and Marketing
Duration: 3FT Hon

Entry Requirements: *GCE:* 220. *IB:* 28.

MN23 BA Business Law and Taxation
Duration: 3FT Hon

Entry Requirements: *GCE:* 220. *IB:* 28.

MN28 BA Business Law and Travel Management
Duration: 3FT Hon

Entry Requirements: *GCE:* 220. *IB:* 28.

NM42 BA/BSc Accounting and Business Law
Duration: 3FT Hon

Entry Requirements: *GCE:* 220. *IB:* 28.

MN2V BA/BSc Business Law and Events Management
Duration: 3FT Hon

Entry Requirements: *GCE:* 220. *IB:* 28.

MN2F BA/BSc Business Law and Management
Duration: 3FT Hon

Entry Requirements: *GCE:* 220. *IB:* 28.

MN22 BA/BSc Business Law and Retail Management
Duration: 3FT Hon

Entry Requirements: *GCE:* 220. *IB:* 28.

P80 UNIVERSITY OF PORTSMOUTH

ACADEMIC REGISTRY
UNIVERSITY HOUSE
WINSTON CHURCHILL AVENUE
PORTSMOUTH PO1 2UP

t: 023 9284 8484 f: 023 9284 3082
e: admissions@port.ac.uk

// www.port.ac.uk

L1M2 BA Business Economics with Business Law

Duration: 3FT/4SW Hon

Entry Requirements: *GCE:* 260-300.

S21 SHEFFIELD HALLAM UNIVERSITY

CITY CAMPUS
HOWARD STREET
SHEFFIELD S1 1WB

t: 0114 225 5555 f: 0114 225 2167
e: admissions@shu.ac.uk

// www.shu.ac.uk

M225 LLB Business Law

Duration: 3FT Hon

Entry Requirements: *GCE:* 260.

S64 ST MARY'S UNIVERSITY COLLEGE, TWICKENHAM

WALDEGRAVE ROAD
STRAWBERRY HILL
MIDDLESEX TW1 4SX

t: 020 8240 4029 f: 020 8240 2361
e: admit@smuc.ac.uk

// www.smuc.ac.uk

MX23 BA Business Law and Education & Employment

Duration: 3FT Hon

Entry Requirements: *GCE:* 160-200. *BTEC NC:* MM. *BTEC ND:* MPP.

MQ23 BA Business Law and English

Duration: 3FT Hon

Entry Requirements: *GCE:* 160-200. *IB:* 28. *BTEC NC:* MM. *BTEC ND:* MPP.

MV21 BA Business Law and History

Duration: 3FT Hon

Entry Requirements: Contact the institution for details.

MQ25 BA Business Law and Irish Studies

Duration: 3FT Hon

Entry Requirements: *GCE:* 160-200. *BTEC NC:* MM. *BTEC ND:* MPP.

MN22 BA Business Law and Management Studies

Duration: 3FT Hon

Entry Requirements: *GCE:* 160-200. *BTEC NC:* MM. *BTEC ND:* MPP.

MV25 BA Business Law and Philosophy

Duration: 3FT Hon

Entry Requirements: *GCE:* 160-200. *BTEC NC:* MM. *BTEC ND:* MPP.

MN28 BA Business Law and Tourism

Duration: 3FT Hon

Entry Requirements: *GCE:* 160-200. *BTEC NC:* MM. *BTEC ND:* MPP.

PM32 BA Film & Popular Culture and Business Law

Duration: 3FT Hon

Entry Requirements: Contact the institution for details.

ML23 BA/BSc Business Law and Sociology

Duration: 3FT Hon

Entry Requirements: *GCE:* 160-200. *BTEC NC:* MM. *BTEC ND:* MPP.

MC26 BSc Business Law and Sport Science

Duration: 3FT Hon

Entry Requirements: Contact the institution for details.

S72 STAFFORDSHIRE UNIVERSITY

COLLEGE ROAD
STOKE ON TRENT ST4 2DE

t: 01782 292753 f: 01782 292740
e: admissions@staffs.ac.uk

// www.staffs.ac.uk

M221 LLB LLB (Business Law)

Duration: 3FT Hon

Entry Requirements: *GCE:* BB-ABB. *SQAAH:* BB-ABB. *IB:* 26. *BTEC NC:* DM. *BTEC ND:* DDM. *OCR ND:* Distinction.

S75 THE UNIVERSITY OF STIRLING
STIRLING FK9 4LA
t: 01786 467044 **f:** 01786 466800
e: admissions@stir.ac.uk
// www.stir.ac.uk

M221 BA Business Law
Duration: 4FT Hon

Entry Requirements: *GCE:* CCC. *SQAH:* BBBB. *SQAAH:* AAA-CCC. *BTEC ND:* DMM.

S78 THE UNIVERSITY OF STRATHCLYDE
GLASGOW G1 1XQ
t: 0141 552 4400 **f:** 0141 552 0775
// www.strath.ac.uk

MN28 BA Business Law and Hospitality & Tourism
Duration: 3FT Hon

Entry Requirements: *GCE:* BBC. *SQAH:* AABB-ABBBC. *IB:* 32.

NM32 BA Finance and Business Law
Duration: 4FT Hon

Entry Requirements: *GCE:* BBC. *SQAH:* AABB-ABBBC. *IB:* 32.

NM62 BA Human Resource Management and Business Law
Duration: 4FT Hon

Entry Requirements: *GCE:* BBC. *SQAH:* AABB-ABBBC. *IB:* 32.

GM22 BA Management Science and Business Law
Duration: 4FT Hon

Entry Requirements: *GCE:* BBC. *SQAH:* AABB-ABBBC. *IB:* 32.

NM52 BA Marketing and Business Law
Duration: 4FT Hon

Entry Requirements: *GCE:* BBC. *SQAH:* AABB-ABBBC. *IB:* 32.

W17 WARRINGTON COLLEGIATE
WINWICK ROAD CAMPUS
WINWICK ROAD
WARRINGTON
CHESHIRE WA2 8QA
t: 01925 494494 **f:** 01925 418328
e: admissions@warrington.ac.uk
// www.warrington.ac.uk

122M HND Business (Law)
Duration: 2FT HND

Entry Requirements: Contact the institution for details.

W75 UNIVERSITY OF WOLVERHAMPTON
ADMISSIONS UNIT
MX207, CAMP STREET
WOLVERHAMPTON
WEST MIDLANDS WV1 1AD
t: 01902 321000 **f:** 01902 321896
e: admissions@wlv.ac.uk
// www.wlv.ac.uk

MN24 BA Business Law and Accounting
Duration: 3FT Hon

Entry Requirements: *GCE:* 220. *IB:* 28. *BTEC NC:* DD. *BTEC ND:* MMM.

MN21 BA Business Law and Business
Duration: 3FT Hon

Entry Requirements: *GCE:* 220. *IB:* 28. *BTEC NC:* DD. *BTEC ND:* MMM.

MN26 BA Business Law and Human Resource Management
Duration: 3FT Hon

Entry Requirements: *GCE:* 220. *IB:* 28. *BTEC NC:* DD. *BTEC ND:* MMM.

GM32 BA/BSc Statistical Sciences and Business Law
Duration: 3FT Hon

Entry Requirements: *GCE:* 160-220. *IB:* 24.

COMMERCIAL LAW

B80 UNIVERSITY OF THE WEST OF ENGLAND, BRISTOL

FRENCHAY CAMPUS
COLDHARBOUR LANE
BRISTOL BS16 1QY

t: +44 (0)117 32 83333 f: +44 (0)117 32 82810
e: admissions@uwe.ac.uk

// www.uwe.ac.uk

M221 LLB LLB (Commercial Law)

Duration: 3FT Hon

Entry Requirements: GCE: 300-340.

E25 EAST LANCASHIRE INSTITUTE OF HIGHER EDUCATION AT BLACKBURN COLLEGE

DUKE STREET
BLACKBURN BB2 1LH

t: 01254 292594 f: 01254 260749
e: he-admissions@blackburn.ac.uk

// www.elihe.ac.uk

M221 LLB LLB Commercial Law

Duration: 3FT Hon

Entry Requirements: GCE: 220.

G14 UNIVERSITY OF GLAMORGAN, CARDIFF AND PONTYPRIDD

ENQUIRIES AND ADMISSIONS UNIT
PONTYPRIDD CF37 1DL

t: 0800 716925 f: 01443 654050
e: enquiries@glam.ac.uk

// www.glam.ac.uk

M221 LLB Commercial Law

Duration: 3FT Hon

Entry Requirements: GCE: 300-340. IB: 30. BTEC NC: DD. BTEC ND: DMM.

H72 THE UNIVERSITY OF HULL

THE UNIVERSITY OF HULL
COTTINGHAM ROAD
HULL HU6 7RX

t: 01482 466100 f: 01482 442290
e: admissions@hull.ac.uk

// www.hull.ac.uk

M221 LLB Commercial Law

Duration: 3FT Hon

Entry Requirements: GCE: 320. IB: 28.

S30 SOUTHAMPTON SOLENT UNIVERSITY

EAST PARK TERRACE
SOUTHAMPTON
HAMPSHIRE SO14 0RT

t: +44 (0) 23 8031 9039 f: + 44 (0)23 8022 2259
e: admissions@solent.ac.uk or ask@solent.ac.uk

// www.solent.ac.uk/

N1M2 BA Business Mgt with Commercial Law

Duration: 3FT Hon

Entry Requirements: GCE: 160.

M225 BA Commercial Law

Duration: 3FT Hon

Entry Requirements: GCE: 120.

M221 BA Commercial Law (with foundation)

Duration: 4FT Hon

Entry Requirements: BTEC NC: PP. BTEC ND: PPP.

W50 UNIVERSITY OF WESTMINSTER

115 NEW CAVENDISH STREET
LONDON W1W 6UW

t: 020 7911 5000 f: 020 7911 5788
e: course-enquiries@westminster.ac.uk

// www.westminster.ac.uk

M221 LLB Commercial Law

Duration: 3FT Hon

Entry Requirements: GCE: ABB. SQAH: AABBB. SQAAH: ABB. IB: 32. BTEC ND: DDM.

NM22 BA Business Management (Commercial Law)

Duration: 3FT Hon

Entry Requirements: GCE: BBB. SQAH: BBBBB. SQAAH: BBB. IB: 28.

N1M2 BA Business Studies (Commercial Law)

Duration: 4SW Hon

Entry Requirements: GCE: BBB. SQAH: BBBBB. SQAAH: BBB. IB: 28.

COMPUTING & MATHEMATICS COMBINATIONS

A40 ABERYSTWYTH UNIVERSITY
WELCOME CENTRE, ABERYSTWYTH UNIVERSITY
PENGLAIS CAMPUS
ABERYSTWYTH
CEREDIGION SY23 3FB

t: 01970 622021 f: 01970 627410
e: ug-admissions@aber.ac.uk
// www.aber.ac.uk

M1G1 BA Law with Mathematics
Duration: 3FT Hon

Entry Requirements: *GCE:* 280. *IB:* 27.

B56 THE UNIVERSITY OF BRADFORD
RICHMOND ROAD
BRADFORD
WEST YORKSHIRE BD7 1DP

t: 0800 073 1225 f: 01274 235585
e: course-enquiries@bradford.ac.uk
// www.bradford.ac.uk

G5M1 BSc ICT with Law
Duration: 3FT Hon

Entry Requirements: *GCE:* 120.

G5MC BSc ICT with Law (4 years)
Duration: 4FT Hon

Entry Requirements: *GCE:* 240. *IB:* 28.

D39 UNIVERSITY OF DERBY
KEDLESTON ROAD
DERBY DE22 1GB

t: 08701 202330 f: 01332 597724
e: askadmissions@derby.ac.uk
// www.derby.ac.uk

GM4C BA/BSc Computer Networks and Law
Duration: 3FT Hon

Entry Requirements: *Foundation:* Merit. *GCE:* 180-240. *IB:* 26. *BTEC NC:* DM. *BTEC ND:* MMP.

GM4D BA/BSc Computing and Law
Duration: 3FT Hon

Entry Requirements: *Foundation:* Merit. *GCE:* 180-240. *IB:* 26. *BTEC NC:* DM. *BTEC ND:* MMP.

E28 UNIVERSITY OF EAST LONDON
DOCKLANDS CAMPUS
UNIVERSITY WAY
LONDON E16 2RD

t: 020 8223 2835 f: 020 8223 2978
e: admiss@uel.ac.uk
// www.uel.ac.uk

GM5C BA/BSc Business Information Systems/Law
Duration: 3FT Hon

Entry Requirements: *GCE:* 240. *IB:* 28. *BTEC NC:* DD. *BTEC ND:* MMM.

GM51 BA/BSc Information Technology/Law
Duration: 3FT Hon

Entry Requirements: *GCE:* 200. *IB:* 28. *BTEC NC:* DD. *BTEC ND:* MMM.

G4M1 BSc Computer Networks with Law
Duration: 3FT Hon

Entry Requirements: *GCE:* 200. *IB:* 24.

G5M1 BEng Computer Technology with Law
Duration: 3FT Hon

Entry Requirements: *GCE:* 220. *IB:* 26.

G14 UNIVERSITY OF GLAMORGAN, CARDIFF AND PONTYPRIDD
ENQUIRIES AND ADMISSIONS UNIT
PONTYPRIDD CF37 1DL

t: 0800 716925 f: 01443 654050
e: enquiries@glam.ac.uk
// www.glam.ac.uk

GM41 BSc Computing and Law
Duration: 3FT Hon

Entry Requirements: *GCE:* 280-320. *IB:* 30. *BTEC NC:* DD. *BTEC ND:* DMM.

G70 UNIVERSITY OF GREENWICH
GREENWICH CAMPUS
OLD ROYAL NAVAL COLLEGE
PARK ROW
LONDON SE10 9LS

t: 0800 005 006 f: 020 8331 8145
e: courseinfo@gre.ac.uk
// www.gre.ac.uk

GM11 LLB Law and Mathematics
Duration: 3FT Hon

Entry Requirements: *GCE:* 180. *SQAH:* BBBBC. *SQAAH:* BCC. *IB:* 24.

H36 UNIVERSITY OF HERTFORDSHIRE

UNIVERSITY ADMISSIONS SERVICE
COLLEGE LANE
HATFIELD
HERTS AL10 9AB

t: 01707 284800 f: 01707 284870

// www.herts.ac.uk

G4M1 BSc Computing/Law

Duration: 3FT/4SW Hon

Entry Requirements: *GCE:* 220.

M1G4 BSc Law/Computing

Duration: 3FT Hon

Entry Requirements: *GCE:* 260.

K12 KEELE UNIVERSITY

STAFFS ST5 5BG

t: 01782 734005 f: 01782 632343
e: undergraduate@keele.ac.uk

// www.keele.ac.uk

GM41 BSc Computer Science and Law

Duration: 3FT Hon

Entry Requirements: *GCE:* 300-320.

GM4C BSc Creative Computing and Law

Duration: 3FT Hon

Entry Requirements: *GCE:* 280-320.

MG14 BSc Information Systems and Law

Duration: 3FT Hon

Entry Requirements: *GCE:* 300-320.

L46 LIVERPOOL HOPE UNIVERSITY

HOPE PARK
LIVERPOOL L16 9JD

t: 0151 291 3295 f: 0151 291 2050
e: admission@hope.ac.uk

// www.hope.ac.uk

MG15 BA Information Technology and Law

Duration: 3FT Hon

Entry Requirements: *GCE:* 240. *IB:* 25.

L68 LONDON METROPOLITAN UNIVERSITY

166-220 HOLLOWAY ROAD
LONDON N7 8DB

t: 020 7133 4200
e: admissions@londonmet.ac.uk

// www.londonmet.ac.uk

GM51 BA/BSc Business Information Technology and Law

Duration: 3FT Hon

Entry Requirements: *GCE:* 240. *IB:* 28.

L75 LONDON SOUTH BANK UNIVERSITY

103 BOROUGH ROAD
LONDON SE1 0AA

t: 020 7815 7815 f: 020 7815 8273
e: enquiry@lsbu.ac.uk

// www.lsbu.ac.uk

M1G5 LLB Law with Business Information Technology

Duration: 3FT Hon

Entry Requirements: *GCE:* 240. *IB:* 24.

S72 STAFFORDSHIRE UNIVERSITY

COLLEGE ROAD
STOKE ON TRENT ST4 2DE

t: 01782 292753 f: 01782 292740
e: admissions@staffs.ac.uk

// www.staffs.ac.uk

MG15 LLB LLB with Information Systems

Duration: 3FT Hon

Entry Requirements: *GCE:* BB-ABB. *SQAAH:* BB-ABB. *IB:* 26. *BTEC NC:* DM. *BTEC ND:* DDM. *OCR ND:* Distinction.

S78 THE UNIVERSITY OF STRATHCLYDE

GLASGOW G1 1XQ

t: 0141 552 4400 f: 0141 552 0775

// www.strath.ac.uk

G4M1 BSc Computer Science with Law

Duration: 4FT Hon

Entry Requirements: *GCE:* BBC. *SQAH:* AABB-BBBBB. *IB:* 32.

S84 UNIVERSITY OF SUNDERLAND

STUDENT HELPLINE
THE STUDENT GATEWAY
CHESTER ROAD
SUNDERLAND SR1 3SD

t: 0191 515 3000 f: 0191 515 3805
e: student-helpline@sunderland.ac.uk

// www.sunderland.ac.uk

GM41 BA/BSc Law and Computing

Duration: 3FT Hon

Entry Requirements: *GCE:* 220-360. *BTEC NC:* DM. *BTEC ND:* MMM.
OCR ND: Distinction. *OCR NED:* Merit.

M1G4 BA/BSc Law with Computing

Duration: 3FT Hon

Entry Requirements: *GCE:* 220-360. *BTEC NC:* DM. *BTEC ND:* MMM.
OCR ND: Distinction. *OCR NED:* Merit.

W75 UNIVERSITY OF WOLVERHAMPTON

ADMISSIONS UNIT
MX207, CAMP STREET
WOLVERHAMPTON
WEST MIDLANDS WV1 1AD

t: 01902 321000 f: 01902 321896
e: admissions@wlv.ac.uk

// www.wlv.ac.uk

GM41 BA Computing and Law

Duration: 3FT Hon

Entry Requirements: HND required.

GM4C BA/BSc Computer Science and Law

Duration: 3FT Hon

Entry Requirements: *GCE:* 160-220.

GM51 BA/BSc Information Systems and Law

Duration: 3FT Hon

Entry Requirements: *GCE:* 160-220.

CONSUMER LAW

N38 UNIVERSITY OF NORTHAMPTON

PARK CAMPUS
BOUGHTON GREEN ROAD
NORTHAMPTON NN2 7AL

t: 0800 358 2232 f: 01604 722083
e: admissions@northampton.ac.uk

// www.northampton.ac.uk

LM5F FdA Advice, Advocacy & Guidance

Duration: 2FT Fdg

Entry Requirements: *GCE:* 40-80. *SQAH:* CC-BC. *IB:* 24.

T20 UNIVERSITY OF TEESSIDE

MIDDLESBROUGH TS1 3BA

t: 01642 218121 f: 01642 384201
e: registry@tees.ac.uk

// www.tees.ac.uk

FM42 BSc Forensic Investigation and Consumer Law

Duration: 3FT/4SW Hon

Entry Requirements: *GCE:* 280. *IB:* 30. *BTEC NC:* DD. *BTEC ND:* DMM. Interview required.

CRIMINAL JUSTICE, CIVIL & COMMUNITY LAW

A40 ABERYSTWYTH UNIVERSITY

WELCOME CENTRE, ABERYSTWYTH UNIVERSITY
PENGLAIS CAMPUS
ABERYSTWYTH
CEREDIGION SY23 3FB

t: 01970 622021 f: 01970 627410
e: ug-admissions@aber.ac.uk

// www.aber.ac.uk

M131 LLB Criminal Law

Duration: 3FT Hon

Entry Requirements: *GCE:* 280. *IB:* 27.

B06 BANGOR UNIVERSITY

BANGOR
GWYNEDD LL57 2DG

t: 01248 382016/2017 f: 01248 370451
e: admissions@bangor.ac.uk

// www.bangor.ac.uk

M1M2 LLB Law with Criminal Justice

Duration: 3FT Hon

Entry Requirements: *GCE:* 280. *IB:* 28.

B41 BLACKPOOL AND THE FYLDE COLLEGE AN ASSOCIATE COLLEGE OF LANCASTER UNIVERSITY

ASHFIELD ROAD
BISPHAM
BLACKPOOL
LANCS FY2 0HB

t: 01253 504346 f: 01253 356127
e: admissions@blackpool.ac.uk

// www.blackpool.ac.uk

M211 FdA Criminology and Criminal Justice

Duration: 2FT Fdg

Entry Requirements: *GCE:* 40. *IB:* 24. *BTEC NC:* PP. *BTEC ND:* PPP.
OCR ND: Pass. *OCR NED:* Pass.

B56 THE UNIVERSITY OF BRADFORD
RICHMOND ROAD
BRADFORD
WEST YORKSHIRE BD7 1DP

t: 0800 073 1225 f: 01274 235585
e: course-enquiries@bradford.ac.uk

// www.bradford.ac.uk

M211 BA Applied Criminal Justice Studies
Duration: 3FT Hon

Entry Requirements: *GCE:* 220. *IB:* 24.

B60 BRADFORD COLLEGE: AN ASSOCIATE COLLEGE OF LEEDS METROPOLITAN UNIVERSITY
GREAT HORTON ROAD
BRADFORD
WEST YORKSHIRE BD7 1AY

t: 01274 433333 f: 01274 433241
e: admissions@bradfordcollege.ac.uk

// www.bradfordcollege.ac.uk

M211 BA Criminal Justice Studies
Duration: 3FT Hon

Entry Requirements: *GCE:* 160.

C30 UNIVERSITY OF CENTRAL LANCASHIRE
PRESTON
LANCS PR1 2HE

t: 01772 201201 f: 01772 894954
e: uadmissions@uclan.ac.uk

// www.uclan.ac.uk

M930 BA Criminology and Criminal Justice
Duration: 3FT Hon

Entry Requirements: *GCE:* 220. *SQAH:* BBBC. *IB:* 28. *BTEC NC:* DD. *BTEC ND:* DMM.

FM42 BSc Forensic Science and Criminal Investigation
Duration: 3FT Hon

Entry Requirements: *GCE:* 260-300. *IB:* 30. *BTEC ND:* DMM. *OCR ND:* Distinction.

FM49 BSc Police and Criminal Investigation
Duration: 3FT Hon

Entry Requirements: *GCE:* 260-300. *IB:* 30. *BTEC NC:* DD. *BTEC ND:* DMM. *OCR ND:* Distinction.

D26 DE MONTFORT UNIVERSITY
THE GATEWAY
LEICESTER LE1 9BH

t: 0116 255 1551 f: 0116 250 6204
e: enquiries@dmu.ac.uk

// www.dmu.ac.uk

M211 LLB Law and Criminal Justice
Duration: 3FT Hon

Entry Requirements: *GCE:* 280. *IB:* 28. *BTEC ND:* DMM. Interview required.

D39 UNIVERSITY OF DERBY
KEDLESTON ROAD
DERBY DE22 1GB

t: 08701 202330 f: 01332 597724
e: askadmissions@derby.ac.uk

// www.derby.ac.uk

ML93 BA Crime and Justice
Duration: 3FT Hon

Entry Requirements: *GCE:* 260. *IB:* 26. *BTEC NC:* DD. *BTEC ND:* MMM. *OCR ND:* Distinction. *OCR NED:* Merit.

E25 EAST LANCASHIRE INSTITUTE OF HIGHER EDUCATION AT BLACKBURN COLLEGE
DUKE STREET
BLACKBURN BB2 1LH

t: 01254 292594 f: 01254 260749
e: he-admissions@blackburn.ac.uk

// www.elihe.ac.uk

M212 LLB LLB Criminal Law
Duration: 3FT Hon

Entry Requirements: *GCE:* 220.

LM32 FdA Criminology and Criminal Justice
Duration: 2FT Fdg

Entry Requirements: *GCE:* 40.

E28 UNIVERSITY OF EAST LONDON
DOCKLANDS CAMPUS
UNIVERSITY WAY
LONDON E16 2RD

t: 020 8223 2835 f: 020 8223 2978
e: admiss@uel.ac.uk

// www.uel.ac.uk

M930 BA Criminology and Criminal Justice
Duration: 3FT Hon

Entry Requirements: *GCE:* 240. *IB:* 28. *BTEC NC:* DD. *BTEC ND:* MMM.

G14 UNIVERSITY OF GLAMORGAN, CARDIFF AND PONTYPRIDD

ENQUIRIES AND ADMISSIONS UNIT
PONTYPRIDD CF37 1DL

t: 0800 716925 f: 01443 654050
e: enquiries@glam.ac.uk

// www.glam.ac.uk

M212 LLB Criminal Law

Duration: 3FT Hon

Entry Requirements: *GCE:* 80-120.

F4M9 BSc Forensic Science with Criminology

Duration: 3FT Hon

Entry Requirements: *GCE:* 220-260. *IB:* 30. *BTEC NC:* DM. *BTEC ND:* MMM.

G53 GLYNDWR UNIVERSITY

PLAS COCH
MOLD ROAD
WREXHAM LL11 2AW

t: 01978 293439 f: 01978 290008
e: SID@glyndwr.ac.uk

// www.glyndwr.ac.uk

M240 BA Criminal Justice (Working with Offending Behaviour)

Duration: 3FT Hon

Entry Requirements: *GCE:* 200.

F4M2 BSc Forensic Science with Criminal Justice

Duration: 3FT Hon

Entry Requirements: *GCE:* 200.

G70 UNIVERSITY OF GREENWICH

GREENWICH CAMPUS
OLD ROYAL NAVAL COLLEGE
PARK ROW
LONDON SE10 9LS

t: 0800 005 006 f: 020 8331 8145
e: courseinfo@gre.ac.uk

// www.gre.ac.uk

MM92 BSc Criminal Justice and Legal Studies

Duration: 3FT Hon

Entry Requirements: Contact the institution for details.

G80 GRIMSBY INSTITUTE OF FURTHER AND HIGHER EDUCATION

NUNS CORNER
GRIMSBY
NE LINCOLNSHIRE DN34 5BQ

t: 0800 328 3631 f: 01472 315506/879924
e: headmissions@grimsby.ac.uk

// www.grimsby.ac.uk

LM42 FdA Criminological Studies

Duration: 2FT Fdg

Entry Requirements: *GCE:* 120-240. *BTEC NC:* MP. *BTEC ND:* PPP. Interview required.

K24 THE UNIVERSITY OF KENT

INFORMATION, RECRUITMENT & ADMISSIONS REGISTRY
UNIVERSITY OF KENT
CANTERBURY. KENT CT2 7NZ

t: 01227 827272 f: 01227 827077
e: information@kent.ac.uk

// www.kent.ac.uk

M900 BA Criminal Justice Studies

Duration: 3FT Hon

Entry Requirements: *GCE:* 200. *BTEC NC:* DD. *BTEC ND:* MMP.

L51 LIVERPOOL JOHN MOORES UNIVERSITY

ROSCOE COURT
4 RODNEY STREET
LIVERPOOL L1 2TZ

t: 0151 231 5090 f: 0151 231 3462
e: recruitment@ljmu.ac.uk

// www.ljmu.ac.uk

M291 BA Criminal Justice

Duration: 3FT Hon

Entry Requirements: *GCE:* 240.

MM21 BA Criminal Justice and Law

Duration: 3FT Hon

Entry Requirements: *GCE:* 240.

CM82 BSc Forensic Psychology and Criminal Justice

Duration: 3FT Hon

Entry Requirements: *GCE:* 240.

L68 LONDON METROPOLITAN UNIVERSITY

166-220 HOLLOWAY ROAD
LONDON N7 8DB

t: 020 7133 4200
e: admissions@londonmet.ac.uk

// www.londonmet.ac.uk

M290 LLB LLB (Social Justice)

Duration: 3FT Hon

Entry Requirements: *GCE:* 320. *IB:* 28.

M80 MIDDLESEX UNIVERSITY

MIDDLESEX UNIVERSITY
THE BURROUGHS
LONDON NW4 4BT

t: 020 8411 5555 f: 020 8411 5649
e: enquiries@mdx.ac.uk

// www.mdx.ac.uk

M930 BA Criminal Justice and Criminology

Duration: 3FT/4SW Hon

Entry Requirements: *GCE:* 200-300. *IB:* 28.

LM32 BA Youth Justice

Duration: 3FT Hon

Entry Requirements: *GCE:* 200-300. *IB:* 28.

N37 UNIVERSITY OF WALES, NEWPORT

CAERLEON CAMPUS
PO BOX 101
NEWPORT
SOUTH WALES NP18 3YH

t: 01633 432030 f: 01633 432850
e: admissions@newport.ac.uk

// www.newport.ac.uk

LM3F BA Criminology & Criminal Justice

Duration: 3FT Hon

Entry Requirements: *GCE:* 280. *IB:* 24. Interview required.

LM3G BA Criminology & Criminal Justice and Youth Justice

Duration: 3FT Hon

Entry Requirements: *GCE:* 280. *IB:* 24. Interview required.

LM52 BA Youth & Community Studies and Youth Justice

Duration: 3FT Hon

Entry Requirements: *GCE:* 280. *IB:* 24. Interview required.

N38 UNIVERSITY OF NORTHAMPTON

PARK CAMPUS
BOUGHTON GREEN ROAD
NORTHAMPTON NN2 7AL

t: 0800 358 2232 f: 01604 722083
e: admissions@northampton.ac.uk

// www.northampton.ac.uk

M211 BA Applied Criiminal Justice (top-up)

Duration: 1FT Hon

Entry Requirements: Contact the institution for details.

M212 BA Applied Criminal Justice

Duration: 3FT Hon

Entry Requirements: Contact the institution for details.

LM49 FdA Criminal Investigation Studies

Duration: 2FT Fdg

Entry Requirements: *GCE:* 40-80. *SQAH:* CC-BC. *IB:* 24.

LM42 FdA Police and Criminal Justice Services

Duration: 2FT Fdg

Entry Requirements: *GCE:* 40-80. *SQAH:* CC-BC. *IB:* 24.

LM52 FdA Prison and Criminal Justice Services

Duration: 2FT Fdg

Entry Requirements: *GCE:* 40-80. *SQAH:* CC-BC. *IB:* 24.

M290 FdA Youth Offending & Criminal Justice Services

Duration: 2FT Fdg

Entry Requirements: *GCE:* 40-80. *SQAH:* CC-BC. *IB:* 24.

N91 NOTTINGHAM TRENT UNIVERSITY

DRYDEN CENTRE
BURTON STREET
NOTTINGHAM NG1 4BU

t: +44 (0) 115 941 8418 f: +44 (0) 115 848 6063
e: admissions@ntu.ac.uk
// www.ntu.ac.uk/

M290 BA Youth Justice

Duration: 1FT Hon

Entry Requirements: Contact the institution for details.

M900 FdA Youth Justice

Duration: 2FT Fdg

Entry Requirements: GCE: 80.

P60 UNIVERSITY OF PLYMOUTH

DRAKE CIRCUS
PLYMOUTH PL4 8AA

t: 01752 588037 f: 01752 588050
e: admissions@plymouth.ac.uk
// www.plymouth.ac.uk

M9LG BSc Criminology & Criminal Justice Studies with International Relations

Duration: 3FT Hon

Entry Requirements: GCE: 260-300. IB: 28.

M213 BSc Criminology and Criminal Justice Studies

Duration: 3FT Hon

Entry Requirements: GCE: 260-300. IB: 28.

M215 BSc Law with Criminology & Criminal Justice Studies

Duration: 3FT Hon

Entry Requirements: GCE: 300. IB: 32.

L3MY BSc Sociology with Criminology & Criminal Justice Studies

Duration: 3FT Hon

Entry Requirements: GCE: 260-300. IB: 28.

P80 UNIVERSITY OF PORTSMOUTH

ACADEMIC REGISTRY
UNIVERSITY HOUSE
WINSTON CHURCHILL AVENUE
PORTSMOUTH PO1 2UP

t: 023 9284 8484 f: 023 9284 3082
e: admissions@port.ac.uk
// www.port.ac.uk

M930 BSc Criminology and Criminal Justice

Duration: 3FT Hon

Entry Requirements: GCE: 120.

S30 SOUTHAMPTON SOLENT UNIVERSITY

EAST PARK TERRACE
SOUTHAMPTON
HAMPSHIRE SO14 0RT

t: +44 (0) 23 8031 9039 f: + 44 (0)23 8022 2259
e: admissions@solent.ac.uk or ask@solent.ac.uk
// www.solent.ac.uk/

M2C8 BA Criminal Justice with Psychology

Duration: 3FT Hon

Entry Requirements: GCE: 240.

S51 ST HELENS COLLEGE

WATER STREET
ST HELENS
MERSEYSIDE WA10 1PP

t: 01744 733766 f: 01744 623400
e: enquiries@sthelens.ac.uk
// www.sthelens.ac.uk

M900 FdA Criminal Justice

Duration: 2FT Fdg

Entry Requirements: GCE: 80-100.

S52 SOUTH TYNESIDE COLLEGE

ST GEORGE'S AVENUE
SOUTH SHIELDS
TYNE & WEAR NE34 6ET

t: 0191 427 3500 f: 0191 427 3535
e: info@stc.ac.uk
// www.stc.ac.uk

M211 FdSc Criminal Justice

Duration: 2FT Fdg

Entry Requirements: GCE: 80-120. Interview required.

S72 STAFFORDSHIRE UNIVERSITY

COLLEGE ROAD
STOKE ON TRENT ST4 2DE
t: 01782 292753 f: 01782 292740
e: admissions@staffs.ac.uk
// www.staffs.ac.uk

MQ93 BA Crime, Deviance & Society and English Literature

Duration: 3FT Hon

Entry Requirements: *GCE:* 180-220. *IB:* 24.

MM12 BA Crime, Deviance & Society and Legal Studies

Duration: 3FT Hon

Entry Requirements: *GCE:* 180-220. *IB:* 24.

LM39 BA Crime, Deviance and Society

Duration: 3FT Hon

Entry Requirements: *GCE:* 160-200. *IB:* 24.

FM4X BSc Policing and Criminal Investigation

Duration: 3FT Hon

Entry Requirements: *GCE:* 180-240. *IB:* 24.

S93 SWANSEA UNIVERSITY

SINGLETON PARK
SWANSEA SA2 8PP
t: 01792 295111 f: 01792 295110
e: admissions@swansea.ac.uk
// www.swansea.ac.uk

M2L4 BSc Criminology and Criminal Justice

Duration: 3FT Hon

Entry Requirements: *GCE:* 280.

U40 UNIVERSITY OF THE WEST OF SCOTLAND

PAISLEY
RENFREWSHIRE
SCOTLAND PA1 2BE
t: 0141 848 3727 f: 0141 848 3623
e: admissions@uws.ac.uk
// www.uws.ac.uk

M211 BA Criminal Justice

Duration: 3FT/3.5FT Ord/Hon

Entry Requirements: *GCE:* CD. *SQAH:* BBC.

W50 UNIVERSITY OF WESTMINSTER

115 NEW CAVENDISH STREET
LONDON W1W 6UW
t: 020 7911 5000 f: 020 7911 5788
e: course-enquiries@westminster.ac.uk
// www.westminster.ac.uk

M211 BA Criminal Justice

Duration: 3FT Hon

Entry Requirements: *GCE:* BCC. *SQAH:* CCCBB. *SQAAH:* BCC. *IB:* 28. *BTEC ND:* DMM.

W75 UNIVERSITY OF WOLVERHAMPTON

ADMISSIONS UNIT
MX207, CAMP STREET
WOLVERHAMPTON
WEST MIDLANDS WV1 1AD
t: 01902 321000 f: 01902 321896
e: admissions@wlv.ac.uk
// www.wlv.ac.uk

TM72 BA American Studies and Criminal Justice

Duration: 3FT Hon

Entry Requirements: *GCE:* 160-220.

M211 BA Criminal Justice

Duration: 3FT Hon

Entry Requirements: *GCE:* 160-220. *IB:* 28.

MM91 BA Criminal Justice and Law

Duration: 3FT Hon

Entry Requirements: *GCE:* 160-220. *IB:* 28.

MP23 BA Criminal Justice and Media & Communication Studies

Duration: 3FT Hon

Entry Requirements: *GCE:* 160-220.

MM29 BA Criminal Justice and Social Welfare Law

Duration: 3FT Hon

Entry Requirements: *GCE:* 160-220. *IB:* 28.

QM32 BA English and Criminal Justice

Duration: 3FT Hon

Entry Requirements: *GCE:* 160-220.

PM32 BA Media & Cultural Studies and Criminal Justice

Duration: 3FT Hon

Entry Requirements: *GCE:* 160-220.

LM49 BA Social Policy and Criminal Justice
Duration: 3FT Hon

Entry Requirements: *GCE:* 160-220. *IB:* 24.

LM39 BA Sociology and Criminal Justice
Duration: 3FT Hon

Entry Requirements: *GCE:* 160-220. *IB:* 24.

CM12 BSc Biological Sciences and Criminal Justice
Duration: 3FT Hon

Entry Requirements: *GCE:* 160-220.

FM42 BSc Forensic Science and Criminal Justice
Duration: 3FT Hon

Entry Requirements: HND required.

CRIMINOLOGY

A40 ABERYSTWYTH UNIVERSITY
WELCOME CENTRE, ABERYSTWYTH UNIVERSITY
PENGLAIS CAMPUS
ABERYSTWYTH
CEREDIGION SY23 3FB

t: 01970 622021 f: 01970 627410
e: ug-admissions@aber.ac.uk
// www.aber.ac.uk

M1M9 BA Law with Criminology
Duration: 3FT Hon

Entry Requirements: *GCE:* 280. *IB:* 27.

M900 BScEcon Criminology
Duration: 3FT Hon

Entry Requirements: *GCE:* 280. *IB:* 27.

M9C8 BScEcon Criminology with Applied Psychology
Duration: 3FT Hon

Entry Requirements: *GCE:* 280. *IB:* 27.

CM89 BScEcon Psychology/Criminology
Duration: 3FT Hon

Entry Requirements: *GCE:* 260. *IB:* 27.

A60 ANGLIA RUSKIN UNIVERSITY
BISHOP HALL LANE
CHELMSFORD
ESSEX CM1 1SQ

t: 0845 271 3333 f: 01245 251789
e: answers@anglia.ac.uk
// www.anglia.ac.uk

M211 BA Criminology
Duration: 3FT Hon

Entry Requirements: *GCE:* 220-260. *SQAH:* AABC. *SQAAH:* AB. *IB:* 30.

ML13 BA Law and Criminology
Duration: 3FT Hon

Entry Requirements: *GCE:* 220-260. *SQAH:* AABC. *SQAAH:* AB. *IB:* 30.

B06 BANGOR UNIVERSITY
BANGOR
GWYNEDD LL57 2DG

t: 01248 382016/2017 f: 01248 370451
e: admissions@bangor.ac.uk
// www.bangor.ac.uk

MR93 BA Criminology & Criminal Justice and Italian
Duration: 4FT Hon

Entry Requirements: *GCE:* 240-280. *IB:* 28.

MC98 BA Criminology & Criminal Justice and Psychology
Duration: 3FT Hon

Entry Requirements: *GCE:* 260-300. *IB:* 28.

MV16 BA Criminology & Criminal Justice and Religious Studies
Duration: 3FT Hon

Entry Requirements: *GCE:* 240-260. *IB:* 28.

MR94 BA Criminology & Criminal Justice and Spanish
Duration: 4FT Hon

Entry Requirements: *GCE:* 240-260. *IB:* 28.

M930 BA Criminology and Criminal Justice
Duration: 3FT Hon

Entry Requirements: *GCE:* 240-260. *IB:* 28.

MQ93 BA English and Criminology & Criminal Justice
Duration: 3FT Hon

Entry Requirements: *GCE:* 240-260. *IB:* 28.

MR91 BA French and Criminology & Criminal Justice
Duration: 4FT Hon

Entry Requirements: *GCE:* 240-260. *IB:* 28.

MR92 BA German and Criminology & Criminal Justice
Duration: 4FT Hon

Entry Requirements: *GCE:* 240-260. *IB:* 28.

MVX1 BA History and Criminology & Criminal Justice
Duration: 3FT Hon

Entry Requirements: *GCE:* 240-260. *IB:* 28.

LM49 BA Social Policy and Criminology & Criminal Justice
Duration: 3FT Hon

Entry Requirements: *GCE:* 240-260. *IB:* 28.

LM39 BA Sociology and Criminology & Criminal Justice
Duration: 3FT Hon

Entry Requirements: *GCE:* 240-260. *IB:* 28.

B22 UNIVERSITY OF BEDFORDSHIRE
PARK SQUARE
LUTON
BEDS LU1 3JU
t: 01582 489286 f: 01582 489323
e: admissions@beds.ac.uk
// www.beds.ac.uk

M931 BA Criminology
Duration: 3FT Hon

Entry Requirements: *GCE:* 160-240. *SQAH:* CCC. *SQAAH:* CCC. *IB:* 30.

ML23 BA Criminology and Sociology
Duration: 3FT Hon

Entry Requirements: *GCE:* 200.

CM89 BSc Psychology and Criminology
Duration: 3FT Hon

Entry Requirements: *GCE:* 160-240. *SQAH:* BBC. *SQAAH:* BBC. *IB:* 30.

B25 BIRMINGHAM CITY UNIVERSITY
PERRY BARR
BIRMINGHAM B42 2SU
t: 0121 331 5595 f: 0121 331 7994
e: choices@bcu.ac.uk
// www.bcu.ac.uk

M1MF LLB Law with Criminology
Duration: 3FT Hon

Entry Requirements: *GCE:* 280. *IB:* 24. *BTEC NC:* DD. *BTEC ND:* DMM. *OCR ND:* Distinction.

M900 BA Criminology
Duration: 3FT Hon

Entry Requirements: *GCE:* 240.

ML9K BA Criminology and Policing
Duration: 3FT Hon

Entry Requirements: *GCE:* 240.

ML94 BA Criminology and Security Studies
Duration: 3FT Hon

Entry Requirements: *GCE:* 240.

LM39 BA Criminology and Sociology
Duration: 3FT Hon

Entry Requirements: *GCE:* 240.

B41 BLACKPOOL AND THE FYLDE COLLEGE AN ASSOCIATE COLLEGE OF LANCASTER UNIVERSITY
ASHFIELD ROAD
BISPHAM
BLACKPOOL
LANCS FY2 0HB
t: 01253 504346 f: 01253 356127
e: admissions@blackpool.ac.uk
// www.blackpool.ac.uk

M212 BA Criminology and Criminal Justice (Top-up)
Duration: 1FT Hon

Entry Requirements: Contact the institution for details.

B72 UNIVERSITY OF BRIGHTON
MITHRAS HOUSE
LEWES ROAD
BRIGHTON BN2 4AT
t: 01273 644644 f: 01273 642607
e: admissions@brighton.ac.uk
// www.brighton.ac.uk

MC98 BA Applied Psychology and Criminology
Duration: 3FT Hon
Entry Requirements: *GCE:* BBB. *IB:* 28. *BTEC ND:* DDM.

LM49 BA Criminology and Social Policy
Duration: 3FT Hon
Entry Requirements: *GCE:* BBC. *IB:* 28. *BTEC ND:* DMM.

LM39 BA Criminology and Sociology
Duration: 3FT Hon
Entry Requirements: *GCE:* BBC. *IB:* 28. *BTEC ND:* DMM.

LM29 BA Politics and Criminology
Duration: 3FT Hon
Entry Requirements: *GCE:* BBB. *IB:* 28. *BTEC ND:* DDM.

B80 UNIVERSITY OF THE WEST OF ENGLAND, BRISTOL
FRENCHAY CAMPUS
COLDHARBOUR LANE
BRISTOL BS16 1QY
t: +44 (0)117 32 83333 f: +44 (0)117 32 82810
e: admissions@uwe.ac.uk
// www.uwe.ac.uk

M900 BA Criminology
Duration: 3FT Hon
Entry Requirements: *GCE:* 280-320.

MW94 BA Criminology and Drama
Duration: 3FT Hon
Entry Requirements: *GCE:* 240-300.

MQ9H BA Criminology and English
Duration: 3FT Hon
Entry Requirements: *GCE:* 240-300.

MV91 BA Criminology and History
Duration: 3FT Hon
Entry Requirements: *GCE:* 260-320.

ML9F BA Criminology and International Relations
Duration: 3FT Hon
Entry Requirements: *GCE:* 240-300.

MM19 BA Criminology and Law
Duration: 3FT Hon
Entry Requirements: *GCE:* 240-300.

MP93 BA Criminology and Media & Cultural Studies
Duration: 3FT Hon
Entry Requirements: *GCE:* 240-300.

MV95 BA Criminology and Philosophy
Duration: 3FT Hon
Entry Requirements: *GCE:* 240-300.

ML92 BA Criminology and Politics
Duration: 3FT Hon
Entry Requirements: *GCE:* 240-300.

ML93 BA Criminology and Sociology
Duration: 3FT Hon
Entry Requirements: *GCE:* 80-120.

MR94 BA Criminology and Spanish
Duration: 3FT Hon
Entry Requirements: *GCE:* 240-300.

MM92 FdA Criminology and Criminal Justice
Duration: 2FT Fdg
Entry Requirements: HND required.

B94 BUCKINGHAMSHIRE NEW UNIVERSITY
QUEEN ALEXANDRA ROAD
HIGH WYCOMBE
BUCKS HP11 2JZ
t: 0800 0565 660 f: 01494 605023
e: admissions@bucks.ac.uk
// www.bucks.ac.uk

M930 BSc Criminology
Duration: 3FT Hon
Entry Requirements: *GCE:* 200-240. *SQAH:* CCCC. *IB:* 27. *BTEC NC:* MM. *BTEC ND:* MPP.

LM39 BSc Criminology and Sociology
Duration: 3FT Hon
Entry Requirements: *GCE:* 200-240. *SQAH:* CCCC. *IB:* 27. *BTEC NC:* MM. *BTEC ND:* MPP.

L4M9 BSc Police Studies with Criminal Investigation
Duration: 3FT Hon
Entry Requirements: *GCE:* 80.

C10 CANTERBURY CHRIST CHURCH UNIVERSITY

NORTH HOLMES ROAD
CANTERBURY
KENT CT1 1QU

t: 01227 782900 f: 01227 782888
e: admissions@canterbury.ac.uk

// www.canterbury.ac.uk

M900 BA Applied Criminology
Duration: 3FT Hon

Entry Requirements: *GCE:* 200. *IB:* 24.

MT97 BA Applied Criminology and American Studies
Duration: 3FT Hon

Entry Requirements: *GCE:* 200. *IB:* 24.

MN91 BA Applied Criminology and Business Studies
Duration: 3FT Hon

Entry Requirements: *GCE:* 200. *IB:* 24.

GM49 BA Applied Criminology and Digital Media
Duration: 3FT Hon

Entry Requirements: *GCE:* 200. *IB:* 24.

MQ93 BA Applied Criminology and English
Duration: 3FT Hon

Entry Requirements: *GCE:* 200. *IB:* 24.

FM89 BA Applied Criminology and Environmental Science
Duration: 3FT Hon

Entry Requirements: *GCE:* 200. *IB:* 24.

MP9H BA Applied Criminology and Film, Radio & Television Studies
Duration: 3FT Hon

Entry Requirements: *GCE:* 200. *IB:* 24.

MF94 BA Applied Criminology and Forensic Investigation
Duration: 3FT Hon

Entry Requirements: *GCE:* 200. *IB:* 24.

MR91 BA Applied Criminology and French
Duration: 3FT Hon

Entry Requirements: *GCE:* 200. *IB:* 24.

MF98 BA Applied Criminology and Geography
Duration: 3FT Hon

Entry Requirements: *GCE:* 200. *IB:* 24.

MV91 BA Applied Criminology and History
Duration: 3FT Hon

Entry Requirements: *GCE:* 200. *IB:* 24.

MN95 BA Applied Criminology and Marketing
Duration: 3FT Hon

Entry Requirements: *GCE:* 200. *IB:* 24.

MW93 BA Applied Criminology and Music
Duration: 3FT Hon

Entry Requirements: *GCE:* 200. *IB:* 24.

MC98 BA Applied Criminology and Psychology
Duration: 3FT Hon

Entry Requirements: *GCE:* 200. *IB:* 24.

MV96 BA Applied Criminology and Religious Studies
Duration: 3FT Hon

Entry Requirements: *GCE:* 200. *IB:* 24.

ML93 BA Applied Criminology and Sociology & Social Science
Duration: 3FT Hon

Entry Requirements: *GCE:* 200. *IB:* 24.

MC96 BA Applied Criminology and Sport & Exercise Science
Duration: 3FT Hon

Entry Requirements: *GCE:* 200. *IB:* 24.

M9T7 BA Applied Criminology with American Studies
Duration: 3FT Hon

Entry Requirements: *GCE:* 200. *IB:* 24.

M9N1 BA Applied Criminology with Business Studies
Duration: 3FT Hon

Entry Requirements: *GCE:* 200. *IB:* 24.

M9GK BA Applied Criminology with Digital Media
Duration: 3FT Hon

Entry Requirements: *GCE:* 200. *IB:* 24.

M9Q3 BA Applied Criminology with English
Duration: 3FT Hon

Entry Requirements: *GCE:* 200. *IB:* 24.

M9NC BA Applied Criminology with Entrepreneurship
Duration: 3FT Hon

Entry Requirements: *GCE:* 200. *IB:* 24.

M9FV BA Applied Criminology with Environmental Science
Duration: 3FT Hon

Entry Requirements: *GCE:* 200. *IB:* 24.

M9F4 BA Applied Criminology with Forensic Investigation
Duration: 3FT Hon

Entry Requirements: *GCE:* 200. *IB:* 24.

M9FK BA Applied Criminology with Forensic Investigation 'International Only'
Duration: 4FT Hon

Entry Requirements: Interview required.

M9R1 BA Applied Criminology with French
Duration: 3FT Hon

Entry Requirements: *GCE:* 200. *IB:* 24.

M9F8 BA Applied Criminology with Geography
Duration: 3FT Hon

Entry Requirements: *GCE:* 200. *IB:* 24.

M9L2 BA Applied Criminology with Global Politics
Duration: 3FT Hon

Entry Requirements: *GCE:* 200. *IB:* 24.

M9V1 BA Applied Criminology with History
Duration: 3FT Hon

Entry Requirements: *GCE:* 200. *IB:* 24.

M9LF BA Applied Criminology with International Relations
Duration: 3FT Hon

Entry Requirements: *GCE:* 200. *IB:* 24.

M9N5 BA Applied Criminology with Marketing
Duration: 3FT Hon

Entry Requirements: *GCE:* 200. *IB:* 24.

M9LG BA Applied Criminology with Politics & Governance
Duration: 3FT Hon

Entry Requirements: *GCE:* 200. *IB:* 24.

M9C8 BA Applied Criminology with Psychology
Duration: 3FT Hon

Entry Requirements: *GCE:* 200. *IB:* 24.

M9V6 BA Applied Criminology with Religious Studies
Duration: 3FT Hon

Entry Requirements: *GCE:* 200. *IB:* 24.

NM19 BA Entrepreneurship and Applied Criminology
Duration: 3FT Hon

Entry Requirements: *GCE:* 200. *IB:* 24.

N1MX BA Entrepreneurship with Applied Criminology
Duration: 3FT Hon

Entry Requirements: *GCE:* 200. *IB:* 24.

LM2X BA Global Politics and Applied Criminology
Duration: 3FT Hon

Entry Requirements: *GCE:* 200. *IB:* 24.

L2MX BA Global Politics with Applied Criminology
Duration: 3FT Hon

Entry Requirements: *GCE:* 200. *IB:* 24.

L2M9 BA International Relations with Applied Criminology
Duration: 3FT Hon

Entry Requirements: *GCE:* 200. *IB:* 24.

LM29 BA Politics & Governance and Applied Criminology
Duration: 3FT Hon

Entry Requirements: *GCE:* 200. *IB:* 24.

L2MY BA Politics & Governance with Applied Criminology
Duration: 3FT Hon

Entry Requirements: *GCE:* 200. *IB:* 24.

Confused about courses?
Indecisive about institutions?
Stressed about student life?
Unsure about UCAS?
Frowning over finance?

Help is available.

Visit www.ucasbooks.com to view our range
of over 75 books covering all aspects
of entry into higher education.

www.ucasbooks.com

> Unlock your potential
It's as easy as 1, 2, 3.

1 Search
Use Course Search to look for courses in your subject; find out about your chosen universities and colleges and lots more.

2 Apply
Use our online system Apply to make your application to higher education.

3 Track
Then use Track to monitor the progress of your application.

UCAS

helping students into higher education

www.ucas.com

T7M9 BA/BSc American Studies with Applied Criminology
Duration: 3FT Hon

Entry Requirements: *GCE:* 200. *IB:* 24.

M9X3 BA/BSc Applied Criminology with Education Studies
Duration: 3FT Hon

Entry Requirements: *GCE:* 200. *IB:* 24.

M292 BA/BSc Applied Criminology with Legal Studies
Duration: 3FT Hon

Entry Requirements: *GCE:* 200. *IB:* 24.

M9L3 BA/BSc Applied Criminology with Sociology & Social Science
Duration: 3FT Hon

Entry Requirements: *GCE:* 200. *IB:* 24.

M9C6 BA/BSc Applied Criminology with Sport & Exercise Science
Duration: 3FT Hon

Entry Requirements: *GCE:* 200. *IB:* 24.

M9VP BA/BSc Applied Criminology with Theology
Duration: 3FT Hon

Entry Requirements: *GCE:* 200. *IB:* 24.

XM39 BA/BSc Education Studies and Applied Criminology
Duration: 3FT Hon

Entry Requirements: *GCE:* 200. *IB:* 24.

X3M9 BA/BSc Education Studies with Applied Criminology
Duration: 3FT Hon

Entry Requirements: *GCE:* 200. *IB:* 24.

Q3M9 BA/BSc English with Applied Criminology
Duration: 3FT Hon

Entry Requirements: *GCE:* 200. *IB:* 24.

F8MX BA/BSc Environmental Science with Applied Criminology
Duration: 3FT Hon

Entry Requirements: *GCE:* 200. *IB:* 24.

F8MY BA/BSc Environmental Science with Applied Criminology (with Foundation Year)
Duration: 4FT Hon

Entry Requirements: *IB:* 24.

P3MX BA/BSc Film, Radio & Television Studies with Applied Criminology
Duration: 3FT Hon

Entry Requirements: *GCE:* 240. *IB:* 24.

W1M9 BA/BSc Fine & Applied Arts with Applied Criminology
Duration: 3FT Hon

Entry Requirements: *GCE:* 200. *IB:* 24.

LM2Y BA/BSc International Relations and Applied Criminology
Duration: 3FT Hon

Entry Requirements: *GCE:* 200. *IB:* 24.

M291 BA/BSc Legal Studies with Applied Criminology
Duration: 3FT Hon

Entry Requirements: *GCE:* 200. *IB:* 24.

C8MX BA/BSc Psychology with Applied Criminology
Duration: 3FT Hon

Entry Requirements: *GCE:* 200. *IB:* 24.

V6M9 BA/BSc Religious Studies with Applied Criminology
Duration: 3FT Hon

Entry Requirements: *GCE:* 200. *IB:* 24.

L3M9 BA/BSc Sociology & Social Science with Applied Criminology
Duration: 3FT Hon

Entry Requirements: *GCE:* 200. *IB:* 24.

VM69 BA/BSc Theology and Applied Criminology
Duration: 3FT Hon

Entry Requirements: *GCE:* 200. *IB:* 24.

V6MX BA/BSc Theology with Applied Criminology
Duration: 3FT Hon

Entry Requirements: *GCE:* 200. *IB:* 24.

N1M9 BSc Business Studies with Applied Criminology

Duration: 3FT Hon

Entry Requirements: *GCE:* 200. *IB:* 24.

N5M9 BSc Marketing with Applied Criminology

Duration: 3FT Hon

Entry Requirements: *GCE:* 200. *IB:* 24.

G4MX BSc/BA Digital Media with Applied Criminology

Duration: 3FT Hon

Entry Requirements: *GCE:* 200. *IB:* 24.

F4M9 BSc/BA Forensic Investigation with Applied Criminology

Duration: 3FT Hon

Entry Requirements: *GCE:* 200. *IB:* 24.

F8M9 BSc/BA Geography with Applied Criminology

Duration: 3FT Hon

Entry Requirements: *GCE:* 200. *IB:* 24.

V1M9 BSc/BA History with Applied Criminology

Duration: 3FT Hon

Entry Requirements: *GCE:* 200. *IB:* 24.

C15 CARDIFF UNIVERSITY

PO BOX 927
30-36 NEWPORT ROAD
CARDIFF CF24 0DE

t: 029 2087 9999 f: 029 2087 6138
e: admissions@cardiff.ac.uk

// www.cardiff.ac.uk

M190 LLB Law and Criminology

Duration: 3FT Hon

Entry Requirements: *GCE:* AAA. Interview required.

XM39 BScEcon Education and Criminology

Duration: 3FT Hon

Entry Requirements: *GCE:* BBB. *SQAAH:* BBB. *IB:* 32. *BTEC ND:* DDM. *OCR ND:* Distinction. *OCR NED:* Distinction.

ML94 BScEcon Social Policy and Criminology

Duration: 3FT Hon

Entry Requirements: *GCE:* BBB. *SQAAH:* BBB. *IB:* 32. *BTEC ND:* DDM. *OCR ND:* Distinction. *OCR NED:* Distinction.

LM39 BScEcon Sociology and Criminology

Duration: 3FT Hon

Entry Requirements: *GCE:* BBB. *SQAAH:* BBB. *IB:* 32. *BTEC ND:* DDM. *OCR ND:* Distinction. *OCR NED:* Distinction.

C30 UNIVERSITY OF CENTRAL LANCASHIRE

PRESTON
LANCS PR1 2HE

t: 01772 201201 f: 01772 894954
e: uadmissions@uclan.ac.uk

// www.uclan.ac.uk

MV95 BA Criminology and Philosophy

Duration: 3FT Hon

Entry Requirements: *GCE:* 220. *IB:* 26. *BTEC NC:* DM. *BTEC ND:* MMP.

LM49 BA Criminology and Social Policy

Duration: 3FT Hon

Entry Requirements: *GCE:* 220. *IB:* 26. *BTEC NC:* DM. *BTEC ND:* MMP.

LM39 BA Criminology and Sociology

Duration: 3FT Hon

Entry Requirements: *GCE:* 220. *IB:* 26. *BTEC NC:* DM. *BTEC ND:* MMP.

ML99 BA Ethnicity & Human Rights and Criminology

Duration: 3FT Hon

Entry Requirements: *GCE:* 220. *IB:* 26. *BTEC NC:* DM. *BTEC ND:* MMP.

M190 BA Law and Criminology

Duration: 3FT Hon

Entry Requirements: *GCE:* 220. *IB:* 28. *BTEC NC:* DM. *BTEC ND:* MMM.

LM31 BA Sociology and Criminology

Duration: 3FT Hon

Entry Requirements: *GCE:* 220. *IB:* 26. *BTEC NC:* DM. *BTEC ND:* MMP.

FM4X BSc Forensic Science and Criminology

Duration: 3FT Hon

Entry Requirements: *GCE:* 260-300. *IB:* 30. *BTEC ND:* DMM. *OCR ND:* Distinction.

CMV9 BSc Psychology and Criminology

Duration: 3FT Hon

Entry Requirements: *GCE:* 240. *IB:* 30. *BTEC ND:* MMM. *OCR ND:* Distinction.

C55 UNIVERSITY OF CHESTER

PARKGATE ROAD
CHESTER CH1 4BJ

t: 01244 511000 **f:** 01244 511300
e: enquiries@chester.ac.uk

// www.chester.ac.uk

M1LH LLB Law with Criminology

Duration: 3FT Hon

Entry Requirements: *GCE:* 240 - 300. *SQAH:* BBBB. *IB:* 24. *BTEC NC:* DM. *BTEC ND:* MMM.

N1M9 BA Business with Criminology

Duration: 3FT Hon

Entry Requirements: *GCE:* 240. *SQAH:* BBBB. *IB:* 24. *BTEC NC:* DM. *BTEC ND:* MMM.

P3M9 BA Communication Studies with Criminology

Duration: 3FT Hon

Entry Requirements: *GCE:* 240. *SQAH:* BBBB. *IB:* 24. *BTEC NC:* DM. *BTEC ND:* MMM.

L5MX BA Counselling Skills with Criminology

Duration: 3FT Hon

Entry Requirements: *GCE:* 240. *SQAH:* BBBB. *IB:* 24. *BTEC NC:* DM. *BTEC ND:* MMM.

MN91 BA Criminology and Business

Duration: 3FT Hon

Entry Requirements: *GCE:* 240. *SQAH:* BBBB. *IB:* 24. *BTEC NC:* DM. *BTEC ND:* MMM.

ML9N BA Criminology and Counselling Skills

Duration: 3FT Hon

Entry Requirements: *GCE:* 240. *SQAH:* BBBB. *IB:* 24. *BTEC NC:* DM. *BTEC ND:* MMM.

MQ93 BA Criminology and English

Duration: 3FT Hon

Entry Requirements: *GCE:* 240. *SQAH:* BBBB. *IB:* 24. *BTEC NC:* DM. *BTEC ND:* MPP.

MR91 BA Criminology and French

Duration: 4FT Hon

Entry Requirements: *GCE:* 240. *SQAH:* BBBB. *IB:* 24. *BTEC NC:* DM. *BTEC ND:* MMM.

MRX4 BA Criminology and Spanish

Duration: 4FT Hon

Entry Requirements: *GCE:* 240. *SQAH:* BBBB. *IB:* 24. *BTEC NC:* DM. *BTEC ND:* MMM.

MV96 BA Criminology and Theology & Religious Studies

Duration: 3FT Hon

Entry Requirements: *GCE:* 240. *SQAH:* BBBB. *IB:* 24. *BTEC NC:* DM. *BTEC ND:* MMM.

Q3M9 BA English with Criminology

Duration: 3FT Hon

Entry Requirements: *GCE:* 240. *SQAH:* BBBB. *IB:* 24. *BTEC NC:* DM. *BTEC ND:* MPP.

R1MY BA French with Criminology

Duration: 4FT Hon

Entry Requirements: *GCE:* 240. *SQAH:* BBBB. *IB:* 24. *BTEC NC:* DM. *BTEC ND:* MMM.

MP95 BA Journalism and Criminology

Duration: 3FT Hon

Entry Requirements: *GCE:* 240. *SQAH:* BBBB. *IB:* 24. *BTEC NC:* DM. *BTEC ND:* MMM.

MM19 BA Law and Criminology

Duration: 3FT Hon

Entry Requirements: *GCE:* 240. *SQAH:* BBBB. *IB:* 24. *BTEC NC:* DM. *BTEC ND:* MMM.

NM29 BA Management and Criminology

Duration: 3FT Hon

Entry Requirements: *GCE:* 240. *SQAH:* BBBB. *IB:* 24. *BTEC NC:* DM. *BTEC ND:* MMM.

N2M9 BA Management with Criminology

Duration: 3FT Hon

Entry Requirements: *GCE:* 240. *SQAH:* BBBB. *IB:* 24. *BTEC NC:* DM. *BTEC ND:* MMM.

LM29 BA Politics and Criminology

Duration: 3FT Hon

Entry Requirements: HND required.

L2M9 BA Politics with Criminology

Duration: 3FT Hon

Entry Requirements: *GCE:* 240. *SQAH:* BBBB. *IB:* 24. *BTEC NC:* DM. *BTEC ND:* MMM.

R4MY BA Spanish with Criminology

Duration: 4FT Hon

Entry Requirements: *GCE:* 240. *SQAH:* BBBB. *IB:* 24. *BTEC NC:* DM. *BTEC ND:* MMM.

V6M9 BA Theology & Religious Studies with Criminology
Duration: 3FT Hon

Entry Requirements: *GCE:* 240. *SQAH:* BBBB. *IB:* 24. *BTEC NC:* DM. *BTEC ND:* MMM.

NM89 BA Tourism and Criminology
Duration: 3FT Hon

Entry Requirements: *Foundation:* Pass. *GCE:* 240. *SQAH:* BBBB. *IB:* 24. *BTEC NC:* DM. *BTEC ND:* MMM.

N8M9 BA Tourism with Criminology
Duration: 3FT Hon

Entry Requirements: *Foundation:* Pass. *GCE:* 240. *SQAH:* BBBB. *IB:* 24. *BTEC NC:* DM. *BTEC ND:* MMM.

G4M9 BSc Computer Science with Criminology
Duration: 3FT Hon

Entry Requirements: *GCE:* 240. *SQAH:* BBBB. *IB:* 24. *BTEC NC:* DM. *BTEC ND:* MMM.

M900 BSc Criminology
Duration: 3FT Hon

Entry Requirements: *GCE:* 220 - 260. *SQAH:* BBBB. *IB:* 24. *BTEC NC:* DM. *BTEC ND:* MMM.

MG94 BSc Criminology and Computer Science
Duration: 3FT Hon

Entry Requirements: *GCE:* 240. *SQAH:* BBBB. *IB:* 24. *BTEC NC:* DM. *BTEC ND:* MMM.

MF94 BSc Criminology and Forensic Biology
Duration: 3FT Hon

Entry Requirements: *GCE:* 240. *SQAH:* BBBB. *IB:* 24. *BTEC NC:* DM. *BTEC ND:* MMM.

MF98 BSc Criminology and Geography
Duration: 3FT Hon

Entry Requirements: *GCE:* 240. *SQAH:* BBBB. *IB:* 24. *BTEC NC:* DM. *BTEC ND:* MMM.

ML99 BSc Criminology and International Development Studies
Duration: 3FT Hon

Entry Requirements: *GCE:* 240. *SQAH:* BBBB. *IB:* 24. *BTEC NC:* DM. *BTEC ND:* MMM.

ML93 BSc Criminology and Sociology
Duration: 3FT Hon

Entry Requirements: *GCE:* 240. *SQAH:* BBBB. *IB:* 24. *BTEC NC:* DM. *BTEC ND:* MMM.

M9N1 BSc Criminology with Business
Duration: 3FT Hon

Entry Requirements: *GCE:* 240. *SQAH:* BBBB. *IB:* 24. *BTEC NC:* DM. *BTEC ND:* MMM.

M9PJ BSc Criminology with Communication Studies
Duration: 3FT Hon

Entry Requirements: *GCE:* 240. *SQAH:* BBBB. *IB:* 24. *BTEC NC:* DM. *BTEC ND:* MMM.

M9G4 BSc Criminology with Computer Science
Duration: 3FT Hon

Entry Requirements: *GCE:* 240. *SQAH:* BBBB. *IB:* 24. *BTEC NC:* DM. *BTEC ND:* MMM.

M9Q3 BSc Criminology with English
Duration: 3FT Hon

Entry Requirements: *GCE:* 240. *SQAH:* BBBB. *IB:* 24. *BTEC NC:* DM. *BTEC ND:* MPP.

M9F4 BSc Criminology with Forensic Biology
Duration: 3FT Hon

Entry Requirements: *GCE:* 240. *SQAH:* BBBB. *IB:* 24. *BTEC NC:* DM. *BTEC ND:* MMM.

M9R1 BSc Criminology with French
Duration: 3FT Hon

Entry Requirements: *GCE:* 240. *SQAH:* BBBB. *IB:* 24. *BTEC NC:* DM. *BTEC ND:* MMM.

M9F8 BSc Criminology with Geography
Duration: 3FT Hon

Entry Requirements: *GCE:* 240. *SQAH:* BBBB. *IB:* 24. *BTEC NC:* DM. *BTEC ND:* MMM.

M9L9 BSc Criminology with International Development Studies
Duration: 3FT Hon

Entry Requirements: *GCE:* 240. *SQAH:* BBBB. *IB:* 24. *BTEC NC:* DM. *BTEC ND:* MMM.

M9M1 BSc Criminology with Law
Duration: 3FT Hon

Entry Requirements: *GCE:* 240. *SQAH:* BBBB. *IB:* 24. *BTEC NC:* DM. *BTEC ND:* MMM.

M9N2 BSc Criminology with Management
Duration: 3FT Hon

Entry Requirements: *GCE:* 240. *SQAH:* BBBB. *IB:* 24. *BTEC NC:* DM. *BTEC ND:* MMM.

M9L2 BSc Criminology with Politics
Duration: 3FT Hon

Entry Requirements: *GCE:* 240. *SQAH:* BBBB. *IB:* 24. *BTEC NC:* DM. *BTEC ND:* MMM.

M9L3 BSc Criminology with Sociology
Duration: 3FT Hon

Entry Requirements: *GCE:* 240. *SQAH:* BBBB. *IB:* 24. *BTEC NC:* DM. *BTEC ND:* MMM.

M9R4 BSc Criminology with Spanish
Duration: 3FT Hon

Entry Requirements: *GCE:* 240. *SQAH:* BBBB. *IB:* 24. *BTEC NC:* DM. *BTEC ND:* MMM.

M9V6 BSc Criminology with Theology & Religious Studies
Duration: 3FT Hon

Entry Requirements: *GCE:* 240. *SQAH:* BBBB. *IB:* 24. *BTEC NC:* DM. *BTEC ND:* MMM.

M9N8 BSc Criminology with Tourism
Duration: 3FT Hon

Entry Requirements: *Foundation:* Pass. *GCE:* 240. *SQAH:* BBBB. *IB:* 24. *BTEC NC:* DM. *BTEC ND:* MMM.

F4M9 BSc Forensic Biology with Criminology
Duration: 3FT Hon

Entry Requirements: *GCE:* 240. *SQAH:* BBBB. *IB:* 24. *BTEC NC:* DM. *BTEC ND:* MMM.

F8M9 BSc Geography with Criminology
Duration: 3FT Hon

Entry Requirements: *GCE:* 240. *SQAH:* BBBB. *IB:* 24. *BTEC NC:* DM. *BTEC ND:* MMM.

L9M9 BSc International Development Studies with Criminology
Duration: 3FT Hon

Entry Requirements: *GCE:* 240. *SQAH:* BBBB. *IB:* 24. *BTEC NC:* DM. *BTEC ND:* MMM.

C8M9 BSc Psychology with Criminology
Duration: 3FT Hon

Entry Requirements: *GCE:* 240. *SQAH:* BBBB. *IB:* 24. *BTEC NC:* DM. *BTEC ND:* MMM.

L3M9 BSc Sociology with Criminology
Duration: 3FT Hon

Entry Requirements: *GCE:* 240. *SQAH:* BBBB. *IB:* 24. *BTEC NC:* DM. *BTEC ND:* MMM.

C85 COVENTRY UNIVERSITY
THE STUDENT CENTRE
COVENTRY UNIVERSITY
1 GULSON RD
COVENTRY CV1 2JH
t: 024 7615 2222 f: 024 7615 2223
e: studentenquiries@coventry.ac.uk
// www.coventry.ac.uk

M930 BA Criminology and Law
Duration: 3FT Hon

Entry Requirements: *GCE:* 260. *BTEC NC:* DD. *BTEC ND:* DMM.

CM89 BA Criminology and Psychology
Duration: 3FT Hon

Entry Requirements: *GCE:* 260. *BTEC NC:* DD. *BTEC ND:* DMM.

LM39 BA Sociology and Criminology
Duration: 3FT Hon

Entry Requirements: *GCE:* 260-280. *BTEC NC:* DD. *BTEC ND:* DMM.

C99 UNIVERSITY OF CUMBRIA
FUSEHILL STREET
CARLISLE
CUMBRIA CA1 2HH
t: 01228 616234 f: 01228 616235
// www.cumbria.ac.uk

LM31 BA Criminology and Law
Duration: 3FT Hon

Entry Requirements: *GCE:* 180-200. *SQAH:* AAAB. *IB:* 30. *BTEC NC:* DD. *BTEC ND:* DDM.

LM39 BA Social Sciences and Criminology
Duration: 3FT Hon

Entry Requirements: *Foundation:* Merit. *GCE:* 200. *IB:* 28. *BTEC NC:* DM. *BTEC ND:* MMP. *OCR ND:* Merit. *OCR NED:* Pass.

LM32 BSc Criminology and Criminal Justice Studies
Duration: 3FT Hon

Entry Requirements: Contact the institution for details.

LM49 BSc Policing (Criminology)
Duration: 3FT Hon

Entry Requirements: Contact the institution for details.

LM3F DipHE Criminology and Criminal Justic Studies
Duration: 2FT Dip

Entry Requirements: Contact the institution for details.

MM91 DipHE Criminology and Law

Duration: 2FT Dip

Entry Requirements: Contact the institution for details.

ML95 DipHE Criminology and Youth Justice Studies

Duration: 2FT Dip

Entry Requirements: *Foundation:* Pass. *GCE:* 80. *IB:* 24. *BTEC NC:* PP. *BTEC ND:* PPP.

LM3Y DipHE Social Sciences and Criminology

Duration: 2FT Dip

Entry Requirements: *Foundation:* Pass. *GCE:* 80. *IB:* 24. *BTEC NC:* PP. *BTEC ND:* PPP.

D39 UNIVERSITY OF DERBY

KEDLESTON ROAD
DERBY DE22 1GB

t: 08701 202330 **f:** 01332 597724
e: askadmissions@derby.ac.uk

// www.derby.ac.uk

M1M2 LLB Law with Criminology

Duration: 3FT Hon

Entry Requirements: *GCE:* 300. *IB:* 30. *BTEC NC:* DD. *BTEC ND:* DMM.

KM19 BA Architectural Design and Criminology

Duration: 3FT Hon

Entry Requirements: *Foundation:* Merit. *GCE:* 180-240. *IB:* 26. *BTEC NC:* DM. *BTEC ND:* MMP.

WM92 BA Creative Design Practices and Criminology

Duration: 3FT Hon

Entry Requirements: *Foundation:* Merit. *GCE:* 180-240. *IB:* 26. *BTEC NC:* DM. *BTEC ND:* MMP.

MG25 BA Criminology and Computing Management

Duration: 3FT Hon

Entry Requirements: *Foundation:* Merit. *GCE:* 180-240. *IB:* 26. *BTEC NC:* DM. *BTEC ND:* MMP.

MX23 BA Criminology and Education Studies

Duration: 3FT Hon

Entry Requirements: *Foundation:* Merit. *GCE:* 180-240. *IB:* 26. *BTEC NC:* DM. *BTEC ND:* MMP.

MQ23 BA Criminology and English

Duration: 3FT Hon

Entry Requirements: *Foundation:* Merit. *GCE:* 180-240. *IB:* 26. *BTEC NC:* DM. *BTEC ND:* MMP.

MP2H BA Criminology and Film & Television Studies

Duration: 3FT Hon

Entry Requirements: *Foundation:* Merit. *GCE:* 180-240. *IB:* 26. *BTEC NC:* DM. *BTEC ND:* MMP.

MF24 BA Criminology and Forensic Studies

Duration: 3FT Hon

Entry Requirements: *Foundation:* Merit. *GCE:* 180-240. *IB:* 26. *BTEC NC:* DM. *BTEC ND:* MMP.

MB23 BA Criminology and Healing Arts

Duration: 3FT Hon

Entry Requirements: *Foundation:* Merit. *GCE:* 180-240. *IB:* 26. *BTEC NC:* DM. *BTEC ND:* MMP.

MV21 BA Criminology and History

Duration: 3FT Hon

Entry Requirements: *Foundation:* Merit. *GCE:* 180-240. *IB:* 26. *BTEC NC:* DM. *BTEC ND:* MMP.

MN26 BA Criminology and Human Resources Management

Duration: 3FT Hon

Entry Requirements: *Foundation:* Merit. *GCE:* 180-240. *IB:* 26. *BTEC NC:* DM. *BTEC ND:* MMP.

MM21 BA Criminology and Law

Duration: 3FT Hon

Entry Requirements: *Foundation:* Merit. *GCE:* 180-240. *IB:* 26. *BTEC NC:* DM. *BTEC ND:* MMP.

MN25 BA Criminology and Marketing

Duration: 3FT Hon

Entry Requirements: *Foundation:* Merit. *GCE:* 180-240. *IB:* 26. *BTEC NC:* DM. *BTEC ND:* MMP.

MW23 BA Criminology and Popular Music Production

Duration: 3FT Hon

Entry Requirements: *Foundation:* Merit. *GCE:* 180-240. *IB:* 26. *BTEC NC:* DM. *BTEC ND:* MMP.

MC28 BA Criminology and Psychology

Duration: 3FT Hon

Entry Requirements: *Foundation:* Merit. *GCE:* 180-240. *IB:* 26. *BTEC NC:* DM. *BTEC ND:* MMP.

ML23 BA Criminology and Sociology

Duration: 3FT Hon

Entry Requirements: *Foundation:* Merit. *GCE:* 180-240. *IB:* 26. *BTEC NC:* DM. *BTEC ND:* MMP.

MW24 BA Criminology and Theatre Arts

Duration: 3FT Hon

Entry Requirements: *Foundation:* Merit. *GCE:* 180-240. *IB:* 26. *BTEC NC:* DM. *BTEC ND:* MMP.

VM39 BA/BSc Art & Design History and Criminology

Duration: 3FT Hon

Entry Requirements: Contact the institution for details.

GM49 BA/BSc Computer Networks and Criminology

Duration: 3FT Hon

Entry Requirements: *Foundation:* Merit. *GCE:* 180-240. *IB:* 26. *BTEC NC:* DM. *BTEC ND:* MMP.

ML27 BA/BSc Criminology and Geography

Duration: 3FT Hon

Entry Requirements: *Foundation:* Merit. *GCE:* 180-240. *IB:* 26. *BTEC NC:* DM. *BTEC ND:* MMP.

MF26 BA/BSc Criminology and Geology

Duration: 3FT Hon

Entry Requirements: *Foundation:* Merit. *GCE:* 180-240. *IB:* 26. *BTEC NC:* DM. *BTEC ND:* MMP.

MG21 BA/BSc Criminology and Mathematics

Duration: 3FT Hon

Entry Requirements: *Foundation:* Merit. *GCE:* 180-240. *IB:* 26. *BTEC NC:* DM. *BTEC ND:* MMP.

MG24 BA/BSc Criminology and Web-based Systems

Duration: 3FT Hon

Entry Requirements: *Foundation:* Merit. *GCE:* 180-240. *IB:* 26. *BTEC NC:* DM. *BTEC ND:* MMP.

LM99 BA/BSc Third World Development and Criminology

Duration: 3FT Hon

Entry Requirements: *Foundation:* Merit. *GCE:* 180-240. *IB:* 26. *BTEC NC:* DM. *BTEC ND:* MMP.

NM89 BA/BSc Travel & Tourism and Criminology

Duration: 3FT Hon

Entry Requirements: *GCE:* 200.

GM42 BSc Computing and Criminology

Duration: 3FT Hon

Entry Requirements: *Foundation:* Merit. *GCE:* 180-240. *IB:* 26. *BTEC NC:* DM. *BTEC ND:* MMP.

MC98 BSc Criminology, Forensic Studies and Psychology

Duration: 3FT Hon

Entry Requirements: *Foundation:* Merit. *GCE:* 180-240. *IB:* 26. *BTEC NC:* DM. *BTEC ND:* MMP.

CM69 BSc Sport & Exercise Science and Criminology

Duration: 3FT Hon

Entry Requirements: *Foundation:* Merit. *GCE:* 180-240. *IB:* 26. *BTEC NC:* DM. *BTEC ND:* MMP.

D52 DONCASTER COLLEGE

THE HUB
CHAPPELL DRIVE
SOUTH YORKSHIRE DN1 2RF

t: 01302 553610
e: he@don.ac.uk

// www.don.ac.uk

ML13 BA Law and Criminology

Duration: 3FT Hon

Entry Requirements: *GCE:* 160.

E25 EAST LANCASHIRE INSTITUTE OF HIGHER EDUCATION AT BLACKBURN COLLEGE

DUKE STREET
BLACKBURN BB2 1LH

t: 01254 292594 **f:** 01254 260749
e: he-admissions@blackburn.ac.uk

// www.elihe.ac.uk

M930 BA Criminology (top-up)

Duration: 1FT Hon

Entry Requirements: HND required.

039M HND Criminology

Duration: 2FT HND

Entry Requirements: *GCE:* 40.

E28 UNIVERSITY OF EAST LONDON

DOCKLANDS CAMPUS
UNIVERSITY WAY
LONDON E16 2RD

t: 020 8223 2835 **f:** 020 8223 2978
e: admiss@uel.ac.uk

// www.uel.ac.uk

L6M2 BA Anthropology with Criminology

Duration: 3FT Hon

Entry Requirements: *GCE:* 200. *IB:* 24. *BTEC NC:* DM. *BTEC ND:* MMP.

WM89 BA Creative & Professional Writing/Criminology

Duration: 3FT Hon

Entry Requirements: *GCE:* 240. *IB:* 28. *BTEC NC:* DD. *BTEC ND:* MMM.

M9F4 BA Criminology with Forensic Science

Duration: 3FT Hon

Entry Requirements: *GCE:* 240. *IB:* 28. *BTEC NC:* DD. *BTEC ND:* MMM. *OCR ND:* Merit. *OCR NED:* Pass.

M9M1 BA Criminology with Law

Duration: 3FT Hon

Entry Requirements: *GCE:* 240. *IB:* 28. *BTEC NC:* DD. *BTEC ND:* MMM.

M9LH BA Criminology with Sociology

Duration: 3FT Hon

Entry Requirements: *GCE:* 240. *IB:* 28. *BTEC NC:* DD. *BTEC ND:* MMM.

M9B2 BA Criminology with Toxicology

Duration: 3FT Hon

Entry Requirements: *GCE:* 240. *IB:* 28. *BTEC NC:* DD. *BTEC ND:* MMM.

MV91 BA Criminology/History

Duration: 3FT Hon

Entry Requirements: *GCE:* 240. *IB:* 28. *BTEC NC:* DD. *BTEC ND:* MMM.

MM19 BA Criminology/Law

Duration: 3FT Hon

Entry Requirements: *GCE:* 240. *IB:* 28. *BTEC NC:* DD. *BTEC ND:* MMM.

M9CW BA Criminology/Psychosocial Studies

Duration: 3FT Hon

Entry Requirements: *GCE:* 240. *IB:* 28. *BTEC NC:* DD. *BTEC ND:* MMM.

M9L3 BA Criminology/Sociology

Duration: 3FT Hon

Entry Requirements: *GCE:* 80.

M1M2 BA Law with Criminology

Duration: 3FT Hon

Entry Requirements: *GCE:* 240. *IB:* 28. *BTEC NC:* DD. *BTEC ND:* MMM.

MF94 BA/BSc Criminology and Forensic Science

Duration: 3FT Hon

Entry Requirements: *GCE:* 240. *IB:* 28. *BTEC NC:* DD. *BTEC ND:* MMM. *OCR ND:* Merit. *OCR NED:* Pass.

F4M9 BSc Forensic Science with Criminology

Duration: 3FT Hon

Entry Requirements: *GCE:* 200. *IB:* 24. *BTEC NC:* DM. *BTEC ND:* MMP. *OCR ND:* Merit. *OCR NED:* Pass.

C5M9 BSc Immunology with Criminology

Duration: 3FT Hon

Entry Requirements: *GCE:* 200. *IB:* 24. *BTEC NC:* DM. *BTEC ND:* MMP. *OCR ND:* Merit. *OCR NED:* Pass.

G5M9 BSc Information Security Systems with Criminology

Duration: 3FT Hon

Entry Requirements: *GCE:* 200. *IB:* 24. *BTEC NC:* DM. *BTEC ND:* MMP.

C8M9 BSc Psychology with Criminology

Duration: 3FT Hon

Entry Requirements: *GCE:* 200. *IB:* 24.

B2MX BSc Toxicology with Criminology

Duration: 3FT Hon

Entry Requirements: *GCE:* 200. *IB:* 24. *BTEC NC:* DM. *BTEC ND:* MMP.

E42 EDGE HILL UNIVERSITY
ORMSKIRK
LANCASHIRE L39 4QP
t: 0800 195 5063 f: 01695 584355
e: enquiries@edgehill.ac.uk
// www.edgehill.ac.uk

M1M9 LLB Law with Criminology

Duration: 3FT Hon

Entry Requirements: *GCE:* 260. *IB:* 28. *BTEC NC:* DD. *BTEC ND:* MMM.

XM32 BA Childhood & Youth Studies and Criminology

Duration: 3FT Hon

Entry Requirements: *GCE:* 220. *IB:* 28. *BTEC NC:* DM. *BTEC ND:* MMP.

M900 BA Criminology & Criminal Justice

Duration: 3FT Hon

Entry Requirements: *GCE:* 240. *IB:* 28. *BTEC NC:* DM. *BTEC ND:* MMP.

VM19 BA Criminology and History
Duration: 3FT Hon

Entry Requirements: *GCE:* 240. *IB:* 28. *BTEC NC:* DM. *BTEC ND:* MMP.

ML93 BA Criminology and Sociology
Duration: 3FT Hon

Entry Requirements: *GCE:* 240. *IB:* 28. *BTEC NC:* DM. *BTEC ND:* MMP.

M9W4 BA Criminology with Drama
Duration: 3FT Hon

Entry Requirements: *GCE:* 240. *IB:* 28. *BTEC NC:* DM. *BTEC ND:* MMP.

M9V1 BA Criminology with History
Duration: 3FT Hon

Entry Requirements: *GCE:* 240. *IB:* 28. *BTEC NC:* DM. *BTEC ND:* MMP.

M9L7 BA Criminology with Human Geography
Duration: 3FT Hon

Entry Requirements: *GCE:* 240. *IB:* 28. *BTEC NC:* DM. *BTEC ND:* MMP.

M9G5 BA Criminology with Information Technology
Duration: 3FT Hon

Entry Requirements: *GCE:* 240. *IB:* 28. *BTEC NC:* DM. *BTEC ND:* MMP.

M9M1 BA Criminology with Law
Duration: 3FT Hon

Entry Requirements: *GCE:* 240. *IB:* 28. *BTEC NC:* DM. *BTEC ND:* MMP.

M9N2 BA Criminology with Management
Duration: 3FT Hon

Entry Requirements: *GCE:* 240. *IB:* 28. *BTEC NC:* DM. *BTEC ND:* MMP.

L7M9 BA Geography with Criminology
Duration: 3FT Hon

Entry Requirements: *GCE:* 220. *IB:* 26. *BTEC NC:* MM. *BTEC ND:* MMP.

V1M9 BA History with Criminology
Duration: 3FT Hon

Entry Requirements: *GCE:* 220. *IB:* 26. *BTEC NC:* DM. *BTEC ND:* MPP.

L7MX BA Human Geography with Criminology
Duration: 3FT Hon

Entry Requirements: *GCE:* 220. *IB:* 26. *BTEC NC:* MM. *BTEC ND:* MMP.

E59 EDINBURGH NAPIER UNIVERSITY
CRAIGLOCKHART CAMPUS
EDINBURGH EH14 1DJ
t: +44 (0)8452 60 60 40 f: 0131 455 6464
e: info@napier.ac.uk
// www.napier.ac.uk

M900 BSc Criminology
Duration: 3FT/4FT Ord/Hon

Entry Requirements: *GCE:* 230.

E70 THE UNIVERSITY OF ESSEX
WIVENHOE PARK
COLCHESTER
ESSEX CO4 3SQ
t: 01206 873666 f: 01206 873423
e: admit@essex.ac.uk
// www.essex.ac.uk

M900 BA Criminology
Duration: 3FT Hon

Entry Requirements: *GCE:* 300 - 320. *SQAH:* AAAB-AABB. *BTEC NC:* DD. *BTEC ND:* DDM.

MT27 BA Criminology and American Studies
Duration: 4FT Hon

Entry Requirements: *GCE:* 300. *SQAH:* AABB. *IB:* 32.

MT2R BA Criminology and American Studies (term abroad)
Duration: 3FT Hon

Entry Requirements: *GCE:* 300. *SQAH:* AABB. *IB:* 32.

MP93 BA Criminology and the Media
Duration: 3FT Hon

Entry Requirements: *GCE:* 300 - 320. *SQAH:* AAAB-AABB. *BTEC NC:* DD. *BTEC ND:* DDM.

MV91 BA History and Criminology
Duration: 3FT Hon

Entry Requirements: *GCE:* 300. *SQAH:* AABB. *IB:* 32. *BTEC NC:* DM. *BTEC ND:* MMP.

MV9C BA History and Criminology (International Exchange)
Duration: 4FT Hon

Entry Requirements: Contact the institution for details.

LM39 BA Sociology and Criminology

Duration: 3FT Hon

Entry Requirements: *GCE:* 300 - 320. *SQAH:* AAAB-AABB. *BTEC NC:* DD. *BTEC ND:* DDM.

G14 UNIVERSITY OF GLAMORGAN, CARDIFF AND PONTYPRIDD

ENQUIRIES AND ADMISSIONS UNIT
PONTYPRIDD CF37 1DL

t: 0800 716925 **f:** 01443 654050
e: enquiries@glam.ac.uk
// www.glam.ac.uk

M1M9 LLB Law with Criminology

Duration: 3FT Hon

Entry Requirements: *GCE:* 280-320.

L7M9 BA Human Geography with Criminology

Duration: 3FT Hon

Entry Requirements: *GCE:* 200-240. *BTEC NC:* DM. *BTEC ND:* MMP.

L2M9 BA Politics with Criminology

Duration: 3FT Hon

Entry Requirements: *GCE:* 200.

M901 BSc Criminology and Criminal Justice

Duration: 3FT Hon

Entry Requirements: *GCE:* 240-280.

MQ93 BSc Criminology and English Studies

Duration: 3FT Hon

Entry Requirements: *GCE:* 220-260. *BTEC NC:* DD. *BTEC ND:* MMM.

MF94 BSc Criminology and Forensic Science

Duration: 3FT Hon

Entry Requirements: *GCE:* 220-260.

ML97 BSc Criminology and Human Geography

Duration: 3FT Hon

Entry Requirements: *GCE:* 220-260.

ML9R BSc Criminology and Human Geography

Duration: 3FT Hon

Entry Requirements: *GCE:* 220-260.

MM91 BSc Criminology and Law

Duration: 3FT Hon

Entry Requirements: *GCE:* 280-320. *IB:* 30. *BTEC NC:* DD. *BTEC ND:* DMM.

ML92 BSc Criminology and Politics

Duration: 3FT Hon

Entry Requirements: *GCE:* 220-260.

MC98 BSc Criminology and Psychology

Duration: 3FT Hon

Entry Requirements: *GCE:* 220-260.

ML93 BSc Criminology and Sociology

Duration: 3FT Hon

Entry Requirements: *GCE:* 220-260.

M9F4 BSc Criminology with Forensic Science

Duration: 3FT Hon

Entry Requirements: *GCE:* 220-260.

M9L7 BSc Criminology with Human Geography

Duration: 3FT Hon

Entry Requirements: *GCE:* 220-260.

M9LF BSc Criminology with International Politics

Duration: 3FT Hon

Entry Requirements: *GCE:* 220-260.

M9M1 BSc Criminology with Law

Duration: 3FT Hon

Entry Requirements: *GCE:* 220-260.

M9L2 BSc Criminology with Politics

Duration: 3FT Hon

Entry Requirements: *GCE:* 220-260.

M9C8 BSc Criminology with Psychology

Duration: 3FT Hon

Entry Requirements: *GCE:* 220-260.

M9L3 BSc Criminology with Sociology

Duration: 3FT Hon

Entry Requirements: *GCE:* 220-260.

B790 BSc Forensic Biology

Duration: 3FT Hon

Entry Requirements: *GCE:* 220-260. *IB:* 30. *BTEC NC:* DD. *BTEC ND:* MMM.

L3M9 BSc Sociology with Criminology

Duration: 3FT Hon

Entry Requirements: *GCE:* 220-260.

G42 GLASGOW CALEDONIAN UNIVERSITY

CITY CAMPUS
COWCADDENS ROAD
GLASGOW G4 0BA

t: 0141 331 3000 f: 0141 331 3449
e: admissions@gcal.ac.uk

// www.gcal.ac.uk

M211 BA Criminology

Duration: 4FT Hon

Entry Requirements: *GCE:* BBD. *SQAH:* BBBBB.

G50 THE UNIVERSITY OF GLOUCESTERSHIRE

HARDWICK CAMPUS
ST PAUL'S ROAD
CHELTENHAM GL50 4BS

t: 01242 714501 f: 01242 543334
e: admissions@glos.ac.uk

// www.glos.ac.uk

MQ9H BA/BSc Criminology and English Language

Duration: 3FT Hon

Entry Requirements: *GCE:* 200-280.

MQ93 BA/BSc Criminology and English Literature

Duration: 3FT Hon

Entry Requirements: *GCE:* 200-280.

MV91 BA/BSc Criminology and History

Duration: 3FT Hon

Entry Requirements: *GCE:* 200-300.

ML93 BA/BSc Criminology and Sociology

Duration: 3FT Hon

Entry Requirements: *GCE:* 200-280.

CM19 BSc Biology and Criminology

Duration: 3FT Hon

Entry Requirements: *GCE:* 200-280.

M900 BSc Criminology

Duration: 3FT Hon

Entry Requirements: *GCE:* 100.

MF94 BSc Criminology and Forensic Investigation

Duration: 3FT Hon

Entry Requirements: *GCE:* 200-300.

MF98 BSc Criminology and Geography

Duration: 3FT Hon

Entry Requirements: *GCE:* 200-280.

G70 UNIVERSITY OF GREENWICH

GREENWICH CAMPUS
OLD ROYAL NAVAL COLLEGE
PARK ROW
LONDON SE10 9LS

t: 0800 005 006 f: 020 8331 8145
e: courseinfo@gre.ac.uk

// www.gre.ac.uk

M211 BA Criminology

Duration: 3FT Hon

Entry Requirements: *IB:* 24.

F4M9 BSc Forensic Science with Criminology

Duration: 3FT Hon

Entry Requirements: Interview required.

H60 THE UNIVERSITY OF HUDDERSFIELD

QUEENSGATE
HUDDERSFIELD HD1 3DH

t: 01484 473969 f: 01484 472765
e: admissionsandrecords@hud.ac.uk

// www.hud.ac.uk

M211 BSc Applied Criminology (Criminal and Community Justice)

Duration: 3FT Hon

Entry Requirements: *GCE:* 200-240. *SQAH:* BBBB. *IB:* 28.

M900 BSc Criminology

Duration: 3FT Hon

Entry Requirements: *GCE:* 150.

ML22 BSc Criminology and Politics

Duration: 3FT Hon

Entry Requirements: *GCE:* 200-240. *SQAH:* BBBB-BBBC. *IB:* 28.

M2L2 BSc Criminology with International Politics

Duration: 1FT Hon

Entry Requirements: *GCE:* 120. *SQAH:* CCC. *IB:* 24.

G4M2 BSc Information & Communication Technology with Criminology

Duration: 4SW/3FT Hon

Entry Requirements: *GCE:* 180.

C8M2 BSc Psychology with Criminology
Duration: 3FT Hon

Entry Requirements: *GCE:* 240. *SQAH:* BBBB. *IB:* 28.

ML93 BSc Sociology and Criminology
Duration: 3FT Hon

Entry Requirements: *GCE:* 200-240. *SQAH:* BBBB-BBBC. *IB:* 28.

L3M9 BSc Sociology with Criminology
Duration: 3FT Hon

Entry Requirements: Contact the institution for details.

H72 THE UNIVERSITY OF HULL
THE UNIVERSITY OF HULL
COTTINGHAM ROAD
HULL HU6 7RX
t: 01482 466100 f: 01482 442290
e: admissions@hull.ac.uk
// www.hull.ac.uk

M1M2 LLB Law with Criminology
Duration: 3FT Hon

Entry Requirements: *GCE:* 200.

M930 BA Criminology
Duration: 3FT Hon

Entry Requirements: *GCE:* 260-300. *IB:* 28.

LM39 BA Criminology and Sociology
Duration: 3FT Hon

Entry Requirements: *GCE:* 260-300. *IB:* 28.

M9F4 BA Criminology with Forensic Science
Duration: 3FT Hon

Entry Requirements: *GCE:* 260-300. *IB:* 28.

M9M1 BA Criminology with Law
Duration: 3FT Hon

Entry Requirements: *GCE:* 40-160.

F4M9 BSc Forensic Science with Criminology
Duration: 3FT Hon

Entry Requirements: *GCE:* 240-300. *IB:* 28.

K12 KEELE UNIVERSITY
STAFFS ST5 5BG
t: 01782 734005 f: 01782 632343
e: undergraduate@keele.ac.uk
// www.keele.ac.uk

M1LH LLB Law with Criminology
Duration: 3FT Hon

Entry Requirements: *GCE:* 340-360. *BTEC ND:* DDD.

NM49 BA Accounting and Criminology
Duration: 3FT Hon

Entry Requirements: *GCE:* 300-320.

MTX7 BA American Studies and Criminology
Duration: 3FT Hon

Entry Requirements: *GCE:* 300-320.

MNX2 BA Business Management and Criminology
Duration: 3FT Hon

Entry Requirements: *GCE:* 300-320.

MXX3 BA Criminology and Educational Studies
Duration: 3FT Hon

Entry Requirements: *GCE:* 300-320.

MQ93 BA Criminology and English
Duration: 3FT Hon

Entry Requirements: *GCE:* 300-320.

MNX3 BA Criminology and Finance
Duration: 3FT Hon

Entry Requirements: *GCE:* 300-320.

LM79 BA Criminology and Geography
Duration: 3FT Hon

Entry Requirements: *GCE:* 300-320.

MVX1 BA Criminology and History
Duration: 3FT Hon

Entry Requirements: *GCE:* 300-320.

LMR9 BA Criminology and Human Geography
Duration: 3FT Hon

Entry Requirements: *GCE:* 300-320.

MN91 BA Criminology and International Business
Duration: 3FT Hon

Entry Requirements: *GCE:* 300-320.

ML92 BA Criminology and International Relations
Duration: 3FT Hon

Entry Requirements: *GCE:* 300-320.

M930 BA Criminology and Law
Duration: 3FT Hon

Entry Requirements: *GCE:* 300-320.

MNC5 BA Criminology and Marketing
Duration: 3FT Hon

Entry Requirements: *GCE:* 300-320.

PM39 BA Criminology and Media, Communications & Culture
Duration: 3FT Hon

Entry Requirements: *GCE:* 300-320.

MVX5 BA Criminology and Philosophy
Duration: 3FT Hon

Entry Requirements: *GCE:* 300-320.

LMH9 BA Criminology and Sociology
Duration: 3FT Hon

Entry Requirements: *GCE:* 300-320.

ML93 BA Criminology with Social Science Foundation Year
Duration: 4FT Deg

Entry Requirements: *GCE:* 160. Interview required.

FM79 BSc Applied Environmental Science and Criminology
Duration: 3FT Hon

Entry Requirements: *GCE:* 280-320.

CM8Y BSc Applied Psychology and Criminology
Duration: 4FT Deg

Entry Requirements: *GCE:* 300-320.

FM59 BSc Astrophysics and Criminology
Duration: 3FT Hon

Entry Requirements: *GCE:* 300-320.

CM19 BSc Biology and Criminology
Duration: 3FT Hon

Entry Requirements: *GCE:* 280-320.

FM19 BSc Chemistry and Criminology
Duration: 3FT Hon

Entry Requirements: *GCE:* 280-320.

GM49 BSc Computer Science and Criminology
Duration: 3FT Hon

Entry Requirements: *GCE:* 300-320.

GM4X BSc Creative Computing and Criminology
Duration: 3FT Hon

Entry Requirements: *GCE:* 300-320.

FM42 BSc Criminology and Forensic Science
Duration: 3FT Hon

Entry Requirements: *GCE:* 280-320.

MC91 BSc Criminology and Human Biology
Duration: 3FT Hon

Entry Requirements: *GCE:* 280-320. *BTEC NC:* DD. *BTEC ND:* DMM.

MG95 BSc Criminology and Information Systems
Duration: 3FT Hon

Entry Requirements: *GCE:* 300-320.

FMC9 BSc Criminology and Medicinal Chemistry
Duration: 3FT Hon

Entry Requirements: *GCE:* 280-320.

FM89 BSc Criminology and Physical Geography
Duration: 3FT Hon

Entry Requirements: *GCE:* 280-320.

FM39 BSc Criminology and Physics
Duration: 3FT Hon

Entry Requirements: *GCE:* 300-320.

GM79 BSc Smart Systems and Criminology
Duration: 3FT Hon

Entry Requirements: *GCE:* 300-320.

K24 THE UNIVERSITY OF KENT

INFORMATION, RECRUITMENT & ADMISSIONS
REGISTRY
UNIVERSITY OF KENT
CANTERBURY. KENT CT2 7NZ

t: 01227 827272 **f:** 01227 827077
e: information@kent.ac.uk

// www.kent.ac.uk

MV99 BA Criminology and Cultural Studies
Duration: 3FT Hon

Entry Requirements: *GCE:* 300. *IB:* 33. *BTEC NC:* DD. *BTEC ND:* DMM. *OCR ND:* Distinction. *OCR NED:* Merit.

LM49 BA Criminology and Social Policy
Duration: 3FT Hon

Entry Requirements: *GCE:* 300. *IB:* 33. *BTEC NC:* DD. *BTEC ND:* DMM. *OCR ND:* Distinction. *OCR NED:* Merit.

LM39 BA Criminology and Sociology
Duration: 3FT Hon

Entry Requirements: *GCE:* 300. *IB:* 33. *BTEC NC:* DD. *BTEC ND:* DMM. *OCR ND:* Distinction. *OCR NED:* Merit.

MM19 BA Law and Criminology
Duration: 3FT Hon

Entry Requirements: *GCE:* 320. *SQAH:* AAAAA. *IB:* 34. *BTEC NC:* DD. *BTEC ND:* DDM.

K84 KINGSTON UNIVERSITY
STUDENT INFORMATION & ADVICE CENTRE
COOPER HOUSE
40-46 SURBITON ROAD
KINGSTON UPON THAMES KT1 2HX
t: 020 8547 7053 f: 020 8547 7080
e: aps@kingston.ac.uk
// www.kingston.ac.uk

M1M9 LLB Law with Criminology
Duration: 3FT Hon

Entry Requirements: *GCE:* 320. *IB:* 26. *BTEC ND:* DDM.

LM39 BA Criminology
Duration: 3FT Hon

Entry Requirements: Interview required.

M9W8 BA Criminology with Creative Writing
Duration: 3FT Hon

Entry Requirements: *GCE:* 220-320. *SQAH:* BBCCC. *SQAAH:* BBC. *IB:* 30.

M9L1 BA Criminology with Economics (Applied)
Duration: 3FT Hon

Entry Requirements: *GCE:* 220-320. *SQAH:* BBCCC. *SQAAH:* BBC.

M9Q1 BA Criminology with English Language & Communications
Duration: 3FT Hon

Entry Requirements: *GCE:* 220-320. *SQAH:* BBCCC. *SQAAH:* BBC.

M9Q3 BA Criminology with English Literature
Duration: 3FT Hon

Entry Requirements: *GCE:* 240-320. *SQAH:* BBCCC. *SQAAH:* BBC.

M9P3 BA Criminology with Film Studies
Duration: 3FT Hon

Entry Requirements: *GCE:* 220-320. *SQAH:* BBCCC. *SQAAH:* BBC.

M9R1 BA Criminology with French
Duration: 3FT Hon

Entry Requirements: *GCE:* 220-320. *SQAH:* BBCCC. *SQAAH:* BBC.

M9V1 BA Criminology with History
Duration: 3FT Hon

Entry Requirements: *GCE:* 220-320. *SQAH:* BBCCC. *SQAAH:* BBC.

M9V3 BA Criminology with History of Art, Design & Film
Duration: 3FT Hon

Entry Requirements: *GCE:* 220-320. *SQAH:* BBCCC. *SQAAH:* BBC.

M9LF BA Criminology with Human Rights
Duration: 3FT Hon

Entry Requirements: *GCE:* 220-320. *SQAH:* BBCCC. *SQAAH:* BBC.

M9LG BA Criminology with International Relations
Duration: 3FT Hon

Entry Requirements: *GCE:* 240-320. *SQAH:* BBCCC. *SQAAH:* BBC.

M9PH BA Criminology with Media & Cultural Studies
Duration: 3FT Hon

Entry Requirements: *GCE:* 240-320. *SQAH:* BBCCC. *SQAAH:* BBC.

M9L2 BA Criminology with Politics
Duration: 3FT Hon

Entry Requirements: *GCE:* 220-320. *SQAH:* BBCCC. *SQAAH:* BBC.

M9L3 BA Criminology with Sociology
Duration: 3FT Hon

Entry Requirements: *GCE:* 220-320. *SQAH:* BBCCC. *SQAAH:* BBC.

M2R4 BA Criminology with Spanish
Duration: 3FT Hon

Entry Requirements: *GCE:* 220-320. *SQAH:* BBCCC. *SQAAH:* BBC.

L1M9 BA Economics (Applied) with Criminology
Duration: 3FT Hon

Entry Requirements: *GCE:* 180-320.

Q1M9 BA English Language & Communication with Criminology
Duration: 3FT Hon

Entry Requirements: *GCE:* 220-320.

Q3M9 BA English Literature with Criminology
Duration: 3FT Hon

Entry Requirements: *GCE:* 220-320.

V3M9 BA History of Art, Design & Film with Criminology
Duration: 3FT Hon

Entry Requirements: *GCE:* 220.

V1M9 BA History with Criminology
Duration: 3FT Hon

Entry Requirements: *GCE:* 220-320.

L0M9 BA Human Rights with Criminology
Duration: 3FT Hon

Entry Requirements: *GCE:* 40.

LM29 BA International Relations and Criminology
Duration: 3FT Hon

Entry Requirements: *GCE:* 240-280.

P3MX BA Media & Cultural Studies with Criminology
Duration: 3FT Hon

Entry Requirements: *GCE:* 240-320.

L2M9 BA Politics with Criminology
Duration: 3FT Hon

Entry Requirements: *GCE:* 220-320.

C8M9 BA Psychology with Criminology
Duration: 3FT Hon

Entry Requirements: *GCE:* 220-320.

L3M9 BA Sociology with Criminology
Duration: 3FT Hon

Entry Requirements: *GCE:* 220-320.

L2MX BSc International Relations with Criminology
Duration: 3FT Hon

Entry Requirements: *GCE:* 240-280.

L14 LANCASTER UNIVERSITY
THE UNIVERSITY
LANCASTER
LANCASHIRE LA1 4YW

t: 01524 592029 f: 01524 846243
e: ugadmissions@lancaster.ac.uk
// www.lancs.ac.uk

MM12 LLB Law and Criminology
Duration: 3FT Hon

Entry Requirements: *GCE:* AAB. *SQAH:* AAABB. *SQAAH:* AAB. *IB:* 31. *BTEC ND:* DDD.

M930 BA Criminology
Duration: 3FT Hon

Entry Requirements: *GCE:* BBB. *SQAH:* BBBBB. *SQAAH:* BBB. *IB:* 29.

LM39 BA Criminology and Sociology
Duration: 3FT Hon

Entry Requirements: *GCE:* BBB. *SQAH:* BBBBB. *SQAAH:* BBB. *IB:* 29.

L23 UNIVERSITY OF LEEDS
THE UNIVERSITY OF LEEDS
LEEDS LS2 9JT

t: 0113 343 3999
e: admissions@adm.leeds.ac.uk
// www.leeds.ac.uk

MM29 BA Criminal Justice & Criminology
Duration: 3FT Hon

Entry Requirements: *GCE:* 320. *IB:* 33.

L27 LEEDS METROPOLITAN UNIVERSITY
COURSE ENQUIRIES OFFICE
CIVIC QUARTER
LEEDS LS1 3HE

t: 0113 81 23113 f: 0113 81 23129
e: course-enquiries@leedsmet.ac.uk
// www.leedsmet.ac.uk

M900 BA Criminology
Duration: 3FT Hon

Entry Requirements: *GCE:* 200. *IB:* 24.

ML93 BA Criminology & Sociology
Duration: 3FT Hon

Entry Requirements: *GCE:* 200. *IB:* 24.

M1M9 BA Law with Criminology
Duration: 3FT Hon

Entry Requirements: *GCE:* 260. *IB:* 28.

C8M9 BSc Psychology with Criminology
Duration: 3FT Hon

Entry Requirements: *GCE:* 240. *IB:* 24. *BTEC NC:* DD. *BTEC ND:* MMM. *OCR ND:* Distinction.

L34 UNIVERSITY OF LEICESTER
UNIVERSITY ROAD
LEICESTER LE1 7RH
t: 0116 252 5281 f: 0116 252 2447
e: admissions@le.ac.uk
// www.le.ac.uk

M930 BA Criminology
Duration: 3FT Hon

Entry Requirements: *GCE:* BBB. *SQAH:* BBBBB. *SQAAH:* BBB. *IB:* 32. *BTEC ND:* DMM.

L39 UNIVERSITY OF LINCOLN
ADMISSIONS
BRAYFORD POOL
LINCOLN LN6 7TS
t: 01522 886097 f: 01522 886146
e: admissions@lincoln.ac.uk
// www.lincoln.ac.uk

M930 LLB Criminology and Law
Duration: 3FT Hon

Entry Requirements: *GCE:* 240.

M931 BA Criminology
Duration: 3FT Hon

Entry Requirements: *GCE:* 220.

MQX3 BA Criminology and English
Duration: 3FT Hon

Entry Requirements: *GCE:* 240.

MVX1 BA Criminology and History
Duration: 3FT Hon

Entry Requirements: *GCE:* 220.

LMF9 BA/BSc Criminology and International Relations
Duration: 3FT Hon

Entry Requirements: *GCE:* 220.

MP95 BA/BSc Criminology and Journalism
Duration: 3FT Hon

Entry Requirements: *GCE:* 260.

LMG9 BA/BSc Criminology and Politics
Duration: 3FT Hon

Entry Requirements: *GCE:* 220.

LM49 BA/BSc Criminology and Social Policy
Duration: 3FT Hon

Entry Requirements: *GCE:* 220.

FM49 BSc Criminology and Forensic Investigation
Duration: 3FT Hon

Entry Requirements: *GCE:* 220.

L46 LIVERPOOL HOPE UNIVERSITY
HOPE PARK
LIVERPOOL L16 9JD
t: 0151 291 3295 f: 0151 291 2050
e: admission@hope.ac.uk
// www.hope.ac.uk

LM39 BA Applied Social Science and Criminology
Duration: 3FT Hon

Entry Requirements: *GCE:* 240. *IB:* 25.

M990 BA Criminology
Duration: 3FT Hon

Entry Requirements: *GCE:* 260. *IB:* 25.

L51 LIVERPOOL JOHN MOORES UNIVERSITY
ROSCOE COURT
4 RODNEY STREET
LIVERPOOL L1 2TZ
t: 0151 231 5090 f: 0151 231 3462
e: recruitment@ljmu.ac.uk
// www.ljmu.ac.uk

M212 BA Criminology
Duration: 3FT Hon

Entry Requirements: *GCE:* 240. *IB:* 28.

ML23 BA Criminology and Sociology
Duration: 3FT Hon

Entry Requirements: *GCE:* 240.

MC28 BA/BSc Criminology and Applied Psychology
Duration: 3FT Hon

Entry Requirements: *GCE:* 240.

M213 FYr Criminology (Year 0 only)
Duration: 1FT FYr

Entry Requirements: *GCE:* 40-100.

MC98 FYr Criminology and Psychology (Year 0 only)
Duration: 1FT FYr

Entry Requirements: *GCE:* 220.

ML2H FYr Criminology and Sociology (Year 0 only)
Duration: 1FT FYr

Entry Requirements: *GCE:* 40-100.

L68 LONDON METROPOLITAN UNIVERSITY
166-220 HOLLOWAY ROAD
LONDON N7 8DB
t: 020 7133 4200
e: admissions@londonmet.ac.uk
// www.londonmet.ac.uk

MNX1 BA Business and Criminology
Duration: 3FT Hon

Entry Requirements: *GCE:* 200. *IB:* 28.

M930 BA Criminology
Duration: 3FT Hon

Entry Requirements: *GCE:* 200. *IB:* 28.

LMFX BA Criminology and International Relations
Duration: 3FT Hon

Entry Requirements: *GCE:* 240. *IB:* 28.

MM1X BA Criminology and Law
Duration: 3FT Hon

Entry Requirements: *GCE:* 240. *IB:* 28.

MPX3 BA Criminology and Media Arts
Duration: 3FT Hon

Entry Requirements: *GCE:* 200. *IB:* 28.

ML9F BA Criminology and Politics
Duration: 3FT Hon

Entry Requirements: *GCE:* 240. *IB:* 28.

NM29 BA/BSc Community Sector Management and Criminology
Duration: 3FT Hon

Entry Requirements: *GCE:* 200. *IB:* 28.

ML92 BA/BSc Criminology and Governance & Law
Duration: 3FT Hon

Entry Requirements: *GCE:* 240. *IB:* 28.

CM8X BA/BSc Criminology and Psychology
Duration: 3FT Hon

Entry Requirements: *GCE:* 280. *IB:* 28.

ML93 BA/BSc Criminology and Sociology
Duration: 3FT Hon

Entry Requirements: *GCE:* 200. *IB:* 28.

ML95 BA/BSc Criminology and Youth Studies
Duration: 3FT Hon

Entry Requirements: *GCE:* 200. *IB:* 28.

L72 LONDON SCHOOL OF ECONOMICS AND POLITICAL SCIENCE (UNIVERSITY OF LONDON)
HOUGHTON STREET
LONDON WC2A 2AE
t: 020 7955 7125/7769 f: 020 7955 6001
e: ug-admissions@lse.ac.uk
// www.lse.ac.uk

LM42 BSc Social Policy and Criminology
Duration: 3FT Hon

Entry Requirements: *GCE:* BBB. *SQAH:* AABBB-ABBBB. *SQAAH:* BBB. *IB:* 36.

L75 LONDON SOUTH BANK UNIVERSITY
103 BOROUGH ROAD
LONDON SE1 0AA
t: 020 7815 7815 f: 020 7815 8273
e: enquiry@lsbu.ac.uk
// www.lsbu.ac.uk

M1M9 LLB Law with Criminology
Duration: 3FT Hon

Entry Requirements: *GCE:* 240. *IB:* 24.

LM22 BA International Politics and Criminology
Duration: 3FT Hon

Entry Requirements: *GCE:* 160. *IB:* 24. *BTEC NC:* MM. *BTEC ND:* MPP.

L2M9 BA International Politics with Criminology
Duration: 3FT Hon

Entry Requirements: *GCE:* 160. *IB:* 24. *BTEC NC:* MM. *BTEC ND:* MPP.

P3M9 BA Media Studies with Criminology

Duration: 3FT Hon

Entry Requirements: *GCE:* 160. *IB:* 24. *BTEC NC:* MM. *BTEC ND:* MPP.

M930 BSc Criminology

Duration: 3FT Hon

Entry Requirements: *GCE:* 160. *IB:* 24. *BTEC NC:* MM. *BTEC ND:* MPP.

ML94 BSc Criminology and Social Policy

Duration: 3FT Hon

Entry Requirements: *GCE:* 160. *IB:* 24. *BTEC NC:* MM. *BTEC ND:* MPP.

ML93 BSc Criminology and Sociology

Duration: 3FT Hon

Entry Requirements: *GCE:* 160. *IB:* 24. *BTEC NC:* MM. *BTEC ND:* MPP.

M9L2 BSc Criminology with International Politics

Duration: 3FT Hon

Entry Requirements: *GCE:* 160. *IB:* 24. *BTEC NC:* MM. *BTEC ND:* MPP.

M9M1 BSc Criminology with Law

Duration: 3FT Hon

Entry Requirements: *GCE:* 240. *IB:* 24.

M9P3 BSc Criminology with Media Studies

Duration: 3FT Hon

Entry Requirements: *GCE:* 160. *IB:* 24. *BTEC NC:* MM. *BTEC ND:* MPP.

M9C8 BSc Criminology with Psychology

Duration: 3FT Hon

Entry Requirements: *GCE:* 240. *IB:* 24.

M9L4 BSc Criminology with Social Policy

Duration: 3FT Hon

Entry Requirements: *GCE:* 160. *IB:* 24.

M9L3 BSc Criminology with Sociology

Duration: 3FT Hon

Entry Requirements: *GCE:* 160. *IB:* 24. *BTEC NC:* MM. *BTEC ND:* MPP.

F4M9 BSc Forensic Science with Criminology

Duration: 3FT Hon

Entry Requirements: *GCE:* 160. *IB:* 24. *BTEC NC:* MM. *BTEC ND:* MPP.

C8M9 BSc (Hons) Psychology with Criminology

Duration: 3FT Hon

Entry Requirements: *GCE:* 240. *IB:* 24.

L4M9 BSc Social Policy with Criminology

Duration: 3FT Hon

Entry Requirements: *GCE:* 160. *IB:* 24. *BTEC NC:* MM. *BTEC ND:* MPP.

L79 LOUGHBOROUGH UNIVERSITY
LOUGHBOROUGH
LEICESTERSHIRE LE11 3TU
t: 01509 223522 f: 01509 223905
e: admissions@lboro.ac.uk
// www.lboro.ac.uk

ML24 BSc Criminology and Social Policy

Duration: 3FT Hon

Entry Requirements: *GCE:* 300. *IB:* 32. *BTEC ND:* DDM.

M20 THE UNIVERSITY OF MANCHESTER
OXFORD ROAD
MANCHESTER M13 9PL
t: 0161 275 2077 f: 0161 275 2106
e: ug-admissions@manchester.ac.uk
// www.manchester.ac.uk

M1M9 LLB Law with Criminology

Duration: 3FT Hon

Entry Requirements: *GCE:* AAA. *SQAH:* AAAAB. *SQAAH:* AAA. *IB:* 37. *BTEC NC:* DD. *BTEC ND:* DDD.

M901 BA Criminology

Duration: 3FT Hon

Entry Requirements: *GCE:* ABB. *SQAH:* AABBB. *SQAAH:* ABB. *IB:* 33.

M900 BAEcon Criminology

Duration: 3FT Hon

Entry Requirements: *GCE:* ABB. *SQAH:* AABBB. *SQAAH:* ABB. *IB:* 34. *BTEC ND:* DDM.

LM19 BAEcon Economics and Criminology

Duration: 3FT Hon

Entry Requirements: *GCE:* ABB. *SQAH:* AABBB. *SQAAH:* ABB. *IB:* 34. *BTEC ND:* DDM.

LM29 BAEcon Politics and Criminology

Duration: 3FT Hon

Entry Requirements: *GCE:* ABB. *SQAH:* AABBB. *SQAAH:* ABB. *IB:* 34. *BTEC ND:* DDM.

LM69 BAEcon Social Anthropology and Criminology

Duration: 3FT Hon

Entry Requirements: *GCE:* ABB. *SQAH:* AABBB. *SQAAH:* ABB. *IB:* 34. *BTEC ND:* DDM.

LM39 BAEcon Sociology and Criminology

Duration: 3FT Hon

Entry Requirements: *GCE:* ABB. *SQAH:* AABBB. *SQAAH:* ABB. *IB:* 34. *BTEC ND:* DDM.

M40 THE MANCHESTER METROPOLITAN UNIVERSITY

ADMISSIONS OFFICE
ALL SAINTS (GMS)
ALL SAINTS
MANCHESTER M15 6BH

t: 0161 247 2000

// www.mmu.ac.uk

ML9J BA Criminology

Duration: 3FT Hon

Entry Requirements: *GCE:* 240. *SQAH:* CCC. *SQAAH:* CC. *IB:* 27. *BTEC NC:* MM. *BTEC ND:* MPP.

M900 BA Criminology (Foundation)

Duration: 4FT Hon

Entry Requirements: *GCE:* 40.

NM19 BA/BSc Business/Criminology

Duration: 3FT Hon

Entry Requirements: *GCE:* 220. *IB:* 26.

MN91 BA/BSc Criminology/Business Enterprise

Duration: 3FT Hon

Entry Requirements: *GCE:* 220. *IB:* 26.

ML96 BA/BSc Criminology/Cultural Studies

Duration: 3FT Hon

Entry Requirements: *GCE:* 220. *IB:* 26.

MG94 BA/BSc Criminology/Digital Media

Duration: 3FT Hon

Entry Requirements: *GCE:* 220. *IB:* 26.

MX93 BA/BSc Criminology/Education Studies

Duration: 3FT Hon

Entry Requirements: *GCE:* 220. *IB:* 26.

MQ93 BA/BSc Criminology/English

Duration: 3FT Hon

Entry Requirements: *GCE:* 240. *IB:* 27.

MR99 BA/BSc Criminology/European Studies

Duration: 3FT Hon

Entry Requirements: *GCE:* 220. *IB:* 26.

ML99 BA/BSc Criminology/Global Studies

Duration: 3FT Hon

Entry Requirements: *GCE:* 220. *IB:* 26.

MN9C BA/BSc Criminology/International Business

Duration: 3FT Hon

Entry Requirements: *GCE:* 220. *IB:* 26.

ML92 BA/BSc Criminology/International Politics

Duration: 3FT Hon

Entry Requirements: *GCE:* 220. *IB:* 26.

MQ91 BA/BSc Criminology/Linguistics

Duration: 3FT Hon

Entry Requirements: *GCE:* 220. *IB:* 26.

MJ99 BA/BSc Criminology/Logistics

Duration: 3FT Hon

Entry Requirements: *GCE:* 220. *IB:* 26.

MN95 BA/BSc Criminology/Marketing

Duration: 3FT Hon

Entry Requirements: *GCE:* 220. *IB:* 26.

ML9F BA/BSc Criminology/Politics

Duration: 3FT Hon

Entry Requirements: *GCE:* 220. *IB:* 26.

MN9G BA/BSc Criminology/Project Management

Duration: 3FT Hon

Entry Requirements: *GCE:* 220. *IB:* 26.

MN9F BA/BSc Criminology/Public Management Studies

Duration: 3FT Hon

Entry Requirements: *GCE:* 220. *IB:* 26.

MV9H BA/BSc Criminology/Social History

Duration: 3FT Hon

Entry Requirements: *GCE:* 220. *IB:* 26.

MX91 BA/BSc Criminology/Teaching English as a Foreign Language

Duration: 3FT Hon

Entry Requirements: *GCE:* 220. *IB:* 26.

MN98 BA/BSc Criminology/Tourism
Duration: 3FT Hon

Entry Requirements: *GCE:* 220. *IB:* 26.

QM39 BA/BSc English as a Foreign Language/Criminology
Duration: 3FT Hon

Entry Requirements: *GCE:* 220. *IB:* 26.

LM19 BSc Business Economics/Criminology
Duration: 3FT Hon

Entry Requirements: *GCE:* 220. *IB:* 26.

FM19 BSc Chemistry/Criminology
Duration: 3FT Hon

Entry Requirements: *GCE:* 220. *IB:* 26.

MF94 BSc Criminology/Forensic Science
Duration: 3FT Hon

Entry Requirements: *GCE:* 220. *IB:* 26.

MF98 BSc Criminology/Geography
Duration: 3FT Hon

Entry Requirements: *GCE:* 240. *IB:* 27.

MP91 BSc Criminology/Information & Communications
Duration: 3FT Hon

Entry Requirements: *GCE:* 220. *IB:* 26.

MG95 BSc Criminology/Information Systems
Duration: 3FT Hon

Entry Requirements: *GCE:* 220. *IB:* 26.

MN92 BSc Criminology/Management Systems
Duration: 3FT Hon

Entry Requirements: *GCE:* 220. *IB:* 26.

MG91 BSc Criminology/Mathematics
Duration: 3FT Hon

Entry Requirements: *GCE:* 220. *IB:* 26.

MLXH BSc Criminology/Sociology
Duration: 3FT Hon

Entry Requirements: *GCE:* 220. *IB:* 26.

M80 MIDDLESEX UNIVERSITY
MIDDLESEX UNIVERSITY
THE BURROUGHS
LONDON NW4 4BT
t: 020 8411 5555 f: 020 8411 5649
e: enquiries@mdx.ac.uk
// www.mdx.ac.uk

L3MX BA Sociology with Criminology
Duration: 3FT/4SW Hon

Entry Requirements: *GCE:* 200-300. *IB:* 28.

CM89 BSc Psychology with Criminology
Duration: 3FT/4SW Hon

Entry Requirements: *GCE:* 200-300. *IB:* 28.

N38 UNIVERSITY OF NORTHAMPTON
PARK CAMPUS
BOUGHTON GREEN ROAD
NORTHAMPTON NN2 7AL
t: 0800 358 2232 f: 01604 722083
e: admissions@northampton.ac.uk
// www.northampton.ac.uk

T7MX BA American Literature & Film/Criminology
Duration: 3FT Hon

Entry Requirements: *GCE:* 220-260. *SQAH:* AAB-BBBB. *IB:* 24.

T7M9 BA American Studies/Criminology
Duration: 3FT Hon

Entry Requirements: *GCE:* 220-260. *SQAH:* AAB-BBBB. *IB:* 24.

N1M9 BA Business/Criminology
Duration: 3FT Hon

Entry Requirements: *GCE:* 220-260. *SQAH:* AAB-BBBB. *IB:* 24.

M930 BA Criminology
Duration: 3FT Hon

Entry Requirements: *GCE:* 220-260. *SQAH:* AAB-BBBB. *IB:* 24.

M9NG BA Criminology with Applied Management
Duration: 3FT Hon

Entry Requirements: *GCE:* 220-260. *SQAH:* AAB-BBBB. *IB:* 24.

M9D4 BA Criminology with Equine Studies
Duration: 3FT Hon

Entry Requirements: *GCE:* 220-260. *SQAH:* AAB-BBBB. *IB:* 24.

M9NM BA Criminology/Advertising
Duration: 3FT Hon

Entry Requirements: *GCE:* 220-260. *SQAH:* AAB-BBBB. *IB:* 24.

M9TR BA Criminology/American Literature & Film
Duration: 3FT Hon

Entry Requirements: *GCE:* 220-260. *SQAH:* AAB-BBBB. *IB:* 24.

M9T7 BA Criminology/American Studies
Duration: 3FT Hon

Entry Requirements: *GCE:* 220-260. *SQAH:* AAB-BBBB. *IB:* 24.

M9C1 BA Criminology/Biological Conservation
Duration: 3FT Hon

Entry Requirements: *GCE:* 220-260. *SQAH:* AAB-BBBB. *IB:* 24.

M9N1 BA Criminology/Business
Duration: 3FT Hon

Entry Requirements: *GCE:* 220-260. *SQAH:* AAB-BBBB. *IB:* 24.

M9G5 BA Criminology/Business Computing Systems
Duration: 3FT Hon

Entry Requirements: *GCE:* 220-260. *SQAH:* AAB-BBBB. *IB:* 24.

M9G4 BA Criminology/Computing
Duration: 3FT Hon

Entry Requirements: *GCE:* 220-260. *SQAH:* AAB-BBBB. *IB:* 24.

M9W4 BA Criminology/Drama
Duration: 3FT Hon

Entry Requirements: *GCE:* 220-260. *SQAH:* AAB-BBBB. *IB:* 24.
Interview required.

M9L1 BA Criminology/Economics
Duration: 3FT Hon

Entry Requirements: *GCE:* 220-260. *SQAH:* AAB-BBBB. *IB:* 24.

M9X3 BA Criminology/Education Studies
Duration: 3FT Hon

Entry Requirements: *GCE:* 220-260. *SQAH:* AAB-BBBB. *IB:* 24.

M9Q3 BA Criminology/English
Duration: 3FT Hon

Entry Requirements: *GCE:* 220-260. *SQAH:* AAB-BBBB. *IB:* 24.

M9NV BA Criminology/Events Management
Duration: 3FT Hon

Entry Requirements: *GCE:* 220-260. *SQAH:* AAB-BBBB. *IB:* 24.

M9R2 BA Criminology/German
Duration: 3FT Hon

Entry Requirements: *GCE:* 220-260. *SQAH:* AAB-BBBB. *IB:* 24.

M9L4 BA Criminology/Health Studies
Duration: 3FT Hon

Entry Requirements: *GCE:* 220-260. *SQAH:* AAB-BBBB. *IB:* 24.

M9M1 BA Criminology/Law
Duration: 3FT Hon

Entry Requirements: *GCE:* 220-260. *SQAH:* AAB-BBBB. *IB:* 24.

M9P4 BA Criminology/Magazine Publishing
Duration: 3FT Hon

Entry Requirements: *GCE:* 220-260. *SQAH:* AAB-BBBB. *IB:* 24.

M9N2 BA Criminology/Management
Duration: 3FT Hon

Entry Requirements: *GCE:* 220-260. *SQAH:* AAB-BBBB. *IB:* 24.

M9N5 BA Criminology/Marketing
Duration: 3FT Hon

Entry Requirements: *GCE:* 220-260. *SQAH:* AAB-BBBB. *IB:* 24.

M9V5 BA Criminology/Philosophy
Duration: 3FT Hon

Entry Requirements: *GCE:* 220-260. *SQAH:* AAB-BBBB. *IB:* 24.

M9F8 BA Criminology/Physical Geography
Duration: 3FT Hon

Entry Requirements: *GCE:* 220-260. *SQAH:* AAB-BBBB. *IB:* 24.

M9L2 BA Criminology/Politics
Duration: 3FT Hon

Entry Requirements: *GCE:* 220-260. *SQAH:* AAB-BBBB. *IB:* 24.

M9NF BA Criminology/Retailing
Duration: 3FT Hon

Entry Requirements: *GCE:* 220-260. *SQAH:* AAB-BBBB. *IB:* 24.

M9NA BA Criminology/Social Enterprise Development

Duration: 3FT Hon

Entry Requirements: *GCE:* 220-260. *SQAH:* AAB-BBBB. *IB:* 24.

M9L3 BA Criminology/Sociology

Duration: 3FT Hon

Entry Requirements: *GCE:* 220-260. *SQAH:* AAB-BBBB. *IB:* 24.

M9LX BA Criminology/Third World Development

Duration: 3FT Hon

Entry Requirements: *GCE:* 220-260. *SQAH:* AAB-BBBB. *IB:* 24.

M9N8 BA Criminology/Tourism

Duration: 3FT Hon

Entry Requirements: *GCE:* 220-260. *SQAH:* AAB-BBBB. *IB:* 24.

M9FV BA Criminology/Wastes Management

Duration: 3FT Hon

Entry Requirements: *GCE:* 220-260. *SQAH:* AAB-BBBB. *IB:* 24.

L1M9 BA Economics/Criminology

Duration: 3FT Hon

Entry Requirements: *GCE:* 220-260. *SQAH:* AAB-BBBB. *IB:* 24.

X3M9 BA Education Studies/Criminology

Duration: 3FT Hon

Entry Requirements: *GCE:* 220-260. *SQAH:* AAB-BBBB. *IB:* 24.

Q3M9 BA English/Criminology

Duration: 3FT Hon

Entry Requirements: *GCE:* 220-260. *SQAH:* AAB-BBBB. *IB:* 24.

N8MX BA Events Management/Criminology

Duration: 3FT Hon

Entry Requirements: *GCE:* 220-260. *SQAH:* AAB-BBBB. *IB:* 24.

R2M9 BA German/Criminology

Duration: 3FT Hon

Entry Requirements: *GCE:* 220-260. *SQAH:* AAB-BBBB. *IB:* 24.

L4M9 BA Health Studies/Criminology

Duration: 3FT Hon

Entry Requirements: *GCE:* 220-260. *SQAH:* AAB-BBBB. *IB:* 24.

M1M9 BA Law/Criminology

Duration: 3FT Hon

Entry Requirements: *GCE:* 220-260. *SQAH:* AAB-BBBB. *IB:* 24.

P4M9 BA Magazine Publishing/Criminology

Duration: 3FT Hon

Entry Requirements: *GCE:* 220-260. *SQAH:* AAB-BBBB. *IB:* 24.

N2M9 BA Management/Criminology

Duration: 3FT Hon

Entry Requirements: *GCE:* 220-260. *SQAH:* AAB-BBBB. *IB:* 24.

N5M9 BA Marketing/Criminology

Duration: 3FT Hon

Entry Requirements: *GCE:* 220-260. *SQAH:* AAB-BBBB. *IB:* 24.

V5M9 BA Philosophy/Criminology

Duration: 3FT Hon

Entry Requirements: *GCE:* 220-260. *SQAH:* AAB-BBBB. *IB:* 24.

L2M9 BA Politics/Criminology

Duration: 3FT Hon

Entry Requirements: *GCE:* 220-260. *SQAH:* AAB-BBBB. *IB:* 24.

C8M9 BA Psychology/Criminology

Duration: 3FT Hon

Entry Requirements: *GCE:* 220-260. *SQAH:* AAB-BBBB. *IB:* 24.

N2MX BA Retailing/Criminology

Duration: 3FT Hon

Entry Requirements: *GCE:* 220-260. *SQAH:* AAB-BBBB. *IB:* 24.

N2MY BA Social Enterprise Development/Criminology

Duration: 3FT Hon

Entry Requirements: *GCE:* 220-260. *SQAH:* AAB-BBBB. *IB:* 24.

L3M9 BA Sociology/Criminology

Duration: 3FT Hon

Entry Requirements: *GCE:* 220-260. *SQAH:* AAB-BBBB. *IB:* 24.

C6M9 BA Sport Studies/Criminology

Duration: 3FT Hon

Entry Requirements: *GCE:* 220-260. *SQAH:* AAB-BBBB. *IB:* 24.

L9MX BA Third World Development/Criminology

Duration: 3FT Hon

Entry Requirements: *GCE:* 220-260. *SQAH:* AAB-BBBB. *IB:* 24.

N8M9 BA Tourism/Criminology

Duration: 3FT Hon

Entry Requirements: *GCE:* 220-260. *SQAH:* AAB-BBBB. *IB:* 24.

N5MX BSc Advertising/Criminology

Duration: 3FT Hon

Entry Requirements: *GCE:* 220-260. *SQAH:* AAB-BBBB. *IB:* 24.

C1M9 BSc Biological Conservation/Criminology

Duration: 3FT Hon

Entry Requirements: *GCE:* 220-260. *SQAH:* AAB-BBBB. *IB:* 24.

G5M9 BSc Business Computing Systems/Criminology

Duration: 3FT Hon

Entry Requirements: *GCE:* 220-260. *SQAH:* AAB-BBBB. *IB:* 24.

G4M9 BSc Computing/Criminology

Duration: 3FT Hon

Entry Requirements: *GCE:* 220-260. *SQAH:* AAB-BBBB. *IB:* 24.

F8M9 BSc Physical Geography/Criminology

Duration: 3FT Hon

Entry Requirements: *GCE:* 220-260. *SQAH:* AAB-BBBB. *IB:* 24.

F8MX BSc Wastes Management/Criminology

Duration: 3FT Hon

Entry Requirements: *GCE:* 220-260. *SQAH:* AAB-BBBB. *IB:* 24.

N77 NORTHUMBRIA UNIVERSITY

TRINITY BUILDING
NORTHUMBERLAND ROAD
NEWCASTLE UPON TYNE NE1 8ST

t: 0191 243 7420 f: 0191 227 4561
e: er.admissions@northumbria.ac.uk

// www.northumbria.ac.uk

M900 BSc Criminology

Duration: 3FT Hon

Entry Requirements: HND required.

MF94 BSc Criminology and Forensic Science

Duration: 3FT Hon

Entry Requirements: *GCE:* 280. *SQAH:* BBCCC. *SQAAH:* BCC. *IB:* 25. *BTEC ND:* DMM. *OCR ND:* Merit. *OCR NED:* Merit.

LM39 BSc Criminology and Sociology

Duration: 3FT Hon

Entry Requirements: *GCE:* 280. *SQAH:* BBCCC. *SQAAH:* BCC. *IB:* 25. *BTEC ND:* DMM.

N91 NOTTINGHAM TRENT UNIVERSITY

DRYDEN CENTRE
BURTON STREET
NOTTINGHAM NG1 4BU

t: +44 (0) 115 941 8418 f: +44 (0) 115 848 6063
e: admissions@ntu.ac.uk

// www.ntu.ac.uk/

M1L3 LLB Law with Criminology

Duration: 3FT Hon

Entry Requirements: *Foundation:* Pass. *GCE:* 280. *SQAH:* BBBBC. *SQAAH:* BBC. *IB:* 24. *BTEC NC:* DM. *BTEC ND:* DMM. *OCR ND:* Merit. *OCR NED:* Merit.

P55 PETERBOROUGH REGIONAL COLLEGE

PARK CRESCENT
PETERBOROUGH PE1 4DZ

t: 0845 8728722 f: 01733 767986
e: info@peterborough.ac.uk

// www.peterborough.ac.uk

M900 BA Criminology

Duration: 3FT Hon

Entry Requirements: Interview required.

P60 UNIVERSITY OF PLYMOUTH

DRAKE CIRCUS
PLYMOUTH PL4 8AA

t: 01752 588037 f: 01752 588050
e: admissions@plymouth.ac.uk

// www.plymouth.ac.uk

M9L4 BSc Criminology & Criminal Justice Studies with International Social Justice

Duration: 3FT Hon

Entry Requirements: Contact the institution for details.

M214 BSc Criminology & Criminal Justice Studies with Law

Duration: 3FT Hon

Entry Requirements: *GCE:* 260-300. *IB:* 28.

M9LF BSc Criminology & Criminal Justice Studies with Politics

Duration: 3FT Hon

Entry Requirements: *GCE:* 260-300. *IB:* 28.

M2LH BSc Criminology & Criminal Justice Studies with Social Research

Duration: 3FT Hon

Entry Requirements: *GCE:* 260-300. *IB:* 28.

M9LH BSc Criminology & Criminal Justice Studies with Sociology

Duration: 3FT Hon

Entry Requirements: *GCE:* 260-300. *IB:* 28.

L2MY BSc International Relations with Criminology & Criminal Justice Studies

Duration: 3FT Hon

Entry Requirements: *GCE:* 240-300.

L2M9 BSc Politics with Criminology & Criminal Justice Studies

Duration: 3FT Hon

Entry Requirements: *GCE:* 240-300.

C8MX BSc Psychology with Criminology and Criminal Justice Studies

Duration: 3FT Hon

Entry Requirements: HND required.

P80 UNIVERSITY OF PORTSMOUTH

ACADEMIC REGISTRY
UNIVERSITY HOUSE
WINSTON CHURCHILL AVENUE
PORTSMOUTH PO1 2UP

t: 023 9284 8484 f: 023 9284 3082
e: admissions@port.ac.uk

// www.port.ac.uk

MMC9 LLB Law and Criminology

Duration: 3FT/4SW Hon

Entry Requirements: *GCE:* 300.

M9C8 BSc Criminology with Psychology

Duration: 3FT Hon

Entry Requirements: *GCE:* 240-300.

LM39 BSc Sociology and Criminology

Duration: 3FT Hon

Entry Requirements: *GCE:* 240-300.

Q75 QUEEN'S UNIVERSITY BELFAST

UNIVERSITY ROAD
BELFAST BT7 1NN

t: 028 9097 2727 f: 028 9097 2828
e: admissions@qub.ac.uk

// www.qub.ac.uk

M900 BA Criminology

Duration: 3FT Hon

Entry Requirements: *GCE:* ABB-BBBb. *SQAH:* AABBB. *SQAAH:* ABB. *IB:* 34.

ML94 BA Criminology/Social Policy

Duration: 3FT Hon

Entry Requirements: *GCE:* ABB-BBBb. *SQAH:* AABBB. *SQAAH:* ABB. *IB:* 34.

ML93 BA Criminology/Sociology

Duration: 3FT Hon

Entry Requirements: *GCE:* ABB-BBBb. *SQAH:* AABBB. *SQAAH:* ABB. *IB:* 34.

R48 ROEHAMPTON UNIVERSITY

ERASMUS HOUSE
ROEHAMPTON LANE
LONDON SW15 5PU

t: 020 8392 3232 f: 020 8392 3470
e: enquiries@roehampton.ac.uk

// www.roehampton.ac.uk

M900 BA Criminology

Duration: 3FT Hon

Entry Requirements: *GCE:* 240-280. *IB:* 24. *BTEC NC:* DD. *BTEC ND:* MMM. *OCR ND:* Distinction. *OCR NED:* Merit.

MN91 BA Criminology and Business Management

Duration: 3FT Hon

Entry Requirements: *GCE:* 240-280. *IB:* 24. *BTEC NC:* DD. *BTEC ND:* MMM. *OCR ND:* Distinction. *OCR NED:* Merit.

ML9P BA Criminology and Social Anthropology

Duration: 3FT Hon

Entry Requirements: *GCE:* 240-280. *IB:* 24. *BTEC NC:* DD. *BTEC ND:* MMM. *OCR ND:* Distinction. *OCR NED:* Merit.

ML93 BA Criminology and Sociology

Duration: 3FT Hon

Entry Requirements: *GCE:* 200-240. *IB:* 24. *BTEC NC:* DM. *BTEC ND:* MMP. *OCR ND:* Merit. *OCR NED:* Pass.

WM69 BA/BSc Photography and Criminology

Duration: 3FT Hon

Entry Requirements: *GCE:* 240-320. *IB:* 24. *BTEC NC:* DD. *BTEC ND:* MMM. *OCR ND:* Distinction. *OCR NED:* Merit.

VM69 BA/BSc Theology & Religious Studies and Criminology

Duration: 3FT Hon

Entry Requirements: Contact the institution for details.

GM49 BSc/BA Computing Studies and Criminology

Duration: 3FT Hon

Entry Requirements: *GCE:* 200-240. *IB:* 24. *BTEC NC:* DM. *BTEC ND:* MMP. *OCR ND:* Merit. *OCR NED:* Pass.

R72 ROYAL HOLLOWAY, UNIVERSITY OF LONDON

ROYAL HOLLOWAY, UNIVERSITY OF LONDON
EGHAM
SURREY TW20 0EX

t: 01784 434455 **f:** 01784 473662
e: Admissions@rhul.ac.uk

// www.rhul.ac.uk

LM39 BSc Criminology and Sociology

Duration: 3FT Hon

Entry Requirements: *GCE:* BBB. *SQAH:* BBBBB. *IB:* 32. *BTEC ND:* DDM.

S03 THE UNIVERSITY OF SALFORD

SALFORD M5 4WT

t: 0161 295 4545 **f:** 0161 295 3126
e: ugadmissions-exrel@salford.ac.uk

// www.salford.ac.uk

M1M9 LLB Law with Criminology

Duration: 3FT Hon

Entry Requirements: *GCE:* 300. *IB:* 29. *BTEC ND:* DMM. *OCR NED:* Merit. Interview required.

M900 BSc Criminology

Duration: 3FT Hon

Entry Requirements: Contact the institution for details.

ML99 BSc Criminology and Cultural Studies

Duration: 3FT Hon

Entry Requirements: *GCE:* 240. *IB:* 27. *BTEC NC:* DD. *BTEC ND:* MMM.

LM29 BSc Criminology and Politics

Duration: 3FT Hon

Entry Requirements: *GCE:* 240. *IB:* 27. *BTEC NC:* DD. *BTEC ND:* MMM.

LM39 BSc Criminology and Sociology

Duration: 3FT Hon

Entry Requirements: *GCE:* 200.

L2M9 BSc Politics with Criminology

Duration: 3FT Hon

Entry Requirements: *GCE:* 200.

CM89 BSc Psychology and Criminology

Duration: 3FT Hon

Entry Requirements: *GCE:* 280. *SQAH:* BBCCC. *IB:* 27. *BTEC ND:* DMM.

L3M9 BSc Sociology with Criminology

Duration: 3FT Hon

Entry Requirements: *GCE:* 240. *IB:* 27. *BTEC NC:* DD. *BTEC ND:* MMM.

S18 THE UNIVERSITY OF SHEFFIELD

9 NORTHUMBERLAND ROAD
SHEFFIELD S10 2TT

t: 0114 222 1255 **f:** 0114 222 8032
e: ask@sheffield.ac.uk

// www.sheffield.ac.uk

M930 LLB Law and Criminology

Duration: 3FT Hon

Entry Requirements: *GCE:* AAB. *SQAH:* AAAA. *SQAAH:* AAB. *IB:* 35.

ML94 BA Social Policy and Criminology

Duration: 3FT Hon

Entry Requirements: *GCE:* BBB. *SQAH:* AABB. *SQAAH:* BBB. *IB:* 32. *BTEC ND:* DMM.

S21 SHEFFIELD HALLAM UNIVERSITY

CITY CAMPUS
HOWARD STREET
SHEFFIELD S1 1WB

t: 0114 225 5555 **f:** 0114 225 2167
e: admissions@shu.ac.uk

// www.shu.ac.uk

M931 BA Criminology

Duration: 3FT Hon

Entry Requirements: *GCE:* 240.

ML93 BA Criminology and Sociology

Duration: 3FT Hon

Entry Requirements: *GCE:* 240.

MV91 BA History and Criminology

Duration: 3FT Hon

Entry Requirements: *GCE:* 260.

M930 BA Law and Criminology

Duration: 3FT Hon

Entry Requirements: *GCE:* 260.

LM29 BA Politics and Criminology

Duration: 3FT Hon

Entry Requirements: *GCE:* 240.

S27 UNIVERSITY OF SOUTHAMPTON
HIGHFIELD
SOUTHAMPTON SO17 1BJ
t: 023 8059 4732 f: 023 8059 3037
e: admissions@soton.ac.uk
// www.southampton.ac.uk

LM39 BSc Applied Social Sciences (Criminology)
Duration: 3FT Hon

Entry Requirements: *GCE:* BBB. *IB:* 32. *BTEC ND:* DMM.

S30 SOUTHAMPTON SOLENT UNIVERSITY
EAST PARK TERRACE
SOUTHAMPTON
HAMPSHIRE SO14 0RT
t: +44 (0) 23 8031 9039 f: + 44 (0)23 8022 2259
e: admissions@solent.ac.uk or ask@solent.ac.uk
// www.solent.ac.uk/

M1M9 LLB LLB (Hons) with Criminology
Duration: 3FT Hon

Entry Requirements: *GCE:* 220.

M930 BA Criminology
Duration: 3FT Hon

Entry Requirements: *GCE:* 120.

S72 STAFFORDSHIRE UNIVERSITY
COLLEGE ROAD
STOKE ON TRENT ST4 2DE
t: 01782 292753 f: 01782 292740
e: admissions@staffs.ac.uk
// www.staffs.ac.uk

M930 LLB LLB (Criminology)
Duration: 3FT Hon

Entry Requirements: *GCE:* BB-ABB. *SQAAH:* BB-ABB. *IB:* 26. *BTEC NC:* DM. *BTEC ND:* DDM. *OCR ND:* Distinction.

FMK9 BSc Forensic Science and Criminology
Duration: 3FT Hon

Entry Requirements: *GCE:* 200-280. *IB:* 24. *BTEC NC:* DM. *BTEC ND:* DMM.

S73 STAFFORDSHIRE UNIVERSITY REGIONAL FEDERATION
COLLEGE ROAD
STOKE ON TRENT ST4 2DE
t: 01782 292753 f: 01782 292740
e: admissions@staffs.ac.uk
// www.surf.ac.uk

FMK9 BSc Forensic Science and Criminology
Duration: 4FT Hon

Entry Requirements: *GCE:* 40-160. *IB:* 24. *BTEC NC:* PP. *BTEC ND:* PPP. Interview required.

S75 THE UNIVERSITY OF STIRLING
STIRLING FK9 4LA
t: 01786 467044 f: 01786 466800
e: admissions@stir.ac.uk
// www.stir.ac.uk

MM91 BA Criminology and Law
Duration: 4FT Hon

Entry Requirements: *GCE:* BCC. *SQAH:* BBBB. *SQAAH:* AAA-CCC. *BTEC ND:* DMM.

MV95 BA Criminology and Philosophy
Duration: 4FT Hon

Entry Requirements: *GCE:* CCC. *SQAH:* BBBC. *SQAAH:* AAA-CCC. *BTEC ND:* DMM.

ML92 BA Criminology and Politics
Duration: 4FT Hon

Entry Requirements: *GCE:* CCC. *SQAH:* BBBC. *SQAAH:* AAA-CCC.

LM39 BA Criminology and Sociology
Duration: 4FT Hon

Entry Requirements: *GCE:* CCC. *SQAH:* BBBC. *SQAAH:* AAA-CCC. *BTEC ND:* DMM.

S82 UNIVERSITY CAMPUS SUFFOLK
WATERFRONT BUILDING
NEPTUNE QUAY
IPSWICH
SUFFOLK IP4 1QJ
t: 01473 338348 f: 01473 339900
e: info@ucs.ac.uk
// www.ucs.ac.uk

ML95 BA Criminology and Youth Studies
Duration: 3FT Hon

Entry Requirements: *GCE:* 200.

ML93 BSc Criminology and Sociology
Duration: 3FT Hon

Entry Requirements: *GCE:* 160.

Confused about courses?
Indecisive about institutions?
Stressed about student life?
Unsure about UCAS?
Frowning over finance?

Help is available.

Visit www.ucasbooks.com to view our range
of over 75 books covering all aspects
of entry into higher education.

www.ucasbooks.com

> **Unlock your potential**
It's as easy as 1, 2, 3.

1 Search

Use Course Search to look for courses in your subject;
find out about your chosen universities and colleges
and lots more.

2 Apply

Use our online system Apply to make your application to
higher education.

3 Track

Then use Track to monitor the progress of your application.

UCAS   helping students into higher education   **www.ucas.com**

S84 UNIVERSITY OF SUNDERLAND

STUDENT HELPLINE
THE STUDENT GATEWAY
CHESTER ROAD
SUNDERLAND SR1 3SD

t: 0191 515 3000 f: 0191 515 3805
e: student-helpline@sunderland.ac.uk

// www.sunderland.ac.uk

TM79 BA American Studies and Criminology
Duration: 3FT Hon

Entry Requirements: *GCE:* 220-360. *BTEC NC:* DM. *BTEC ND:* MMM. *OCR ND:* Distinction. *OCR NED:* Merit.

T7M9 BA American Studies with Criminology
Duration: 3FT Hon

Entry Requirements: *GCE:* 220-360. *BTEC NC:* DM. *BTEC ND:* MMM. *OCR ND:* Distinction. *OCR NED:* Merit.

NM19 BA Business Management and Criminology
Duration: 3FT Hon

Entry Requirements: *GCE:* 220-360. *IB:* 31. *BTEC NC:* DM. *BTEC ND:* MMM. *OCR ND:* Distinction. *OCR NED:* Merit.

N1M9 BA Business Management with Criminology
Duration: 3FT Hon

Entry Requirements: *GCE:* 220-360. *IB:* 31. *BTEC NC:* DM. *BTEC ND:* MMM. *OCR ND:* Distinction. *OCR NED:* Merit.

M930 BA Criminology
Duration: 3FT Hon

Entry Requirements: *GCE:* 220-360. *SQAH:* AAAA-CCCC. *BTEC NC:* DM. *BTEC ND:* MMM.

MN91 BA Criminology and Business Management
Duration: 3FT Hon

Entry Requirements: *GCE:* 220-360. *BTEC NC:* DM. *BTEC ND:* MMM. *OCR ND:* Distinction. *OCR NED:* Merit.

GM49 BA Criminology and Computing
Duration: 3FT Hon

Entry Requirements: *GCE:* 220-360. *BTEC NC:* DM. *BTEC ND:* MMM. *OCR ND:* Distinction. *OCR NED:* Merit.

MX93 BA Criminology and Education
Duration: 3FT Hon

Entry Requirements: *GCE:* 220-360. *BTEC NC:* DM. *BTEC ND:* MMM. *OCR ND:* Distinction. *OCR NED:* Merit.

MQ91 BA Criminology and English Language/Linguistics
Duration: 3FT Hon

Entry Requirements: *GCE:* 220-360. *BTEC NC:* DM. *BTEC ND:* MMM. *OCR ND:* Distinction. *OCR NED:* Merit.

MQ93 BA Criminology and English Studies
Duration: 3FT Hon

Entry Requirements: *GCE:* 220-360. *BTEC NC:* DM. *BTEC ND:* MMM. *OCR ND:* Distinction. *OCR NED:* Merit.

FM8Y BA Criminology and Geography
Duration: 3FT Hon

Entry Requirements: *GCE:* 220-360. *IB:* 31. *BTEC NC:* DM. *BTEC ND:* MMM. *OCR ND:* Distinction. *OCR NED:* Merit.

MV9C BA Criminology and History
Duration: 3FT Hon

Entry Requirements: *GCE:* 220-360. *BTEC NC:* DM. *BTEC ND:* MMM. *OCR ND:* Distinction. *OCR NED:* Merit.

MQ9H BA Criminology and Modern Foreign Language (English)
Duration: 3FT Hon

Entry Requirements: *GCE:* 220-360. *BTEC NC:* DM. *BTEC ND:* MMM. *OCR ND:* Distinction. *OCR NED:* Merit.

LM29 BA Criminology and Politics
Duration: 3FT Hon

Entry Requirements: *GCE:* 220-360. *BTEC NC:* DM. *BTEC ND:* MMM. *OCR ND:* Distinction. *OCR NED:* Merit.

CM89 BA Criminology and Psychology
Duration: 3FT Hon

Entry Requirements: *GCE:* 220-360. *BTEC NC:* DM. *BTEC ND:* MMM. *OCR ND:* Distinction. *OCR NED:* Merit.

MP92 BA Criminology and Public Relations
Duration: 3FT Hon

Entry Requirements: *GCE:* 220-360. *BTEC NC:* DM. *BTEC ND:* MMM. *OCR ND:* Distinction. *OCR NED:* Merit.

LM39 BA Criminology and Sociology
Duration: 3FT Hon

Entry Requirements: *GCE:* 220-360. *BTEC NC:* DM. *BTEC ND:* MMM. *OCR ND:* Distinction. *OCR NED:* Merit.

MX91 BA Criminology and TESOL
Duration: 3FT Hon

Entry Requirements: *GCE:* 220-360. *BTEC NC:* DM. *BTEC ND:* MMM. *OCR ND:* Distinction. *OCR NED:* Merit.

M9T7 BA Criminology with American Studies
Duration: 3FT Hon

Entry Requirements: *GCE:* 220-360. *BTEC NC:* DM. *BTEC ND:* MMM. *OCR ND:* Distinction. *OCR NED:* Merit.

M9N1 BA Criminology with Business Management
Duration: 3FT Hon

Entry Requirements: *GCE:* 220-360. *BTEC NC:* DM. *BTEC ND:* MMM. *OCR ND:* Distinction. *OCR NED:* Merit.

M9G4 BA Criminology with Computing
Duration: 3FT Hon

Entry Requirements: *GCE:* 220-360. *BTEC NC:* DM. *BTEC ND:* MMM. *OCR ND:* Distinction. *OCR NED:* Merit.

M9Q1 BA Criminology with English Language/Linguistics
Duration: 3FT Hon

Entry Requirements: *GCE:* 220-360. *BTEC NC:* DM. *BTEC ND:* MMM. *OCR ND:* Distinction. *OCR NED:* Merit.

M9QH BA Criminology with English Studies
Duration: 3FT Hon

Entry Requirements: *GCE:* 220-360. *BTEC NC:* DM. *BTEC ND:* MMM. *OCR ND:* Distinction. *OCR NED:* Merit.

M9N3 BA Criminology with Financial Management
Duration: 3FT Hon

Entry Requirements: *GCE:* 220-360. *BTEC NC:* DM. *BTEC ND:* MMM. *OCR ND:* Distinction. *OCR NED:* Merit.

M9L7 BA Criminology with Geography
Duration: 3FT Hon

Entry Requirements: *GCE:* 220-360. *IB:* 31. *BTEC NC:* DM. *BTEC ND:* MMM. *OCR ND:* Distinction. *OCR NED:* Merit.

M9V1 BA Criminology with History
Duration: 3FT Hon

Entry Requirements: *GCE:* 220-360. *BTEC NC:* DM. *BTEC ND:* MMM. *OCR ND:* Distinction. *OCR NED:* Merit.

M9NP BA Criminology with Human Resource Management
Duration: 3FT Hon

Entry Requirements: *GCE:* 220-360. *BTEC NC:* DM. *BTEC ND:* MMM. *OCR ND:* Distinction. *OCR NED:* Merit.

M9P5 BA Criminology with Journalism
Duration: 3FT Hon

Entry Requirements: *GCE:* 220-360. *BTEC NC:* DM. *BTEC ND:* MMM. *OCR ND:* Distinction. *OCR NED:* Merit.

M9N5 BA Criminology with Marketing Management
Duration: 3FT Hon

Entry Requirements: *GCE:* 220-360. *BTEC NC:* DM. *BTEC ND:* MMM. *OCR ND:* Distinction. *OCR NED:* Merit.

M9P3 BA Criminology with Media Studies
Duration: 3FT Hon

Entry Requirements: *GCE:* 220-360. *BTEC NC:* DM. *BTEC ND:* MMM. *OCR ND:* Distinction. *OCR NED:* Merit.

M9R1 BA Criminology with MFL (French)
Duration: 3FT Hon

Entry Requirements: *GCE:* 220-360. *BTEC NC:* DM. *BTEC ND:* MMM. *OCR ND:* Distinction. *OCR NED:* Merit.

M9R2 BA Criminology with MFL (German)
Duration: 3FT Hon

Entry Requirements: *GCE:* 220-360. *BTEC NC:* DM. *BTEC ND:* MMM. *OCR ND:* Distinction. *OCR NED:* Merit.

M9R4 BA Criminology with MFL (Spanish)
Duration: 3FT Hon

Entry Requirements: *GCE:* 220-360. *BTEC NC:* DM. *BTEC ND:* MMM. *OCR ND:* Distinction. *OCR NED:* Merit.

M9QJ BA Criminology with Modern Foreign Languages (English)
Duration: 3FT Hon

Entry Requirements: *GCE:* 220-360. *BTEC NC:* DM. *BTEC ND:* MMM. *OCR ND:* Distinction. *OCR NED:* Merit.

M9W3 BA Criminology with Music
Duration: 3FT Hon

Entry Requirements: *GCE:* 220-360. *IB:* 31. *BTEC NC:* DM. *BTEC ND:* MMM. *OCR ND:* Distinction. *OCR NED:* Merit.

M9W6 BA Criminology with Photography
Duration: 3FT Hon

Entry Requirements: *GCE:* 220-360. *BTEC NC:* DM. *BTEC ND:* MMM. *OCR ND:* Distinction. *OCR NED:* Merit.

M9L2 BA Criminology with Politics
Duration: 3FT Hon

Entry Requirements: *GCE:* 220-360. *BTEC NC:* DM. *BTEC ND:* MMM. *OCR ND:* Distinction. *OCR NED:* Merit.

M9L3 BA Criminology with Sociology

Duration: 3FT Hon

Entry Requirements: *GCE:* 220-360. *BTEC NC:* DM. *BTEC ND:* MMM. *OCR ND:* Distinction. *OCR NED:* Merit.

M9X1 BA Criminology with TESOL

Duration: 3FT Hon

Entry Requirements: *GCE:* 220-360. *BTEC NC:* DM. *BTEC ND:* MMM. *OCR ND:* Distinction. *OCR NED:* Merit.

Q1M9 BA English Language & Linguistics with Criminology

Duration: 3FT Hon

Entry Requirements: *GCE:* 220-360. *BTEC NC:* DM. *BTEC ND:* MMM. *OCR ND:* Distinction. *OCR NED:* Merit.

Q3M9 BA English Studies with Criminology

Duration: 3FT Hon

Entry Requirements: *GCE:* 220-360. *IB:* 31. *BTEC NC:* DM. *BTEC ND:* MMM. *OCR ND:* Distinction. *OCR NED:* Merit.

N3M9 BA Financial Management with Criminology

Duration: 3FT Hon

Entry Requirements: *GCE:* 220-360. *BTEC NC:* DM. *BTEC ND:* MMM. *OCR ND:* Distinction. *OCR NED:* Merit.

L7M9 BA Geography with Criminology

Duration: 3FT Hon

Entry Requirements: *GCE:* 220-360. *IB:* 31. *BTEC NC:* DM. *BTEC ND:* MMM. *OCR ND:* Distinction. *OCR NED:* Merit.

V1M9 BA History with Criminology

Duration: 3FT Hon

Entry Requirements: *GCE:* 220-360. *IB:* 31. *BTEC NC:* DM. *BTEC ND:* MMM. *OCR ND:* Distinction. *OCR NED:* Merit.

MN96 BA Human Resource Management and Criminology

Duration: 3FT Hon

Entry Requirements: *GCE:* 220-360. *BTEC NC:* DM. *BTEC ND:* MMM. *OCR ND:* Distinction. *OCR NED:* Merit.

P5M9 BA Journalism with Criminology

Duration: 3FT Hon

Entry Requirements: *GCE:* 220-360. *IB:* 32. *BTEC NC:* DM. *BTEC ND:* MMM. *OCR ND:* Distinction. *OCR NED:* Merit.

MM19 BA Law and Criminology

Duration: 3FT Hon

Entry Requirements: *GCE:* 220-360. *BTEC NC:* DM. *BTEC ND:* MMM. *OCR ND:* Distinction. *OCR NED:* Merit.

M1M9 BA Law with Criminology

Duration: 3FT Hon

Entry Requirements: *GCE:* 220-360. *BTEC NC:* DM. *BTEC ND:* MMM. *OCR ND:* Distinction. *OCR NED:* Merit.

NM59 BA Marketing Management and Criminology

Duration: 3FT Hon

Entry Requirements: *GCE:* 220-360. *BTEC NC:* DM. *BTEC ND:* MMM. *OCR ND:* Distinction. *OCR NED:* Merit.

N5M9 BA Marketing Management with Criminology

Duration: 3FT Hon

Entry Requirements: *GCE:* 220-360. *BTEC NC:* DM. *BTEC ND:* MMM. *OCR ND:* Distinction. *OCR NED:* Merit.

P3M9 BA Media Studies with Criminology

Duration: 3FT Hon

Entry Requirements: *GCE:* 220-360. *IB:* 32. *BTEC NC:* DM. *BTEC ND:* MMM. *OCR ND:* Distinction. *OCR NED:* Merit.

MR91 BA Modern Foreign Languages (French) and Criminology

Duration: 3FT Hon

Entry Requirements: *GCE:* 220-360. *IB:* 31. *BTEC NC:* DM. *BTEC ND:* MMM. *OCR ND:* Distinction. *OCR NED:* Merit.

MR94 BA Modern Foreign Languages (Spanish) and Criminology

Duration: 3FT Hon

Entry Requirements: *GCE:* 220-360. *IB:* 31. *BTEC NC:* DM. *BTEC ND:* MMM. *OCR ND:* Distinction. *OCR NED:* Merit.

L2M9 BA Politics with Criminology

Duration: 3FT Hon

Entry Requirements: *GCE:* 220-360. *IB:* 31. *BTEC NC:* DM. *BTEC ND:* MMM. *OCR ND:* Distinction. *OCR NED:* Merit.

PM29 BA Public Relations and Criminology

Duration: 3FT Hon

Entry Requirements: *GCE:* 220-360. *BTEC NC:* DM. *BTEC ND:* MMM. *OCR ND:* Distinction. *OCR NED:* Merit.

L3M9 BA Sociology with Criminology

Duration: 3FT Hon

Entry Requirements: *GCE:* 220-360. *IB:* 31. *BTEC NC:* DM. *BTEC ND:* MMM. *OCR ND:* Distinction. *OCR NED:* Merit.

X1M9 BA TESOL with Criminology

Duration: 3FT Hon

Entry Requirements: *GCE:* 220-360. *BTEC NC:* DM. *BTEC ND:* MMM. *OCR ND:* Distinction. *OCR NED:* Merit.

NM89 BA Tourism and Criminology

Duration: 3FT Hon

Entry Requirements: *GCE:* 220-360. *IB:* 31. *BTEC NC:* DM. *BTEC ND:* MMM. *OCR ND:* Distinction. *OCR NED:* Merit.

N8M9 BA Tourism with Criminology

Duration: 3FT Hon

Entry Requirements: *GCE:* 220-360. *IB:* 31. *BTEC NC:* DM. *BTEC ND:* MMM. *OCR ND:* Distinction. *OCR NED:* Merit.

MN98 BA/BSc Criminology and Tourism

Duration: 3FT Hon

Entry Requirements: *GCE:* 220-360. *BTEC NC:* DM. *BTEC ND:* MMM. *OCR ND:* Distinction. *OCR NED:* Merit.

M9B9 BA/BSc Criminology with Community Health

Duration: 3FT Hon

Entry Requirements: *GCE:* 220-360. *BTEC NC:* DM. *BTEC ND:* MMM. *OCR ND:* Distinction. *OCR NED:* Merit.

CM69 BA/BSc Sport and Criminology

Duration: 3FT Hon

Entry Requirements: *GCE:* 220-360. *BTEC NC:* DM. *BTEC ND:* MMM. *OCR ND:* Distinction. *OCR NED:* Merit.

B9M9 BSc Community Health with Criminology

Duration: 3FT Hon

Entry Requirements: *GCE:* 220-360. *IB:* 31. *BTEC NC:* DM. *BTEC ND:* MMM. *OCR ND:* Distinction. *OCR NED:* Merit.

G4M9 BSc Computing with Criminology

Duration: 3FT Hon

Entry Requirements: *GCE:* 220-360. *IB:* 31. *BTEC NC:* DM. *BTEC ND:* MMM. *OCR ND:* Distinction. *OCR NED:* Merit.

C6M9 BSc Sport with Criminology

Duration: 3FT Hon

Entry Requirements: *GCE:* 220-360. *BTEC NC:* DM. *BTEC ND:* MMM. *OCR ND:* Distinction. *OCR NED:* Merit.

S85 UNIVERSITY OF SURREY

STAG HILL
GUILDFORD
SURREY GU2 7XH

t: +44(0)1483 689305 f: +44(0)1483 689388
e: admissions@surrey.ac.uk
// www.surrey.ac.uk

M1M9 LLB Law with Criminology

Duration: 3FT/4SW Hon

Entry Requirements: *GCE:* ABB.

LM39 BSc Criminology and Sociology (3 years)

Duration: 3FT Hon

Entry Requirements: *GCE:* 300.

ML93 BSc Criminology and Sociology (4 years)

Duration: 4SW Hon

Entry Requirements: *GCE:* 300.

S93 SWANSEA UNIVERSITY

SINGLETON PARK
SWANSEA SA2 8PP

t: 01792 295111 f: 01792 295110
e: admissions@swansea.ac.uk
// www.swansea.ac.uk

MM19 LLB Law and Criminology

Duration: 3FT Hon

Entry Requirements: *GCE:* 280-300. *IB:* 25.

MLF4 BSc Criminology and Social Policy

Duration: 3FT Hon

Entry Requirements: *GCE:* 280.

T20 UNIVERSITY OF TEESSIDE

MIDDLESBROUGH TS1 3BA

t: 01642 218121 f: 01642 384201
e: registry@tees.ac.uk
// www.tees.ac.uk

M1M2 LLB Law with Criminology

Duration: 3FT Hon

Entry Requirements: *GCE:* 240.

FM49 BSc Crime and Investigation

Duration: 3FT Hon

Entry Requirements: *GCE:* 240.

BF14 BSc Crime Scene Science

Duration: 3FT/4SW Hon

Entry Requirements: *GCE:* 280. *IB:* 30. *BTEC NC:* DD. *BTEC ND:* DMM. Interview required.

M980 BSc Criminology

Duration: 3FT Hon

Entry Requirements: *GCE:* 240.

LM39 BSc Criminology and Sociology

Duration: 3FT Hon

Entry Requirements: *GCE:* 240.

M2M1 BSc Criminology with Law

Duration: 3FT Hon

Entry Requirements: *GCE:* 240.

CM89 BSc Psychology and Criminology

Duration: 3FT Hon

Entry Requirements: *GCE:* 240-260.

L5M9 BSc Youth Studies with Criminology

Duration: 3FT Hon

Entry Requirements: *GCE:* 200-220.

T40 THAMES VALLEY UNIVERSITY

ST MARY'S ROAD
EALING
LONDON W5 5RF

t: 0800 036 8888 **f:** 020 8566 1353
e: learning.advice@tvu.ac.uk

// www.tvu.ac.uk

M2M1 BA Criminology with Law

Duration: 3FT Hon

Entry Requirements: *GCE:* 200. *IB:* 28. Interview required.

M2B2 BA Criminology with Substance Use & Misuse

Duration: 3FT Hon

Entry Requirements: *GCE:* 200. *IB:* 28. Interview required.

U20 UNIVERSITY OF ULSTER

COLERAINE
CO. LONDONDERRY
NORTHERN IRELAND BT52 1SA

t: 028 7032 4221 **f:** 028 7032 4908
e: online@ulster.ac.uk

// www.ulster.ac.uk

M1M9 LLB Law with Criminology

Duration: 3FT Hon

Entry Requirements: *GCE:* ABB. *SQAH:* AAABC. *SQAAH:* ABB. *IB:* 26. *BTEC ND:* DDM.

M931 BSc Criminology and Criminal Justice

Duration: 3FT Hon

Entry Requirements: *GCE:* 300. *IB:* 25. *BTEC ND:* DDM.

L2M9 BSc Politics with Criminology

Duration: 3FT Hon

Entry Requirements: *GCE:* 240. *IB:* 24. *BTEC NC:* MM. *BTEC ND:* MMM.

L4M9 BSc Social Policy with Criminology

Duration: 3FT Hon

Entry Requirements: *GCE:* 240. *IB:* 24. *BTEC NC:* MM. *BTEC ND:* MMM.

L3M9 BSc Sociology with Criminology

Duration: 3FT Hon

Entry Requirements: *GCE:* 260. *IB:* 24. *BTEC NC:* MM. *BTEC ND:* DMM.

W75 UNIVERSITY OF WOLVERHAMPTON

ADMISSIONS UNIT
MX207, CAMP STREET
WOLVERHAMPTON
WEST MIDLANDS WV1 1AD

t: 01902 321000 **f:** 01902 321896
e: admissions@wlv.ac.uk

// www.wlv.ac.uk

MM92 BA(HONS) Criminology and Criminal Justice

Duration: 3FT Hon

Entry Requirements: Contact the institution for details.

ECONOMICS, ACCOUNTING & FINANCE COMBINATIONS

A40 ABERYSTWYTH UNIVERSITY

WELCOME CENTRE, ABERYSTWYTH UNIVERSITY
PENGLAIS CAMPUS
ABERYSTWYTH
CEREDIGION SY23 3FB

t: 01970 622021 **f:** 01970 627410
e: ug-admissions@aber.ac.uk

// www.aber.ac.uk

L1M1 BScEcon Economics with Law

Duration: 3FT Hon

Entry Requirements: *GCE:* 280. *IB:* 27.

B22 UNIVERSITY OF BEDFORDSHIRE

PARK SQUARE
LUTON
BEDS LU1 3JU

t: 01582 489286 **f:** 01582 489323
e: admissions@beds.ac.uk

// www.beds.ac.uk

N3M1 BA Accounting and Law

Duration: 3FT Hon

Entry Requirements: Interview required.

B44 THE UNIVERSITY OF BOLTON

DEANE ROAD
BOLTON BL3 5AB

t: 01204 900600 f: 01204 399074
e: enquiries@bolton.ac.uk

// www.bolton.ac.uk

M1N4 LLB LLB Law with Accountancy

Duration: 3FT Hon

Entry Requirements: *GCE:* 240. *IB:* 24. *BTEC ND:* MMM.

NM41 BA Accountancy and Law

Duration: 3FT Hon

Entry Requirements: *GCE:* 220. *IB:* 20. *BTEC NC:* DD. *BTEC ND:* MMM.

B50 BOURNEMOUTH UNIVERSITY

TALBOT CAMPUS
FERN BARROW
POOLE
DORSET BH12 5BB

t: 01202 524111

// www.bournemouth.ac.uk

NM41 BA Accounting and Law

Duration: 3FT Hon

Entry Requirements: *GCE:* 260.

B60 BRADFORD COLLEGE: AN ASSOCIATE COLLEGE OF LEEDS METROPOLITAN UNIVERSITY

GREAT HORTON ROAD
BRADFORD
WEST YORKSHIRE BD7 1AY

t: 01274 433333 f: 01274 433241
e: admissions@bradfordcollege.ac.uk

// www.bradfordcollege.ac.uk

NM41 BA Accountancy and Law

Duration: 3FT Hon

Entry Requirements: *GCE:* 100-140. *BTEC NC:* MM. *BTEC ND:* MPP.

B90 THE UNIVERSITY OF BUCKINGHAM

YEOMANRY HOUSE
HUNTER STREET
BUCKINGHAM MK18 1EG

t: 01280 820313 f: 01280 822245
e: info@buckingham.ac.uk

// www.buckingham.ac.uk

M1N3 LLB Law with Business Finance

Duration: 2FT Hon

Entry Requirements: *GCE:* 300. *IB:* 28. *BTEC NC:* DD. *BTEC ND:* DMM.

M1L1 LLB Law with Economics

Duration: 2FT Hon

Entry Requirements: *GCE:* 300. *IB:* 28. *BTEC NC:* DD. *BTEC ND:* DMM.

C30 UNIVERSITY OF CENTRAL LANCASHIRE

PRESTON
LANCS PR1 2HE

t: 01772 201201 f: 01772 894954
e: uadmissions@uclan.ac.uk

// www.uclan.ac.uk

MN14 BA Accounting and Law

Duration: 3FT Hon

Entry Requirements: *GCE:* 220. *IB:* 26. *BTEC NC:* DM. *BTEC ND:* MMP.

C55 UNIVERSITY OF CHESTER

PARKGATE ROAD
CHESTER CH1 4BJ

t: 01244 511000 f: 01244 511300
e: enquiries@chester.ac.uk

// www.chester.ac.uk

N4M1 BA Accounting & Finance with Law

Duration: 3FT Hon

Entry Requirements: *GCE:* 240. *SQAH:* BBBB. *IB:* 24. *BTEC NC:* DM. *BTEC ND:* MMM.

M1N4 BA Law with Accounting & Finance

Duration: 3FT Hon

Entry Requirements: *GCE:* 240. *SQAH:* BBBB. *IB:* 24. *BTEC NC:* DM. *BTEC ND:* MMM.

M1L1 BA Law with Economics

Duration: 3FT Hon

Entry Requirements: *GCE:* 240. *SQAH:* BBBB. *IB:* 24. *BTEC NC:* DM. *BTEC ND:* MMM.

L1M1 BSc Economics with Law

Duration: 3FT Hon

Entry Requirements: *GCE:* 240. *SQAH:* BBBB. *IB:* 24. *BTEC NC:* DM. *BTEC ND:* MMM.

D39 UNIVERSITY OF DERBY

KEDLESTON ROAD
DERBY DE22 1GB

t: 08701 202330 f: 01332 597724
e: askadmissions@derby.ac.uk

// www.derby.ac.uk

MN1K BA Accounting and Law

Duration: 3FT Hon

Entry Requirements: *Foundation:* Merit. *GCE:* 180-240. *IB:* 26.
BTEC NC: DM. *BTEC ND:* MMP.

E14 UNIVERSITY OF EAST ANGLIA

NORWICH NR4 7TJ

t: 01603 456161 f: 01603 458596
e: admissions@uea.ac.uk

// www.uea.ac.uk

N4M1 BSc Accounting with Law

Duration: 3FT Hon

Entry Requirements: *GCE:* 280. *IB:* 30. *BTEC ND:* DMM.

E28 UNIVERSITY OF EAST LONDON

DOCKLANDS CAMPUS
UNIVERSITY WAY
LONDON E16 2RD

t: 020 8223 2835 f: 020 8223 2978
e: admiss@uel.ac.uk

// www.uel.ac.uk

M1NK BA Law with Accounting

Duration: 3FT Hon

Entry Requirements: *GCE:* 240. *IB:* 28. *BTEC NC:* DD. *BTEC ND:*
MMM.

E56 THE UNIVERSITY OF EDINBURGH

STUDENT RECRUITMENT & ADMISSIONS
57 GEORGE SQUARE
EDINBURGH EH8 9JU

t: 0131 650 4360 f: 0131 651 1236
e: sra.enquiries@ed.ac.uk

// www.ed.ac.uk/studying/undergraduate/

MN14 LLB Law and Accountancy

Duration: 4FT Hon

Entry Requirements: *GCE:* BBB. *SQAH:* BBBB. *IB:* 34.

ML11 LLB Law and Economics

Duration: 4FT Hon

Entry Requirements: *GCE:* BBB. *SQAH:* BBBB. *IB:* 34.

LM11 MA Economics and Law

Duration: 4FT Hon

Entry Requirements: *GCE:* BBB. *SQAH:* BBBB. *IB:* 34.

E59 EDINBURGH NAPIER UNIVERSITY

CRAIGLOCKHART CAMPUS
EDINBURGH EH14 1DJ

t: +44 (0)8452 60 60 40 f: 0131 455 6464
e: info@napier.ac.uk

// www.napier.ac.uk

N4M1 BA Accounting with Law

Duration: 3FT/4FT Ord/Hon

Entry Requirements: *GCE:* 240.

G14 UNIVERSITY OF GLAMORGAN, CARDIFF AND PONTYPRIDD

ENQUIRIES AND ADMISSIONS UNIT
PONTYPRIDD CF37 1DL

t: 0800 716925 f: 01443 654050
e: enquiries@glam.ac.uk

// www.glam.ac.uk

MN14 BA Accounting and Law

Duration: 3FT Hon

Entry Requirements: *GCE:* 220-260. *BTEC NC:* DD. *BTEC ND:* MMM.
Interview required.

N4M1 BA Accounting with Law

Duration: 3FT Hon

Entry Requirements: *GCE:* 220-260. *BTEC NC:* DD. *BTEC ND:* MMM.
Interview required.

G28 UNIVERSITY OF GLASGOW

THE UNIVERSITY OF GLASGOW
THE FRASER BUILDING
65 HILLHEAD STREET
GLASGOW G12 8QF

t: 0141 330 6062 f: 0141 330 2961
e: ugenquiries@gla.ac.uk (UK/EU undergrad
enquiries only)

// www.glasgow.ac.uk

MN11 LLB Law/Business Economics

Duration: 4FT Hon

Entry Requirements: *GCE:* AAB. *SQAH:* AAAAB. *IB:* 34. Admissions
Test required.

MV13 LLB Law/Economic and Social History

Duration: 4FT Hon

Entry Requirements: *GCE:* AAB. *SQAH:* AAAAB. *IB:* 34. Admissions
Test required.

ML11 LLB Law/Economics

Duration: 4FT Hon

Entry Requirements: *GCE:* AAB. *SQAH:* AAAAB. *IB:* 34. Admissions Test required.

G70 UNIVERSITY OF GREENWICH

GREENWICH CAMPUS
OLD ROYAL NAVAL COLLEGE
PARK ROW
LONDON SE10 9LS

t: 0800 005 006 f: 020 8331 8145
e: courseinfo@gre.ac.uk

// www.gre.ac.uk

ML11 BA Law and Economics

Duration: 3FT Hon

Entry Requirements: *GCE:* 180. *IB:* 24.

H36 UNIVERSITY OF HERTFORDSHIRE

UNIVERSITY ADMISSIONS SERVICE
COLLEGE LANE
HATFIELD
HERTS AL10 9AB

t: 01707 284800 f: 01707 284870

// www.herts.ac.uk

L1M1 BSc Economics/Law

Duration: 3FT Hon

Entry Requirements: *GCE:* 260.

H60 THE UNIVERSITY OF HUDDERSFIELD

QUEENSGATE
HUDDERSFIELD HD1 3DH

t: 01484 473969 f: 01484 472765
e: admissionsandrecords@hud.ac.uk

// www.hud.ac.uk

MN14 BA Law and Accountancy

Duration: 3FT/4SW Hon

Entry Requirements: *GCE:* 280. *SQAH:* BBCC. *IB:* 28.

K12 KEELE UNIVERSITY

STAFFS ST5 5BG

t: 01782 734005 f: 01782 632343
e: undergraduate@keele.ac.uk

// www.keele.ac.uk

NM41 BA Accounting and Law

Duration: 3FT Hon

Entry Requirements: *GCE:* 300-320.

L23 UNIVERSITY OF LEEDS

THE UNIVERSITY OF LEEDS
LEEDS LS2 9JT

t: 0113 343 3999
e: admissions@adm.leeds.ac.uk

// www.leeds.ac.uk

MN14 BA Accounting and Law

Duration: 4FT Hon

Entry Requirements: *GCE:* AAB. *SQAAH:* AAB. *IB:* 37.

L34 UNIVERSITY OF LEICESTER

UNIVERSITY ROAD
LEICESTER LE1 7RH

t: 0116 252 5281 f: 0116 252 2447
e: admissions@le.ac.uk

// www.le.ac.uk

LM11 BA Economics and Law

Duration: 3FT Hon

Entry Requirements: *GCE:* ABB. *SQAH:* AABBB. *SQAAH:* ABB. *IB:* 32. *BTEC ND:* DDM.

L68 LONDON METROPOLITAN UNIVERSITY

166-220 HOLLOWAY ROAD
LONDON N7 8DB

t: 020 7133 4200
e: admissions@londonmet.ac.uk

// www.londonmet.ac.uk

LM1C BA Economics and Law

Duration: 3FT Hon

Entry Requirements: *GCE:* 240. *IB:* 28.

LM1D BA/BSc Economics and International Law & International Politics

Duration: 3FT Hon

Entry Requirements: *GCE:* 240. *IB:* 28.

LM11 BA/BSc Financial Economics and Law

Duration: 3FT Hon

Entry Requirements: *GCE:* 240. *IB:* 28.

L75 LONDON SOUTH BANK UNIVERSITY

103 BOROUGH ROAD
LONDON SE1 0AA

t: 020 7815 7815 f: 020 7815 8273
e: enquiry@lsbu.ac.uk

// www.lsbu.ac.uk

N4M1 BA Accounting with Law

Duration: 3FT Hon

Entry Requirements: *GCE:* 240. *IB:* 24.

N37 UNIVERSITY OF WALES, NEWPORT

CAERLEON CAMPUS
PO BOX 101
NEWPORT
SOUTH WALES NP18 3YH
t: 01633 432030 f: 01633 432850
e: admissions@newport.ac.uk
// www.newport.ac.uk

LM11 BSc Economics and Law

Duration: 3FT Hon

Entry Requirements: *GCE:* 240. *IB:* 24.

N38 UNIVERSITY OF NORTHAMPTON

PARK CAMPUS
BOUGHTON GREEN ROAD
NORTHAMPTON NN2 7AL
t: 0800 358 2232 f: 01604 722083
e: admissions@northampton.ac.uk
// www.northampton.ac.uk

L1M1 BA Economics/Law

Duration: 3FT Hon

Entry Requirements: *GCE:* 220-260. *SQAH:* AAB-BBBB. *IB:* 24.

M1N4 BA Law/Accounting

Duration: 3FT Hon

Entry Requirements: *GCE:* 220-260. *SQAH:* AAB-BBBB. *IB:* 24.

S03 THE UNIVERSITY OF SALFORD

SALFORD M5 4WT
t: 0161 295 4545 f: 0161 295 3126
e: ugadmissions-exrel@salford.ac.uk
// www.salford.ac.uk

M1N3 LLB Law with Finance

Duration: 3FT Hon

Entry Requirements: *GCE:* 300. *IB:* 29. *BTEC ND:* DMM. *OCR NED:*
Merit. Interview required.

S72 STAFFORDSHIRE UNIVERSITY

COLLEGE ROAD
STOKE ON TRENT ST4 2DE
t: 01782 292753 f: 01782 292740
e: admissions@staffs.ac.uk
// www.staffs.ac.uk

M1N4 LLB LLB with Accounting

Duration: 3FT Hon

Entry Requirements: *GCE:* BB-ABB. *SQAAH:* BB-ABB. *IB:* 26. *BTEC
NC:* DM. *BTEC ND:* DDM. *OCR ND:* Distinction.

S75 THE UNIVERSITY OF STIRLING

STIRLING FK9 4LA
t: 01786 467044 f: 01786 466800
e: admissions@stir.ac.uk
// www.stir.ac.uk

MN13 BA Finance and Law

Duration: 4FT Hon

Entry Requirements: *GCE:* CCC. *SQAH:* BBBB. *SQAAH:* AAA-CCC.
BTEC ND: DMM.

S78 THE UNIVERSITY OF STRATHCLYDE

GLASGOW G1 1XQ
t: 0141 552 4400 f: 0141 552 0775
// www.strath.ac.uk

LM11 BA Economics and Law

Duration: 4FT Hon

Entry Requirements: *GCE:* BBC. *SQAH:* ABBB-BBBBC. *IB:* 30.

S84 UNIVERSITY OF SUNDERLAND

STUDENT HELPLINE
THE STUDENT GATEWAY
CHESTER ROAD
SUNDERLAND SR1 3SD
t: 0191 515 3000 f: 0191 515 3805
e: student-helpline@sunderland.ac.uk
// www.sunderland.ac.uk

NM31 BA Financial Management and Law

Duration: 3FT Hon

Entry Requirements: *GCE:* 220-360. *BTEC NC:* DM. *BTEC ND:* MMM.
OCR ND: Distinction. *OCR NED:* Merit.

N3M1 BA Financial Management with Law

Duration: 3FT Hon

Entry Requirements: *GCE:* 220-360. *BTEC NC:* DM. *BTEC ND:* MMM.
OCR ND: Distinction. *OCR NED:* Merit.

U20 UNIVERSITY OF ULSTER

COLERAINE
CO. LONDONDERRY
NORTHERN IRELAND BT52 1SA

t: 028 7032 4221 **f:** 028 7032 4908
e: online@ulster.ac.uk

// www.ulster.ac.uk

M1N4 LLB Law with Accounting

Duration: 3FT Hon

Entry Requirements: *GCE:* ABB. *SQAH:* AAABC. *SQAAH:* ABB. *IB:* 26.
BTEC ND: DDM.

W75 UNIVERSITY OF WOLVERHAMPTON

ADMISSIONS UNIT
MX207, CAMP STREET
WOLVERHAMPTON
WEST MIDLANDS WV1 1AD

t: 01902 321000 **f:** 01902 321896
e: admissions@wlv.ac.uk

// www.wlv.ac.uk

M221 LLB Corporate and Financial Law

Duration: 3FT Hon

Entry Requirements: *GCE:* 240-280.

MN1L BA Accounting and Law

Duration: 3FT Hon

Entry Requirements: HND required.

W76 UNIVERSITY OF WINCHESTER

WINCHESTER
HANTS SO22 4NR

t: 01962 827234 **f:** 01962 827288
e: course.enquiries@winchester.ac.uk

// www.winchester.ac.uk

NM4C DipHE Accounting and Law

Duration: 2FT Dip

Entry Requirements: *Foundation:* Pass. *GCE:* 120. *IB:* 20. *BTEC NC:*
MP. *BTEC ND:* PPP.

EUROPEAN LAW

A20 THE UNIVERSITY OF ABERDEEN

UNIVERSITY OFFICE
KING'S COLLEGE
ABERDEEN AB24 3FX

t: +44 (0) 1224 273504 **f:** +44 (0) 1224 272034
e: sras@abdn.ac.uk

// www.abdn.ac.uk/sras

M120 LLB Law with Belgian Law

Duration: 4FT/5FT Ord/Hon

Entry Requirements: *GCE:* BBB. *SQAH:* ABBBB-AABB. *SQAAH:* BBB.
IB: 34.

M121 LLB Law with French Law

Duration: 4FT/5FT Ord/Hon

Entry Requirements: *GCE:* BBB. *SQAH:* ABBBB-AABB. *SQAAH:* BBB.
IB: 34.

M123 LLB Law with German Law

Duration: 4FT/5FT Ord/Hon

Entry Requirements: *GCE:* BBB. *SQAH:* ABBBB-AABB. *SQAAH:* BBB.
IB: 34.

M126 LLB Law with Spanish Law

Duration: 4FT/5FT Ord/Hon

Entry Requirements: *GCE:* BBB. *SQAH:* ABBBB-AABB. *SQAAH:* BBB.
IB: 34.

A30 UNIVERSITY OF ABERTAY DUNDEE

BELL STREET
DUNDEE DD1 1HG

t: 01382 308080 **f:** 01382 308081
e: sro@abertay.ac.uk

// www.abertay.ac.uk

M120 BA European Business Law

Duration: 2FT Hon

Entry Requirements: HND required.

A40 ABERYSTWYTH UNIVERSITY

WELCOME CENTRE, ABERYSTWYTH UNIVERSITY
PENGLAIS CAMPUS
ABERYSTWYTH
CEREDIGION SY23 3FB

t: 01970 622021 **f:** 01970 627410
e: ug-admissions@aber.ac.uk

// www.aber.ac.uk

M120 LLB European Law

Duration: 3FT Hon

Entry Requirements: *GCE:* 280. *IB:* 27.

B80 UNIVERSITY OF THE WEST OF ENGLAND, BRISTOL

FRENCHAY CAMPUS
COLDHARBOUR LANE
BRISTOL BS16 1QY

t: +44 (0)117 32 83333 **f:** +44 (0)117 32 82810
e: admissions@uwe.ac.uk

// www.uwe.ac.uk

M121 LLB LLB (European and International)
Duration: 3FT Hon

Entry Requirements: *GCE:* 300-340.

E14 UNIVERSITY OF EAST ANGLIA
NORWICH NR4 7TJ

t: 01603 456161 **f:** 01603 458596
e: admissions@uea.ac.uk

// www.uea.ac.uk

M121 LLB Law with French Law and Language (4 years)
Duration: 4FT Hon

Entry Requirements: *GCE:* 320. *IB:* 32.

E70 THE UNIVERSITY OF ESSEX
WIVENHOE PARK
COLCHESTER
ESSEX CO4 3SQ

t: 01206 873666 **f:** 01206 873423
e: admit@essex.ac.uk

// www.essex.ac.uk

M122 LLB English & French Laws (with Maitrise Masters 1)
Duration: 4FT Hon

Entry Requirements: *GCE:* AAB. *SQAH:* AAAA-AAAB. *IB:* 36. *BTEC NC:* DD. *BTEC ND:* DDD. Interview required.

M120 LLB Laws (International Exchange) (four-years)
Duration: 4FT Hon

Entry Requirements: *GCE:* AAB. *SQAH:* AAAA-AAAB. *IB:* 36. *BTEC NC:* DD. *BTEC ND:* DDD.

E84 UNIVERSITY OF EXETER
LAVER BUILDING
NORTH PARK ROAD
EXETER
DEVON EX4 4QE

t: 01392 263855 **f:** 01392 263857/262479
e: admissions@exeter.ac.uk

// www.exeter.ac.uk/admissions

M120 LLB Law (European) (4 years)
Duration: 4FT Hon

Entry Requirements: *GCE:* AAA-AAB. Admissions Test required.

H72 THE UNIVERSITY OF HULL
THE UNIVERSITY OF HULL
COTTINGHAM ROAD
HULL HU6 7RX

t: 01482 466100 **f:** 01482 442290
e: admissions@hull.ac.uk

// www.hull.ac.uk

M1R1 LLB Law with French Law and Language (4 years)
Duration: 4FT Hon

Entry Requirements: *GCE:* 320. *IB:* 28.

M1R2 LLB Law with German Law and Language (4 years)
Duration: 4FT Hon

Entry Requirements: *GCE:* 320. *IB:* 28.

K24 THE UNIVERSITY OF KENT
INFORMATION, RECRUITMENT & ADMISSIONS REGISTRY
UNIVERSITY OF KENT
CANTERBURY. KENT CT2 7NZ

t: 01227 827272 **f:** 01227 827077
e: information@kent.ac.uk

// www.kent.ac.uk

M121 LLB English and French Law (4 years)
Duration: 4FT Hon

Entry Requirements: *GCE:* 320. *SQAH:* AAAAA. *IB:* 34. *BTEC NC:* DD. *BTEC ND:* DDM.

M122 LLB English and German Law (4 years)
Duration: 4FT Hon

Entry Requirements: *GCE:* 320. *SQAH:* AAAAA. *IB:* 34. *BTEC NC:* DD. *BTEC ND:* DDM.

M123 LLB English and Italian Law (4 years)
Duration: 4FT Hon

Entry Requirements: *GCE:* 320. *SQAH:* AAAAA. *IB:* 34. *BTEC NC:* DD. *BTEC ND:* DDM.

M125 LLB English and Spanish Law (4 years)

Duration: 4FT Hon

Entry Requirements: *GCE:* 320. *SQAH:* AAAAA. *IB:* 34. *BTEC NC:* DD. *BTEC ND:* DDM.

K60 KING'S COLLEGE LONDON (UNIVERSITY OF LONDON)

STRAND
LONDON WC2R 2LS
t: 020 7836 5454 f: 020 7836 1799
e: ucas.enquiries@kcl.ac.uk
// www.kcl.ac.uk

M121 LLB English and French Law (LLB Honours)

Duration: 4FT Hon

Entry Requirements: *GCE:* AAAb. *SQAH:* AAB. *SQAAH:* AA. *IB:* 38. *BTEC NC:* DD. Admissions Test required.

M122 LLB Law with German Law

Duration: 4FT Hon

Entry Requirements: *GCE:* AAAb. *SQAH:* AAB. *SQAAH:* AA. *IB:* 38. *BTEC NC:* DD. Admissions Test required.

L34 UNIVERSITY OF LEICESTER

UNIVERSITY ROAD
LEICESTER LE1 7RH
t: 0116 252 5281 f: 0116 252 2447
e: admissions@le.ac.uk
// www.le.ac.uk

M120 LLB English and French Law (LLB/Maitrise)

Duration: 4FT Hon

Entry Requirements: *GCE:* AAA. *SQAH:* AAAAA. *SQAAH:* AAA. *IB:* 36. *BTEC ND:* DDD.

M1R1 LLB Law with French Law and Language (4 years)

Duration: 4FT Hon

Entry Requirements: *GCE:* AAA. *SQAH:* AAAAA. *SQAAH:* AAA. *IB:* 36. *BTEC ND:* DDD.

M20 THE UNIVERSITY OF MANCHESTER

OXFORD ROAD
MANCHESTER M13 9PL
t: 0161 275 2077 f: 0161 275 2106
e: ug-admissions@manchester.ac.uk
// www.manchester.ac.uk

M121 LLB English Law with French Law (4 Years)

Duration: 4FT Hon

Entry Requirements: *GCE:* AAA. *SQAH:* AAAAB. *SQAAH:* AAA. *IB:* 37. *BTEC ND:* DDD.

O33 OXFORD UNIVERSITY

UNDERGRADUATE ADMISSIONS OFFICE
UNIVERSITY OF OXFORD
WELLINGTON SQUARE
OXFORD OX1 2JD
t: 01865 288000 f: 01865 270212
e: undergraduate.admissions@admin.ox.ac.uk
// www.admissions.ox.ac.uk

M190 BA Law with European Law

Duration: 4FT Hon

Entry Requirements: *GCE:* AAA. *SQAH:* AAAAA-AAAAB. *SQAAH:* AAB. Interview required. Admissions Test required.

M191 BA Law with French Law

Duration: 4FT Hon

Entry Requirements: *GCE:* AAA. *SQAH:* AAAAA-AAAAB. *SQAAH:* AAB. Interview required. Admissions Test required.

M192 BA Law with German Law

Duration: 4FT Hon

Entry Requirements: *GCE:* AAA. *SQAH:* AAAAA-AAAAB. *SQAAH:* AAB. Interview required. Admissions Test required.

M193 BA Law with Italian Law

Duration: 4FT Hon

Entry Requirements: *GCE:* AAA. *SQAH:* AAAAA-AAAAB. *SQAAH:* AAB. Interview required. Admissions Test required.

M194 BA Law with Spanish Law

Duration: 4FT Hon

Entry Requirements: *GCE:* AAA. *SQAH:* AAAAA-AAAAB. *SQAAH:* AAB. Interview required. Admissions Test required.

Q50 QUEEN MARY, UNIVERSITY OF LONDON

MILE END ROAD
LONDON E1 4NS
t: 020 7882 5555 f: 020 7882 5500
e: admissions@qmul.ac.uk
// www.qmul.ac.uk

M120 LLB English and European Law (4 years)

Duration: 4FT Hon

Entry Requirements: *GCE:* AAA. *SQAAH:* AAA. *IB:* 36. *BTEC NC:* DD. *BTEC ND:* DDD.

S18 THE UNIVERSITY OF SHEFFIELD
9 NORTHUMBERLAND ROAD
SHEFFIELD S10 2TT
t: 0114 222 1255 f: 0114 222 8032
e: ask@sheffield.ac.uk
// www.sheffield.ac.uk

M120 LLB LLB in Law (European and International)
Duration: 4FT Hon

Entry Requirements: *GCE:* AAA. *SQAH:* AAAA. *SQAAH:* AAA. *IB:* 37. *BTEC ND:* DDD.

S21 SHEFFIELD HALLAM UNIVERSITY
CITY CAMPUS
HOWARD STREET
SHEFFIELD S1 1WB
t: 0114 225 5555 f: 0114 225 2167
e: admissions@shu.ac.uk
// www.shu.ac.uk

M101 LLB LLB/Maitrise en Droit Francais
Duration: 3FT Hon

Entry Requirements: *GCE:* 260.

S85 UNIVERSITY OF SURREY
STAG HILL
GUILDFORD
SURREY GU2 7XH
t: +44(0)1483 689305 f: +44(0)1483 689388
e: admissions@surrey.ac.uk
// www.surrey.ac.uk

M1R1 LLB Law with French Law (4 years)
Duration: 4SW Hon

Entry Requirements: *GCE:* ABB.

M1R2 LLB Law with German Law (4 years)
Duration: 4SW Hon

Entry Requirements: *GCE:* ABB.

M1R4 LLB Law with Spanish Law (4 years)
Duration: 4SW Hon

Entry Requirements: *GCE:* ABB.

U80 UNIVERSITY COLLEGE LONDON (UNIVERSITY OF LONDON)
GOWER STREET
LONDON WC1E 6BT
t: 020 7679 3000 f: 020 7679 3001
// www.ucl.ac.uk

M146 LLB English and German Law (4 years)
Duration: 4FT Hon

Entry Requirements: *GCE:* AAAe. *SQAAH:* AAA. *IB:* 38. Admissions Test required.

M141 LLB Law with French Law (4 years)
Duration: 4FT Hon

Entry Requirements: *GCE:* AAAe. *SQAAH:* AAA. *IB:* 38. Admissions Test required.

M142 LLB Law with German Law (4 years)
Duration: 4FT Hon

Entry Requirements: *GCE:* AAAe. *SQAAH:* AAA. *IB:* 38. Admissions Test required.

M144 LLB Law with Hispanic Law (4 years)
Duration: 4FT Hon

Entry Requirements: *GCE:* AAAe. *SQAAH:* AAA. *IB:* 38. Admissions Test required.

M143 LLB Law with Italian Law (4 years)
Duration: 4FT Hon

Entry Requirements: *GCE:* AAAe. *SQAAH:* AAA. *IB:* 38. Admissions Test required.

W20 THE UNIVERSITY OF WARWICK
COVENTRY CV4 8UW
t: 024 7652 3723 f: 024 7652 4649
e: ugadmissions@warwick.ac.uk
// www.warwick.ac.uk

M125 LLB European Law (4 years including year abroad)
Duration: 4FT Hon

Entry Requirements: *GCE:* AAAc-AABb. *SQAAH:* AAA-AAB.

EUROPEAN LEGAL STUDIES

A20 THE UNIVERSITY OF ABERDEEN

UNIVERSITY OFFICE
KING'S COLLEGE
ABERDEEN AB24 3FX

t: +44 (0) 1224 273504 f: +44 (0) 1224 272034
e: sras@abdn.ac.uk

// www.abdn.ac.uk/sras

M127 LLB Law with European Legal Studies

Duration: 4FT/5FT Ord/Hon

Entry Requirements: *GCE:* BBB. *SQAH:* ABBBB-AABB. *SQAAH:* BBB. *IB:* 34.

M125 LLB Law with options in French

Duration: 3FT/4FT Ord/Hon

Entry Requirements: *GCE:* BBB. *SQAH:* ABBBB-AABB. *SQAAH:* BBB. *IB:* 34.

M124 LLB Law with options in German

Duration: 3FT/4FT Ord/Hon

Entry Requirements: *GCE:* BBB. *SQAH:* ABBBB-AABB. *SQAAH:* BBB. *IB:* 34.

E14 UNIVERSITY OF EAST ANGLIA

NORWICH NR4 7TJ

t: 01603 456161 f: 01603 458596
e: admissions@uea.ac.uk

// www.uea.ac.uk

M120 LLB Law with European Legal Systems (4 years)

Duration: 4FT Hon

Entry Requirements: *GCE:* 340. *IB:* 33.

G28 UNIVERSITY OF GLASGOW

THE UNIVERSITY OF GLASGOW
THE FRASER BUILDING
65 HILLHEAD STREET
GLASGOW G12 8QF

t: 0141 330 6062 f: 0141 330 2961
e: ugenquiries@gla.ac.uk (UK/EU undergrad enquiries only)

// www.glasgow.ac.uk

M121 LLB Law with French Legal Studies

Duration: 4FT Hon

Entry Requirements: *GCE:* AAB. *SQAH:* AAAAB. *IB:* 34. Admissions Test required.

M122 LLB Law with German Legal Studies

Duration: 4FT Hon

Entry Requirements: *GCE:* AAB. *SQAH:* AAAAB. *IB:* 34. Admissions Test required.

M1M9 LLB Law with Italian Legal Studies

Duration: 4FT Hon

Entry Requirements: *GCE:* AAB. *SQAH:* AAAAB. *IB:* 34. Admissions Test required.

M123 LLB Law with Spanish Legal Studies

Duration: 4FT Hon

Entry Requirements: *GCE:* AAB. *SQAH:* AAAAB. *IB:* 34. Admissions Test required.

H60 THE UNIVERSITY OF HUDDERSFIELD

QUEENSGATE
HUDDERSFIELD HD1 3DH

t: 01484 473969 f: 01484 472765
e: admissionsandrecords@hud.ac.uk

// www.hud.ac.uk

M120 LLB LLB European Legal Studies

Duration: 3FT Hon

Entry Requirements: *GCE:* 300. *SQAH:* BBBB. *IB:* 28.

K24 THE UNIVERSITY OF KENT

INFORMATION, RECRUITMENT & ADMISSIONS REGISTRY
UNIVERSITY OF KENT
CANTERBURY. KENT CT2 7NZ

t: 01227 827272 f: 01227 827077
e: information@kent.ac.uk

// www.kent.ac.uk

M120 LLB European Legal Studies (4 years)

Duration: 4FT Hon

Entry Requirements: *GCE:* 320. *SQAH:* AAAAA. *IB:* 34. *BTEC NC:* DD. *BTEC ND:* DDM.

L14 LANCASTER UNIVERSITY

THE UNIVERSITY
LANCASTER
LANCASHIRE LA1 4YW

t: 01524 592029 f: 01524 846243
e: ugadmissions@lancaster.ac.uk

// www.lancs.ac.uk

M120 LLB European Legal Studies (4 years)

Duration: 4SW Hon

Entry Requirements: *GCE:* AAA. *SQAH:* AAAAA. *SQAAH:* AAA. *IB:* 31.

S27 UNIVERSITY OF SOUTHAMPTON
HIGHFIELD
SOUTHAMPTON SO17 1BJ
t: 023 8059 4732 **f:** 023 8059 3037
e: admissions@soton.ac.uk
// www.southampton.ac.uk

M125 LLB Law (European Legal Studies)
Duration: 4FT Hon

Entry Requirements: *GCE:* AAA-AAB. *SQAAH:* AAA. *IB:* 36. *BTEC NC:* DD.

W50 UNIVERSITY OF WESTMINSTER
115 NEW CAVENDISH STREET
LONDON W1W 6UW
t: 020 7911 5000 **f:** 020 7911 5788
e: course-enquiries@westminster.ac.uk
// www.westminster.ac.uk

M125 LLB European Legal Studies (4 years)
Duration: 4FT Hon

Entry Requirements: *GCE:* ABC. *SQAH:* ABBBC. *SQAAH:* ABC. *IB:* 30. *BTEC ND:* DDM.

HUMAN RIGHTS

A40 ABERYSTWYTH UNIVERSITY
WELCOME CENTRE, ABERYSTWYTH UNIVERSITY
PENGLAIS CAMPUS
ABERYSTWYTH
CEREDIGION SY23 3FB
t: 01970 622021 **f:** 01970 627410
e: ug-admissions@aber.ac.uk
// www.aber.ac.uk

M990 LLB Human Rights
Duration: 3FT Hon

Entry Requirements: *GCE:* 280. *IB:* 27.

B25 BIRMINGHAM CITY UNIVERSITY
PERRY BARR
BIRMINGHAM B42 2SU
t: 0121 331 5595 **f:** 0121 331 7994
e: choices@bcu.ac.uk
// www.bcu.ac.uk

M1L3 LLB Law with Human Rights
Duration: 3FT Hon

Entry Requirements: *GCE:* 280. *IB:* 24. *BTEC NC:* DD. *BTEC ND:* DMM. *OCR ND:* Distinction.

D26 DE MONTFORT UNIVERSITY
THE GATEWAY
LEICESTER LE1 9BH
t: 0116 255 1551 **f:** 0116 250 6204
e: enquiries@dmu.ac.uk
// www.dmu.ac.uk

M200 LL.B Law, Human Rights and Social Justice
Duration: 3FT Hon

Entry Requirements: *GCE:* 240. *IB:* 28. *BTEC ND:* DMM. Interview required.

E70 THE UNIVERSITY OF ESSEX
WIVENHOE PARK
COLCHESTER
ESSEX CO4 3SQ
t: 01206 873666 **f:** 01206 873423
e: admit@essex.ac.uk
// www.essex.ac.uk

MM19 LLB Law and Human Rights (4 years)
Duration: 4FT Hon

Entry Requirements: *GCE:* AAB. *SQAH:* AAAA-AAAB. *IB:* 36. *BTEC NC:* DM. *BTEC ND:* DDD.

T7M9 BA Latin American Studies with Human Rights
Duration: 4FT Hon

Entry Requirements: *GCE:* 300-340. *SQAH:* AAAA-AABB. *SQAAH:* AAB-ABB. *BTEC NC:* DM. *BTEC ND:* DDM.

M1M9 BA Law and Human Rights
Duration: 3FT Hon

Entry Requirements: *GCE:* 300-340. *SQAH:* AAAA-AABB. *SQAAH:* AAB-ABB. *BTEC NC:* DM. *BTEC ND:* DDM.

V5M9 BA Philosophy with Human Rights
Duration: 3FT Hon

Entry Requirements: *GCE:* 300-340. *SQAH:* AAAA-AABB. *SQAAH:* AAB-ABB. *BTEC NC:* DM. *BTEC ND:* DDM.

L2M9 BA Politics with Human Rights
Duration: 3FT Hon

Entry Requirements: *GCE:* 300-340. *SQAH:* AAAA-AABB. *SQAAH:* AAB-ABB. *BTEC NC:* DM. *BTEC ND:* DDM.

L3M9 BA Sociology with Human Rights
Duration: 3FT Hon

Entry Requirements: *GCE:* 300-340. *SQAH:* AAAA-AABB. *SQAAH:* AAB-ABB. *BTEC NC:* DM. *BTEC ND:* DDM.

K84 KINGSTON UNIVERSITY
STUDENT INFORMATION & ADVICE CENTRE
COOPER HOUSE
40-46 SURBITON ROAD
KINGSTON UPON THAMES KT1 2HX

t: 020 8547 7053 f: 020 8547 7080
e: aps@kingston.ac.uk
// www.kingston.ac.uk

L3M1 BA Human Rights with Law
Duration: 3FT Hon

Entry Requirements: *GCE:* 220-320.

ML13 BA Law and Human Rights
Duration: 3FT Hon

Entry Requirements: *GCE:* 280-320.

R48 ROEHAMPTON UNIVERSITY
ERASMUS HOUSE
ROEHAMPTON LANE
LONDON SW15 5PU

t: 020 8392 3232 f: 020 8392 3470
e: enquiries@roehampton.ac.uk
// www.roehampton.ac.uk

ML9F BA Human Rights and Criminology
Duration: 3FT Hon

Entry Requirements: *GCE:* 200-240. *IB:* 24. *BTEC NC:* DM. *BTEC ND:* MMP. *OCR ND:* Merit. *OCR NED:* Pass.

S72 STAFFORDSHIRE UNIVERSITY
COLLEGE ROAD
STOKE ON TRENT ST4 2DE

t: 01782 292753 f: 01782 292740
e: admissions@staffs.ac.uk
// www.staffs.ac.uk

M291 LLB LLB (Human Rights)
Duration: 3FT Hon

Entry Requirements: *GCE:* BB-ABB. *SQAAH:* BB-ABB. *IB:* 26. *BTEC NC:* DM. *BTEC ND:* DDM. *OCR ND:* Distinction.

INTERNATIONAL LAW

A60 ANGLIA RUSKIN UNIVERSITY
BISHOP HALL LANE
CHELMSFORD
ESSEX CM1 1SQ

t: 0845 271 3333 f: 01245 251789
e: answers@anglia.ac.uk
// www.anglia.ac.uk

M221 LLB International Business Law
Duration: 3FT Hon

Entry Requirements: *GCE:* 220-260. *SQAH:* AABC. *SQAAH:* AB. *IB:* 30.

B25 BIRMINGHAM CITY UNIVERSITY
PERRY BARR
BIRMINGHAM B42 2SU

t: 0121 331 5595 f: 0121 331 7994
e: choices@bcu.ac.uk
// www.bcu.ac.uk

M130 LLB Law with American Legal Studies
Duration: 3FT Hon

Entry Requirements: *GCE:* 280. *IB:* 24. *BTEC NC:* DD. *BTEC ND:* DMM. *OCR ND:* Distinction.

C10 CANTERBURY CHRIST CHURCH UNIVERSITY
NORTH HOLMES ROAD
CANTERBURY
KENT CT1 1QU

t: 01227 782900 f: 01227 782888
e: admissions@canterbury.ac.uk
// www.canterbury.ac.uk

M101 LLB Law 'International only'
Duration: 4FT Hon

Entry Requirements: Interview required.

Q3MG BA English Language & Communication with Legal Studies 'International Only'
Duration: 4FT Hon

Entry Requirements: Interview required.

L2MF BA Politics & Governance with Legal Studies 'International Only'
Duration: 4FT Hon

Entry Requirements: Interview required.

C60 CITY UNIVERSITY

NORTHAMPTON SQUARE
LONDON EC1V 0HB

t: 020 7040 5060 f: 020 7040 8995
e: ugadmissions@city.ac.uk

// www.city.ac.uk

M101 LLB International Foundation Programme (Law routes)

Duration: 4FT Hon

Entry Requirements: Contact the institution for details.

H72 THE UNIVERSITY OF HULL

THE UNIVERSITY OF HULL
COTTINGHAM ROAD
HULL HU6 7RX

t: 01482 466100 f: 01482 442290
e: admissions@hull.ac.uk

// www.hull.ac.uk

M130 LLB International Law

Duration: 3FT Hon

Entry Requirements: GCE: 60.

K60 KING'S COLLEGE LONDON (UNIVERSITY OF LONDON)

STRAND
LONDON WC2R 2LS

t: 020 7836 5454 f: 020 7836 1799
e: ucas.enquiries@kcl.ac.uk

// www.kcl.ac.uk

M190 LLB English Law and Hong Kong Law

Duration: 5FT Hon

Entry Requirements: Contact the institution for details.

K84 KINGSTON UNIVERSITY

STUDENT INFORMATION & ADVICE CENTRE
COOPER HOUSE
40-46 SURBITON ROAD
KINGSTON UPON THAMES KT1 2HX

t: 020 8547 7053 f: 020 8547 7080
e: aps@kingston.ac.uk

// www.kingston.ac.uk

M130 LLB International Law

Duration: 3FT Hon

Entry Requirements: GCE: 320. IB: 26. BTEC ND: DDM.

L14 LANCASTER UNIVERSITY

THE UNIVERSITY
LANCASTER
LANCASHIRE LA1 4YW

t: 01524 592029 f: 01524 846243
e: ugadmissions@lancaster.ac.uk

// www.lancs.ac.uk

M101 LLB Law (International)

Duration: 4FT Hon

Entry Requirements: GCE: AAA. SQAH: AAAAA. SQAAH: AAA. IB: 31. BTEC ND: DDD.

L68 LONDON METROPOLITAN UNIVERSITY

166-220 HOLLOWAY ROAD
LONDON N7 8DB

t: 020 7133 4200
e: admissions@londonmet.ac.uk

// www.londonmet.ac.uk

ML1G BA International Law & International Politics and Peace & Conflict Studies

Duration: 3FT Hon

Entry Requirements: GCE: 240. IB: 28.

MLC2 BA International Law and International Politics

Duration: 3FT Hon

Entry Requirements: GCE: 240. IB: 28.

TM31 BA/BSc Asia-Pacific Studies and International Law & International Politics

Duration: 3FT Hon

Entry Requirements: GCE: 240. IB: 28.

NMC1 BA/BSc Business and International Law & International Politics

Duration: 3FT Hon

Entry Requirements: GCE: 240. IB: 28.

LM2C BA/BSc International Development and International Law & International Politics

Duration: 3FT Hon

Entry Requirements: GCE: 240. IB: 28.

ML13 BA/BSc International Law & International Politics and Sociology

Duration: 3FT Hon

Entry Requirements: GCE: 240. IB: 28.

LANGUAGE COMBINATIONS

A20 THE UNIVERSITY OF ABERDEEN
UNIVERSITY OFFICE
KING'S COLLEGE
ABERDEEN AB24 3FX

t: +44 (0) 1224 273504 f: +44 (0) 1224 272034
e: sras@abdn.ac.uk
// www.abdn.ac.uk/sras

M128 LLB Law with options in Gaelic Language
Duration: 3FT/4FT Ord/Hon

Entry Requirements: *GCE:* BBB. *SQAH:* ABBBB-AABB. *SQAAH:* BBB. *IB:* 34.

M122 LLB Law with options in Spanish
Duration: 3FT/4FT Ord/Hon

Entry Requirements: *GCE:* BBB. *SQAH:* ABBBB-AABB. *SQAAH:* BBB. *IB:* 34.

A40 ABERYSTWYTH UNIVERSITY
WELCOME CENTRE, ABERYSTWYTH UNIVERSITY
PENGLAIS CAMPUS
ABERYSTWYTH
CEREDIGION SY23 3FB

t: 01970 622021 f: 01970 627410
e: ug-admissions@aber.ac.uk
// www.aber.ac.uk

M1R1 LLB Law with French (4 years)
Duration: 4FT Hon

Entry Requirements: *GCE:* 280. *IB:* 27.

M1R2 LLB Law with German (4 years)
Duration: 4FT Hon

Entry Requirements: *GCE:* 280. *IB:* 27.

M1R4 LLB Law with Spanish (4 years)
Duration: 4FT Hon

Entry Requirements: *GCE:* 280. *IB:* 27.

M1Q5 BA Law with Cymraeg
Duration: 3FT Hon

Entry Requirements: *GCE:* 280. *IB:* 27.

M1RC BA Law with French (4 years)
Duration: 4FT Hon

Entry Requirements: *GCE:* 280. *IB:* 27.

M1RF BA Law with German (4 years)
Duration: 4FT Hon

Entry Requirements: *GCE:* 280. *IB:* 27.

M1RK BA Law with Spanish (4 years)
Duration: 4FT Hon

Entry Requirements: *GCE:* 280. *IB:* 27.

B06 BANGOR UNIVERSITY
BANGOR
GWYNEDD LL57 2DG

t: 01248 382016/2017 f: 01248 370451
e: admissions@bangor.ac.uk
// www.bangor.ac.uk

M1R1 LLB Law with French
Duration: 4FT Hon

Entry Requirements: *GCE:* 280. *IB:* 28.

M1R2 LLB Law with German
Duration: 4FT Hon

Entry Requirements: *GCE:* 280. *IB:* 28.

M1R3 LLB Law with Italian
Duration: 4FT Hon

Entry Requirements: *GCE:* 280. *IB:* 28.

M1R4 LLB Law with Spanish
Duration: 4FT Hon

Entry Requirements: *GCE:* 280. *IB:* 28.

M1Q5 LLB Law with Welsh
Duration: 3FT Hon

Entry Requirements: *GCE:* 280. *IB:* 28.

B32 THE UNIVERSITY OF BIRMINGHAM
EDGBASTON
BIRMINGHAM B15 2TT

t: 0121 415 8900 f: 0121 414 7159
e: admissions@bham.ac.uk
// www.bham.ac.uk

MR11 LLB Law with French (4 years)
Duration: 4FT Hon

Entry Requirements: *GCE:* AAA. *SQAAH:* AAA. *IB:* 36. *BTEC NC:* DD. *BTEC ND:* DDD. Admissions Test required.

MR12 LLB Law with German (4 years)
Duration: 4FT Hon

Entry Requirements: *GCE:* AAA. *SQAAH:* AAA. *IB:* 36. *BTEC NC:* DD. *BTEC ND:* DDD. Admissions Test required.

B78 UNIVERSITY OF BRISTOL

UNDERGRADUATE ADMISSIONS OFFICE
SENATE HOUSE
TYNDALL AVENUE
BRISTOL BS8 1TH

t: 0117 928 9000 f: 0117 925 1424
e: ug-admissions@bristol.ac.uk

// www.bristol.ac.uk

MR11 LLB Law and French (4 years)

Duration: 4FT Hon

Entry Requirements: *GCE:* AAA. *SQAH:* AAAAA. *SQAAH:* AA. *IB:* 37.
BTEC ND: DDD. Admissions Test required.

MR12 LLB Law and German (4 years)

Duration: 4FT Hon

Entry Requirements: *GCE:* AAA. *SQAH:* AAAAA. *SQAAH:* AA. *IB:* 37.
BTEC ND: DDD. Admissions Test required.

B80 UNIVERSITY OF THE WEST OF ENGLAND, BRISTOL

FRENCHAY CAMPUS
COLDHARBOUR LANE
BRISTOL BS16 1QY

t: +44 (0)117 32 83333 f: +44 (0)117 32 82810
e: admissions@uwe.ac.uk

// www.uwe.ac.uk

M1R1 LLB LLB (with French)

Duration: 4SW Hon

Entry Requirements: *GCE:* 300-340.

M1R4 LLB LLB (with Spanish)

Duration: 4SW Hon

Entry Requirements: *GCE:* 300-340.

B90 THE UNIVERSITY OF BUCKINGHAM

YEOMANRY HOUSE
HUNTER STREET
BUCKINGHAM MK18 1EG

t: 01280 820313 f: 01280 822245
e: info@buckingham.ac.uk

// www.buckingham.ac.uk

M1Q1 LLB Law with English as a Foreign Language

Duration: 2FT Hon

Entry Requirements: *GCE:* 300. *IB:* 28. *BTEC NC:* DD. *BTEC ND:*
DMM.

M1R1 LLB Law with French

Duration: 2FT Hon

Entry Requirements: *GCE:* 300. *IB:* 28. *BTEC NC:* DD. *BTEC ND:*
DMM.

M1R4 LLB Law with Spanish

Duration: 2FT Hon

Entry Requirements: *GCE:* 300. *IB:* 28. *BTEC NC:* DD. *BTEC ND:*
DMM.

C15 CARDIFF UNIVERSITY

PO BOX 927
30-36 NEWPORT ROAD
CARDIFF CF24 0DE

t: 029 2087 9999 f: 029 2087 6138
e: admissions@cardiff.ac.uk

// www.cardiff.ac.uk

RM11 LLB Law and French (4 years)

Duration: 4FT Hon

Entry Requirements: *GCE:* ABB. *SQAAH:* ABB. *IB:* 32. Interview
required. Admissions Test required.

RM21 LLB Law and German (4 years)

Duration: 4FT Hon

Entry Requirements: *GCE:* BBB.

MQ15 LLB Law and Welsh

Duration: 3FT Hon

Entry Requirements: *GCE:* BBB. Interview required.

C30 UNIVERSITY OF CENTRAL LANCASHIRE

PRESTON
LANCS PR1 2HE

t: 01772 201201 f: 01772 894954
e: uadmissions@uclan.ac.uk

// www.uclan.ac.uk

M1T6 LLB Law with Arabic

Duration: 4FT Hon

Entry Requirements: Contact the institution for details.

M1T1 LLB Law with Chinese

Duration: 4FT Hon

Entry Requirements: Contact the institution for details.

M1T2 LLB Law with Japanese

Duration: 4FT Hon

Entry Requirements: Contact the institution for details.

C55 UNIVERSITY OF CHESTER

PARKGATE ROAD
CHESTER CH1 4BJ

t: 01244 511000 f: 01244 511300
e: enquiries@chester.ac.uk

// www.chester.ac.uk

R1M1 BA French with Law

Duration: 4FT Hon

Entry Requirements: *GCE:* 240. *SQAH:* BBBB. *IB:* 24. *BTEC NC:* DM. *BTEC ND:* MMM.

R2M1 BA German with Law

Duration: 4FT Hon

Entry Requirements: *GCE:* 240. *SQAH:* BBBB. *IB:* 24. *BTEC NC:* DM. *BTEC ND:* MMM.

MR11 BA Law and French

Duration: 4FT Hon

Entry Requirements: *GCE:* 240. *SQAH:* BBBB. *IB:* 24. *BTEC NC:* DM. *BTEC ND:* MMM.

MR12 BA Law and German

Duration: 4FT Hon

Entry Requirements: *GCE:* 240. *SQAH:* BBBB. *IB:* 24. *BTEC NC:* DM. *BTEC ND:* MMM.

MR14 BA Law and Spanish

Duration: 4FT Hon

Entry Requirements: *GCE:* 240. *SQAH:* BBBB. *IB:* 24. *BTEC NC:* DM. *BTEC ND:* MMM.

M1R1 BA Law with French

Duration: 3FT Hon

Entry Requirements: *GCE:* 240. *SQAH:* BBBB. *IB:* 24. *BTEC NC:* DM. *BTEC ND:* MMM.

M1R2 BA Law with German

Duration: 3FT Hon

Entry Requirements: *GCE:* 240. *SQAH:* BBBB. *IB:* 24. *BTEC NC:* DM. *BTEC ND:* MMM.

M1R4 BA Law with Spanish

Duration: 3FT Hon

Entry Requirements: *GCE:* 240. *SQAH:* BBBB. *IB:* 24. *BTEC NC:* DM. *BTEC ND:* MMM.

R4M1 BA Spanish with Law

Duration: 4FT Hon

Entry Requirements: *GCE:* 240. *SQAH:* BBBB. *IB:* 24. *BTEC NC:* DM. *BTEC ND:* MMM.

C85 COVENTRY UNIVERSITY

THE STUDENT CENTRE
COVENTRY UNIVERSITY
1 GULSON RD
COVENTRY CV1 2JH

t: 024 7615 2222 f: 024 7615 2223
e: studentenquiries@coventry.ac.uk

// www.coventry.ac.uk

MR11 LLB Law and French

Duration: 3FT Hon

Entry Requirements: *GCE:* 300. *BTEC ND:* DDM.

MR14 LLB Law and Spanish

Duration: 3FT Hon

Entry Requirements: *GCE:* 300. *BTEC ND:* DDM.

D65 UNIVERSITY OF DUNDEE

DUNDEE DD1 4HN

t: 01382 383838 f: 01382 388150
e: srs@dundee.ac.uk

// www.dundee.ac.uk/admissions/undergraduate

M1RC LLB Law (Eng/NI) with French

Duration: 4FT Hon

Entry Requirements: *GCE:* BBB. *SQAH:* AABB-ABBBB. *IB:* 33.

M1RF LLB Law (Eng/NI) with German

Duration: 4FT Hon

Entry Requirements: *GCE:* BBB. *SQAH:* AABB-ABBBB. *IB:* 33.

M1RK LLB Law (Eng/NI) with Spanish

Duration: 4FT Hon

Entry Requirements: *GCE:* BBB. *SQAH:* AABB-ABBBB. *IB:* 33.

M1R1 LLB Law (Scots) with French

Duration: 4FT Hon

Entry Requirements: *GCE:* BBB. *SQAH:* AABB-ABBBB. *IB:* 33.

M1R2 LLB Law (Scots) with German

Duration: 4FT Hon

Entry Requirements: *GCE:* BBB. *SQAH:* AABB-ABBBB. *IB:* 33.

M1R4 LLB Law (Scots) with Spanish

Duration: 4FT Hon

Entry Requirements: *GCE:* BBB. *SQAH:* AABB-ABBBB. *IB:* 33.

E56 THE UNIVERSITY OF EDINBURGH

STUDENT RECRUITMENT & ADMISSIONS
57 GEORGE SQUARE
EDINBURGH EH8 9JU

t: 0131 650 4360 f: 0131 651 1236
e: sra.enquiries@ed.ac.uk
// www.ed.ac.uk/studying/undergraduate/

MQ15 LLB Law and Celtic

Duration: 4FT Hon

Entry Requirements: *GCE:* BBB. *SQAH:* BBBB. *IB:* 34.

MR11 LLB Law and French

Duration: 4FT Hon

Entry Requirements: *GCE:* BBB. *SQAH:* BBBB. *IB:* 34.

MR12 LLB Law and German

Duration: 4FT Hon

Entry Requirements: *GCE:* BBB. *SQAH:* BBBB. *IB:* 34.

MR14 LLB Law and Spanish

Duration: 4FT Hon

Entry Requirements: *GCE:* BBB. *SQAH:* BBBB. *IB:* 34.

E77 EUROPEAN BUSINESS SCHOOL, LONDON

INNER CIRCLE
REGENT'S PARK
LONDON NW1 4NS

t: +44 (0)20 7487 7505 f: +44 (0)20 7487 7425
e: ebsl@regents.ac.uk
// www.ebslondon.ac.uk

N1M1 BA International Business with Law and one language

Duration: 3FT/4FT Hon

Entry Requirements: *SQAH:* BBCC. *SQAAH:* CC. *IB:* 28.

G14 UNIVERSITY OF GLAMORGAN, CARDIFF AND PONTYPRIDD

ENQUIRIES AND ADMISSIONS UNIT
PONTYPRIDD CF37 1DL

t: 0800 716925 f: 01443 654050
e: enquiries@glam.ac.uk
// www.glam.ac.uk

M1Q5 LLB Law with Professional Welsh

Duration: 3FT Hon

Entry Requirements: *GCE:* 280-320.

M2R4 LLB Law with Spanish

Duration: 3FT Hon

Entry Requirements: *GCE:* 280-320. *IB:* 30. *BTEC NC:* DD. *BTEC ND:* DMM.

MQ15 BA Law and Professional Welsh

Duration: 3FT Hon

Entry Requirements: *GCE:* 280-320. *IB:* 30. *BTEC NC:* DD. *BTEC ND:* DMM.

Q5M1 BA Professional Welsh with Law

Duration: 3FT Hon

Entry Requirements: *GCE:* 220-280. *IB:* 27. *BTEC NC:* MM. *BTEC ND:* MMP.

G28 UNIVERSITY OF GLASGOW

THE UNIVERSITY OF GLASGOW
THE FRASER BUILDING
65 HILLHEAD STREET
GLASGOW G12 8QF

t: 0141 330 6062 f: 0141 330 2961
e: ugenquiries@gla.ac.uk (UK/EU undergrad enquiries only)
// www.glasgow.ac.uk

M1R7 LLB Law with Czech Language

Duration: 4FT Hon

Entry Requirements: *GCE:* AAB. *SQAH:* AAAAB. *IB:* 34. Admissions Test required.

M1R1 LLB Law with French Language

Duration: 4FT Hon

Entry Requirements: *GCE:* AAB. *SQAH:* AAAAB. *IB:* 34. Admissions Test required.

M1R2 LLB Law with German Language

Duration: 4FT Hon

Entry Requirements: *GCE:* AAB. *SQAH:* AAAAB. *IB:* 34. Admissions Test required.

M1R3 LLB Law with Italian Language

Duration: 4FT Hon

Entry Requirements: *GCE:* AAB. *SQAH:* AAAAB. *IB:* 34. Admissions Test required.

M1RR LLB Law with Polish Language

Duration: 4FT Hon

Entry Requirements: *GCE:* AAB. *SQAH:* AAAAB. *IB:* 34. Admissions Test required.

M1R4 LLB Law with Spanish Language

Duration: 4FT Hon

Entry Requirements: *GCE:* AAB. *SQAH:* AAAAB. *IB:* 34. Admissions Test required.

MQ15 LLB Law/Gaelic Language

Duration: 4FT Hon

Entry Requirements: *GCE:* AAB. *SQAH:* AAAAB. *IB:* 34. Admissions Test required.

G70 UNIVERSITY OF GREENWICH

GREENWICH CAMPUS
OLD ROYAL NAVAL COLLEGE
PARK ROW
LONDON SE10 9LS

t: 0800 005 006 f: 020 8331 8145
e: courseinfo@gre.ac.uk
// www.gre.ac.uk

MR11 BA Law and French
Duration: 3FT Hon

Entry Requirements: *GCE:* 180. *IB:* 24.

MR12 BA Law and German
Duration: 3FT Hon

Entry Requirements: *GCE:* 180. *IB:* 24.

MR13 BA Law and Italian
Duration: 3FT Hon

Entry Requirements: *GCE:* 180. *SQAH:* BBBBC. *SQAAH:* BCC. *IB:* 24.

MR14 BA Law and Spanish
Duration: 3FT Hon

Entry Requirements: *GCE:* 180. *IB:* 24.

H36 UNIVERSITY OF HERTFORDSHIRE

UNIVERSITY ADMISSIONS SERVICE
COLLEGE LANE
HATFIELD
HERTS AL10 9AB

t: 01707 284800 f: 01707 284870
// www.herts.ac.uk

M1R1 BSc Law/French
Duration: 3FT Hon

Entry Requirements: *GCE:* 260.

M1R4 BSc Law/Spanish
Duration: 3FT Hon

Entry Requirements: *GCE:* 220.

H72 THE UNIVERSITY OF HULL

THE UNIVERSITY OF HULL
COTTINGHAM ROAD
HULL HU6 7RX

t: 01482 466100 f: 01482 442290
e: admissions@hull.ac.uk
// www.hull.ac.uk

M1R4 BA Law with Spanish Law & Language
Duration: 4FT Hon

Entry Requirements: *GCE:* 320. *IB:* 28.

K24 THE UNIVERSITY OF KENT

INFORMATION, RECRUITMENT & ADMISSIONS
REGISTRY
UNIVERSITY OF KENT
CANTERBURY. KENT CT2 7NZ

t: 01227 827272 f: 01227 827077
e: information@kent.ac.uk
// www.kent.ac.uk

M124 LLB Law with a Language
Duration: 3FT Hon

Entry Requirements: *GCE:* 300. *SQAH:* AAAAA. *IB:* 34. *BTEC NC:* DD. *BTEC ND:* DDM.

M1R4 LLB Law with Spanish
Duration: 3FT Hon

Entry Requirements: *GCE:* 320. *SQAH:* AAAAA. *IB:* 34. *BTEC NC:* DD. *BTEC ND:* DDM.

L23 UNIVERSITY OF LEEDS

THE UNIVERSITY OF LEEDS
LEEDS LS2 9JT

t: 0113 343 3999
e: admissions@adm.leeds.ac.uk
// www.leeds.ac.uk

MR11 LLB Law and French (4 Years)
Duration: 4FT Hon

Entry Requirements: *GCE:* AAA. *SQAAH:* AAA. *IB:* 37.

N38 UNIVERSITY OF NORTHAMPTON

PARK CAMPUS
BOUGHTON GREEN ROAD
NORTHAMPTON NN2 7AL

t: 0800 358 2232 f: 01604 722083
e: admissions@northampton.ac.uk
// www.northampton.ac.uk

R1M1 BA French/Law
Duration: 3FT Hon

Entry Requirements: *GCE:* 220-260. *SQAH:* AAB-BBBB. *IB:* 24.

R2M1 BA German/Law
Duration: 3FT Hon

Entry Requirements: *GCE:* 220-260. *SQAH:* AAB-BBBB. *IB:* 24.

M1R1 BA Law/French
Duration: 3FT Hon

Entry Requirements: *GCE:* 220-260. *SQAH:* AAB-BBBB. *IB:* 24.

M1R2 BA Law/German
Duration: 3FT Hon

Entry Requirements: *GCE:* 220-260. *SQAH:* AAB-BBBB. *IB:* 24.

N84 THE UNIVERSITY OF NOTTINGHAM
THE ADMISSIONS OFFICE
THE UNIVERSITY OF NOTTINGHAM
UNIVERSITY PARK
NOTTINGHAM NG7 2RD

t: 0115 951 5151 f: 0115 951 4668

// www.nottingham.ac.uk

M1R1 BA Law with French
Duration: 4FT Hon

Entry Requirements: *GCE:* AAA. *SQAAH:* AAA. *IB:* 38. Admissions Test required.

M1R2 BA Law with German
Duration: 4FT Hon

Entry Requirements: *GCE:* AAA. *SQAAH:* AAA. *IB:* 38. Admissions Test required.

N91 NOTTINGHAM TRENT UNIVERSITY
DRYDEN CENTRE
BURTON STREET
NOTTINGHAM NG1 4BU

t: +44 (0) 115 941 8418 f: +44 (0) 115 848 6063
e: admissions@ntu.ac.uk

// www.ntu.ac.uk/

M1R4 LLB Law with Spanish
Duration: 4SW Hon

Entry Requirements: *Foundation:* Pass. *GCE:* 280. *SQAH:* BBBBC. *SQAAH:* BBC. *IB:* 24. *BTEC NC:* DM. *BTEC ND:* DMM. *OCR ND:* Merit. *OCR NED:* Merit.

O66 OXFORD BROOKES UNIVERSITY
ADMISSIONS OFFICE
HEADINGTON CAMPUS
GIPSY LANE
OXFORD OX3 0BP

t: 01865 483040 f: 01865 483983
e: admissions@brookes.ac.uk

// www.brookes.ac.uk

QM31 BA English/Law
Duration: 3FT Hon

Entry Requirements: *GCE:* BBB.

RM11 BA/BSc French Studies/Law
Duration: 4SW Hon

Entry Requirements: *GCE:* BCC.

TM21 BA/BSc Japanese Studies/Law
Duration: 4SW Hon

Entry Requirements: *GCE:* BBC.

P80 UNIVERSITY OF PORTSMOUTH
ACADEMIC REGISTRY
UNIVERSITY HOUSE
WINSTON CHURCHILL AVENUE
PORTSMOUTH PO1 2UP

t: 023 9284 8484 f: 023 9284 3082
e: admissions@port.ac.uk

// www.port.ac.uk

MR18 BA Law and Languages
Duration: 4SW Hon

Entry Requirements: *GCE:* 200-280.

Q75 QUEEN'S UNIVERSITY BELFAST
UNIVERSITY ROAD
BELFAST BT7 1NN

t: 028 9097 2727 f: 028 9097 2828
e: admissions@qub.ac.uk

// www.qub.ac.uk

M2R1 LLB Common & Civil Law with French (4 years)
Duration: 4FT Hon

Entry Requirements: *GCE:* AAA-AABa. *SQAH:* AAAAB-AAABB. *SQAAH:* AAA-AAB. *IB:* 36.

M2R4 LLB Common & Civil Law with Spanish (4 years)
Duration: 4FT Hon

Entry Requirements: *GCE:* AAA-AABa. *SQAH:* AAAAB-AAABB. *SQAAH:* AAA-AAB. *IB:* 36.

S09 SCHOOL OF ORIENTAL AND AFRICAN STUDIES (UNIVERSITY OF LONDON)
THORNHAUGH STREET
RUSSELL SQUARE
LONDON WC1H 0XG

t: 020 7074 5106 f: 020 7898 4039
e: undergradadmissions@soas.ac.uk

// www.soas.ac.uk

TM41 BA Bengali and Law
Duration: 4FT Hon

Entry Requirements: *GCE:* AAA. *SQAH:* AAAAA. *SQAAH:* AAA. *IB:* 37.

MT16 BA Law and Arabic
Duration: 4FT Hon

Entry Requirements: *GCE:* AAA. *SQAH:* AAAAA. *SQAAH:* AAA. *IB:* 38. *BTEC ND:* DDD.

MTCH BA Law and Burmese
Duration: 3FT Hon

Entry Requirements: *GCE:* AAA. *SQAH:* AAAAA. *SQAAH:* AAA. *IB:* 38. *BTEC ND:* DDD.

MT11 BA Law and Chinese
Duration: 4FT Hon

Entry Requirements: *GCE:* AAA. *SQAH:* AAAAA. *SQAAH:* AAA. *IB:* 38. *BTEC ND:* DDD.

MT19 BA Law and Georgian
Duration: 3FT Hon

Entry Requirements: *GCE:* AAA. *SQAH:* AAAAA. *SQAAH:* AAA. *IB:* 38. *BTEC ND:* DDD.

MTC5 BA Law and Hausa
Duration: 4FT Hon

Entry Requirements: *GCE:* AAA. *SQAH:* AAAAA. *SQAAH:* AAA. *IB:* 38. *BTEC ND:* DDD.

MQ14 BA Law and Hebrew
Duration: 4FT Hon

Entry Requirements: *GCE:* AAA. *SQAH:* AAAAA. *SQAAH:* AAA. *IB:* 38. *BTEC ND:* DDD.

MTCJ BA Law and Hindi
Duration: 4FT Hon

Entry Requirements: *GCE:* AAA. *SQAH:* AAAAA. *SQAAH:* AAA. *IB:* 38. *BTEC ND:* DDD.

MTDH BA Law and Indonesian
Duration: 3FT Hon

Entry Requirements: *GCE:* AAA. *SQAH:* AAAAA. *SQAAH:* AAA. *IB:* 38. *BTEC ND:* DDD.

MTDL BA Law and Korean
Duration: 4FT Hon

Entry Requirements: *GCE:* AAA. *SQAH:* AAAAA. *SQAAH:* AAA. *IB:* 38. *BTEC ND:* DDD.

MQ11 BA Law and Linguistics
Duration: 3FT Hon

Entry Requirements: *GCE:* AAA. *SQAH:* AAAAA. *SQAAH:* AAA. *IB:* 38. *BTEC ND:* DDD.

MTC3 BA Nepali and Law
Duration: 4FT Hon

Entry Requirements: *GCE:* AAA. *SQAH:* AAAAA. *SQAAH:* AAA. *IB:* 38. *BTEC ND:* DDD.

MTD6 BA Persian and Law
Duration: 3FT Hon

Entry Requirements: *GCE:* AAA. *SQAH:* AAAAA. *SQAAH:* AAA. *IB:* 38. *BTEC ND:* DDD.

MQ1K BA Sanskrit and Law
Duration: 3FT Hon

Entry Requirements: *GCE:* AAA. *SQAH:* AAAAA. *SQAAH:* AAA. *IB:* 38. *BTEC ND:* DDD.

MTD5 BA Swahili and Law
Duration: 4FT Hon

Entry Requirements: *GCE:* AAA. *SQAH:* AAAAA. *SQAAH:* AAA. *IB:* 38. *BTEC ND:* DDD.

TM31 BA Thai and Law
Duration: 3FT Hon

Entry Requirements: *GCE:* AAA. *SQAH:* AAAAA. *SQAAH:* AAA. *IB:* 38. *BTEC ND:* DDD.

MTC6 BA Turkish and Law
Duration: 4FT Hon

Entry Requirements: *GCE:* AAB. *SQAH:* AAABB. *SQAAH:* AAB. *IB:* 37. *BTEC ND:* DDM.

MT1H BA Vietnamese and Law
Duration: 3FT Hon

Entry Requirements: *GCE:* AAA. *SQAH:* AAAAA. *SQAAH:* AAA. *IB:* 38. *BTEC ND:* DDD.

S18 THE UNIVERSITY OF SHEFFIELD
9 NORTHUMBERLAND ROAD
SHEFFIELD S10 2TT
t: 0114 222 1255 f: 0114 222 8032
e: ask@sheffield.ac.uk
// www.sheffield.ac.uk

M1R1 LLB Law with French
Duration: 4FT Hon

Entry Requirements: *GCE:* AAB. *SQAH:* AAAA. *SQAAH:* AAB. *IB:* 35.

M1R2 LLB Law with German
Duration: 4FT Hon

Entry Requirements: *GCE:* AAB. *SQAH:* AAAA. *SQAAH:* AAB. *IB:* 35.

M1R4 LLB Law with Spanish
Duration: 4FT Hon

Entry Requirements: *GCE:* AAB. *SQAH:* AAAA. *SQAAH:* AAB. *IB:* 35.

S30 SOUTHAMPTON SOLENT UNIVERSITY
EAST PARK TERRACE
SOUTHAMPTON
HAMPSHIRE SO14 0RT
t: +44 (0) 23 8031 9039 f: + 44 (0)23 8022 2259
e: admissions@solent.ac.uk or ask@solent.ac.uk
// www.solent.ac.uk/

M1Q3 LLB LLB (Hons) with Language Foundation Year
Duration: 4FT Hon

Entry Requirements: Contact the institution for details.

S75 THE UNIVERSITY OF STIRLING
STIRLING FK9 4LA
t: 01786 467044 f: 01786 466800
e: admissions@stir.ac.uk
// www.stir.ac.uk

RM11 BA French and Law
Duration: 4FT Hon

Entry Requirements: *GCE:* CCC. *SQAH:* BBBC. *SQAAH:* AAA-CCC. *BTEC ND:* DMM.

MR14 BA Law and Spanish
Duration: 4FT Hon

Entry Requirements: *GCE:* CCC. *SQAH:* BBBC. *SQAAH:* AAA-CCC. *BTEC ND:* DMM.

S78 THE UNIVERSITY OF STRATHCLYDE
GLASGOW G1 1XQ
t: 0141 552 4400 f: 0141 552 0775
// www.strath.ac.uk

M1R2 LLB Law(Scots) with German
Duration: 5FT Hon

Entry Requirements: *GCE:* AAB. *SQAH:* AAAAB. *IB:* 38.

M1R3 LLB Law(Scots) with Italian
Duration: 5FT Hon

Entry Requirements: *GCE:* AAB. *SQAH:* AAAAB. *IB:* 38.

M1R4 LLB Law(Scots) with Spanish
Duration: 5FT Hon

Entry Requirements: *GCE:* AAB. *SQAH:* AAAAB. *IB:* 38.

RM11 BA French and Law
Duration: 5FT Hon

Entry Requirements: *GCE:* BBC. *SQAH:* ABBB-BBBBC. *IB:* 30.

RM21 BA German and Law
Duration: 5FT Hon

Entry Requirements: *GCE:* BBC. *SQAH:* ABBB-BBBBC. *IB:* 30.

RM31 BA Italian and Law
Duration: 5FT Hon

Entry Requirements: *GCE:* BBC. *SQAH:* ABBB-BBBBC. *IB:* 30.

MR14 BA Law and Spanish
Duration: 5FT Hon

Entry Requirements: *GCE:* BBC. *SQAH:* ABBB-BBBBC. *IB:* 30.

S84 UNIVERSITY OF SUNDERLAND
STUDENT HELPLINE
THE STUDENT GATEWAY
CHESTER ROAD
SUNDERLAND SR1 3SD
t: 0191 515 3000 f: 0191 515 3805
e: student-helpline@sunderland.ac.uk
// www.sunderland.ac.uk

M1Q1 BA Law with English Language/Linguistics
Duration: 3FT Hon

Entry Requirements: *GCE:* 220-360. *BTEC NC:* DM. *BTEC ND:* MMM. *OCR ND:* Distinction. *OCR NED:* Merit.

M1R1 BA Law with Modern Foreign Language (French)
Duration: 3FT Hon

Entry Requirements: *GCE:* 220-360. *BTEC NC:* DM. *BTEC ND:* MMM. *OCR ND:* Distinction. *OCR NED:* Merit.

M1R2 BA Law with Modern Foreign Language (German)
Duration: 3FT Hon

Entry Requirements: *GCE:* 220-360. *BTEC NC:* DM. *BTEC ND:* MMM. *OCR ND:* Distinction. *OCR NED:* Merit.

M1R4 BA Law with Modern Foreign Language (Spanish)
Duration: 3FT Hon

Entry Requirements: *GCE:* 220-360. *BTEC NC:* DM. *BTEC ND:* MMM. *OCR ND:* Distinction. *OCR NED:* Merit.

RM11 BA Modern Foreign Languages (French) and Law
Duration: 3FT Hon

Entry Requirements: *GCE:* 220-360. *IB:* 31. *BTEC NC:* DM. *BTEC ND:* MMM. *OCR ND:* Distinction. *OCR NED:* Merit.

MR92 BA Modern Foreign Languages (German) and Criminology
Duration: 3FT Hon

Entry Requirements: *GCE:* 220-360. *IB:* 31. *BTEC NC:* DM. *BTEC ND:* MMM. *OCR ND:* Distinction. *OCR NED:* Merit.

MR12 BA Modern Foreign Languages (German) and Law

Duration: 3FT Hon

Entry Requirements: *GCE:* 220-360. *IB:* 31. *BTEC NC:* DM. *BTEC ND:* MMM. *OCR ND:* Distinction. *OCR NED:* Merit.

MR14 BA Modern Foreign Languages (Spanish) and Law

Duration: 3FT Hon

Entry Requirements: *GCE:* 220-360. *IB:* 31. *BTEC NC:* DM. *BTEC ND:* MMM. *OCR ND:* Distinction. *OCR NED:* Merit.

MQ11 BA/BSc Law and English Language/Linguistics

Duration: 3FT Hon

Entry Requirements: *GCE:* 220-360. *BTEC NC:* DM. *BTEC ND:* MMM. *OCR ND:* Distinction. *OCR NED:* Merit.

S90 UNIVERSITY OF SUSSEX

UNDERGRADUATE ADMISSIONS
SUSSEX HOUSE
UNIVERSITY OF SUSSEX
BRIGHTON BN1 9RH

t: 01273 678416 f: 01273 678545
e: ug.applicants@sussex.ac.uk
// www.sussex.ac.uk

M1RY LLB Law with a Language (French, German, Italian or Spanish) (4 years)

Duration: 4FT Hon

Entry Requirements: *GCE:* AAB-ABB. *SQAH:* AAABB-AABBB.

S93 SWANSEA UNIVERSITY

SINGLETON PARK
SWANSEA SA2 8PP

t: 01792 295111 f: 01792 295110
e: admissions@swansea.ac.uk
// www.swansea.ac.uk

MR11 LLB Law and French (4 years)

Duration: 4FT Hon

Entry Requirements: *GCE:* 280-300.

MR12 LLB Law and German (4 years)

Duration: 4FT Hon

Entry Requirements: *GCE:* 240-300.

MR13 LLB Law and Italian (4 years)

Duration: 4FT Hon

Entry Requirements: *GCE:* 240-300.

MR14 LLB Law and Spanish (4 years)

Duration: 4FT Hon

Entry Requirements: *GCE:* 240-300.

MQ15 LLB Law and Welsh (4 years)

Duration: 4FT Hon

Entry Requirements: *GCE:* 260-300.

U20 UNIVERSITY OF ULSTER

COLERAINE
CO. LONDONDERRY
NORTHERN IRELAND BT52 1SA

t: 028 7032 4221 f: 028 7032 4908
e: online@ulster.ac.uk
// www.ulster.ac.uk

M1R1 LLB Law with French

Duration: 3FT Hon

Entry Requirements: *GCE:* ABB. *SQAH:* AAABC. *SQAAH:* ABB. *IB:* 26. *BTEC ND:* DDM.

M1Q5 LLB Law with Irish

Duration: 3FT Hon

Entry Requirements: *GCE:* ABB. *SQAH:* AAABC. *SQAAH:* ABB. *IB:* 26. *BTEC ND:* DDM.

M1R4 LLB Law with Spanish

Duration: 3FT Hon

Entry Requirements: *GCE:* ABB. *SQAH:* AAABC. *SQAAH:* ABB. *IB:* 26. *BTEC ND:* DDM.

W50 UNIVERSITY OF WESTMINSTER

115 NEW CAVENDISH STREET
LONDON W1W 6UW

t: 020 7911 5000 f: 020 7911 5788
e: course-enquiries@westminster.ac.uk
// www.westminster.ac.uk

M1R1 LLB Law with French

Duration: 4FT Hon

Entry Requirements: *GCE:* ABC. *SQAH:* ABBBC. *SQAAH:* ABC. *IB:* 30. *BTEC ND:* DDM.

W75 UNIVERSITY OF WOLVERHAMPTON

ADMISSIONS UNIT
MX207, CAMP STREET
WOLVERHAMPTON
WEST MIDLANDS WV1 1AD

t: 01902 321000 f: 01902 321896
e: admissions@wlv.ac.uk

// www.wlv.ac.uk

RM11 BA French and Law

Duration: 3FT Hon

Entry Requirements: *GCE:* 160-220.

LAW

A20 THE UNIVERSITY OF ABERDEEN

UNIVERSITY OFFICE
KING'S COLLEGE
ABERDEEN AB24 3FX

t: +44 (0) 1224 273504 f: +44 (0) 1224 272034
e: sras@abdn.ac.uk

// www.abdn.ac.uk/sras

M114 LLB Law

Duration: 3FT/4FT Ord/Hon

Entry Requirements: *GCE:* BBB. *SQAH:* ABBBB-AABB. *SQAAH:* BBB.
IB: 34.

M115 LLB Law - Accelerated (Graduates only)

Duration: 2FT Hon

Entry Requirements: Contact the institution for details.

A30 UNIVERSITY OF ABERTAY DUNDEE

BELL STREET
DUNDEE DD1 1HG

t: 01382 308080 f: 01382 308081
e: sro@abertay.ac.uk

// www.abertay.ac.uk

M114 LLB Law

Duration: 4FT Hon

Entry Requirements: *GCE:* BCC. *SQAH:* BBBB. *IB:* 26. *BTEC NC:* DD.
BTEC ND: DMM.

A40 ABERYSTWYTH UNIVERSITY

WELCOME CENTRE, ABERYSTWYTH UNIVERSITY
PENGLAIS CAMPUS
ABERYSTWYTH
CEREDIGION SY23 3FB

t: 01970 622021 f: 01970 627410
e: ug-admissions@aber.ac.uk

// www.aber.ac.uk

M100 LLB Law

Duration: 3FT Hon

Entry Requirements: *GCE:* 280. *IB:* 27.

M101 LLB Law (2 years)

Duration: 2FT Hon

Entry Requirements: Contact the institution for details.

M103 BA Law

Duration: 3FT Hon

Entry Requirements: *GCE:* 280. *IB:* 27.

A60 ANGLIA RUSKIN UNIVERSITY

BISHOP HALL LANE
CHELMSFORD
ESSEX CM1 1SQ

t: 0845 271 3333 f: 01245 251789
e: answers@anglia.ac.uk

// www.anglia.ac.uk

M100 LLB Law

Duration: 3FT Hon

Entry Requirements: *GCE:* 240. *SQAH:* AABC. *SQAAH:* AB. *IB:* 30.

B06 BANGOR UNIVERSITY

BANGOR
GWYNEDD LL57 2DG

t: 01248 382016/2017 f: 01248 370451
e: admissions@bangor.ac.uk

// www.bangor.ac.uk

M100 LLB Law

Duration: 3FT Hon

Entry Requirements: *GCE:* 280. *IB:* 28.

M101 LLB Law (2 year programme)

Duration: 2FT Hon

Entry Requirements: *GCE:* 280. *IB:* 28.

B22 UNIVERSITY OF BEDFORDSHIRE
PARK SQUARE
LUTON
BEDS LU1 3JU
t: 01582 489286 **f:** 01582 489323
e: admissions@beds.ac.uk
// www.beds.ac.uk

M100 LLB Law
Duration: 3FT Hon

Entry Requirements: *GCE:* 160-240. *SQAH:* BCC. *SQAAH:* BCC. *IB:* 32.

M102 BA Extended Degree of Higher Education - Law
Duration: 4FT Hon

Entry Requirements: Contact the institution for details.

M103 BA Extended Degree of Higher Education - Law (English Pathway)
Duration: 4FT Hon

Entry Requirements: Contact the institution for details.

B25 BIRMINGHAM CITY UNIVERSITY
PERRY BARR
BIRMINGHAM B42 2SU
t: 0121 331 5595 **f:** 0121 331 7994
e: choices@bcu.ac.uk
// www.bcu.ac.uk

M100 LLB Law
Duration: 3FT Hon

Entry Requirements: *GCE:* 280. *IB:* 24. *BTEC NC:* DD. *BTEC ND:* DMM. *OCR ND:* Distinction.

B32 THE UNIVERSITY OF BIRMINGHAM
EDGBASTON
BIRMINGHAM B15 2TT
t: 0121 415 8900 **f:** 0121 414 7159
e: admissions@bham.ac.uk
// www.bham.ac.uk

M100 LLB Law
Duration: 3FT Hon

Entry Requirements: *GCE:* AAA. *SQAAH:* AAA. *IB:* 36. *BTEC NC:* DD. *BTEC ND:* DDD. Admissions Test required.

M990 LLB LLB for Graduates (2 years)
Duration: 2FT Hon

Entry Requirements: Contact the institution for details.

B44 THE UNIVERSITY OF BOLTON
DEANE ROAD
BOLTON BL3 5AB
t: 01204 900600 **f:** 01204 399074
e: enquiries@bolton.ac.uk
// www.bolton.ac.uk

M100 LLB LLB Law
Duration: 3FT Hon

Entry Requirements: *GCE:* 240. *IB:* 24. *BTEC ND:* MMM.

M1N2 LLB LLB Law with Business Management
Duration: 3FT Hon

Entry Requirements: *GCE:* 240. *IB:* 24. *BTEC ND:* MMM.

B50 BOURNEMOUTH UNIVERSITY
TALBOT CAMPUS
FERN BARROW
POOLE
DORSET BH12 5BB
t: 01202 524111
// www.bournemouth.ac.uk

M100 LLB Law
Duration: 4SW Hon

Entry Requirements: *GCE:* 320.

M100 LLB Law
Duration: 4SW Hon

Entry Requirements: *GCE:* 320.

M100 LLB Law
Duration: 4SW Hon

Entry Requirements: *GCE:* 300.

M100 LLB Law
Duration: 4SW Hon

Entry Requirements: *GCE:* 320. *IB:* 32.

B54 BPP COLLEGE OF PROFESSIONAL STUDIES
68-70 RED LION STREET
LONDON WC1R 4NY
t: +44 (0) 845 678 6868 **f:** +44 (0) 20 7404 1389
e: law@bpp.com
// www.bppuc.com/index.htm

M100 LLB LLB
Duration: 3FT Hon

Entry Requirements: Contact the institution for details.

Confused about courses?
Indecisive about institutions?
Stressed about student life?
Unsure about UCAS?
Frowning over finance?

Help is available.

Visit www.ucasbooks.com to view our range
of over 75 books covering all aspects
of entry into higher education.

www.ucasbooks.com

> Unlock your potential
It's as easy as 1, 2, 3.

1 Search
Use Course Search to look for courses in your subject; find out about your chosen universities and colleges and lots more.

2 Apply
Use our online system Apply to make your application to higher education.

3 Track
Then use Track to monitor the progress of your application.

UCAS   helping students into higher education   **www.ucas.com**

M101 LLB LLB (2 years)
Duration: 2FT Hon

Entry Requirements: Contact the institution for details.

M221 LLB LLB (Business Law)
Duration: 3FT Hon

Entry Requirements: *GCE:* 240.

M225 LLB LLB (Business Law) (2 years)
Duration: 2FT Hon

Entry Requirements: Contact the institution for details.

B56 THE UNIVERSITY OF BRADFORD
RICHMOND ROAD
BRADFORD
WEST YORKSHIRE BD7 1DP

t: 0800 073 1225 **f:** 01274 235585
e: course-enquiries@bradford.ac.uk

// www.bradford.ac.uk

M100 LLB Law
Duration: 3FT Hon

Entry Requirements: *GCE:* 300. *IB:* 30. Interview required.

B60 BRADFORD COLLEGE: AN ASSOCIATE COLLEGE OF LEEDS METROPOLITAN UNIVERSITY
GREAT HORTON ROAD
BRADFORD
WEST YORKSHIRE BD7 1AY

t: 01274 433333 **f:** 01274 433241
e: admissions@bradfordcollege.ac.uk

// www.bradfordcollege.ac.uk

M100 LLB Law
Duration: 3FT Hon

Entry Requirements: *GCE:* 160. *IB:* 24.

ML14 BA Law and Social Welfare
Duration: 3FT Hon

Entry Requirements: Contact the institution for details.

M190 BA Law IPOS
Duration: 3FT Hon

Entry Requirements: *GCE:* 120.

B78 UNIVERSITY OF BRISTOL
UNDERGRADUATE ADMISSIONS OFFICE
SENATE HOUSE
TYNDALL AVENUE
BRISTOL BS8 1TH

t: 0117 928 9000 **f:** 0117 925 1424
e: ug-admissions@bristol.ac.uk

// www.bristol.ac.uk

M100 LLB Law
Duration: 3FT Hon

Entry Requirements: *GCE:* AAA. *SQAH:* AAAAA. *SQAAH:* AA. *IB:* 37. *BTEC ND:* DDD. Admissions Test required.

B80 UNIVERSITY OF THE WEST OF ENGLAND, BRISTOL
FRENCHAY CAMPUS
COLDHARBOUR LANE
BRISTOL BS16 1QY

t: +44 (0)117 32 83333 **f:** +44 (0)117 32 82810
e: admissions@uwe.ac.uk

// www.uwe.ac.uk

M100 LLB Law
Duration: 3FT Hon

Entry Requirements: *GCE:* 300-340.

M101 BA Law
Duration: 3FT Hon

Entry Requirements: *GCE:* 300-340.

B84 BRUNEL UNIVERSITY
UXBRIDGE
MIDDLESEX UB8 3PH

t: 01895 265265 **f:** 01895 269790
e: admissions@brunel.ac.uk

// www.brunel.ac.uk

M103 LLB Law
Duration: 3FT Hon

Entry Requirements: Interview required.

M101 LLB Law (4 year Thick SW)
Duration: 4SW Hon

Entry Requirements: *GCE:* 390. *IB:* 32. *BTEC NC:* DM. *BTEC ND:* DDM.

B90 THE UNIVERSITY OF BUCKINGHAM

YEOMANRY HOUSE
HUNTER STREET
BUCKINGHAM MK18 1EG

t: 01280 820313 f: 01280 822245
e: info@buckingham.ac.uk

// www.buckingham.ac.uk

M100 LLB Law

Duration: 2FT Hon

Entry Requirements: *GCE:* 300. *IB:* 28. *BTEC NC:* DD. *BTEC ND:* DMM.

B94 BUCKINGHAMSHIRE NEW UNIVERSITY

QUEEN ALEXANDRA ROAD
HIGH WYCOMBE
BUCKS HP11 2JZ

t: 0800 0565 660 f: 01494 605023
e: admissions@bucks.ac.uk

// www.bucks.ac.uk

M100 LLB Law

Duration: 3FT Hon

Entry Requirements: *GCE:* 240-280. *IB:* 24. *BTEC NC:* DD. *BTEC ND:* MMM. *OCR ND:* Distinction. *OCR NED:* Merit.

C05 UNIVERSITY OF CAMBRIDGE

CAMBRIDGE ADMISSIONS OFFICE
FITZWILLIAM HOUSE
32 TRUMPINGTON STREET
CAMBRIDGE CB2 1QY

t: 01223 333 308 f: 01223 366 383
e: admissions@cam.ac.uk

// www.cam.ac.uk/admissions/undergraduate/

M100 BA Law

Duration: 3FT Hon

Entry Requirements: *GCE:* AAA. *SQAAH:* AAA-AAB. Interview required.

C10 CANTERBURY CHRIST CHURCH UNIVERSITY

NORTH HOLMES ROAD
CANTERBURY
KENT CT1 1QU

t: 01227 782900 f: 01227 782888
e: admissions@canterbury.ac.uk

// www.canterbury.ac.uk

M100 LLB Law

Duration: 3FT Hon

Entry Requirements: *GCE:* 260. *IB:* 24.

M102 BA Law

Duration: 3FT Hon

Entry Requirements: *GCE:* 260. *IB:* 24.

C15 CARDIFF UNIVERSITY

PO BOX 927
30-36 NEWPORT ROAD
CARDIFF CF24 0DE

t: 029 2087 9999 f: 029 2087 6138
e: admissions@cardiff.ac.uk

// www.cardiff.ac.uk

M100 LLB Law

Duration: 3FT Hon

Entry Requirements: *GCE:* AAA. *SQAAH:* AAA. Interview required.

C30 UNIVERSITY OF CENTRAL LANCASHIRE

PRESTON
LANCS PR1 2HE

t: 01772 201201 f: 01772 894954
e: uadmissions@uclan.ac.uk

// www.uclan.ac.uk

M100 LLB Law

Duration: 3FT Hon

Entry Requirements: *GCE:* BBC. *SQAH:* AAAB. *IB:* 30. *BTEC NC:* DD. *BTEC ND:* DDM.

M101 FYr LLB Foundation Entry

Duration: 4FT Hon

Entry Requirements: Contact the institution for details.

C55 UNIVERSITY OF CHESTER

PARKGATE ROAD
CHESTER CH1 4BJ

t: 01244 511000 f: 01244 511300
e: enquiries@chester.ac.uk

// www.chester.ac.uk

M100 LLB Law

Duration: 3FT Hon

Entry Requirements: *GCE:* 240 - 300. *SQAH:* BBBB. *IB:* 24. *BTEC NC:* DM. *BTEC ND:* MMM.

C60 CITY UNIVERSITY

NORTHAMPTON SQUARE
LONDON EC1V 0HB

t: 020 7040 5060 f: 020 7040 8995
e: ugadmissions@city.ac.uk

// www.city.ac.uk

M100 LLB Law

Duration: 3FT Hon

Entry Requirements: *GCE:* AAB. *SQAH:* ABBBB. *IB:* 35.

C85 COVENTRY UNIVERSITY

THE STUDENT CENTRE
COVENTRY UNIVERSITY
1 GULSON RD
COVENTRY CV1 2JH

t: 024 7615 2222 f: 024 7615 2223
e: studentenquiries@coventry.ac.uk

// www.coventry.ac.uk

M100 LLB Law
Duration: 3FT Hon

Entry Requirements: *GCE:* 300. *BTEC ND:* DDM.

M205 LLB Law (Senior Status) (2 years)
Duration: 2FT Hon

Entry Requirements: Contact the institution for details.

M101 Foundation Law Foundation Year
Duration: 1FT FYr

Entry Requirements: *GCE:* 100. *BTEC NC:* MP. *BTEC ND:* PPP.

C92 CROYDON COLLEGE

COLLEGE ROAD
CROYDON CR9 1DX

t: 020 8760 5914 f: 020 8760 5880
e: info@croydon.ac.uk

// www.croydon.ac.uk

M100 LLB Law
Duration: 3FT Hon

Entry Requirements: *GCE:* 60-80.

C99 UNIVERSITY OF CUMBRIA

FUSEHILL STREET
CARLISLE
CUMBRIA CA1 2HH

t: 01228 616234 f: 01228 616235

// www.cumbria.ac.uk

M100 LLB Law
Duration: 3FT Hon

Entry Requirements: *GCE:* 40.

D26 DE MONTFORT UNIVERSITY

THE GATEWAY
LEICESTER LE1 9BH

t: 0116 255 1551 f: 0116 250 6204
e: enquiries@dmu.ac.uk

// www.dmu.ac.uk

M100 LLB Law
Duration: 3FT Hon

Entry Requirements: *GCE:* 280. *IB:* 28. *BTEC ND:* DMM. Interview required.

D39 UNIVERSITY OF DERBY

KEDLESTON ROAD
DERBY DE22 1GB

t: 08701 202330 f: 01332 597724
e: askadmissions@derby.ac.uk

// www.derby.ac.uk

M100 LLB Law
Duration: 3FT Hon

Entry Requirements: *GCE:* 300. *IB:* 30. *BTEC NC:* DD. *BTEC ND:* DMM.

M101 BA Law
Duration: 3FT Hon

Entry Requirements: *Foundation:* Merit. *GCE:* 260. *IB:* 26. *BTEC NC:* DD. *BTEC ND:* MMM. *OCR ND:* Distinction. *OCR NED:* Merit.

D65 UNIVERSITY OF DUNDEE

DUNDEE DD1 4HN

t: 01382 383838 f: 01382 388150
e: srs@dundee.ac.uk

// www.dundee.ac.uk/admissions/undergraduate

M111 LLB Law (Eng/NI)
Duration: 4FT Hon

Entry Requirements: *GCE:* BBB. *SQAH:* AABB-ABBBB. *IB:* 33.

M111 LLB Law (Eng/NI)
Duration: 4FT Hon

Entry Requirements: *GCE:* BBB. *SQAH:* AABB-ABBBB. *IB:* 33.

M111 LLB Law (Eng/NI)
Duration: 4FT Hon

Entry Requirements: *GCE:* BBB. *SQAH:* AABB-ABBBB. *IB:* 33.

M111 LLB Law (Eng/NI)
Duration: 4FT Hon

Entry Requirements: *GCE:* BBB. *SQAH:* AABB-ABBBB. *IB:* 33.

M111 LLB Law (Eng/NI)
Duration: 4FT Hon

Entry Requirements: *GCE:* BBB. *SQAH:* AABB-ABBBB. *IB:* 33.

M101 LLB Law (Eng/NI) - Accelerated
Duration: 2FT Ord

Entry Requirements: Contact the institution for details.

D86 DURHAM UNIVERSITY

DURHAM UNIVERSITY
UNIVERSITY OFFICE
DURHAM DH1 3HP

t: 0191 334 2000 **f:** 0191 334 6055
e: admissions@durham.ac.uk
// www.durham.ac.uk

M101 LLB Law

Duration: 3FT Hon

Entry Requirements: *GCE:* AAA. *SQAH:* AAAAA. *SQAAH:* AAA. *IB:* 38.
Admissions Test required.

M102 BA Law with Foundation

Duration: 4FT Fdg

Entry Requirements: Contact the institution for details.

E14 UNIVERSITY OF EAST ANGLIA

NORWICH NR4 7TJ

t: 01603 456161 **f:** 01603 458596
e: admissions@uea.ac.uk
// www.uea.ac.uk

M100 LLB Law

Duration: 3FT Hon

Entry Requirements: *GCE:* 340. *IB:* 33.

E21 EAST END COMPUTING AND BUSINESS COLLEGE

149 COMERCIAL ROAD
LONDON E1 1PX

t: 020 7247 8447 **f:** 020 7247 0942
e: info@eastendcbc.co.uk
// www.eastendcbc.co.uk

M100 LLB Batchelor of Law (LLB)

Duration: 3FT Hon

Entry Requirements: Contact the institution for details.

E25 EAST LANCASHIRE INSTITUTE OF HIGHER EDUCATION AT BLACKBURN COLLEGE

DUKE STREET
BLACKBURN BB2 1LH

t: 01254 292594 **f:** 01254 260749
e: he-admissions@blackburn.ac.uk
// www.elihe.ac.uk

M100 LLB Law: Multimode (3 years)

Duration: 3FT Hon

Entry Requirements: *GCE:* 40.

M102 LLB LLB Fast Track (2 years) (top-up)

Duration: 2FT Hon

Entry Requirements: *GCE:* 40.

E28 UNIVERSITY OF EAST LONDON

DOCKLANDS CAMPUS
UNIVERSITY WAY
LONDON E16 2RD

t: 020 8223 2835 **f:** 020 8223 2978
e: admiss@uel.ac.uk
// www.uel.ac.uk

M100 LLB Law

Duration: 3FT Hon

Entry Requirements: *GCE:* 240. *IB:* 28. *BTEC NC:* DD. *BTEC ND:* MMM.

E42 EDGE HILL UNIVERSITY

ORMSKIRK
LANCASHIRE L39 4QP

t: 0800 195 5063 **f:** 01695 584355
e: enquiries@edgehill.ac.uk
// www.edgehill.ac.uk

M100 LLB Law

Duration: 3FT Hon

Entry Requirements: *GCE:* 260. *IB:* 28. *BTEC NC:* DD. *BTEC ND:* MMM.

E56 THE UNIVERSITY OF EDINBURGH

STUDENT RECRUITMENT & ADMISSIONS
57 GEORGE SQUARE
EDINBURGH EH8 9JU

t: 0131 650 4360 **f:** 0131 651 1236
e: sra.enquiries@ed.ac.uk
// www.ed.ac.uk/studying/undergraduate/

M114 LLB Law

Duration: 4FT Hon

Entry Requirements: *GCE:* BBB. *SQAH:* BBBB. *IB:* 34.

M115 LLB Law (Graduate Entry)

Duration: 2FT Deg

Entry Requirements: Contact the institution for details.

E59 EDINBURGH NAPIER UNIVERSITY

CRAIGLOCKHART CAMPUS
EDINBURGH EH14 1DJ

t: +44 (0)8452 60 60 40 **f:** 0131 455 6464
e: info@napier.ac.uk
// www.napier.ac.uk

M115 LLB Law

Duration: 2FT/3FT Ord/Hon

Entry Requirements: *GCE:* 240.

M100 LLB LLB (Accelerated)

Duration: 2FT Ord

Entry Requirements: *GCE:* 240.

M114 BA Law (LLB)

Duration: 3FT/4FT Ord/Hon

Entry Requirements: *GCE:* 230.

E70 THE UNIVERSITY OF ESSEX

WIVENHOE PARK
COLCHESTER
ESSEX CO4 3SQ

t: 01206 873666 **f:** 01206 873423
e: admit@essex.ac.uk

// www.essex.ac.uk

M100 LLB Law

Duration: 3FT Hon

Entry Requirements: *GCE:* AAB. *SQAH:* AAAA-AAAB. *IB:* 36. *BTEC NC:* DM. *BTEC ND:* DDD.

E84 UNIVERSITY OF EXETER

LAVER BUILDING
NORTH PARK ROAD
EXETER
DEVON EX4 4QE

t: 01392 263855 **f:** 01392 263857/262479
e: admissions@exeter.ac.uk

// www.exeter.ac.uk/admissions

M103 LLB Law

Duration: 3FT Hon

Entry Requirements: *GCE:* AAA-AAB. Admissions Test required.

M105 LLB Law (Cornwall campus)

Duration: 3FT Hon

Entry Requirements: *GCE:* AAB-ABB. Admissions Test required.

G14 UNIVERSITY OF GLAMORGAN, CARDIFF AND PONTYPRIDD

ENQUIRIES AND ADMISSIONS UNIT
PONTYPRIDD CF37 1DL

t: 0800 716925 **f:** 01443 654050
e: enquiries@glam.ac.uk

// www.glam.ac.uk

M100 LLB Law

Duration: 3FT Hon

Entry Requirements: *GCE:* 300-340. *IB:* 30. *BTEC NC:* DD. *BTEC ND:* DMM.

M108 FYr Law Foundation Year

Duration: 1FT FYr

Entry Requirements: Contact the institution for details.

G28 UNIVERSITY OF GLASGOW

THE UNIVERSITY OF GLASGOW
THE FRASER BUILDING
65 HILLHEAD STREET
GLASGOW G12 8QF

t: 0141 330 6062 **f:** 0141 330 2961
e: ugenquiries@gla.ac.uk (UK/EU undergrad enquiries only)

// www.glasgow.ac.uk

M114 LLB Law

Duration: 4FT Hon

Entry Requirements: *GCE:* AAB. *SQAH:* AAAAB. *IB:* 34. Admissions Test required.

M115 LLB Law (Fast-track) (Graduates Only)

Duration: 2FT Hon

Entry Requirements: Contact the institution for details.

G42 GLASGOW CALEDONIAN UNIVERSITY

CITY CAMPUS
COWCADDENS ROAD
GLASGOW G4 0BA

t: 0141 331 3000 **f:** 0141 331 3449
e: admissions@gcal.ac.uk

// www.gcal.ac.uk

M114 LLB LLB Law

Duration: 4FT Hon

Entry Requirements: *GCE:* ABB. *SQAH:* AABBB.

M115 LLB LLB Law (Fast Track)

Duration: 2FT Hon

Entry Requirements: *GCE:* CCC.

G50 THE UNIVERSITY OF GLOUCESTERSHIRE

HARDWICK CAMPUS
ST PAUL'S ROAD
CHELTENHAM GL50 4BS

t: 01242 714501 **f:** 01242 543334
e: admissions@glos.ac.uk

// www.glos.ac.uk

M100 LLB Law

Duration: 3FT Hon

Entry Requirements: *GCE:* 280-300. Interview required.

M101 LLB Law

Duration: 2FT Hon

Entry Requirements: *GCE:* 280-300. Interview required.

G70 UNIVERSITY OF GREENWICH

GREENWICH CAMPUS
OLD ROYAL NAVAL COLLEGE
PARK ROW
LONDON SE10 9LS

t: 0800 005 006 f: 020 8331 8145
e: courseinfo@gre.ac.uk
// www.gre.ac.uk

M100 LLB Law

Duration: 3FT Hon

Entry Requirements: *GCE:* 240. *IB:* 30.

G80 GRIMSBY INSTITUTE OF FURTHER AND HIGHER EDUCATION

NUNS CORNER
GRIMSBY
NE LINCOLNSHIRE DN34 5BQ

t: 0800 328 3631 f: 01472 315506/879924
e: headmissions@grimsby.ac.uk
// www.grimsby.ac.uk

M100 LLB Law

Duration: 2FT Dip

Entry Requirements: *GCE:* 120-240. *BTEC NC:* MP. *BTEC ND:* PPP.

H36 UNIVERSITY OF HERTFORDSHIRE

UNIVERSITY ADMISSIONS SERVICE
COLLEGE LANE
HATFIELD
HERTS AL10 9AB

t: 01707 284800 f: 01707 284870
// www.herts.ac.uk

M100 LLB Law

Duration: 3FT Hon

Entry Requirements: *GCE:* 280.

H50 HOLBORN COLLEGE

WOOLWICH ROAD
LONDON SE7 8LN

t: 020 8317 6000 f: 020 8317 6001
e: admissions@holborncollege.ac.uk
// www.holborncollege.ac.uk

M103 LLB Law

Duration: 3FT Hon

Entry Requirements: Contact the institution for details.

M101 LLB Law (External)

Duration: 3FT Hon

Entry Requirements: *SQAH:* BCCCC.

H60 THE UNIVERSITY OF HUDDERSFIELD

QUEENSGATE
HUDDERSFIELD HD1 3DH

t: 01484 473969 f: 01484 472765
e: admissionsandrecords@hud.ac.uk
// www.hud.ac.uk

M100 LLB Law (Exempting)

Duration: 3FT/4FT Hon

Entry Requirements: *GCE:* 300. *SQAH:* BBBB. *IB:* 28.

M102 BA Law (Top-up)

Duration: 1FT Hon

Entry Requirements: HND required.

H72 THE UNIVERSITY OF HULL

THE UNIVERSITY OF HULL
COTTINGHAM ROAD
HULL HU6 7RX

t: 01482 466100 f: 01482 442290
e: admissions@hull.ac.uk
// www.hull.ac.uk

M100 LLB Law

Duration: 3FT Hon

Entry Requirements: *GCE:* 320. *IB:* 28.

M101 LLB LLB Senior Status

Duration: 2FT Hon

Entry Requirements: Contact the institution for details.

K12 KEELE UNIVERSITY

STAFFS ST5 5BG

t: 01782 734005 f: 01782 632343
e: undergraduate@keele.ac.uk
// www.keele.ac.uk

M100 LLB Law (Single Honours)

Duration: 3FT Hon

Entry Requirements: *GCE:* 340-360. *BTEC ND:* DDD.

K24 THE UNIVERSITY OF KENT

INFORMATION, RECRUITMENT & ADMISSIONS
REGISTRY
UNIVERSITY OF KENT
CANTERBURY. KENT CT2 7NZ

t: 01227 827272 f: 01227 827077
e: information@kent.ac.uk
// www.kent.ac.uk

M100 LLB Law

Duration: 3FT Hon

Entry Requirements: *GCE:* 320. *SQAH:* AAAAA. *IB:* 34. *BTEC NC:* DD. *BTEC ND:* DDM.

M102 LLB Law

Duration: 3FT Hon

Entry Requirements: *GCE:* 320. *SQAH:* AAAAA. *IB:* 34. *BTEC NC:* DD. *BTEC ND:* DDM.

K60 KING'S COLLEGE LONDON (UNIVERSITY OF LONDON)
STRAND
LONDON WC2R 2LS
t: 020 7836 5454 f: 020 7836 1799
e: ucas.enquiries@kcl.ac.uk
// www.kcl.ac.uk

M100 LLB Law

Duration: 3FT Hon

Entry Requirements: *GCE:* AAAb. *SQAH:* AAB. *SQAAH:* AA. *IB:* 38. *BTEC NC:* DD. Admissions Test required.

K84 KINGSTON UNIVERSITY
STUDENT INFORMATION & ADVICE CENTRE
COOPER HOUSE
40-46 SURBITON ROAD
KINGSTON UPON THAMES KT1 2HX
t: 020 8547 7053 f: 020 8547 7080
e: aps@kingston.ac.uk
// www.kingston.ac.uk

M100 LLB Law

Duration: 3FT Hon

Entry Requirements: *GCE:* 40.

M101 LLB Law Senior Status

Duration: 2FT Hon

Entry Requirements: *GCE:* 220.

M990 BA Law

Duration: 3FT Hon

Entry Requirements: *GCE:* 140.

L14 LANCASTER UNIVERSITY
THE UNIVERSITY
LANCASTER
LANCASHIRE LA1 4YW
t: 01524 592029 f: 01524 846243
e: ugadmissions@lancaster.ac.uk
// www.lancs.ac.uk

M100 LLB Law

Duration: 3FT Hon

Entry Requirements: *GCE:* AAA. *SQAH:* AAAAA. *SQAAH:* AAA. *IB:* 31. *BTEC ND:* DDD.

L23 UNIVERSITY OF LEEDS
THE UNIVERSITY OF LEEDS
LEEDS LS2 9JT
t: 0113 343 3999
e: admissions@adm.leeds.ac.uk
// www.leeds.ac.uk

M101 LLB Law (2 years)

Duration: 2FT Hon

Entry Requirements: Contact the institution for details.

M100 LLB Law (3 years)

Duration: 3FT Hon

Entry Requirements: *GCE:* AAA. *SQAH:* AAAAA. *SQAAH:* AAA. *IB:* 38.

L27 LEEDS METROPOLITAN UNIVERSITY
COURSE ENQUIRIES OFFICE
CIVIC QUARTER
LEEDS LS1 3HE
t: 0113 81 23113 f: 0113 81 23129
e: course-enquiries@leedsmet.ac.uk
// www.leedsmet.ac.uk

M100 LLB Law

Duration: 3FT Hon

Entry Requirements: *GCE:* 260. *IB:* 28.

L34 UNIVERSITY OF LEICESTER
UNIVERSITY ROAD
LEICESTER LE1 7RH
t: 0116 252 5281 f: 0116 252 2447
e: admissions@le.ac.uk
// www.le.ac.uk

M100 LLB Law

Duration: 3FT Hon

Entry Requirements: *GCE:* AAA. *SQAH:* AAAAA. *SQAAH:* AAA. *IB:* 36. *BTEC ND:* DDD.

M101 LLB LLB (Senior Status)

Duration: 2FT Hon

Entry Requirements: Contact the institution for details.

L39 UNIVERSITY OF LINCOLN
ADMISSIONS
BRAYFORD POOL
LINCOLN LN6 7TS
t: 01522 886097 f: 01522 886146
e: admissions@lincoln.ac.uk
// www.lincoln.ac.uk

M100 LLB Law

Duration: 3FT Hon

Entry Requirements: *GCE:* 260.

L41 THE UNIVERSITY OF LIVERPOOL

THE FOUNDATION BUILDING
BROWNLOW HILL
LIVERPOOL L69 7ZX

t: 0151 794 2000 f: 0151 708 6502
e: ugrecruitment@liv.ac.uk

// www.liv.ac.uk

M100 LLB Law (LLB Honours)

Duration: 3FT Hon

Entry Requirements: *GCE:* AAB-AAA. *SQAH:* AABB. *IB:* 35. *BTEC NC:* DD. *BTEC ND:* DDD. *OCR ND:* Distinction. *OCR NED:* Distinction.

L51 LIVERPOOL JOHN MOORES UNIVERSITY

ROSCOE COURT
4 RODNEY STREET
LIVERPOOL L1 2TZ

t: 0151 231 5090 f: 0151 231 3462
e: recruitment@ljmu.ac.uk

// www.ljmu.ac.uk

M100 LLB Law

Duration: 3FT Hon

Entry Requirements: *GCE:* 260. *IB:* 30.

L68 LONDON METROPOLITAN UNIVERSITY

166-220 HOLLOWAY ROAD
LONDON N7 8DB

t: 020 7133 4200
e: admissions@londonmet.ac.uk

// www.londonmet.ac.uk

M100 LLB LLB

Duration: 3FT Hon

Entry Requirements: *GCE:* 320. *IB:* 28.

M102 LLB LLB Law (with ILEX Exemption)

Duration: 3FT Hon

Entry Requirements: HND required.

M103 LLB LLB Law (with International Development)

Duration: 3FT Hon

Entry Requirements: *GCE:* 320. *IB:* 28.

M1L2 LLB LLB Law (with International Relations)

Duration: 3FT Hon

Entry Requirements: *GCE:* 320. *IB:* 28.

M101 BA Law

Duration: 3FT Hon

Entry Requirements: *GCE:* 240. *IB:* 28.

MM12 BA Law & Practice (Top-up)

Duration: 1FT Hon

Entry Requirements: Contact the institution for details.

L72 LONDON SCHOOL OF ECONOMICS AND POLITICAL SCIENCE (UNIVERSITY OF LONDON)

HOUGHTON STREET
LONDON WC2A 2AE

t: 020 7955 7125/7769 f: 020 7955 6001
e: ug-admissions@lse.ac.uk

// www.lse.ac.uk

M100 LLB Law (Bachelor of Laws)

Duration: 3FT Hon

Entry Requirements: *GCE:* AAA. *SQAH:* AAAAA-AAAAB. *SQAAH:* AAA. *IB:* 38.

L75 LONDON SOUTH BANK UNIVERSITY

103 BOROUGH ROAD
LONDON SE1 0AA

t: 020 7815 7815 f: 020 7815 8273
e: enquiry@lsbu.ac.uk

// www.lsbu.ac.uk

M100 LLB Law

Duration: 3FT Hon

Entry Requirements: HND required.

M20 THE UNIVERSITY OF MANCHESTER

OXFORD ROAD
MANCHESTER M13 9PL

t: 0161 275 2077 f: 0161 275 2106
e: ug-admissions@manchester.ac.uk

// www.manchester.ac.uk

M100 LLB Law

Duration: 3FT Hon

Entry Requirements: *GCE:* AAA. *SQAH:* AAAAB. *SQAAH:* AAA. *IB:* 37. *BTEC ND:* DDD.

M40 THE MANCHESTER METROPOLITAN UNIVERSITY

ADMISSIONS OFFICE
ALL SAINTS (GMS)
ALL SAINTS
MANCHESTER M15 6BH

t: 0161 247 2000

// www.mmu.ac.uk

M100 LLB Law

Duration: 3FT Hon

Entry Requirements: *GCE:* 40.

M101 LLB Law (Foundation)

Duration: 4FT Hon

Entry Requirements: *GCE:* 120.

M80 MIDDLESEX UNIVERSITY

MIDDLESEX UNIVERSITY
THE BURROUGHS
LONDON NW4 4BT

t: 020 8411 5555 f: 020 8411 5649
e: enquiries@mdx.ac.uk
// www.mdx.ac.uk

M100 LLB Law

Duration: 3FT Hon

Entry Requirements: *GCE:* 200-360. *IB:* 28.

M101 BA Law

Duration: 3FT Hon

Entry Requirements: *GCE:* 200-300. *IB:* 28.

N21 NEWCASTLE UNIVERSITY

6 KENSINGTON TERRACE
NEWCASTLE UPON TYNE NE1 7RU

t: 0191 222 5594 f: 0191 222 6143
e: enquiries@ncl.ac.uk
// www.ncl.ac.uk

M101 LLB Law

Duration: 3FT Hon

Entry Requirements: *GCE:* AAA. *SQAH:* AAAAB. *IB:* 34. *BTEC ND:* DDD.

N30 NEW COLLEGE NOTTINGHAM

ADAMS BUILDING
STONEY STREET
THE LACE MARKET
NOTTINGHAM NG1 1NG

t: 0115 910 0100 f: 0115 953 4349
e: enquiries@ncn.ac.uk
// www.ncn.ac.uk

M100 FdA Law

Duration: 2FT Fdg

Entry Requirements: HND required.

N38 UNIVERSITY OF NORTHAMPTON

PARK CAMPUS
BOUGHTON GREEN ROAD
NORTHAMPTON NN2 7AL

t: 0800 358 2232 f: 01604 722083
e: admissions@northampton.ac.uk
// www.northampton.ac.uk

M100 LLB Law

Duration: 3FT Hon

Entry Requirements: *GCE:* 220-260. *SQAH:* AAB-BBBB. *IB:* 24.

M101 LLB Law (2 year fast track)

Duration: 2FT Hon

Entry Requirements: *GCE:* 220-260. *SQAH:* AAB-BBBB. *IB:* 24.

N77 NORTHUMBRIA UNIVERSITY

TRINITY BUILDING
NORTHUMBERLAND ROAD
NEWCASTLE UPON TYNE NE1 8ST

t: 0191 243 7420 f: 0191 227 4561
e: er.admissions@northumbria.ac.uk
// www.northumbria.ac.uk

M100 LLB Law (Exempting)

Duration: 4FT Hon

Entry Requirements: *GCE:* ABB. *SQAH:* BBBBB. *SQAAH:* BBB. *IB:* 27. *BTEC ND:* DDM. *OCR NED:* Distinction.

N84 THE UNIVERSITY OF NOTTINGHAM

THE ADMISSIONS OFFICE
THE UNIVERSITY OF NOTTINGHAM
UNIVERSITY PARK
NOTTINGHAM NG7 2RD

t: 0115 951 5151 f: 0115 951 4668
// www.nottingham.ac.uk

M101 LLB Senior Status Bachelor of Laws with Honours

Duration: 2FT Hon

Entry Requirements: Contact the institution for details.

M100 BA Law

Duration: 3FT Hon

Entry Requirements: *GCE:* AAA. *SQAAH:* AAA. *IB:* 38. Admissions Test required.

N91 NOTTINGHAM TRENT UNIVERSITY

DRYDEN CENTRE
BURTON STREET
NOTTINGHAM NG1 4BU

t: +44 (0) 115 941 8418 **f:** +44 (0) 115 848 6063
e: admissions@ntu.ac.uk

// www.ntu.ac.uk/

M100 LLB Law FT

Duration: 3FT Hon

Entry Requirements: *Foundation:* Pass. *GCE:* 300. *SQAH:* ABBBC.
SQAAH: BBB. *IB:* 25. *BTEC NC:* DM. *BTEC ND:* DDM. *OCR ND:* Merit.

M101 LLB Law SW

Duration: 4SW Hon

Entry Requirements: *Foundation:* Pass. *GCE:* 320. *SQAH:* AABBB.
SQAAH: ABB. *IB:* 26. *BTEC NC:* DD. *BTEC ND:* DDM. *OCR ND:*
Distinction.

O33 OXFORD UNIVERSITY

UNDERGRADUATE ADMISSIONS OFFICE
UNIVERSITY OF OXFORD
WELLINGTON SQUARE
OXFORD OX1 2JD

t: 01865 288000 **f:** 01865 270212
e: undergraduate.admissions@admin.ox.ac.uk

// www.admissions.ox.ac.uk

M100 BA Law

Duration: 3FT Hon

Entry Requirements: *GCE:* AAA. *SQAH:* AAAAA-AAAAB. *SQAAH:* AAB.
Interview required. Admissions Test required.

O66 OXFORD BROOKES UNIVERSITY

ADMISSIONS OFFICE
HEADINGTON CAMPUS
GIPSY LANE
OXFORD OX3 0BP

t: 01865 483040 **f:** 01865 483983
e: admissions@brookes.ac.uk

// www.brookes.ac.uk

M100 LLB Law

Duration: 3FT Hon

Entry Requirements: *GCE:* BBC.

P60 UNIVERSITY OF PLYMOUTH

DRAKE CIRCUS
PLYMOUTH PL4 8AA

t: 01752 588037 **f:** 01752 588050
e: admissions@plymouth.ac.uk

// www.plymouth.ac.uk

M200 LLB Law

Duration: 3FT Hon

Entry Requirements: *GCE:* 300. *IB:* 32.

P80 UNIVERSITY OF PORTSMOUTH

ACADEMIC REGISTRY
UNIVERSITY HOUSE
WINSTON CHURCHILL AVENUE
PORTSMOUTH PO1 2UP

t: 023 9284 8484 **f:** 023 9284 3082
e: admissions@port.ac.uk

// www.port.ac.uk

M100 LLB Law

Duration: 3FT/4SW Hon

Entry Requirements: *GCE:* 240.

Q50 QUEEN MARY, UNIVERSITY OF LONDON

MILE END ROAD
LONDON E1 4NS

t: 020 7882 5555 **f:** 020 7882 5500
e: admissions@qmul.ac.uk

// www.qmul.ac.uk

M101 LLB Law - Senior Status

Duration: 2FT Hon

Entry Requirements: Contact the institution for details.

M100 LLB Law (3 years)

Duration: 3FT Hon

Entry Requirements: *GCE:* AAA. *SQAAH:* AAA. *IB:* 36. *BTEC NC:* DD.
BTEC ND: DDD.

Q75 QUEEN'S UNIVERSITY BELFAST

UNIVERSITY ROAD
BELFAST BT7 1NN

t: 028 9097 2727 **f:** 028 9097 2828
e: admissions@qub.ac.uk

// www.qub.ac.uk

M100 LLB Law

Duration: 3FT Hon

Entry Requirements: *GCE:* AAA-AABa. *SQAH:* AAAAB. *SQAAH:* AAA.
IB: 36.

R12 THE UNIVERSITY OF READING

THE UNIVERSITY OF READING
PO BOX 217
READING RG6 6AH

t: 0118 378 8619 **f:** 0118 378 8924
e: student.recruitment@reading.ac.uk

// www.reading.ac.uk

M100 LLB Law

Duration: 3FT Hon

Entry Requirements: *GCE:* AAB. *SQAH:* AAAAA-AAABB. *SQAAH:* AAB.

R36 THE ROBERT GORDON UNIVERSITY

ROBERT GORDON UNIVERSITY
SCHOOLHILL
ABERDEEN
SCOTLAND AB10 1FR

t: 01224 26 27 28 **f:** 01224 262147
e: admissions@rgu.ac.uk

// www.rgu.ac.uk

M114 LLB Law

Duration: 4FT Hon

Entry Requirements: *GCE:* 280-300. *SQAH:* BBBB. *IB:* 28.

R90 RUSKIN COLLEGE OXFORD

WALTON STREET
OXFORD OX1 2HE

t: 01865 517832 **f:** 01865 554372
e: enquiries@ruskin.ac.uk

// www.ruskin.ac.uk

M100 CertHE Law

Duration: 1FT Cer

Entry Requirements: Interview required.

S03 THE UNIVERSITY OF SALFORD

SALFORD M5 4WT

t: 0161 295 4545 **f:** 0161 295 3126
e: ugadmissions-exrel@salford.ac.uk

// www.salford.ac.uk

M100 LLB LLB (Hons) Bachelor of Laws

Duration: 3FT Hon

Entry Requirements: *IB:* 30. *BTEC ND:* DDM. Interview required.

S09 SCHOOL OF ORIENTAL AND AFRICAN STUDIES (UNIVERSITY OF LONDON)

THORNHAUGH STREET
RUSSELL SQUARE
LONDON WC1H 0XG

t: 020 7074 5106 **f:** 020 7898 4039
e: undergradadmissions@soas.ac.uk

// www.soas.ac.uk

M100 LLB Law

Duration: 3FT Hon

Entry Requirements: *GCE:* AAA. *SQAH:* AAAAA. *SQAAH:* AAA. *IB:* 38. *BTEC ND:* DDD.

S18 THE UNIVERSITY OF SHEFFIELD

9 NORTHUMBERLAND ROAD
SHEFFIELD S10 2TT

t: 0114 222 1255 **f:** 0114 222 8032
e: ask@sheffield.ac.uk

// www.sheffield.ac.uk

M100 LLB Law

Duration: 3FT Hon

Entry Requirements: *GCE:* AAA. *SQAH:* AAAA. *SQAAH:* AAA. *IB:* 37. *BTEC ND:* DDD.

S21 SHEFFIELD HALLAM UNIVERSITY

CITY CAMPUS
HOWARD STREET
SHEFFIELD S1 1WB

t: 0114 225 5555 **f:** 0114 225 2167
e: admissions@shu.ac.uk

// www.shu.ac.uk

M100 LLB LLB (Law)

Duration: 3FT Hon

Entry Requirements: *GCE:* 260.

S27 UNIVERSITY OF SOUTHAMPTON

HIGHFIELD
SOUTHAMPTON SO17 1BJ

t: 023 8059 4732 **f:** 023 8059 3037
e: admissions@soton.ac.uk

// www.southampton.ac.uk

M100 LLB Law

Duration: 3FT Hon

Entry Requirements: *GCE:* AAA-AAB. *SQAAH:* AAA. *IB:* 36. *BTEC NC:* DD.

M101 LLB Law (Accelerated Programme)

Duration: 2FT Hon

Entry Requirements: *GCE:* AAA-AAB. *SQAAH:* AAA. *IB:* 36. *BTEC NC:* DD.

M130 LLB Law (International Legal Studies)

Duration: 4FT Hon

Entry Requirements: Contact the institution for details.

S30 SOUTHAMPTON SOLENT UNIVERSITY

EAST PARK TERRACE
SOUTHAMPTON
HAMPSHIRE SO14 0RT
t: +44 (0) 23 8031 9039 **f:** + 44 (0)23 8022 2259
e: admissions@solent.ac.uk or ask@solent.ac.uk
// www.solent.ac.uk/

M100 LLB LLB (Hons)

Duration: 3FT Hon

Entry Requirements: *GCE:* 220. *IB:* 32. *BTEC NC:* MM. *BTEC ND:* PPP.

M104 FdA Law

Duration: 2FT Fdg

Entry Requirements: *GCE:* 80. *BTEC NC:* MM. *BTEC ND:* PPP.

001M HND Law

Duration: 2FT HND

Entry Requirements: *GCE:* 80. *BTEC NC:* PP. *BTEC ND:* PPP.

S32 SOUTH DEVON COLLEGE

LONG ROAD
PAIGNTON
DEVON TQ4 7EJ
t: 08000 380123 **f:** 01803 540541
e: highereducation@southdevon.ac.uk
// www.southdevon.ac.uk

M100 FdSc Law

Duration: 2FT Fdg

Entry Requirements: Contact the institution for details.

S72 STAFFORDSHIRE UNIVERSITY

COLLEGE ROAD
STOKE ON TRENT ST4 2DE
t: 01782 292753 **f:** 01782 292740
e: admissions@staffs.ac.uk
// www.staffs.ac.uk

M100 LLB LLB

Duration: 3FT Hon

Entry Requirements: *GCE:* BB-ABB. *SQAAH:* BB-ABB. *IB:* 26. *BTEC NC:* DM. *BTEC ND:* DDM. *OCR ND:* Distinction.

M101 LLB LLB (2 year)

Duration: 2FT Hon

Entry Requirements: *GCE:* BB-ABB. *SQAAH:* BB-ABB. *IB:* 26. *BTEC NC:* DM. *BTEC ND:* DDM. *OCR ND:* Distinction. Interview required.

S75 THE UNIVERSITY OF STIRLING

STIRLING FK9 4LA
t: 01786 467044 **f:** 01786 466800
e: admissions@stir.ac.uk
// www.stir.ac.uk

M114 LLB Law

Duration: 4FT Hon

Entry Requirements: *GCE:* BBB. *SQAH:* AABB.

M115 LLB Law Accelerated Entry (graduates only)

Duration: 4FT Hon

Entry Requirements: Contact the institution for details.

M110 BA Law

Duration: 4FT Hon

Entry Requirements: *GCE:* CCC. *SQAH:* BBBB. *SQAAH:* AAA-CCC. *BTEC ND:* DMM.

S78 THE UNIVERSITY OF STRATHCLYDE

GLASGOW G1 1XQ
t: 0141 552 4400 **f:** 0141 552 0775
// www.strath.ac.uk

M115 LLB Law(Scots) - Accelerated (for Graduates)

Duration: 2FT Ord

Entry Requirements: Contact the institution for details.

S84 UNIVERSITY OF SUNDERLAND

STUDENT HELPLINE
THE STUDENT GATEWAY
CHESTER ROAD
SUNDERLAND SR1 3SD
t: 0191 515 3000 **f:** 0191 515 3805
e: student-helpline@sunderland.ac.uk
// www.sunderland.ac.uk

M100 LLB LLB Law (Qualifying)

Duration: 3FT Hon

Entry Requirements: *GCE:* 260-360. *IB:* 33. *BTEC NC:* DD. *BTEC ND:* DMM. *OCR ND:* Distinction. *OCR NED:* Merit.

M200 FdA Law

Duration: 2FT Fdg

Entry Requirements: *GCE:* 100-240. *BTEC NC:* MP. *BTEC ND:* PPP. *OCR ND:* Pass. *OCR NED:* Pass.

S85 UNIVERSITY OF SURREY

STAG HILL
GUILDFORD
SURREY GU2 7XH

t: +44(0)1483 689305 **f:** +44(0)1483 689388
e: admissions@surrey.ac.uk

// www.surrey.ac.uk

M100 LLB Law (3 or 4 years)

Duration: 3FT/4SW Hon

Entry Requirements: *GCE:* ABB.

S90 UNIVERSITY OF SUSSEX

UNDERGRADUATE ADMISSIONS
SUSSEX HOUSE
UNIVERSITY OF SUSSEX
BRIGHTON BN1 9RH

t: 01273 678416 **f:** 01273 678545
e: ug.applicants@sussex.ac.uk

// www.sussex.ac.uk

M100 LLB Law

Duration: 3FT Hon

Entry Requirements: *GCE:* AAB-ABB. *SQAH:* AAABB-AABBB.

S93 SWANSEA UNIVERSITY

SINGLETON PARK
SWANSEA SA2 8PP

t: 01792 295111 **f:** 01792 295110
e: admissions@swansea.ac.uk

// www.swansea.ac.uk

M100 LLB Law

Duration: 3FT Hon

Entry Requirements: *GCE:* 280.

T20 UNIVERSITY OF TEESSIDE

MIDDLESBROUGH TS1 3BA

t: 01642 218121 **f:** 01642 384201
e: registry@tees.ac.uk

// www.tees.ac.uk

M100 LLB Law

Duration: 3FT Hon

Entry Requirements: *GCE:* 280.

M101 LLB Senior Status LLB

Duration: 2FT Hon

Entry Requirements: Contact the institution for details.

M201 FdA Law

Duration: 2FT Fdg

Entry Requirements: *GCE:* 120.

T40 THAMES VALLEY UNIVERSITY

ST MARY'S ROAD
EALING
LONDON W5 5RF

t: 0800 036 8888 **f:** 020 8566 1353
e: learning.advice@tvu.ac.uk

// www.tvu.ac.uk

M101 LLB LLB (Hons)

Duration: 3FT Hon

Entry Requirements: *GCE:* 240-260. *IB:* 28. Interview required.

M100 LLB LLB (Hons) (with foundation year)

Duration: 4FT Hon

Entry Requirements: *GCE:* 150-170. *IB:* 24. Interview required.

T85 TRURO AND PENWITH COLLEGE (FORMERLY TRURO COLLEGE)

TRURO COLLEGE
COLLEGE ROAD
TRURO
CORNWALL TR1 3XX

t: 01872 267122 **f:** 01872 267526
e: heinfo@trurocollege.ac.uk

// www.trurocollege.ac.uk

M201 FdSc Law

Duration: 2FT Fdg

Entry Requirements: *GCE:* 60. *IB:* 24. *BTEC NC:* PP. *BTEC ND:* PPP.

U20 UNIVERSITY OF ULSTER

COLERAINE
CO. LONDONDERRY
NORTHERN IRELAND BT52 1SA

t: 028 7032 4221 **f:** 028 7032 4908
e: online@ulster.ac.uk

// www.ulster.ac.uk

M100 LLB Law

Duration: 3FT Hon

Entry Requirements: *GCE:* ABB. *SQAH:* AAABC. *SQAAH:* ABB. *IB:* 26. *BTEC ND:* DDM.

U40 UNIVERSITY OF THE WEST OF SCOTLAND

PAISLEY
RENFREWSHIRE
SCOTLAND PA1 2BE

t: 0141 848 3727 **f:** 0141 848 3623
e: admissions@uws.ac.uk

// www.uws.ac.uk

M100 BA Law

Duration: 3FT/4FT/5SW Ord/Hon

Entry Requirements: *GCE:* CC. *SQAH:* BBCC. *BTEC NC:* PP.

U80 UNIVERSITY COLLEGE LONDON (UNIVERSITY OF LONDON)
GOWER STREET
LONDON WC1E 6BT
t: 020 7679 3000 f: 020 7679 3001
// www.ucl.ac.uk

M100 LLB Law
Duration: 3FT Hon

Entry Requirements: *GCE:* AAAe. *SQAAH:* AAA. *IB:* 38. Admissions Test required.

M101 LLB Law with Advanced Studies (4 years)
Duration: 4FT Hon

Entry Requirements: *GCE:* AAAe. *SQAAH:* AAA. *IB:* 38. Admissions Test required.

W20 THE UNIVERSITY OF WARWICK
COVENTRY CV4 8UW
t: 024 7652 3723 f: 024 7652 4649
e: ugadmissions@warwick.ac.uk
// www.warwick.ac.uk

M100 LLB Law
Duration: 3FT Hon

Entry Requirements: *GCE:* AAAc. *SQAAH:* AAA. *OCR ND:* Distinction.

M101 LLB Law (4 years)
Duration: 4FT Hon

Entry Requirements: *GCE:* AAAc. *SQAAH:* AAA. *OCR ND:* Distinction.

M108 LLB Law (4 Years) - Study Abroad in English
Duration: 4FT Hon

Entry Requirements: *GCE:* AAAc. *SQAAH:* AAA. *OCR ND:* Distinction.

W50 UNIVERSITY OF WESTMINSTER
115 NEW CAVENDISH STREET
LONDON W1W 6UW
t: 020 7911 5000 f: 020 7911 5788
e: course-enquiries@westminster.ac.uk
// www.westminster.ac.uk

M100 LLB Law
Duration: 3FT Hon

Entry Requirements: *GCE:* ABB. *SQAH:* AABBB. *SQAAH:* ABB. *IB:* 32. *BTEC ND:* DDM.

M190 LLB LLB (Solicitor's Exempting)
Duration: 4FT Hon

Entry Requirements: *GCE:* AAB. *SQAH:* AAABB. *SQAAH:* AAB.

W75 UNIVERSITY OF WOLVERHAMPTON
ADMISSIONS UNIT
MX207, CAMP STREET
WOLVERHAMPTON
WEST MIDLANDS WV1 1AD
t: 01902 321000 f: 01902 321896
e: admissions@wlv.ac.uk
// www.wlv.ac.uk

M100 LLB Law
Duration: 3FT Hon

Entry Requirements: *GCE:* 160-220. *IB:* 28.

W76 UNIVERSITY OF WINCHESTER
WINCHESTER
HANTS SO22 4NR
t: 01962 827234 f: 01962 827288
e: course.enquiries@winchester.ac.uk
// www.winchester.ac.uk

M100 LLB Law
Duration: 3FT Hon

Entry Requirements: *Foundation:* Distinction. *GCE:* 260-300. *IB:* 26. *BTEC NC:* DD. *BTEC ND:* MMM. *OCR ND:* Distinction.

W81 WORCESTER COLLEGE OF TECHNOLOGY
DEANSWAY
WORCESTER
NULL
NULL WR1 2JF
t: 01905 725555 f: 01905 28906
e: null
// www.wortech.ac.uk

M100 LLB LLB Bachelor of Law
Duration: 4FT Hon

Entry Requirements: Contact the institution for details.

003M HND Law
Duration: 2FT HND

Entry Requirements: *GCE:* 40.

Y50 THE UNIVERSITY OF YORK
ADMISSIONS AND UK/EU STUDENT RECRUITMENT
UNIVERSITY OF YORK
HESLINGTON
YORK YO10 5DD
t: 01904 433533 f: 01904 433538
e: admissions@york.ac.uk
// www.york.ac.uk

M100 LLB Law
Duration: 3FT Hon

Entry Requirements: *GCE:* AAA. *SQAH:* AAAAA. *SQAAH:* AA. *IB:* 36. *BTEC ND:* DDD.

A20 THE UNIVERSITY OF ABERDEEN

UNIVERSITY OFFICE
KING'S COLLEGE
ABERDEEN AB24 3FX

t: +44 (0) 1224 273504 f: +44 (0) 1224 272034
e: sras@abdn.ac.uk

// www.abdn.ac.uk/sras

MV96 MA Divinity and Legal Studies
Duration: 4FT Hon

Entry Requirements: *GCE:* CCC. *SQAH:* BBBB. *SQAAH:* BCC. *IB:* 28.
BTEC ND: MMM.

MQ93 MA English and Legal Studies
Duration: 4FT Hon

Entry Requirements: *GCE:* CCC. *SQAH:* BBBB. *SQAAH:* BCC. *IB:* 28.
BTEC ND: MMM.

MN91 MA Entrepreneurship and Legal Studies
Duration: 4FT Hon

Entry Requirements: *GCE:* CCC. *SQAH:* BBBB. *SQAAH:* BCC. *IB:* 28.
BTEC ND: MMM.

MR91 MA French and Legal Studies
Duration: 5FT Hon

Entry Requirements: *GCE:* CCC. *SQAH:* BBBB. *SQAAH:* BCC. *IB:* 28.
BTEC ND: MMM.

MRX1 MA French and Legal Studies (4 years)
Duration: 4FT Hon

Entry Requirements: *GCE:* CCC. *SQAH:* BBBB. *SQAAH:* BCC. *IB:* 28.
BTEC ND: MMM.

MR92 MA German and Legal Studies
Duration: 5FT Hon

Entry Requirements: *GCE:* CCC. *SQAH:* BBBB. *SQAAH:* BCC. *IB:* 28.
BTEC ND: MMM.

MRX2 MA German and Legal Studies (4 years)
Duration: 4FT Hon

Entry Requirements: *GCE:* CCC. *SQAH:* BBBB. *SQAAH:* BCC. *IB:* 28.
BTEC ND: MMM.

MR94 MA Hispanic Studies and Legal Studies
Duration: 5FT Hon

Entry Requirements: *GCE:* CCC. *SQAH:* BBBB. *SQAAH:* BCC. *IB:* 28.
BTEC ND: MMM.

MRX4 MA Hispanic Studies and Legal Studies (4 years)
Duration: 4FT Hon

Entry Requirements: *GCE:* CCC. *SQAH:* BBBB. *SQAAH:* BCC. *IB:* 28.
BTEC ND: MMM.

VM12 MA History and Legal Studies
Duration: 4FT Hon

Entry Requirements: *GCE:* CCC. *SQAH:* BBBB. *SQAAH:* BCC. *IB:* 28.
BTEC ND: MMM.

MLC2 MA International Relations and Legal Studies
Duration: 4FT Hon

Entry Requirements: *GCE:* CCC. *SQAH:* BBBB. *SQAAH:* BCC. *IB:* 28.
BTEC ND: MMM.

MN92 MA Legal Studies and Management Studies
Duration: 4FT Hon

Entry Requirements: *GCE:* CCC. *SQAH:* BBBB. *SQAAH:* BCC. *IB:* 28.
BTEC ND: MMM.

VM51 MA Legal Studies and Philosophy
Duration: 4FT Hon

Entry Requirements: *GCE:* CCC. *SQAH:* BBBB. *SQAAH:* BCC. *IB:* 28.
BTEC ND: MMM.

ML12 MA Legal Studies and Politics
Duration: 4FT Hon

Entry Requirements: *GCE:* CCC. *SQAH:* BBBB. *SQAAH:* BCC. *IB:* 28.
BTEC ND: MMM.

CM89 MA Legal Studies and Psychology
Duration: 4FT Hon

Entry Requirements: *GCE:* CCC. *SQAH:* BBBB. *SQAAH:* BCC. *IB:* 28.
BTEC ND: MMM.

ML13 MA Legal Studies and Sociology
Duration: 4FT Hon

Entry Requirements: *GCE:* CCC. *SQAH:* BBBB. *SQAAH:* BCC. *IB:* 28.
BTEC ND: MMM.

A60 ANGLIA RUSKIN UNIVERSITY

BISHOP HALL LANE
CHELMSFORD
ESSEX CM1 1SQ

t: 0845 271 3333 f: 01245 251789
e: answers@anglia.ac.uk

// www.anglia.ac.uk

M250 LLB Professional Legal Studies
Duration: 3FT Hon

Entry Requirements: *GCE:* 300-340. *SQAH:* AABB. *SQAAH:* AB. *IB:* 30.

B25 BIRMINGHAM CITY UNIVERSITY
PERRY BARR
BIRMINGHAM B42 2SU

t: 0121 331 5595 f: 0121 331 7994
e: choices@bcu.ac.uk

// www.bcu.ac.uk

039M HND Legal Studies
Duration: 2FT HND

Entry Requirements: *GCE:* 120. *SQAAH:* B. *IB:* 24. *BTEC NC:* DD. *BTEC ND:* MMM.

B60 BRADFORD COLLEGE: AN ASSOCIATE COLLEGE OF LEEDS METROPOLITAN UNIVERSITY
GREAT HORTON ROAD
BRADFORD
WEST YORKSHIRE BD7 1AY

t: 01274 433333 f: 01274 433241
e: admissions@bradfordcollege.ac.uk

// www.bradfordcollege.ac.uk

MM12 FdA Law & Legal Practice
Duration: 2FT Fdg

Entry Requirements: *GCE:* 80.

C10 CANTERBURY CHRIST CHURCH UNIVERSITY
NORTH HOLMES ROAD
CANTERBURY
KENT CT1 1QU

t: 01227 782900 f: 01227 782888
e: admissions@canterbury.ac.uk

// www.canterbury.ac.uk

GM52 BA Business Computing and Legal Studies
Duration: 3FT Hon

Entry Requirements: *GCE:* 80.

G5M2 BA Business Computing with Legal Studies
Duration: 3FT Hon

Entry Requirements: *GCE:* 200. *IB:* 24.

QM32 BA English Language & Communication and Legal Studies
Duration: 3FT Hon

Entry Requirements: *GCE:* 200. *IB:* 24.

Q3MF BA English Language & Communication with Legal Studies
Duration: 3FT Hon

Entry Requirements: *GCE:* 200. *IB:* 24.

NM12 BA Entrepreneurship and Legal Studies
Duration: 3FT Hon

Entry Requirements: *GCE:* 200. *IB:* 24.

N1MF BA Entrepreneurship with Legal Studies
Duration: 3FT Hon

Entry Requirements: *GCE:* 200. *IB:* 24.

LM2F BA Global Politics and Legal Studies
Duration: 3FT Hon

Entry Requirements: *GCE:* 200. *IB:* 24.

L2MG BA Global Politics with Legal Studies
Duration: 3FT Hon

Entry Requirements: *GCE:* 200. *IB:* 24.

GM42 BA Internet Computing and Legal Studies
Duration: 3FT Hon

Entry Requirements: *GCE:* 200. *IB:* 24.

G4MF BA Internet Computing with Legal Studies
Duration: 3FT Hon

Entry Requirements: *GCE:* 200. *IB:* 24.

M2M9 BA Legal Studies with Applied Criminology 'International Only'
Duration: 4FT Hon

Entry Requirements: Interview required.

M2GM BA Legal Studies with Business Computing
Duration: 3FT Hon

Entry Requirements: *GCE:* 200. *IB:* 24.

M2QH BA Legal Studies with English Language & Communication
Duration: 3FT Hon

Entry Requirements: *GCE:* 200. *IB:* 24.

M2NC BA Legal Studies with Entrepreneurship
Duration: 3FT Hon

Entry Requirements: *GCE:* 200. *IB:* 24.

M2LF BA Legal Studies with Global Politics
Duration: 3FT Hon

Entry Requirements: *GCE:* 200. *IB:* 24.

M2G4 BA Legal Studies with Internet Computing
Duration: 3FT Hon

Entry Requirements: *GCE:* 200. *IB:* 24.

M2L2 BA Legal Studies with Politics & Governance
Duration: 3FT Hon
Entry Requirements: *GCE:* 200. *IB:* 24.

LM22 BA Politics & Governance and Legal Studies
Duration: 3FT Hon
Entry Requirements: *GCE:* 200. *IB:* 24.

L2M2 BA Politics & Governance with Legal Studies
Duration: 3FT Hon
Entry Requirements: *GCE:* 80.

T7M2 BA/BSc American Studies with Legal Studies
Duration: 3FT Hon
Entry Requirements: *GCE:* 200. *IB:* 24.

DM32 BA/BSc Animal Science and Legal Studies
Duration: 3FT Hon
Entry Requirements: *GCE:* 200. *IB:* 24.

D3M2 BA/BSc Animal Science with Legal Studies
Duration: 3FT Hon
Entry Requirements: *GCE:* 200. *IB:* 24.

G4M2 BA/BSc Computing with Legal Studies
Duration: 3FT Hon
Entry Requirements: *GCE:* 200. *IB:* 24.

X3M2 BA/BSc Early Childhood Studies with Legal Studies
Duration: 3FT Hon
Entry Requirements: *GCE:* 200. *IB:* 24.

XM32 BA/BSc Education Studies and Legal Studies
Duration: 3FT Hon
Entry Requirements: *GCE:* 200.

X3MF BA/BSc Education Studies with Legal Studies
Duration: 3FT Hon
Entry Requirements: *GCE:* 200.

Q3M2 BA/BSc English with Legal Studies
Duration: 3FT Hon
Entry Requirements: *GCE:* 200. *IB:* 24.

F8M2 BA/BSc Environmental Science with Legal Studies
Duration: 3FT Hon
Entry Requirements: *GCE:* 200. *IB:* 24.

F4M2 BA/BSc Forensic Investigation with Legal Studies
Duration: 3FT Hon
Entry Requirements: *GCE:* 200. *IB:* 24.

V1M2 BA/BSc History with Legal Studies
Duration: 3FT Hon
Entry Requirements: *GCE:* 200. *IB:* 24.

LM2G BA/BSc International Relations and Legal Studies
Duration: 3FT Hon
Entry Requirements: *GCE:* 200. *IB:* 24.

L9M2 BA/BSc International Relations with Legal Studies
Duration: 3FT Hon
Entry Requirements: *GCE:* 200. *IB:* 24.

MT27 BA/BSc Legal Studies and American Studies
Duration: 3FT Hon
Entry Requirements: *IB:* 24.

M290 BA/BSc Legal Studies and Applied Criminology
Duration: 3FT Hon
Entry Requirements: *GCE:* 200. *IB:* 24.

MC21 BA/BSc Legal Studies and Biosciences
Duration: 3FT Hon
Entry Requirements: *GCE:* 200. *IB:* 24.

MN21 BA/BSc Legal Studies and Business Studies
Duration: 3FT Hon
Entry Requirements: *GCE:* 200. *IB:* 24.

MG24 BA/BSc Legal Studies and Computing
Duration: 3FT Hon
Entry Requirements: *GCE:* 200. *IB:* 24.

MX23 BA/BSc Legal Studies and Early Childhood Studies
Duration: 3FT Hon
Entry Requirements: *GCE:* 200. *IB:* 24.

MQ23 BA/BSc Legal Studies and English

Duration: 3FT Hon

Entry Requirements: *GCE:* 200. *IB:* 24.

MF28 BA/BSc Legal Studies and Environmental Science

Duration: 3FT Hon

Entry Requirements: *GCE:* 200. *IB:* 24.

M2P6 BA/BSc Legal Studies and Film, Radio & Television Studies

Duration: 3FT Hon

Entry Requirements: *GCE:* 240. *IB:* 24.

MW21 BA/BSc Legal Studies and Fine & Applied Arts

Duration: 3FT Hon

Entry Requirements: *GCE:* 200. *IB:* 24.

FM42 BA/BSc Legal Studies and Forensic Investigation

Duration: 3FT Hon

Entry Requirements: *GCE:* 200. *IB:* 24.

MV21 BA/BSc Legal Studies and History

Duration: 3FT Hon

Entry Requirements: *GCE:* 200. *IB:* 24.

MN25 BA/BSc Legal Studies and Marketing

Duration: 3FT Hon

Entry Requirements: *GCE:* 200. *IB:* 24.

MW23 BA/BSc Legal Studies and Music

Duration: 3FT Hon

Entry Requirements: *GCE:* 200. *IB:* 24.

ML23 BA/BSc Legal Studies and Sociology & Social Science

Duration: 3FT Hon

Entry Requirements: *GCE:* 200. *IB:* 24.

MC26 BA/BSc Legal Studies and Sport & Exercise Science

Duration: 3FT Hon

Entry Requirements: *GCE:* 200. *IB:* 24.

MN28 BA/BSc Legal Studies and Tourism & Leisure Studies

Duration: 3FT Hon

Entry Requirements: *GCE:* 200. *IB:* 24.

M2T7 BA/BSc Legal Studies with American Studies

Duration: 3FT Hon

Entry Requirements: *GCE:* 200. *IB:* 24.

M2D3 BA/BSc Legal Studies with Animal Science

Duration: 3FT Hon

Entry Requirements: *GCE:* 200. *IB:* 24.

M2C1 BA/BSc Legal Studies with Biosciences

Duration: 3FT Hon

Entry Requirements: *GCE:* 200. *IB:* 24.

M2N1 BA/BSc Legal Studies with Business Studies

Duration: 3FT Hon

Entry Requirements: *GCE:* 200. *IB:* 24.

M2G5 BA/BSc Legal Studies with Computing

Duration: 3FT Hon

Entry Requirements: *GCE:* 200. *IB:* 24.

MWX3 BA/BSc Legal Studies with Early Childhood Studies

Duration: 3FT Hon

Entry Requirements: *GCE:* 200. *IB:* 24.

M2X3 BA/BSc Legal Studies with Education Studies

Duration: 3FT Hon

Entry Requirements: *GCE:* 200. *IB:* 24.

M2Q3 BA/BSc Legal Studies with English

Duration: 3FT Hon

Entry Requirements: *GCE:* 200. *IB:* 24.

M2F8 BA/BSc Legal Studies with Environmental Science

Duration: 3FT Hon

Entry Requirements: *GCE:* 200. *IB:* 24.

M2F4 BA/BSc Legal Studies with Forensic Investigation

Duration: 3FT Hon

Entry Requirements: *GCE:* 200. *IB:* 24.

M2V1 BA/BSc Legal Studies with History

Duration: 3FT Hon

Entry Requirements: *GCE:* 200. *IB:* 24.

M2LG BA/BSc Legal Studies with International Relations

Duration: 3FT Hon

Entry Requirements: *GCE:* 200. *IB:* 24.

M2N5 BA/BSc Legal Studies with Marketing

Duration: 3FT Hon

Entry Requirements: *GCE:* 200. *IB:* 24.

M2W3 BA/BSc Legal Studies with Music

Duration: 3FT Hon

Entry Requirements: *GCE:* 200. *IB:* 24.

M2N8 BA/BSc Legal Studies with Tourism & Leisure Studies

Duration: 3FT Hon

Entry Requirements: *GCE:* 200. *IB:* 24.

W3M2 BA/BSc Music with Legal Studies

Duration: 3FT Hon

Entry Requirements: *GCE:* 200. *IB:* 24.

N8M2 BA/BSc Tourism & Leisure Studies with Legal Studies

Duration: 3FT Hon

Entry Requirements: *GCE:* 200. *IB:* 24.

N1M2 BSc Business Studies with Legal Studies

Duration: 3FT Hon

Entry Requirements: *GCE:* 200. *IB:* 24.

BM92 BSc Health Studies and Legal Studies

Duration: 3FT Hon

Entry Requirements: *GCE:* 200. *IB:* 24.

N5M2 BSc Marketing with Legal Studies

Duration: 3FT Hon

Entry Requirements: *GCE:* 200. *IB:* 24.

C1M2 BSc/BA Biosciences with Legal Studies

Duration: 3FT Hon

Entry Requirements: *GCE:* 200. *IB:* 24.

C92 CROYDON COLLEGE

COLLEGE ROAD
CROYDON CR9 1DX

t: 020 8760 5914 f: 020 8760 5880
e: info@croydon.ac.uk

// www.croydon.ac.uk

M250 FdA Legal Practice

Duration: 2FT Fdg

Entry Requirements: Contact the institution for details.

E25 EAST LANCASHIRE INSTITUTE OF HIGHER EDUCATION AT BLACKBURN COLLEGE

DUKE STREET
BLACKBURN BB2 1LH

t: 01254 292594 f: 01254 260749
e: he-admissions@blackburn.ac.uk

// www.elihe.ac.uk

009M HND Legal Studies

Duration: 2FT HND

Entry Requirements: *GCE:* 160.

E81 EXETER COLLEGE

HELE ROAD
EXETER
DEVON EX4 4JS

t: 01392 205582 f: 01392 279972
e: ebs@exe-coll.ac.uk

// www.exe-coll.ac.uk

052M HND Legal Practice

Duration: 2FT HND

Entry Requirements: *GCE:* 40.

H72 THE UNIVERSITY OF HULL

THE UNIVERSITY OF HULL
COTTINGHAM ROAD
HULL HU6 7RX

t: 01482 466100 f: 01482 442290
e: admissions@hull.ac.uk

// www.hull.ac.uk

ML12 LLB Law and Legislative Studies

Duration: 4FT Hon

Entry Requirements: *GCE:* 340. *IB:* 28.

L21 LEEDS: PARK LANE COLLEGE

PARK LANE
LEEDS LS3 1AA

t: 0113 216 2406 f: 0113 216 2401
e: h.middleton@parklanecoll.ac.uk

// www.parklane.ac.uk

M990 FdA Legal Studies

Duration: 2FT Fdg

Entry Requirements: Contact the institution for details.

L39 UNIVERSITY OF LINCOLN

ADMISSIONS
BRAYFORD POOL
LINCOLN LN6 7TS

t: 01522 886097 f: 01522 886146
e: admissions@lincoln.ac.uk

// www.lincoln.ac.uk

NM29 BA Legal and Administration Studies (top-up)

Duration: 1FT Hon

Entry Requirements: HND required.

L62 THE LONDON COLLEGE, UCK

VICTORIA GARDENS
NOTTING HILL GATE
LONDON W11 3PE

t: 020 7243 4000 f: 020 7243 1484
e: admissions@lcuck.ac.uk

// www.lcuck.ac.uk

M250 Diploma Legal Studies

Duration: 1FT FYr

Entry Requirements: *BTEC NC:* PP. *BTEC ND:* PPP.

M251 APDip Legal Studies

Duration: 3FT/4SW Deg

Entry Requirements: *BTEC NC:* PP. *BTEC ND:* PPP.

M40 THE MANCHESTER METROPOLITAN UNIVERSITY

ADMISSIONS OFFICE
ALL SAINTS (GMS)
ALL SAINTS
MANCHESTER M15 6BH

t: 0161 247 2000

// www.mmu.ac.uk

CM6F BA Coaching Studies/Legal Studies

Duration: 3FT Hon

Entry Requirements: *BTEC ND:* MMM.

LM92 BA Justice and the Environment/Legal Studies

Duration: 3FT Hon

Entry Requirements: Contact the institution for details.

MN2C BA Legal Studies/Business

Duration: 3FT Hon

Entry Requirements: *GCE:* 260. *BTEC ND:* MMM.

ML25 BA Legal Studies/Childhood & Youth Studies

Duration: 3FT Hon

Entry Requirements: *GCE:* 260. *BTEC ND:* MMM.

MW28 BA Legal Studies/Creative Writing

Duration: 3FT Hon

Entry Requirements: *GCE:* 260. *BTEC ND:* DMM.

MLG3 BA Legal Studies/Crime Studies

Duration: 3FT Hon

Entry Requirements: Contact the institution for details.

MQ2H BA Legal Studies/English

Duration: 3FT Hon

Entry Requirements: *GCE:* 260. *BTEC ND:* MMM.

MN2P BA Legal Studies/Human Resource Management

Duration: 3FT Hon

Entry Requirements: *GCE:* 260. *BTEC ND:* MMM.

MN2M BA Legal Studies/Marketing

Duration: 3FT Hon

Entry Requirements: *GCE:* 260. *BTEC ND:* MMM.

MV2M BA Legal Studies/Philosophy

Duration: 3FT Hon

Entry Requirements: *GCE:* 260. *BTEC ND:* MMM.

MLFJ BA Legal Studies/Sociology

Duration: 3FT Hon

Entry Requirements: *GCE:* 260. *BTEC ND:* MMM.

MF28 BA/BSc Legal Studies/Geography

Duration: 3FT Hon

Entry Requirements: *GCE:* 260. *BTEC ND:* MMM.

MC2P BA/BSc Legal Studies/Sport

Duration: 3FT Hon

Entry Requirements: *GCE:* 260. *BTEC ND:* MMM.

P60 UNIVERSITY OF PLYMOUTH
DRAKE CIRCUS
PLYMOUTH PL4 8AA
t: 01752 588037 f: 01752 588050
e: admissions@plymouth.ac.uk
// www.plymouth.ac.uk

M290 FdSc Legal Studies
Duration: 2FT Fdg

Entry Requirements: *GCE:* 60. *IB:* 24. *BTEC NC:* PP. *BTEC ND:* PPP. *OCR ND:* Pass. *OCR NED:* Pass.

R12 THE UNIVERSITY OF READING
THE UNIVERSITY OF READING
PO BOX 217
READING RG6 6AH
t: 0118 378 8619 f: 0118 378 8924
e: student.recruitment@reading.ac.uk
// www.reading.ac.uk

M125 LLB Law with Legal Studies in Europe
Duration: 4FT Hon

Entry Requirements: *GCE:* AAB. *SQAH:* AAAAA-AAABB. *SQAAH:* AAB.

S72 STAFFORDSHIRE UNIVERSITY
COLLEGE ROAD
STOKE ON TRENT ST4 2DE
t: 01782 292753 f: 01782 292740
e: admissions@staffs.ac.uk
// www.staffs.ac.uk

NM42 BA Accounting and Legal Studies
Duration: 3FT Hon

Entry Requirements: *GCE:* BCC-BB. *IB:* 24.

MN91 BA Business Studies and Legal Studies
Duration: 3FT Hon

Entry Requirements: *GCE:* BCC -BB. *IB:* 24.

QM32 BA English Communication for Legal Studies
Duration: 1FT Hon

Entry Requirements: *IB:* 24.

QM39 BA English Literature and Legal Studies
Duration: 3FT Hon

Entry Requirements: *GCE:* 180-220. *IB:* 24.

MG95 BA Information Systems and Legal Studies
Duration: 3FT Hon

Entry Requirements: *GCE:* 180-220. *IB:* 24.

MV91 BA Modern History and Legal Studies
Duration: 3FT Hon

Entry Requirements: *GCE:* 180-220. *IB:* 24.

GM49 BA Multimedia Systems and Legal Studies
Duration: 3FT Hon

Entry Requirements: *GCE:* 200-240. *IB:* 24.

VM59 BA Philosophy and Legal Studies
Duration: 3FT Hon

Entry Requirements: *GCE:* 180-220. *IB:* 24.

LMH1 BA Sociology and Legal Studies
Duration: 3FT Hon

Entry Requirements: *GCE:* 180-220. *IB:* 24.

MN92 BA/BSc Internet Commerce and Legal Studies
Duration: 3FT Hon

Entry Requirements: *GCE:* 180-220. *IB:* 24.

S84 UNIVERSITY OF SUNDERLAND
STUDENT HELPLINE
THE STUDENT GATEWAY
CHESTER ROAD
SUNDERLAND SR1 3SD
t: 0191 515 3000 f: 0191 515 3805
e: student-helpline@sunderland.ac.uk
// www.sunderland.ac.uk

M250 BA Legal Studies
Duration: 1FT Hon

Entry Requirements: Contact the institution for details.

S93 SWANSEA UNIVERSITY
SINGLETON PARK
SWANSEA SA2 8PP
t: 01792 295111 f: 01792 295110
e: admissions@swansea.ac.uk
// www.swansea.ac.uk

R1M9 BA French with Legal Studies (4 years)
Duration: 4FT Hon

Entry Requirements: *GCE:* 240.

R2M9 BA German with Legal Studies (4 years)
Duration: 4FT Hon

Entry Requirements: *GCE:* 240-300.

R3M9 BA Italian with Legal Studies (4 years)
Duration: 4FT Hon

Entry Requirements: *GCE:* 280.

R4M9 BA Spanish with Legal Studies (4 years)
Duration: 4FT Hon

Entry Requirements: *GCE:* 240-300.

Q5M9 BA Welsh with Legal Studies (3 or 4 years)
Duration: 3FT Hon

Entry Requirements: *GCE:* 240.

U40 UNIVERSITY OF THE WEST OF SCOTLAND
PAISLEY
RENFREWSHIRE
SCOTLAND PA1 2BE
t: 0141 848 3727 f: 0141 848 3623
e: admissions@uws.ac.uk
// www.uws.ac.uk

M900 CertHE Legal Studies
Duration: 1FT Cer

Entry Requirements: *SQAH:* C.

U80 UNIVERSITY COLLEGE LONDON (UNIVERSITY OF LONDON)
GOWER STREET
LONDON WC1E 6BT
t: 020 7679 3000 f: 020 7679 3001
// www.ucl.ac.uk

M102 LLB Law with Another Legal System (4 years)
Duration: 4FT Hon

Entry Requirements: *GCE:* AAAe. *SQAAH:* AAA. *IB:* 38. Admissions Test required.

M102 LLB Law with Another Legal System (4 years)
Duration: 4FT Hon

Entry Requirements: *GCE:* AAAe. *SQAAH:* AAA. *IB:* 38. Admissions Test required.

M102 LLB Law with Another Legal System (4 years)
Duration: 4FT Hon

Entry Requirements: *GCE:* AAAe. *SQAAH:* AAA. *IB:* 38. Admissions Test required.

M102 LLB Law with Another Legal System (4 years)
Duration: 4FT Hon

Entry Requirements: *GCE:* AAAe. *SQAAH:* AAA. *IB:* 38. Admissions Test required.

M102 LLB Law with Another Legal System (4 years)
Duration: 4FT Hon

Entry Requirements: *GCE:* AAAe. *SQAAH:* AAA. *IB:* 38. Admissions Test required.

MARITIME LAW

P60 UNIVERSITY OF PLYMOUTH
DRAKE CIRCUS
PLYMOUTH PL4 8AA
t: 01752 588037 f: 01752 588050
e: admissions@plymouth.ac.uk
// www.plymouth.ac.uk

NM12 BSc Maritime Business and Maritime Law
Duration: 3FT Hon

Entry Requirements: *GCE:* 240. *IB:* 26.

OTHER LAW COMBINATIONS

A40 ABERYSTWYTH UNIVERSITY
WELCOME CENTRE, ABERYSTWYTH UNIVERSITY
PENGLAIS CAMPUS
ABERYSTWYTH
CEREDIGION SY23 3FB
t: 01970 622021 f: 01970 627410
e: ug-admissions@aber.ac.uk
// www.aber.ac.uk

M1P1 BA Law with Information Management
Duration: 3FT Hon

Entry Requirements: *GCE:* 280. *IB:* 27.

M1LF BA Law with International Politics
Duration: 3FT Hon

Entry Requirements: *GCE:* 280. *IB:* 27.

M1N5 BA Law with Marketing
Duration: 3FT Hon

Entry Requirements: *GCE:* 280. *IB:* 27.

M1L2 BA Law with Politics
Duration: 3FT Hon

Entry Requirements: *GCE:* 280. *IB:* 27.

P1M1 BScEcon Information Management with Law

Duration: 3FT Hon

Entry Requirements: *GCE:* 180. *IB:* 24.

L2M1 BScEcon International Politics with Law

Duration: 3FT Hon

Entry Requirements: *GCE:* 280. *IB:* 28.

N5M1 BScEcon Marketing with Law

Duration: 3FT Hon

Entry Requirements: *GCE:* 260. *IB:* 27.

L2MC BScEcon Politics with Law

Duration: 3FT Hon

Entry Requirements: *GCE:* 280. *IB:* 28.

B06 BANGOR UNIVERSITY
BANGOR
GWYNEDD LL57 2DG
t: 01248 382016/2017 **f:** 01248 370451
e: admissions@bangor.ac.uk
// www.bangor.ac.uk

M1QJ LLB Law with English

Duration: 3FT Hon

Entry Requirements: *GCE:* 280. *IB:* 28.

M1QH LLB Law with Professional English

Duration: 3FT Hon

Entry Requirements: *GCE:* 280. *IB:* 28.

W9M1 BA Creative Studies with Law

Duration: 3FT Hon

Entry Requirements: *GCE:* 280. *IB:* 28.

P3M1 BA Media Studies with Law

Duration: 3FT Hon

Entry Requirements: *GCE:* 280. *IB:* 28.

B25 BIRMINGHAM CITY UNIVERSITY
PERRY BARR
BIRMINGHAM B42 2SU
t: 0121 331 5595 **f:** 0121 331 7994
e: choices@bcu.ac.uk
// www.bcu.ac.uk

M200 LLB Law and Practice

Duration: 3FT Hon

Entry Requirements: *GCE:* 280. *IB:* 24. *BTEC NC:* DD. *BTEC ND:* DMM. *OCR ND:* Distinction.

B44 THE UNIVERSITY OF BOLTON
DEANE ROAD
BOLTON BL3 5AB
t: 01204 900600 **f:** 01204 399074
e: enquiries@bolton.ac.uk
// www.bolton.ac.uk

M1N6 LLB LLB Law with Human Resource Management

Duration: 3FT Hon

Entry Requirements: *GCE:* 240. *IB:* 24. *BTEC ND:* MMM.

M1N5 LLB LLB Law with Marketing

Duration: 3FT Hon

Entry Requirements: *GCE:* 240. *IB:* 24. *BTEC ND:* MMM.

LM51 BA Community Studies and Law

Duration: 3FT Hon

Entry Requirements: *GCE:* 220. *IB:* 20. *BTEC NC:* DD. *BTEC ND:* MMM.

MX13 BA Education Studies and Law

Duration: 3FT Hon

Entry Requirements: *GCE:* 220. *IB:* 20. *BTEC NC:* DD. *BTEC ND:* MMM.

MQ13 BA English and Law

Duration: 3FT Hon

Entry Requirements: *GCE:* 220. *IB:* 20. *BTEC NC:* DD. *BTEC ND:* MMM.

VM11 BA Modern & Contemporary History and Law

Duration: 3FT Hon

Entry Requirements: *GCE:* 220. *IB:* 20. *BTEC NC:* DD. *BTEC ND:* MMM.

CM91 BA/BSc Human Sciences and Law

Duration: 3FT Hon

Entry Requirements: *GCE:* 220. *IB:* 20. *BTEC NC:* DD. *BTEC ND:* MMM.

CM11 BSc/BA Biology and Law

Duration: 3FT Hon

Entry Requirements: *GCE:* 220. *IB:* 20. *BTEC NC:* DD. *BTEC ND:* MMM.

FM81 BSc/BA Environmental Studies and Law

Duration: 3FT Hon

Entry Requirements: *GCE:* 220. *IB:* 20. *BTEC NC:* DD. *BTEC ND:* MMM.

NM21 BSc/BA Law and Logistics & Supply Chain Management
Duration: 3FT Hon

Entry Requirements: *GCE:* 220. *IB:* 20. *BTEC NC:* DD. *BTEC ND:* MMM.

B50 BOURNEMOUTH UNIVERSITY
TALBOT CAMPUS
FERN BARROW
POOLE
DORSET BH12 5BB

t: 01202 524111
// www.bournemouth.ac.uk

M296 LLB Law and Taxation
Duration: 3FT/4SW Hon

Entry Requirements: *GCE:* 320. *IB:* 32.

B56 THE UNIVERSITY OF BRADFORD
RICHMOND ROAD
BRADFORD
WEST YORKSHIRE BD7 1DP

t: 0800 073 1225 f: 01274 235585
e: course-enquiries@bradford.ac.uk
// www.bradford.ac.uk

MV11 BA History and Law
Duration: 3FT Hon

Entry Requirements: *GCE:* 240. *IB:* 26.

LM21 BA Politics and Law
Duration: 3FT Hon

Entry Requirements: *GCE:* 280. *IB:* 26.

B60 BRADFORD COLLEGE: AN ASSOCIATE COLLEGE OF LEEDS METROPOLITAN UNIVERSITY
GREAT HORTON ROAD
BRADFORD
WEST YORKSHIRE BD7 1AY

t: 01274 433333 f: 01274 433241
e: admissions@bradfordcollege.ac.uk
// www.bradfordcollege.ac.uk

MN15 BA Marketing and Law
Duration: 3FT Hon

Entry Requirements: *GCE:* 100-140. *BTEC NC:* MM. *BTEC ND:* MPP.

B78 UNIVERSITY OF BRISTOL
UNDERGRADUATE ADMISSIONS OFFICE
SENATE HOUSE
TYNDALL AVENUE
BRISTOL BS8 1TH

t: 0117 928 9000 f: 0117 925 1424
e: ug-admissions@bristol.ac.uk
// www.bristol.ac.uk

M1F1 LLB Law with Chemistry
Duration: 4FT Hon

Entry Requirements: *GCE:* AAB-ABB. *SQAH:* AAAAB. *SQAAH:* AB. *BTEC ND:* DDM.

B80 UNIVERSITY OF THE WEST OF ENGLAND, BRISTOL
FRENCHAY CAMPUS
COLDHARBOUR LANE
BRISTOL BS16 1QY

t: +44 (0)117 32 83333 f: +44 (0)117 32 82810
e: admissions@uwe.ac.uk
// www.uwe.ac.uk

QMH1 BA English and Law
Duration: 3FT Hon

Entry Requirements: *GCE:* 240-300.

QM3C BA English Language and Law
Duration: 3FT Hon

Entry Requirements: *GCE:* 240-300.

PM91 BA Intercultural Communication and Law
Duration: 3FT Hon

Entry Requirements: *GCE:* 240-300.

LMF1 BA International Relations and Law
Duration: 3FT Hon

Entry Requirements: *GCE:* 240-300.

MV11 BA Law and History
Duration: 3FT Hon

Entry Requirements: *GCE:* 260-320.

LM21 BA Law and Politics
Duration: 3FT Hon

Entry Requirements: *GCE:* 240-300.

CM8C BSc Law and Psychology
Duration: 3FT Hon

Entry Requirements: *GCE:* 240-300.

B90 THE UNIVERSITY OF BUCKINGHAM

YEOMANRY HOUSE
HUNTER STREET
BUCKINGHAM MK18 1EG

t: 01280 820313 **f:** 01280 822245
e: info@buckingham.ac.uk

// www.buckingham.ac.uk

M1Q3 LLB Law with English Language Studies

Duration: 2FT Hon

Entry Requirements: *GCE:* 300. *IB:* 28. *BTEC NC:* DD. *BTEC ND:* DMM.

M1L2 LLB Law with Politics

Duration: 2FT Hon

Entry Requirements: *GCE:* 300. *IB:* 28. *BTEC NC:* DD. *BTEC ND:* DMM.

C15 CARDIFF UNIVERSITY

PO BOX 927
30-36 NEWPORT ROAD
CARDIFF CF24 0DE

t: 029 2087 9999 **f:** 029 2087 6138
e: admissions@cardiff.ac.uk

// www.cardiff.ac.uk

ML12 LLB Law and Politics

Duration: 3FT Hon

Entry Requirements: *GCE:* AAB. *SQAAH:* AAB. *IB:* 35. Interview required.

C30 UNIVERSITY OF CENTRAL LANCASHIRE

PRESTON
LANCS PR1 2HE

t: 01772 201201 **f:** 01772 894954
e: uadmissions@uclan.ac.uk

// www.uclan.ac.uk

MV11 BA History and Law

Duration: 3FT Hon

Entry Requirements: HND required.

ML12 BA Law and Politics

Duration: 3FT Hon

Entry Requirements: *GCE:* 220. *IB:* 26. *BTEC NC:* DM. *BTEC ND:* MMP.

MC18 BA Law and Psychology

Duration: 3FT Hon

Entry Requirements: *GCE:* 220. *IB:* 26. *BTEC NC:* DM. *BTEC ND:* MMP.

C55 UNIVERSITY OF CHESTER

PARKGATE ROAD
CHESTER CH1 4BJ

t: 01244 511000 **f:** 01244 511300
e: enquiries@chester.ac.uk

// www.chester.ac.uk

NM41 BA Accounting & Finance and Law

Duration: 3FT Hon

Entry Requirements: *GCE:* 240. *SQAH:* BBBB. *IB:* 24. *BTEC NC:* DM. *BTEC ND:* MMM.

X3M1 BA Education Studies with Law

Duration: 3FT Hon

Entry Requirements: *IB:* 24.

QM31 BA English Language and Law

Duration: 3FT Hon

Entry Requirements: *GCE:* 240. *SQAH:* BBBB. *IB:* 24. *BTEC NC:* DM. *BTEC ND:* MPP.

Q3MC BA English Language with Law

Duration: 3FT Hon

Entry Requirements: *GCE:* 240. *SQAH:* BBBB. *IB:* 24. *BTEC NC:* DM. *BTEC ND:* MPP.

Q3M1 BA English with Law

Duration: 3FT Hon

Entry Requirements: *GCE:* 240. *SQAH:* BBBB. *IB:* 24. *BTEC NC:* DM. *BTEC ND:* MPP.

F4M1 BA Forensic Biology with Law

Duration: 3FT Hon

Entry Requirements: *GCE:* 240. *SQAH:* BBBB. *IB:* 24. *BTEC NC:* DM. *BTEC ND:* MMM.

V1M1 BA History with Law

Duration: 3FT Hon

Entry Requirements: *GCE:* 240. *SQAH:* BBBB. *IB:* 24. *BTEC NC:* DM. *BTEC ND:* MPP.

NM11 BA International Business and Law

Duration: 3FT Hon

Entry Requirements: *GCE:* 240. *SQAH:* BBBB. *IB:* 24. *BTEC NC:* DM. *BTEC ND:* MMM.

N1MC BA International Business with Law

Duration: 3FT Hon

Entry Requirements: *GCE:* 240. *SQAH:* BBBB. *IB:* 24. *BTEC NC:* DM. *BTEC ND:* MMM.

MX13 BA Law and Education Studies

Duration: 3FT Hon

Entry Requirements: *IB:* 24.

MQ13 BA Law and English

Duration: 3FT Hon

Entry Requirements: *GCE:* 240. *SQAH:* BBBB. *IB:* 24. *BTEC NC:* DM. *BTEC ND:* MPP.

MF14 BA Law and Forensic Biology

Duration: 3FT Hon

Entry Requirements: *GCE:* 240. *SQAH:* BBBB. *IB:* 24. *BTEC NC:* DM. *BTEC ND:* MMM.

MV11 BA Law and History

Duration: 3FT Hon

Entry Requirements: *GCE:* 240. *SQAH:* BBBB. *IB:* 24. *BTEC NC:* DM. *BTEC ND:* MPP.

ML19 BA Law and International Development Studies

Duration: 3FT Hon

Entry Requirements: *GCE:* 240. *SQAH:* BBBB. *IB:* 24. *BTEC NC:* DM. *BTEC ND:* MMM.

MP15 BA Law and Journalism

Duration: 3FT Hon

Entry Requirements: *GCE:* 240. *SQAH:* BBBB. *IB:* 24. *BTEC NC:* DM. *BTEC ND:* MMM.

MC18 BA Law and Psychology

Duration: 3FT Hon

Entry Requirements: *GCE:* 240. *SQAH:* BBBB. *IB:* 24. *BTEC NC:* DM. *BTEC ND:* MMM.

MCC6 BA Law and Sport & Exercise Sciences

Duration: 3FT Hon

Entry Requirements: *GCE:* 240. *SQAH:* BBBB. *IB:* 24. *BTEC NC:* DM. *BTEC ND:* MMM.

MN18 BA Law and Tourism

Duration: 3FT Hon

Entry Requirements: *GCE:* 240. *SQAH:* BBBB. *IB:* 24. *BTEC NC:* DM. *BTEC ND:* MMM.

M1X3 BA Law with Education Studies

Duration: 3FT Hon

Entry Requirements: *IB:* 24.

M1Q3 BA Law with English

Duration: 3FT Hon

Entry Requirements: *GCE:* 240. *SQAH:* BBBB. *IB:* 24. *BTEC NC:* DM. *BTEC ND:* MPP.

M1QH BA Law with English Language

Duration: 3FT Hon

Entry Requirements: *GCE:* 240. *SQAH:* BBBB. *IB:* 24. *BTEC NC:* DM. *BTEC ND:* MPP.

M1F4 BA Law with Forensic Biology

Duration: 3FT Hon

Entry Requirements: *GCE:* 240. *SQAH:* BBBB. *IB:* 24. *BTEC NC:* DM. *BTEC ND:* MMM.

M1V1 BA Law with History

Duration: 3FT Hon

Entry Requirements: *GCE:* 240. *SQAH:* BBBB. *IB:* 24. *BTEC NC:* DM. *BTEC ND:* MPP.

M1NC BA Law with International Business

Duration: 3FT Hon

Entry Requirements: *GCE:* 240. *SQAH:* BBBB. *IB:* 24. *BTEC NC:* DM. *BTEC ND:* MMM.

M1L9 BA Law with International Development Studies

Duration: 3FT Hon

Entry Requirements: *GCE:* 240. *SQAH:* BBBB. *IB:* 24. *BTEC NC:* DM. *BTEC ND:* MMM.

M1L2 BA Law with Politics

Duration: 3FT Hon

Entry Requirements: *GCE:* 240. *SQAH:* BBBB. *IB:* 24. *BTEC NC:* DM. *BTEC ND:* MMM.

M1C6 BA Law with Sport & Exercise Sciences

Duration: 3FT Hon

Entry Requirements: *GCE:* 240. *SQAH:* BBBB. *IB:* 24. *BTEC NC:* DM. *BTEC ND:* MMM.

M1N8 BA Law with Tourism

Duration: 3FT Hon

Entry Requirements: *GCE:* 240. *SQAH:* BBBB. *IB:* 24. *BTEC NC:* DM. *BTEC ND:* MMM.

LM21 BA Politics and Law

Duration: 3FT Hon

Entry Requirements: *GCE:* 240. *SQAH:* BBBB. *IB:* 24. *BTEC NC:* DM. *BTEC ND:* MMM.

L2M1 BA Politics with Law

Duration: 3FT Hon

Entry Requirements: *GCE:* 240. *SQAH:* BBBB. *IB:* 24. *BTEC NC:* DM. *BTEC ND:* MMM.

Confused about courses?
Indecisive about institutions?
Stressed about student life?
Unsure about UCAS?
Frowning over finance?

Help is available.

Visit www.ucasbooks.com to view our range
of over 75 books covering all aspects
of entry into higher education.

www.ucasbooks.com

> Unlock your potential
It's as easy as 1, 2, 3.

1 Search

Use Course Search to look for courses in your subject;
find out about your chosen universities and colleges
and lots more.

2 Apply

Use our online system Apply to make your application to
higher education.

3 Track

Then use Track to monitor the progress of your application.

UCAS   helping students into higher education   www.ucas.com

N8M1 BA Tourism with Law
Duration: 3FT Hon

Entry Requirements: *GCE:* 240. *SQAH:* BBBB. *IB:* 24. *BTEC NC:* DM. *BTEC ND:* MMM.

L9M1 BSc International Development Studies with Law
Duration: 3FT Hon

Entry Requirements: *GCE:* 240. *SQAH:* BBBB. *IB:* 24. *BTEC NC:* DM. *BTEC ND:* MMM.

C6M1 BSc Sport & Exercise Sciences with Law
Duration: 3FT Hon

Entry Requirements: *GCE:* 240. *SQAH:* BBBB. *IB:* 24. *BTEC NC:* DM. *BTEC ND:* MMM.

C60 CITY UNIVERSITY
NORTHAMPTON SQUARE
LONDON EC1V 0HB
t: 020 7040 5060 f: 020 7040 8995
e: ugadmissions@city.ac.uk
// www.city.ac.uk

M190 LLB English and French Laws
Duration: 4FT Hon

Entry Requirements: *GCE:* AAB. *SQAH:* ABBBB. *IB:* 35.

MN12 LLB Law and Property Valuation
Duration: 3FT Hon

Entry Requirements: *GCE:* AAB. *SQAH:* ABBBB. *IB:* 32.

C85 COVENTRY UNIVERSITY
THE STUDENT CENTRE
COVENTRY UNIVERSITY
1 GULSON RD
COVENTRY CV1 2JH
t: 024 7615 2222 f: 024 7615 2223
e: studentenquiries@coventry.ac.uk
// www.coventry.ac.uk

QM3C BA English and Law
Duration: 3FT Hon

Entry Requirements: *GCE:* 260-280. *BTEC NC:* DD. *BTEC ND:* DMM.

ML1F BA Law and International Studies
Duration: 3FT Hon

Entry Requirements: *GCE:* 260-280. *BTEC NC:* DD. *BTEC ND:* DMM.

D26 DE MONTFORT UNIVERSITY
THE GATEWAY
LEICESTER LE1 9BH
t: 0116 255 1551 f: 0116 250 6204
e: enquiries@dmu.ac.uk
// www.dmu.ac.uk

M1N6 BA Human Resource Management and Law
Duration: 3FT/4SW Hon

Entry Requirements: *IB:* 28.

M1N5 BA Law and Marketing
Duration: 3FT/4SW Hon

Entry Requirements: *IB:* 28.

MP13 BA Law and Media & Communication
Duration: 3FT Hon

Entry Requirements: *GCE:* 240. *IB:* 28. *BTEC NC:* DD. *BTEC ND:* MMM. Interview required.

LMF1 BA Law and Politics
Duration: 3FT Hon

Entry Requirements: *GCE:* 240. *IB:* 28. *BTEC NC:* DD. *BTEC ND:* MMM. Interview required.

CM81 BA Law and Psychology
Duration: 3FT Hon

Entry Requirements: *GCE:* 180-200. *IB:* 24. Interview required.

M1L4 BA Law and Public Policy
Duration: 3FT/4SW Hon

Entry Requirements: *GCE:* 240. *IB:* 28. *BTEC NC:* DD. *BTEC ND:* MMM. Interview required.

D39 UNIVERSITY OF DERBY
KEDLESTON ROAD
DERBY DE22 1GB
t: 08701 202330 f: 01332 597724
e: askadmissions@derby.ac.uk
// www.derby.ac.uk

MT17 BA American Studies and Law
Duration: 3FT Hon

Entry Requirements: *Foundation:* Merit. *GCE:* 180-240. *IB:* 26. *BTEC NC:* DM. *BTEC ND:* MMP.

KM11 BA Architectural Design and Law
Duration: 3FT Hon

Entry Requirements: *Foundation:* Merit. *GCE:* 180-240. *IB:* 26. *BTEC NC:* DM. *BTEC ND:* MMP.

VM31 BA Art & Design History and Law

Duration: 3FT Hon

Entry Requirements: Contact the institution for details.

PMH1 BA Broadcast Media and Law

Duration: 3FT Hon

Entry Requirements: *Foundation:* Merit. *GCE:* 180-240. *IB:* 26. *BTEC NC:* DM. *BTEC ND:* MMP.

WM81 BA Creative Writing and Law

Duration: 3FT Hon

Entry Requirements: *Foundation:* Merit. *GCE:* 180-240. *IB:* 26. *BTEC NC:* DM. *BTEC ND:* MMP.

WM51 BA Dance & Movement Studies and Law

Duration: 3FT Hon

Entry Requirements: *Foundation:* Merit. *GCE:* 180-240. *IB:* 26. *BTEC NC:* DM. *BTEC ND:* MMP.

XM31 BA Education Studies and Law

Duration: 3FT Hon

Entry Requirements: *Foundation:* Merit. *GCE:* 180-240. *IB:* 26. *BTEC NC:* DM. *BTEC ND:* MMP.

MQ13 BA English and Law

Duration: 3FT Hon

Entry Requirements: *Foundation:* Merit. *GCE:* 180-240. *IB:* 26. *BTEC NC:* DM. *BTEC ND:* MMP.

NM2C BA Enterprise Management and Law

Duration: 3FT Hon

Entry Requirements: *Foundation:* Merit. *GCE:* 180-240. *IB:* 26. *BTEC NC:* DM. *BTEC ND:* MMP.

MW19 BA Healing Arts and Law

Duration: 3FT Hon

Entry Requirements: *Foundation:* Merit. *GCE:* 180-240. *IB:* 26. *BTEC NC:* DM. *BTEC ND:* MMP.

MV11 BA History and Law

Duration: 3FT Hon

Entry Requirements: *Foundation:* Merit. *GCE:* 180-240. *IB:* 26. *BTEC NC:* DM. *BTEC ND:* MMP.

NM61 BA Human Resource Management and Law

Duration: 3FT Hon

Entry Requirements: *Foundation:* Merit. *GCE:* 180-240. *IB:* 26. *BTEC NC:* DM. *BTEC ND:* MMP

MN15 BA Law and Marketing

Duration: 3FT Hon

Entry Requirements: *Foundation:* Merit. *GCE:* 180-240. *IB:* 26. *BTEC NC:* DM. *BTEC ND:* MMP.

MW18 BA Law and Media Writing

Duration: 3FT Hon

Entry Requirements: *Foundation:* Merit. *GCE:* 180-240. *IB:* 26. *BTEC NC:* DM. *BTEC ND:* MMP.

MW14 BA Law and Theatre Arts

Duration: 3FT Hon

Entry Requirements: *Foundation:* Merit. *GCE:* 180-240. *IB:* 26. *BTEC NC:* DM. *BTEC ND:* MMP.

PM31 BA Popular Culture & Media and Law

Duration: 3FT Hon

Entry Requirements: *Foundation:* Merit. *GCE:* 180-240. *IB:* 26. *BTEC NC:* DM. *BTEC ND:* MMP.

LM21 BA/BSc International Relations & Global Development and Law

Duration: 3FT Hon

Entry Requirements: *Foundation:* Merit. *GCE:* 180-240. *IB:* 26. *BTEC NC:* DM. *BTEC ND:* MMP.

CM6C BA/BSc Sport & Exercise Science and Law

Duration: 3FT Hon

Entry Requirements: *Foundation:* Merit. *GCE:* 180-240. *IB:* 26. *BTEC NC:* DM. *BTEC ND:* MMP.

CM1C BSc Biology and Law

Duration: 3FT Hon

Entry Requirements: *Foundation:* Merit. *GCE:* 180-240. *IB:* 26. *BTEC NC:* DM. *BTEC ND:* MMP.

FM71 BSc Environmental Hazards and Law

Duration: 3FT Hon

Entry Requirements: *GCE:* 60-80.

FM8C BSc Geography and Law

Duration: 3FT Hon

Entry Requirements: *Foundation:* Merit. *GCE:* 180-240. *IB:* 26. *BTEC NC:* DM. *BTEC ND:* MMP.

E14 UNIVERSITY OF EAST ANGLIA
NORWICH NR4 7TJ

t: 01603 456161 f: 01603 458596
e: admissions@uea.ac.uk

// www.uea.ac.uk

M123 LLB Law with American Law
Duration: 4FT Hon

Entry Requirements: *GCE:* 360. *IB:* 34.

E25 EAST LANCASHIRE INSTITUTE OF HIGHER EDUCATION AT BLACKBURN COLLEGE
DUKE STREET
BLACKBURN BB2 1LH

t: 01254 292594 f: 01254 260749
e: he-admissions@blackburn.ac.uk

// www.elihe.ac.uk

M1C8 LLB Law with Psychology
Duration: 3FT Hon

Entry Requirements: *GCE:* 220.

E28 UNIVERSITY OF EAST LONDON
DOCKLANDS CAMPUS
UNIVERSITY WAY
LONDON E16 2RD

t: 020 8223 2835 f: 020 8223 2978
e: admiss@uel.ac.uk

// www.uel.ac.uk

X3MC BA Education & Community Development with Law
Duration: 3FT Hon

Entry Requirements: *GCE:* 200. *IB:* 28.

Q3MC BA English Literature with Law
Duration: 3FT Hon

Entry Requirements: *GCE:* 200. *IB:* 24. *BTEC NC:* DM. *BTEC ND:* MMP.

Q3M1 BA English Literature/Law
Duration: 3FT Hon

Entry Requirements: *GCE:* 240. *IB:* 28. *BTEC NC:* DD. *BTEC ND:* MMM.

V1M1 BA History with Law
Duration: 3FT Hon

Entry Requirements: *GCE:* 200. *IB:* 28.

L2M1 BA International Politics with Law
Duration: 3FT Hon

Entry Requirements: *GCE:* 200. *IB:* 28.

ML12 BA Law / International Politics
Duration: 3FT Hon

Entry Requirements: *GCE:* 240. *IB:* 28. *BTEC NC:* DD. *BTEC ND:* MMM.

M1Q3 BA Law with English Language
Duration: 3FT Hon

Entry Requirements: *GCE:* 240. *IB:* 28. *BTEC NC:* DD. *BTEC ND:* MMM.

M1QH BA Law with English Literature
Duration: 3FT Hon

Entry Requirements: *GCE:* 240. *IB:* 28. *BTEC NC:* DD. *BTEC ND:* MMM.

M1V1 BA Law with History
Duration: 3FT Hon

Entry Requirements: *GCE:* 240. *IB:* 28. *BTEC NC:* DD. *BTEC ND:* MMM.

M1W4 BA Law with Theatre Studies
Duration: 3FT Hon

Entry Requirements: *GCE:* 240. *IB:* 28. *BTEC NC:* DD. *BTEC ND:* MMM.

CM81 BA Law/Psychosocial Studies
Duration: 3FT Hon

Entry Requirements: *GCE:* 240. *IB:* 28. *BTEC NC:* DD. *BTEC ND:* MMM.

X3M1 BA Special Educational Needs with Law
Duration: 3FT Hon

Entry Requirements: *GCE:* 200. *IB:* 24.

FM41 BA/BSc Forensic Science/Law
Duration: 3FT Hon

Entry Requirements: *GCE:* 240. *IB:* 28. *BTEC NC:* DD. *BTEC ND:* MMM.

BM91 BA/BSc Health Studies/Law
Duration: 3FT Hon

Entry Requirements: *GCE:* 240. *IB:* 28. *BTEC NC:* DD. *BTEC ND:* MMM.

F4M1 BSc Forensic Science with Law
Duration: 3FT Hon

Entry Requirements: *GCE:* 200. *IB:* 24. *BTEC NC:* DM. *BTEC ND:* MMP. *OCR ND:* Merit. *OCR NED:* Pass.

N2M1 BSc Health Services Management with Law
Duration: 3FT Hon

Entry Requirements: *GCE:* 200. *IB:* 28.

G5MC BSc Information Security Systems with Law
Duration: 3FT Hon

Entry Requirements: *GCE:* 200. *IB:* 28.

E56 THE UNIVERSITY OF EDINBURGH
STUDENT RECRUITMENT & ADMISSIONS
57 GEORGE SQUARE
EDINBURGH EH8 9JU
t: 0131 650 4360 f: 0131 651 1236
e: sra.enquiries@ed.ac.uk
// www.ed.ac.uk/studying/undergraduate/

MV11 LLB Law and History
Duration: 4FT Hon

Entry Requirements: *GCE:* BBB. *SQAH:* BBBB. *IB:* 34.

ML12 LLB Law and Politics
Duration: 4FT Hon

Entry Requirements: *GCE:* BBB. *SQAH:* BBBB. *IB:* 34.

E70 THE UNIVERSITY OF ESSEX
WIVENHOE PARK
COLCHESTER
ESSEX CO4 3SQ
t: 01206 873666 f: 01206 873423
e: admit@essex.ac.uk
// www.essex.ac.uk

MV15 LLB Law and Philosophy (4 years)
Duration: 4FT Hon

Entry Requirements: *GCE:* AAB. *SQAH:* AAAA-AAAB. *IB:* 36. *BTEC NC:* DM. *BTEC ND:* DDD.

ML12 LLB Law and Politics (4 years)
Duration: 4FT Hon

Entry Requirements: *GCE:* AAB. *SQAH:* AAAA-AAAB. *IB:* 36. *BTEC NC:* DM. *BTEC ND:* DDD.

MVC5 BA Philosophy and Law
Duration: 3FT Hon

Entry Requirements: *GCE:* 300. *SQAH:* AABB. *IB:* 32. *BTEC ND:* DDM.

LM21 BA Politics and Law
Duration: 3FT Hon

Entry Requirements: *GCE:* 320. *SQAH:* AAAB. *IB:* 34. *BTEC ND:* DDM.

LM2C BA Politics and Law (International Exchange)
Duration: 4FT Hon

Entry Requirements: Contact the institution for details.

E84 UNIVERSITY OF EXETER
LAVER BUILDING
NORTH PARK ROAD
EXETER
DEVON EX4 4QE
t: 01392 263855 f: 01392 263857/262479
e: admissions@exeter.ac.uk
// www.exeter.ac.uk/admissions

M124 LLB Law with European Study (4 years)
Duration: 4FT Hon

Entry Requirements: *GCE:* AAA-AAB. Admissions Test required.

VM12 BA History and Law (Cornwall campus)
Duration: 3FT Hon

Entry Requirements: *GCE:* AAB-ABB. *BTEC ND:* DDM.

LM21 BA Politics and Law (Cornwall campus)
Duration: 3FT Hon

Entry Requirements: *GCE:* AAB-ABB. *BTEC ND:* DDM.

G14 UNIVERSITY OF GLAMORGAN, CARDIFF AND PONTYPRIDD
ENQUIRIES AND ADMISSIONS UNIT
PONTYPRIDD CF37 1DL
t: 0800 716925 f: 01443 654050
e: enquiries@glam.ac.uk
// www.glam.ac.uk

M1Q3 LLB Law with English Studies
Duration: 3FT Hon

Entry Requirements: *GCE:* 280-320.

M1V1 LLB Law with History
Duration: 3FT Hon

Entry Requirements: *GCE:* 280-320.

M2LF LLB Law with International Politics
Duration: 3FT Hon

Entry Requirements: *GCE:* 280-320. *IB:* 30. *BTEC NC:* DD. *BTEC ND:* DMM.

M1L2 LLB Law with Politics
Duration: 3FT Hon

Entry Requirements: *GCE:* 280-320.

QM31 BA English and Law
Duration: 3FT Hon

Entry Requirements: *GCE:* 280-320. *BTEC NC:* DD. *BTEC ND:* DDM.

Q3M1 BA English Studies with Law
Duration: 3FT Hon

Entry Requirements: *GCE:* 220-260.

VM11 BA History and Law
Duration: 3FT Hon

Entry Requirements: *GCE:* 280-320.

V1M1 BA History with Law
Duration: 3FT Hon

Entry Requirements: *GCE:* 200-240.

ML12 BA Law and Politics
Duration: 3FT Hon

Entry Requirements: *GCE:* 280-320. *IB:* 30. *BTEC NC:* DD. *BTEC ND:* DMM.

M1F4 BA Law with Forensic Science
Duration: 3FT Hon

Entry Requirements: *GCE:* 280. *IB:* 30. *BTEC NC:* DD. *BTEC ND:* DMM.

L2M1 BA Politics with Law
Duration: 3FT Hon

Entry Requirements: *GCE:* 200.

FM41 BSc Forensic Science and Law
Duration: 3FT Hon

Entry Requirements: *GCE:* 280-320. *IB:* 30.

F4M1 BSc Forensic Science with Law
Duration: 3FT Hon

Entry Requirements: *GCE:* 220-260. *IB:* 30. *BTEC NC:* DM. *BTEC ND:* MMM.

CM81 BSc Psychology and Law
Duration: 3FT Hon

Entry Requirements: *GCE:* 220-260.

G28 UNIVERSITY OF GLASGOW
THE UNIVERSITY OF GLASGOW
THE FRASER BUILDING
65 HILLHEAD STREET
GLASGOW G12 8QF

t: 0141 330 6062 f: 0141 330 2961
e: ugenquiries@gla.ac.uk (UK/EU undergrad enquiries only)
// www.glasgow.ac.uk

MQ13 LLB Law/English Literature
Duration: 4FT Hon

Entry Requirements: *GCE:* AAB. *SQAH:* AAAAB. *IB:* 34. Admissions Test required.

ML17 LLB Law/Geography
Duration: 4FT Hon

Entry Requirements: *GCE:* AAB. *SQAH:* AAAAB. *IB:* 34. Admissions Test required.

MV11 LLB Law/History
Duration: 4FT Hon

Entry Requirements: *GCE:* AAB. *SQAH:* AAAAB. *IB:* 34. Admissions Test required.

MV15 LLB Law/Philosophy
Duration: 4FT Hon

Entry Requirements: *GCE:* AAB. *SQAH:* AAAAB. *IB:* 34. Admissions Test required.

ML12 LLB Law/Politics
Duration: 4FT Hon

Entry Requirements: *GCE:* AAB. *SQAH:* AAAAB. *IB:* 34. Admissions Test required.

MR17 LLB Law/Slavonic Studies
Duration: 4FT Hon

Entry Requirements: *GCE:* AAB. *SQAH:* AAAAB. *IB:* 34. Admissions Test required.

G53 GLYNDWR UNIVERSITY
PLAS COCH
MOLD ROAD
WREXHAM LL11 2AW

t: 01978 293439 f: 01978 290008
e: SID@glyndwr.ac.uk
// www.glyndwr.ac.uk

N1MC FdA Business with Law
Duration: 2FT Fdg

Entry Requirements: *GCE:* 100.

G70 UNIVERSITY OF GREENWICH
GREENWICH CAMPUS
OLD ROYAL NAVAL COLLEGE
PARK ROW
LONDON SE10 9LS

t: 0800 005 006 f: 020 8331 8145
e: courseinfo@gre.ac.uk
// www.gre.ac.uk

V1M1 BA History with Law
Duration: 3FT Hon

Entry Requirements: *GCE:* 180. *IB:* 24.

LM31 BA Law and Citizenship
Duration: 3FT Hon

Entry Requirements: *GCE:* 180. *SQAH:* BBBBC. *SQAAH:* BCC. *IB:* 24.

MQ13 BA Law and English
Duration: 3FT Hon

Entry Requirements: *GCE:* 180. *IB:* 24.

MV11 BA Law and History
Duration: 3FT Hon

Entry Requirements: *GCE:* 180. *IB:* 24.

MV15 BA Law and Philosophy
Duration: 3FT Hon

Entry Requirements: *GCE:* 180. *IB:* 24.

ML12 BA Law and Politics
Duration: 3FT Hon

Entry Requirements: *GCE:* 180. *IB:* 24.

MC18 BA Law and Psychology
Duration: 3FT Hon

Entry Requirements: *GCE:* 180. *IB:* 24.

V5M1 BA Philosophy with Law
Duration: 3FT Hon

Entry Requirements: *GCE:* 180. *IB:* 24.

L2M1 BA Politics with Law
Duration: 3FT Hon

Entry Requirements: *GCE:* 180. *IB:* 24.

H36 UNIVERSITY OF HERTFORDSHIRE
UNIVERSITY ADMISSIONS SERVICE
COLLEGE LANE
HATFIELD
HERTS AL10 9AB
t: 01707 284800 **f:** 01707 284870
// www.herts.ac.uk

F9M1 BSc Environmental Studies/Law
Duration: 3FT Hon

Entry Requirements: *GCE:* 220.

RM81 BSc European Studies/Law
Duration: 3FT/4SW Hon

Entry Requirements: Contact the institution for details.

B9M1 BSc Health Studies/Law
Duration: 3FT/4SW Hon

Entry Requirements: Contact the institution for details.

L7M1 BSc Human Geography/Law
Duration: 3FT/4SW Hon

Entry Requirements: *GCE:* 220.

M1H6 BSc Law/Digital Media Technology
Duration: 3FT/4SW Hon

Entry Requirements: *GCE:* 260.

M1F9 BSc Law/Environmental Studies
Duration: 3FT Hon

Entry Requirements: *GCE:* 260.

M1B1 BSc Law/Human Biology
Duration: 3FT Hon

Entry Requirements: *GCE:* 260.

M1L7 BSc Law/Human Geography
Duration: 3FT/4SW Hon

Entry Requirements: *GCE:* 260.

M1P5 BSc Law/Journalism & Media Cultures
Duration: 3FT/4SW Hon

Entry Requirements: *GCE:* 260.

M1V5 BSc Law/Philosophy
Duration: 3FT Hon

Entry Requirements: *GCE:* 260.

M1C8 BSc Law/Psychology
Duration: 3FT/4SW Hon

Entry Requirements: *GCE:* 220.

V5M1 BSc Philosophy/Law
Duration: 3FT Hon

Entry Requirements: *GCE:* 260.

H60 THE UNIVERSITY OF HUDDERSFIELD
QUEENSGATE
HUDDERSFIELD HD1 3DH
t: 01484 473969 **f:** 01484 472765
e: admissionsandrecords@hud.ac.uk
// www.hud.ac.uk

N2M1 BA Corporate Management with Law
Duration: 3FT/4SW Hon

Entry Requirements: *GCE:* 280. *SQAH:* BBCC. *IB:* 28.

H72 THE UNIVERSITY OF HULL
THE UNIVERSITY OF HULL
COTTINGHAM ROAD
HULL HU6 7RX
t: 01482 466100 f: 01482 442290
e: admissions@hull.ac.uk
// www.hull.ac.uk

M1Q3 LLB Law (including Foundation English Language)
Duration: 4FT Hon

Entry Requirements: *GCE:* 320. *IB:* 28.

M1QH LLB Law with Literature
Duration: 3FT Hon

Entry Requirements: *GCE:* 320. *IB:* 28.

M1V5 LLB Law with Philosophy
Duration: 3FT Hon

Entry Requirements: *GCE:* 320. *IB:* 28.

M1L2 LLB Law with Politics
Duration: 3FT Hon

Entry Requirements: *GCE:* 320. *IB:* 28.

Q3M1 BA English with Law
Duration: 3FT Hon

Entry Requirements: *GCE:* 320. *IB:* 28.

K12 KEELE UNIVERSITY
STAFFS ST5 5BG
t: 01782 734005 f: 01782 632343
e: undergraduate@keele.ac.uk
// www.keele.ac.uk

M1L2 LLB Law with Politics
Duration: 3FT Hon

Entry Requirements: *GCE:* 340-360. *BTEC ND:* DDD.

MT17 BA American Studies and Law
Duration: 3FT Hon

Entry Requirements: *GCE:* 300-320.

MX13 BA Educational Studies and Law
Duration: 3FT Hon

Entry Requirements: *GCE:* 300-320.

MQ13 BA English and Law
Duration: 3FT Hon

Entry Requirements: *GCE:* 300-320.

MV11 BA History and Law
Duration: 3FT Hon

Entry Requirements: *GCE:* 300-320.

MN16 BA Human Resource Management and Law
Duration: 3FT Hon

Entry Requirements: *GCE:* 300-320.

LM2C BA International Relations and Law
Duration: 3FT Hon

Entry Requirements: *GCE:* 300-320.

MN15 BA Law and Marketing
Duration: 3FT Hon

Entry Requirements: *GCE:* 300-320.

PM31 BA Law and Media, Communications & Culture
Duration: 3FT Hon

Entry Requirements: *GCE:* 300-320.

MW13 BA Law and Music
Duration: 3FT Hon

Entry Requirements: *GCE:* 300-320.

MWD3 BA Law and Music Technology
Duration: 3FT Hon

Entry Requirements: *GCE:* 300-320.

MV15 BA Law and Philosophy
Duration: 3FT Hon

Entry Requirements: *GCE:* 300-320.

LM21 BA Law and Politics
Duration: 3FT Hon

Entry Requirements: *GCE:* 300-320.

FMX1 BSc Applied Environmental Science and Law
Duration: 3FT Hon

Entry Requirements: *GCE:* 280-320.

CM71 BSc Biochemistry and Law
Duration: 3FT Hon

Entry Requirements: *GCE:* 280-320.

CM11 BSc Biology and Law
Duration: 3FT Hon

Entry Requirements: *GCE:* 280-320.

FM11 BSc Chemistry and Law
Duration: 3FT Hon

Entry Requirements: *GCE:* 280-320.

FM41 BSc Forensic Science and Law
Duration: 3FT Hon

Entry Requirements: *GCE:* 280-320.

FM61 BSc Geology and Law
Duration: 3FT Hon

Entry Requirements: *GCE:* 280-320.

CM1C BSc Human Biology and Law
Duration: 3FT Hon

Entry Requirements: *GCE:* 280-320. *BTEC NC:* DD. *BTEC ND:* DMM.

FMCC BSc Law and Medicinal Chemistry
Duration: 3FT Hon

Entry Requirements: *GCE:* 280-320.

BM11 BSc Law and Neuroscience
Duration: 3FT Hon

Entry Requirements: *GCE:* 300-320.

GM71 BSc Smart Systems and Law
Duration: 3FT Hon

Entry Requirements: *GCE:* 300-320.

K24 THE UNIVERSITY OF KENT
INFORMATION, RECRUITMENT & ADMISSIONS
REGISTRY
UNIVERSITY OF KENT
CANTERBURY. KENT CT2 7NZ

t: 01227 827272 f: 01227 827077
e: information@kent.ac.uk

// www.kent.ac.uk

M103 LLB Law with a Year in China
Duration: 4FT Hon

Entry Requirements: *GCE:* 320. *SQAH:* AAAAA. *IB:* 34. *BTEC NC:* DD. *BTEC ND:* DDM.

M104 LLB Law with a Year in the Hong Kong Special Administrative Region (China)
Duration: 4FT Hon

Entry Requirements: *GCE:* 320. *SQAH:* AAAAA. *IB:* 34. *BTEC NC:* DD. *BTEC ND:* DDM.

M101 LLB Law with an optional deferred subject
Duration: 3FT Hon

Entry Requirements: *GCE:* 320. *SQAH:* AAAAA. *IB:* 34. *BTEC NC:* DD. *BTEC ND:* DDM.

MN26 BA Industrial Relations and Human Resource Management (Law)
Duration: 3FT Hon

Entry Requirements: *GCE:* 300. *IB:* 33. *BTEC NC:* DD. *BTEC ND:* DMM. *OCR ND:* Distinction.

MQ13 BA Law and English
Duration: 4FT Hon

Entry Requirements: *GCE:* 320. *SQAH:* AAAAA. *IB:* 34. *BTEC NC:* DD. *BTEC ND:* DDM.

VM1C BA Law and History
Duration: 3FT Hon

Entry Requirements: *GCE:* 320. *SQAH:* AAAAA. *IB:* 34. *BTEC NC:* DD. *BTEC ND:* DDM.

MV15 BA Law and Philosophy
Duration: 3FT Hon

Entry Requirements: *GCE:* 320. *SQAH:* AAAAA. *IB:* 34. *BTEC NC:* DD. *BTEC ND:* DDM.

ML14 BA Law and Welfare
Duration: 3FT Hon

Entry Requirements: *GCE:* 320. *SQAH:* AAAAA. *IB:* 34. *BTEC NC:* DD. *BTEC ND:* DDM.

LM21 BA Politics and Law
Duration: 3FT Hon

Entry Requirements: *GCE:* 320. *SQAH:* AAAAA. *IB:* 34. *BTEC NC:* DD. *BTEC ND:* DDM.

CM81 BSc Psychology and Law (4 years)
Duration: 4FT Hon

Entry Requirements: *GCE:* ABB-AAC. *SQAH:* AAAAB. *IB:* 35. *BTEC NC:* DD. *BTEC ND:* DDM. *OCR ND:* Distinction.

K84 KINGSTON UNIVERSITY
STUDENT INFORMATION & ADVICE CENTRE
COOPER HOUSE
40-46 SURBITON ROAD
KINGSTON UPON THAMES KT1 2HX

t: 020 8547 7053 f: 020 8547 7080
e: aps@kingston.ac.uk

// www.kingston.ac.uk

W8M1 BA Creative Writing with Law
Duration: 3FT Hon

Entry Requirements: *GCE:* 220-320.

Q3M1 BA English Literature with Law
Duration: 3FT Hon

Entry Requirements: *GCE:* 220-320.

MQC3 BA Law and English Literature
Duration: 3FT Hon

Entry Requirements: *GCE:* 280-320.

MP13 BA Law and Film Studies
Duration: 3FT Hon

Entry Requirements: *GCE:* 280-320.

ML12 BA Law and Politics
Duration: 3FT Hon

Entry Requirements: *GCE:* 280-320.

M1L2 BA Law with International Relations
Duration: 3FT Hon

Entry Requirements: *GCE:* 280-320.

L2M1 BA Politics with Law
Duration: 3FT Hon

Entry Requirements: *GCE:* 220-320.

P3MC BA Television & New Broadcasting Media with Law
Duration: 3FT Hon

Entry Requirements: *GCE:* 220-320.

F8M1 BSc Environmental Studies with Law
Duration: 4SW Hon

Entry Requirements: *GCE:* 200-280.

F8MC BSc Environmental Studies with Law
Duration: 3FT Hon

Entry Requirements: *GCE:* 200-280.

FM41 BSc Forensic Science and Law
Duration: 3FT Hon

Entry Requirements: *GCE:* 200-280.

L2MC BSc International Relations with Law
Duration: 3FT Hon

Entry Requirements: *GCE:* 240-280.

CM61 BSc Sports Science and Law
Duration: 4SW Hon

Entry Requirements: *GCE:* 220-280.

CM6C BSc Sports Science and Law
Duration: 3FT Hon

Entry Requirements: *GCE:* 220-280.

C6M1 BSc Sports Science with Law
Duration: 4SW Hon

Entry Requirements: *GCE:* 220-280.

L39 UNIVERSITY OF LINCOLN
ADMISSIONS
BRAYFORD POOL
LINCOLN LN6 7TS
t: 01522 886097 f: 01522 886146
e: admissions@lincoln.ac.uk
// www.lincoln.ac.uk

ML12 LLB Law and Politics
Duration: 3FT Hon

Entry Requirements: *GCE:* 200.

L46 LIVERPOOL HOPE UNIVERSITY
HOPE PARK
LIVERPOOL L16 9JD
t: 0151 291 3295 f: 0151 291 2050
e: admission@hope.ac.uk
// www.hope.ac.uk

LM51 BA Childhood & Youth Studies and Law
Duration: 3FT Hon

Entry Requirements: *GCE:* 240. *IB:* 25.

XM31 BA Early Childhood Studies and Law
Duration: 3FT Hon

Entry Requirements: *GCE:* 240. *IB:* 25.

XM3C BA Education Studies and Law
Duration: 3FT Hon

Entry Requirements: *GCE:* 240. *IB:* 25.

QM31 BA English Language and Law
Duration: 3FT Hon

Entry Requirements: *GCE:* 240. *IB:* 25.

CM11 BA Environmental Biology and Law
Duration: 3FT Hon

Entry Requirements: *GCE:* 240. *IB:* 25.

CM6C BA Football Studies and Law
Duration: 3FT Hon

Entry Requirements: *GCE:* 240. *IB:* 25.

MXCH BA Inclusive Education and Law
Duration: 3FT Hon

Entry Requirements: *GCE:* 240. *IB:* 25.

LM2C BA International Studies and Law
Duration: 3FT Hon

Entry Requirements: *GCE:* 240. *IB:* 25.

NM21 BA Law and Leisure
Duration: 3FT Hon

Entry Requirements: *GCE:* 240. *IB:* 25.

MB14 BA Law and Nutrition
Duration: 3FT Hon

Entry Requirements: *GCE:* 240. *IB:* 25.

MV15 BA Law and Philosophy & Ethics
Duration: 3FT Hon

Entry Requirements: *GCE:* 240. *IB:* 25.

LM21 BA Law and Politics
Duration: 3FT Hon

Entry Requirements: *GCE:* 240. *IB:* 25.

MC18 BA Law and Psychology
Duration: 3FT Hon

Entry Requirements: *GCE:* 240. *IB:* 25.

MC16 BA Law and Sport Studies
Duration: 3FT Hon

Entry Requirements: *GCE:* 240. *IB:* 25.

MV16 BA Law and Theology & Religous Studies
Duration: 3FT Hon

Entry Requirements: *GCE:* 240. *IB:* 25.

MN18 BA Law and Tourism
Duration: 3FT Hon

Entry Requirements: *GCE:* 240. *IB:* 25.

L68 LONDON METROPOLITAN UNIVERSITY
166-220 HOLLOWAY ROAD
LONDON N7 8DB
t: 020 7133 4200
e: admissions@londonmet.ac.uk
// www.londonmet.ac.uk

QM31 BA English Language Studies and Law
Duration: 3FT Hon

Entry Requirements: *GCE:* 240. *IB:* 28.

QM3C BA English Literature and Law
Duration: 3FT Hon

Entry Requirements: *GCE:* 240. *IB:* 28.

LM91 BA International Development and Law
Duration: 3FT Hon

Entry Requirements: *GCE:* 240. *IB:* 28.

ML1F BA International Relations and Law
Duration: 3FT Hon

Entry Requirements: *GCE:* 240. *IB:* 28.

MN15 BA Law and Marketing
Duration: 3FT Hon

Entry Requirements: *GCE:* 240. *IB:* 28.

MP13 BA Law and Media Arts
Duration: 3FT Hon

Entry Requirements: *GCE:* 240. *IB:* 28.

MLD2 BA Law and Peace & Conflict Studies
Duration: 3FT Hon

Entry Requirements: *GCE:* 240. *IB:* 28.

MV15 BA Law and Philosophy
Duration: 3FT Hon

Entry Requirements: *GCE:* 240. *IB:* 28.

LM21 BA Law and Politics
Duration: 3FT Hon

Entry Requirements: *GCE:* 240. *IB:* 28.

TM3C BA/BSc Asia-Pacific Studies and Law
Duration: 3FT Hon

Entry Requirements: *GCE:* 240. *IB:* 28.

NM21 BA/BSc Community Sector Management and Law
Duration: 3FT Hon

Entry Requirements: *GCE:* 240. *IB:* 28.

FM41 BA/BSc Forensic Science and Law
Duration: 3FT Hon

Entry Requirements: *GCE:* 240. *IB:* 28.

LM4C BA/BSc Health Studies and Law
Duration: 3FT Hon

Entry Requirements: *GCE:* 240. *IB:* 28.

MP19 BA/BSc Law and Mass Communications
Duration: 3FT Hon

Entry Requirements: *GCE:* 240. *IB:* 28.

L75 LONDON SOUTH BANK UNIVERSITY

103 BOROUGH ROAD
LONDON SE1 0AA
t: 020 7815 7815 **f:** 020 7815 8273
e: enquiry@lsbu.ac.uk
// www.lsbu.ac.uk

M1N6 LLB Law with Human Resource Management
Duration: 3FT Hon

Entry Requirements: *GCE:* 240. *IB:* 24.

M1C8 LLB Law with Psychology
Duration: 3FT Hon

Entry Requirements: *GCE:* 240. *IB:* 24.

N5M1 BA Digital Marketing with Law
Duration: 3FT Hon

Entry Requirements: *GCE:* 240. *IB:* 24.

L2M1 BA International Politics with Law
Duration: 3FT Hon

Entry Requirements: *GCE:* 240. *IB:* 24.

N5MC BA Marketing with Law
Duration: 3FT Hon

Entry Requirements: *GCE:* 240. *IB:* 24.

F4M1 BSc Forensic Science with Law
Duration: 3FT Hon

Entry Requirements: *GCE:* 240. *IB:* 24. *BTEC NC:* MM. *BTEC ND:* MPP.

M20 THE UNIVERSITY OF MANCHESTER

OXFORD ROAD
MANCHESTER M13 9PL
t: 0161 275 2077 **f:** 0161 275 2106
e: ug-admissions@manchester.ac.uk
// www.manchester.ac.uk

M1L2 BA Law with Politics
Duration: 3FT Hon

Entry Requirements: *GCE:* AAB. *SQAH:* AAABB. *SQAAH:* AAB. *IB:* 35. *BTEC NC:* DD. *BTEC ND:* DDD.

N37 UNIVERSITY OF WALES, NEWPORT

CAERLEON CAMPUS
PO BOX 101
NEWPORT
SOUTH WALES NP18 3YH
t: 01633 432030 **f:** 01633 432850
e: admissions@newport.ac.uk
// www.newport.ac.uk

CM62 BA/BSc Sport and Youth Justice
Duration: 3FT Hon

Entry Requirements: *GCE:* 200-240. *IB:* 24. Interview required.

N38 UNIVERSITY OF NORTHAMPTON

PARK CAMPUS
BOUGHTON GREEN ROAD
NORTHAMPTON NN2 7AL
t: 0800 358 2232 **f:** 01604 722083
e: admissions@northampton.ac.uk
// www.northampton.ac.uk

T7MC BA American Literature & Film/Law
Duration: 3FT Hon

Entry Requirements: *GCE:* 220-260. *SQAH:* AAB-BBBB. *IB:* 24.

T7M1 BA American Studies/Law
Duration: 3FT Hon

Entry Requirements: *GCE:* 220-260. *SQAH:* AAB-BBBB. *IB:* 24.

LM32 BA Citizenship, Law & Ethics
Duration: 3FT Hon

Entry Requirements: *GCE:* 220-260. *SQAH:* AAB-BBBB. *IB:* 24.

W8M1 BA Creative Writing/Law
Duration: 3FT Hon

Entry Requirements: *GCE:* 220-260. *SQAH:* AAB-BBBB. *IB:* 24.

X3M1 BA Education Studies/Law
Duration: 3FT Hon

Entry Requirements: *GCE:* 220-260. *SQAH:* AAB-BBBB. *IB:* 24.

QM31 BA English Language/Law
Duration: 3FT Hon

Entry Requirements: *GCE:* 220-260. *SQAH:* AAB-BBBB. *IB:* 24.

N8M1 BA Events Management/Law
Duration: 3FT Hon

Entry Requirements: *GCE:* 220-260. *SQAH:* AAB-BBBB. *IB:* 24.

W6M1 BA Film & Television Studies/Law
Duration: 3FT Hon

Entry Requirements: *GCE:* 220-260. *SQAH:* AAB-BBBB. *IB:* 24.

W1M1 BA Fine Art Painting & Drawing/Law
Duration: 3FT Hon

Entry Requirements: *GCE:* 220-260. *SQAH:* AAB-BBBB. *IB:* 24.

L4M1 BA Health Studies/Law
Duration: 3FT Hon

Entry Requirements: *GCE:* 220-260. *SQAH:* AAB-BBBB. *IB:* 24.

V1M1 BA History/Law
Duration: 3FT Hon

Entry Requirements: *GCE:* 220-260. *SQAH:* AAB-BBBB. *IB:* 24.

L7M1 BA Human Geography/Law
Duration: 3FT Hon

Entry Requirements: *GCE:* 220-260. *SQAH:* AAB-BBBB. *IB:* 24.

N6M1 BA Human Resource Management/Law
Duration: 3FT Hon

Entry Requirements: *GCE:* 220-260. *SQAH:* AAB-BBBB. *IB:* 24.

P5M1 BA Journalism/Law
Duration: 3FT Hon

Entry Requirements: *GCE:* 220-260. *SQAH:* AAB-BBBB. *IB:* 24.

M1Q3 BA Law with English Language
Duration: 3FT Hon

Entry Requirements: *GCE:* 220-260. *SQAH:* AAB-BBBB. *IB:* 24.

M1D4 BA Law with Equine Studies
Duration: 3FT Hon

Entry Requirements: *GCE:* 220-260. *SQAH:* AAB-BBBB. *IB:* 24.

M1TR BA Law/American Literature & Film
Duration: 3FT Hon

Entry Requirements: *GCE:* 220-260. *SQAH:* AAB-BBBB. *IB:* 24.

M1T7 BA Law/American Studies
Duration: 3FT Hon

Entry Requirements: *GCE:* 220-260. *SQAH:* AAB-BBBB. *IB:* 24.

M1C1 BA Law/Biological Conservation
Duration: 3FT Hon

Entry Requirements: *GCE:* 220-260. *SQAH:* AAB-BBBB. *IB:* 24.

M1G5 BA Law/Business Computing Systems
Duration: 3FT Hon

Entry Requirements: *GCE:* 220-260. *SQAH:* AAB-BBBB. *IB:* 24.

M1W8 BA Law/Creative Writing
Duration: 3FT Hon

Entry Requirements: *GCE:* 220-260. *SQAH:* AAB-BBBB. *IB:* 24.

M1W5 BA Law/Dance
Duration: 3FT Hon

Entry Requirements: *GCE:* 220-260. *SQAH:* AAB-BBBB. *IB:* 24.
Interview required.

M1X3 BA Law/Education Studies
Duration: 3FT Hon

Entry Requirements: *GCE:* 220-260. *SQAH:* AAB-BBBB. *IB:* 24.

M1N8 BA Law/Events Management
Duration: 3FT Hon

Entry Requirements: *GCE:* 220-260. *SQAH:* AAB-BBBB. *IB:* 24.

M1L4 BA Law/Health Studies
Duration: 3FT Hon

Entry Requirements: *GCE:* 220-260. *SQAH:* AAB-BBBB. *IB:* 24.

M1V1 BA Law/History
Duration: 3FT Hon

Entry Requirements: *GCE:* 220-260. *SQAH:* AAB-BBBB. *IB:* 24.

M1B1 BA Law/Human Bioscience
Duration: 3FT Hon

Entry Requirements: *GCE:* 220-260. *SQAH:* AAB-BBBB. *IB:* 24.

M1L7 BA Law/Human Geography
Duration: 3FT Hon

Entry Requirements: *GCE:* 220-260. *SQAH:* AAB-BBBB. *IB:* 24.

M1N6 BA Law/Human Resource Management
Duration: 3FT Hon

Entry Requirements: *GCE:* 220-260. *SQAH:* AAB-BBBB. *IB:* 24.

M1P5 BA Law/Journalism
Duration: 3FT Hon

Entry Requirements: *GCE:* 220-260. *SQAH:* AAB-BBBB. *IB:* 24.

M1P4 BA Law/Magazine Publishing
Duration: 3FT Hon

Entry Requirements: *GCE:* 220-260. *SQAH:* AAB-BBBB. *IB:* 24.

M1P3 BA Law/Media Studies
Duration: 3FT Hon

Entry Requirements: *GCE:* 220-260. *SQAH:* AAB-BBBB. *IB:* 24.

M1V5 BA Law/Philosophy
Duration: 3FT Hon

Entry Requirements: *GCE:* 220-260. *SQAH:* AAB-BBBB. *IB:* 24.

M1F8 BA Law/Physical Geography
Duration: 3FT Hon

Entry Requirements: *GCE:* 220-260. *SQAH:* AAB-BBBB. *IB:* 24.

M1L2 BA Law/Politics
Duration: 3FT Hon

Entry Requirements: *GCE:* 220-260. *SQAH:* AAB-BBBB. *IB:* 24.

M1PH BA Law/Popular Cultures
Duration: 3FT Hon

Entry Requirements: *GCE:* 220-260. *SQAH:* AAB-BBBB. *IB:* 24.

M1W3 BA Law/Popular Music
Duration: 3FT Hon

Entry Requirements: *GCE:* 220-260. *SQAH:* AAB-BBBB. *IB:* 24.

M1L5 BA Law/Social Care
Duration: 3FT Hon

Entry Requirements: *GCE:* 220-260. *SQAH:* AAB-BBBB. *IB:* 24.

M1N9 BA Law/Social Enterprise Development
Duration: 3FT Hon

Entry Requirements: *GCE:* 220-260. *SQAH:* AAB-BBBB. *IB:* 24.

M1FV BA Law/Wastes Management
Duration: 3FT Hon

Entry Requirements: *GCE:* 220-260. *SQAH:* AAB-BBBB. *IB:* 24.

P4M1 BA Magazine Publishing/Law
Duration: 3FT Hon

Entry Requirements: *GCE:* 220-260. *SQAH:* AAB-BBBB. *IB:* 24.

P3M1 BA Media Studies/Law
Duration: 3FT Hon

Entry Requirements: *GCE:* 220-260. *SQAH:* AAB-BBBB. *IB:* 24.

V5M1 BA Philosophy/Law
Duration: 3FT Hon

Entry Requirements: *GCE:* 220-260. *SQAH:* AAB-BBBB. *IB:* 24.

L2M1 BA Politics/Law
Duration: 3FT Hon

Entry Requirements: *GCE:* 220-260. *SQAH:* AAB-BBBB. *IB:* 24.

P3MC BA Popular Cultures/Law
Duration: 3FT Hon

Entry Requirements: *GCE:* 220-260. *SQAH:* AAB-BBBB. *IB:* 24.

C8M1 BA Psychology/Law
Duration: 3FT Hon

Entry Requirements: *GCE:* 220-260. *SQAH:* AAB-BBBB. *IB:* 24.

N2MC BA Social Enterprise Development/Law
Duration: 3FT Hon

Entry Requirements: *GCE:* 220-260. *SQAH:* AAB-BBBB. *IB:* 24.

C1M1 BSc Biological Conservation/Law
Duration: 3FT Hon

Entry Requirements: *GCE:* 220-260. *SQAH:* AAB-BBBB. *IB:* 24.

G5M1 BSc Business Computing Systems/Law
Duration: 3FT Hon

Entry Requirements: *GCE:* 220-260. *SQAH:* AAB-BBBB. *IB:* 24.

B1M1 BSc Human Bioscience/Law
Duration: 3FT Hon

Entry Requirements: *GCE:* 220-260. *SQAH:* AAB-BBBB. *IB:* 24.

G1M1 BSc Mathematics/Law
Duration: 3FT Hon

Entry Requirements: *GCE:* 220-260. *SQAH:* AAB-BBBB. *IB:* 24.

F8M1 BSc Physical Geography/Law
Duration: 3FT Hon

Entry Requirements: *GCE:* 220-260. *SQAH:* AAB-BBBB. *IB:* 24.

F8MC BSc Wastes Management/Law
Duration: 3FT Hon

Entry Requirements: *GCE:* 220-260. *SQAH:* AAB-BBBB. *IB:* 24.

N91 NOTTINGHAM TRENT UNIVERSITY
DRYDEN CENTRE
BURTON STREET
NOTTINGHAM NG1 4BU
t: +44 (0) 115 941 8418 **f:** +44 (0) 115 848 6063
e: admissions@ntu.ac.uk

// www.ntu.ac.uk/

M102 LLB Law and Professional Practice
Duration: 4SW Hon

Entry Requirements: HND required.

O66 OXFORD BROOKES UNIVERSITY
ADMISSIONS OFFICE
HEADINGTON CAMPUS
GIPSY LANE
OXFORD OX3 0BP
t: 01865 483040 f: 01865 483983
e: admissions@brookes.ac.uk
// www.brookes.ac.uk

LM71 BA/BSc Geography/Law
Duration: 3FT Hon
Entry Requirements: GCE: AAB.

MV11 BA/BSc History/Law
Duration: 3FT Hon
Entry Requirements: GCE: BBC.

MV15 BA/BSc Law/Philosophy
Duration: 3FT Hon
Entry Requirements: GCE: BBB.

ML12 BA/BSc Law/Politics
Duration: 3FT Hon
Entry Requirements: GCE: BBB.

MY10 BSc/BA Combined Studies/Law
Duration: 3FT Hon
Entry Requirements: Contact the institution for details.

P55 PETERBOROUGH REGIONAL COLLEGE
PARK CRESCENT
PETERBOROUGH PE1 4DZ
t: 0845 8728722 f: 01733 767986
e: info@peterborough.ac.uk
// www.peterborough.ac.uk

MV11 BA History and Law
Duration: 3FT Hon
Entry Requirements: Interview required.

P60 UNIVERSITY OF PLYMOUTH
DRAKE CIRCUS
PLYMOUTH PL4 8AA
t: 01752 588037 f: 01752 588050
e: admissions@plymouth.ac.uk
// www.plymouth.ac.uk

L2MF BSc International Relations with Law
Duration: 3FT Hon
Entry Requirements: GCE: E.

M2LF BSc Law with International Relations
Duration: 3FT Hon
Entry Requirements: GCE: 300. IB: 32.

M2L2 BSc Law with Politics
Duration: 3FT Hon
Entry Requirements: GCE: 300. IB: 32.

P80 UNIVERSITY OF PORTSMOUTH
ACADEMIC REGISTRY
UNIVERSITY HOUSE
WINSTON CHURCHILL AVENUE
PORTSMOUTH PO1 2UP
t: 023 9284 8484 f: 023 9284 3082
e: admissions@port.ac.uk
// www.port.ac.uk

MR39 LLB Law and European Studies
Duration: 3FT/4SW Hon
Entry Requirements: GCE: 260.

ML12 LLB Law and International Relations
Duration: 3FT/4SW Hon
Entry Requirements: GCE: 160.

Q50 QUEEN MARY, UNIVERSITY OF LONDON
MILE END ROAD
LONDON E1 4NS
t: 020 7882 5555 f: 020 7882 5500
e: admissions@qmul.ac.uk
// www.qmul.ac.uk

ML12 BA Law and Politics
Duration: 3FT Hon
Entry Requirements: GCE: AAB. SQAH: AAAAB. SQAAH: AAB. IB: 36. BTEC NC: DD. BTEC ND: DDD.

Q75 QUEEN'S UNIVERSITY BELFAST
UNIVERSITY ROAD
BELFAST BT7 1NN
t: 028 9097 2727 f: 028 9097 2828
e: admissions@qub.ac.uk
// www.qub.ac.uk

M1L2 LLB Law with Politics
Duration: 3FT Hon
Entry Requirements: GCE: AAA-AABa. SQAH: AAAAB. SQAAH: AAA. IB: 36.

S09 SCHOOL OF ORIENTAL AND AFRICAN STUDIES (UNIVERSITY OF LONDON)

THORNHAUGH STREET
RUSSELL SQUARE
LONDON WC1H 0XG

t: 020 7074 5106 f: 020 7898 4039
e: undergradadmissions@soas.ac.uk
// www.soas.ac.uk

VM31 BA History of Art/Archaeology and Law

Duration: 3FT Hon

Entry Requirements: *GCE:* AAA. *SQAH:* AAAAA. *SQAAH:* AAA. *IB:* 38. *BTEC ND:* DDD.

LM91 BA Law and Development Studies

Duration: 3FT Hon

Entry Requirements: *GCE:* AAA. *SQAH:* AAAAA. *SQAAH:* AAA. *IB:* 38. *BTEC ND:* DDD.

LM71 BA Law and Geography

Duration: 3FT Hon

Entry Requirements: *GCE:* AAA. *SQAH:* AAAAA. *SQAAH:* AAA. *IB:* 38. *BTEC ND:* DDD.

MV11 BA Law and History

Duration: 3FT Hon

Entry Requirements: *GCE:* AAA. *SQAH:* AAAAA. *SQAAH:* AAA. *IB:* 38. *BTEC ND:* DDD.

TMJC BA Law and South-East Asian Studies

Duration: 3FT Hon

Entry Requirements: *GCE:* AAA. *SQAH:* AAAAA. *SQAAH:* AAA. *IB:* 38. *BTEC ND:* DDD.

TM61 BA Middle Eastern Studies and Law

Duration: 3FT Hon

Entry Requirements: *GCE:* AAA. *SQAH:* AAAAA. *SQAAH:* AAA. *IB:* 38. *BTEC ND:* DDD.

LM21 BA Politics and Law

Duration: 3FT Hon

Entry Requirements: *GCE:* AAA. *SQAH:* AAAAA. *SQAAH:* AAA. *IB:* 38. *BTEC ND:* DDD.

TMH1 BA South Asian Studies and Law

Duration: 3FT Hon

Entry Requirements: *GCE:* AAA. *SQAH:* AAAAA. *SQAAH:* AAA. *IB:* 38. *BTEC ND:* DDD.

MV16 BA Study of Religions and Law

Duration: 3FT Hon

Entry Requirements: *GCE:* AAA. *SQAH:* AAAAA. *SQAAH:* AAA. *IB:* 38. *BTEC ND:* DDD.

S21 SHEFFIELD HALLAM UNIVERSITY

CITY CAMPUS
HOWARD STREET
SHEFFIELD S1 1WB

t: 0114 225 5555 f: 0114 225 2167
e: admissions@shu.ac.uk
// www.shu.ac.uk

MC18 BSc Psychology and Law

Duration: 4FT Hon

Entry Requirements: *GCE:* 260.

S30 SOUTHAMPTON SOLENT UNIVERSITY

EAST PARK TERRACE
SOUTHAMPTON
HAMPSHIRE SO14 0RT

t: +44 (0) 23 8031 9039 f: + 44 (0)23 8022 2259
e: admissions@solent.ac.uk or ask@solent.ac.uk
// www.solent.ac.uk/

M190 LLB LLB (Hons) with European Studies

Duration: 3FT Hon

Entry Requirements: *GCE:* 220. *BTEC NC:* MM. *BTEC ND:* PPP.

M1N6 LLB LLB (Hons) with Human Resource Management

Duration: 3FT Hon

Entry Requirements: *GCE:* 220. *BTEC NC:* MM. *BTEC ND:* PPP.

S72 STAFFORDSHIRE UNIVERSITY

COLLEGE ROAD
STOKE ON TRENT ST4 2DE

t: 01782 292753 f: 01782 292740
e: admissions@staffs.ac.uk
// www.staffs.ac.uk

M292 LLB Clinical Advice Work

Duration: 3FT Hon

Entry Requirements: *GCE:* 160-200. *IB:* 24.

M111 LLB Law with a Foundation Year

Duration: 4FT Hon

Entry Requirements: *GCE:* D. *SQAH:* C. *SQAAH:* D. *IB:* 24. *BTEC NC:* PP. *BTEC ND:* PPP. Interview required.

M290 LLB LLB (Advice Work)

Duration: 3FT Hon

Entry Requirements: *GCE:* 180-240. *IB:* 24. *BTEC NC:* MM. *BTEC ND:* MMM.

M1N6 LLB LLB (Human Resource Management)

Duration: 3FT Hon

Entry Requirements: *GCE:* BB-ABB. *SQAAH:* BB-ABB. *IB:* 26. *BTEC NC:* DM. *BTEC ND:* DDM. *OCR ND:* Distinction.

M293 LLB LLB (Sports Law)

Duration: 3FT Hon

Entry Requirements: *GCE:* BB-ABB. *SQAAH:* BB-ABB. *IB:* 26. *BTEC NC:* DM. *BTEC ND:* DDM. *OCR ND:* Distinction.

QM31 LLB LLB with English Literature

Duration: 3FT Hon

Entry Requirements: *GCE:* BB-ABB. *SQAAH:* BB-ABB. *IB:* 26. *BTEC NC:* DM. *BTEC ND:* DDM. *OCR ND:* Distinction.

M1F4 LLB LLB with Forensic Science

Duration: 3FT Hon

Entry Requirements: *GCE:* BB-ABB. *SQAAH:* BB-ABB. *IB:* 26. *BTEC NC:* DM. *BTEC ND:* DDM. *OCR ND:* Distinction.

MV11 LLB LLB with Modern History

Duration: 3FT Hon

Entry Requirements: *GCE:* BB-ABB. *SQAAH:* BB-ABB. *IB:* 26. *BTEC NC:* DM. *BTEC ND:* DDM. *OCR ND:* Distinction.

VM51 LLB LLB with Philosophy

Duration: 3FT Hon

Entry Requirements: *GCE:* BB-ABB. *SQAAH:* BB-ABB. *IB:* 26. *BTEC NC:* DM. *BTEC ND:* DDM. *OCR ND:* Distinction.

MNC2 BA/BSc LLB with Internet Commerce

Duration: 3FT Hon

Entry Requirements: *GCE:* BB-ABB. *SQAAH:* BB-ABB. *IB:* 26. *BTEC NC:* DM. *BTEC ND:* DDM. *OCR ND:* Distinction.

M991 DipHE Advice Work and Law

Duration: 2FT Dip

Entry Requirements: *GCE:* 160-200. *IB:* 24.

S75 THE UNIVERSITY OF STIRLING

STIRLING FK9 4LA
t: 01786 467044 f: 01786 466800
e: admissions@stir.ac.uk
// www.stir.ac.uk

MV11 BA History and Law

Duration: 4FT Hon

Entry Requirements: *GCE:* CCC. *SQAH:* BBBB. *SQAAH:* AAA-CCC. *BTEC ND:* DMM.

MN16 BA Human Resource Management and Law

Duration: 4FT Hon

Entry Requirements: *GCE:* CCC. *SQAH:* BBBB. *SQAAH:* AAA-CCC. *BTEC ND:* DMM.

MN15 BA Law and Marketing

Duration: 4FT Hon

Entry Requirements: *GCE:* BCC. *SQAH:* BBBB. *SQAAH:* AAA-CCC. *BTEC ND:* DMM.

MV15 BA Law and Philosophy

Duration: 5FT Hon

Entry Requirements: *GCE:* CCC. *SQAH:* BBBB. *SQAAH:* AAA-CCC. *BTEC ND:* DMM.

ML12 BA Law and Politics

Duration: 4FT Hon

Entry Requirements: *GCE:* CCC. *SQAH:* BBBB. *SQAAH:* AAA-CCC. *BTEC ND:* DMM.

MC16 BA Law and Sports Studies

Duration: 4FT Hon

Entry Requirements: *GCE:* CCC. *SQAH:* BBBB. *SQAAH:* AAA-CCC. *BTEC ND:* DMM.

S78 THE UNIVERSITY OF STRATHCLYDE

GLASGOW G1 1XQ
t: 0141 552 4400 f: 0141 552 0775
// www.strath.ac.uk

QM31 BA English and Law

Duration: 4FT Hon

Entry Requirements: *GCE:* BBC. *SQAH:* ABBB-BBBBC. *IB:* 30.

LM71 BA Geography and Law

Duration: 4FT Hon

Entry Requirements: *GCE:* BBC. *SQAH:* ABBB-BBBBC. *IB:* 30.

VM11 BA History and Law

Duration: 4FT Hon

Entry Requirements: *GCE:* BBC. *SQAH:* ABBB-BBBBC. *IB:* 30.

NM61 BA Human Resource Management and Law

Duration: 4FT Hon

Entry Requirements: *GCE:* BBC. *SQAH:* ABBB-BBBBC. *IB:* 30.

ML12 BA Law and Politics

Duration: 4FT Hon

Entry Requirements: *GCE:* BBC. *SQAH:* ABBB-BBBBC. *IB:* 30.

MC18 BA Law and Psychology

Duration: 4FT Hon

Entry Requirements: *GCE:* BBC. *SQAH:* ABBB-BBBBC. *IB:* 30.

S84 UNIVERSITY OF SUNDERLAND

STUDENT HELPLINE
THE STUDENT GATEWAY
CHESTER ROAD
SUNDERLAND SR1 3SD

t: 0191 515 3000 f: 0191 515 3805
e: student-helpline@sunderland.ac.uk

// www.sunderland.ac.uk

B9M1 BA Community Health with Law
Duration: 3FT Hon

Entry Requirements: *GCE:* 220-360. *BTEC NC:* DM. *BTEC ND:* MMM. *OCR ND:* Distinction. *OCR NED:* Merit.

Q1M1 BA English Language & Linguistics with Law
Duration: 3FT Hon

Entry Requirements: *GCE:* 220-360. *BTEC NC:* DM. *BTEC ND:* MMM. *OCR ND:* Distinction. *OCR NED:* Merit.

MQ1H BA Law and Modern Foreign Language (English)
Duration: 3FT Hon

Entry Requirements: *GCE:* 220-360. *BTEC NC:* DM. *BTEC ND:* MMM. *OCR ND:* Distinction. *OCR NED:* Merit.

MT17 BA Law and American Studies
Duration: 3FT Hon

Entry Requirements: *GCE:* 220-360. *BTEC NC:* DM. *BTEC ND:* MMM. *OCR ND:* Distinction. *OCR NED:* Merit.

MX13 BA Law and Education
Duration: 3FT Hon

Entry Requirements: *GCE:* 220-360. *BTEC NC:* DM. *BTEC ND:* MMM. *OCR ND:* Distinction. *OCR NED:* Merit.

MQ13 BA Law and English
Duration: 3FT Hon

Entry Requirements: *GCE:* 220-360. *BTEC NC:* DM. *BTEC ND:* MMM. *OCR ND:* Distinction. *OCR NED:* Merit.

MV11 BA Law and History
Duration: 3FT Hon

Entry Requirements: *GCE:* 220-360. *BTEC NC:* DM. *BTEC ND:* MMM. *OCR ND:* Distinction. *OCR NED:* Merit.

MP15 BA Law and Journalism
Duration: 3FT Hon

Entry Requirements: *GCE:* 220-360. *BTEC NC:* DM. *BTEC ND:* MMM. *OCR ND:* Distinction. *OCR NED:* Merit.

MP13 BA Law and Media Studies
Duration: 3FT Hon

Entry Requirements: *GCE:* 220-360. *BTEC NC:* DM. *BTEC ND:* MMM. *OCR ND:* Distinction. *OCR NED:* Merit.

LM21 BA Law and Politics
Duration: 3FT Hon

Entry Requirements: *GCE:* 220-360. *BTEC NC:* DM. *BTEC ND:* MMM. *OCR ND:* Distinction. *OCR NED:* Merit.

MX11 BA Law and TESOL
Duration: 3FT Hon

Entry Requirements: *GCE:* 220-360. *BTEC NC:* DM. *BTEC ND:* MMM. *OCR ND:* Distinction. *OCR NED:* Merit.

M1T7 BA Law with American Studies
Duration: 3FT Hon

Entry Requirements: *GCE:* 220-360. *BTEC NC:* DM. *BTEC ND:* MMM. *OCR ND:* Distinction. *OCR NED:* Merit.

M1X3 BA Law with Education
Duration: 3FT Hon

Entry Requirements: *GCE:* 220-360. *BTEC NC:* DM. *BTEC ND:* MMM. *OCR ND:* Distinction. *OCR NED:* Merit.

M1V1 BA Law with History
Duration: 3FT Hon

Entry Requirements: *GCE:* 220-360. *BTEC NC:* DM. *BTEC ND:* MMM. *OCR ND:* Distinction. *OCR NED:* Merit.

M1P5 BA Law with Journalism
Duration: 3FT Hon

Entry Requirements: *GCE:* 220-360. *BTEC NC:* DM. *BTEC ND:* MMM. *OCR ND:* Distinction. *OCR NED:* Merit.

M1N5 BA Law with Marketing Management
Duration: 3FT Hon

Entry Requirements: *GCE:* 220-360. *BTEC NC:* DM. *BTEC ND:* MMM. *OCR ND:* Distinction. *OCR NED:* Merit.

M1P3 BA Law with Media Studies
Duration: 3FT Hon

Entry Requirements: *GCE:* 220-360. *BTEC NC:* DM. *BTEC ND:* MMM. *OCR ND:* Distinction. *OCR NED:* Merit.

M1Q3 BA Law with Modern Foreign Languages (English)
Duration: 3FT Hon

Entry Requirements: *GCE:* 220-360. *BTEC NC:* DM. *BTEC ND:* MMM. *OCR ND:* Distinction. *OCR NED:* Merit.

M1W6 BA Law with Photography
Duration: 3FT Hon

Entry Requirements: *GCE:* 220-360. *BTEC NC:* DM. *BTEC ND:* MMM. *OCR ND:* Distinction. *OCR NED:* Merit.

M1L2 BA Law with Politics
Duration: 3FT Hon

Entry Requirements: *GCE:* 220-360. *BTEC NC:* DM. *BTEC ND:* MMM. *OCR ND:* Distinction. *OCR NED:* Merit.

M1P2 BA Law with Public Relations
Duration: 3FT Hon

Entry Requirements: *GCE:* 220-360. *BTEC NC:* DM. *BTEC ND:* MMM. *OCR ND:* Distinction. *OCR NED:* Merit.

M1C6 BA Law with Sport
Duration: 3FT Hon

Entry Requirements: *GCE:* 220-360. *BTEC NC:* DM. *BTEC ND:* MMM. *OCR ND:* Distinction. *OCR NED:* Merit.

M1X1 BA Law with TESOL
Duration: 3FT Hon

Entry Requirements: *GCE:* 220-360. *BTEC NC:* DM. *BTEC ND:* MMM. *OCR ND:* Distinction. *OCR NED:* Merit.

M1N8 BA Law with Tourism
Duration: 3FT Hon

Entry Requirements: *GCE:* 220-360. *BTEC NC:* DM. *BTEC ND:* MMM. *OCR ND:* Distinction. *OCR NED:* Merit.

BM91 BA/BSc Law and Community Health
Duration: 3FT Hon

Entry Requirements: *GCE:* 220-360. *BTEC NC:* DM. *BTEC ND:* MMM. *OCR ND:* Distinction. *OCR NED:* Merit.

LM71 BA/BSc Law and Geography
Duration: 3FT Hon

Entry Requirements: *GCE:* 220-360. *BTEC NC:* DM. *BTEC ND:* MMM. *OCR ND:* Distinction. *OCR NED:* Merit.

MN18 BA/BSc Law and Tourism
Duration: 3FT Hon

Entry Requirements: *GCE:* 220-360. *BTEC NC:* DM. *BTEC ND:* MMM. *OCR ND:* Distinction. *OCR NED:* Merit.

M1L7 BA/BSc Law with Geography
Duration: 3FT Hon

Entry Requirements: *GCE:* 220-360. *BTEC NC:* DM. *BTEC ND:* MMM. *OCR ND:* Distinction. *OCR NED:* Merit.

M1C8 BA/BSc Law with Psychology
Duration: 3FT Hon

Entry Requirements: *GCE:* 220-360. *BTEC NC:* DM. *BTEC ND:* MMM. *OCR ND:* Distinction. *OCR NED:* Merit.

CM61 BSc Sport and Law
Duration: 3FT Hon

Entry Requirements: *GCE:* 220-360. *BTEC NC:* DM. *BTEC ND:* MMM. *OCR ND:* Distinction. *OCR NED:* Merit.

S85 UNIVERSITY OF SURREY
STAG HILL
GUILDFORD
SURREY GU2 7XH

t: +44(0)1483 689305 f: +44(0)1483 689388
e: admissions@surrey.ac.uk

// www.surrey.ac.uk

M1T9 LLB Law with International Studies (4 years)
Duration: 3FT/4SW Hon

Entry Requirements: *GCE:* ABB.

S90 UNIVERSITY OF SUSSEX
UNDERGRADUATE ADMISSIONS
SUSSEX HOUSE
UNIVERSITY OF SUSSEX
BRIGHTON BN1 9RH

t: 01273 678416 f: 01273 678545
e: ug.applicants@sussex.ac.uk

// www.sussex.ac.uk

M1TT LLB Law with American Studies
Duration: 3FT Hon

Entry Requirements: *GCE:* AAB-ABB. *SQAH:* AAABB-AABBB.

M1TP LLB Law with American Studies (4 years)
Duration: 4FT Hon

Entry Requirements: *GCE:* AAB-ABB. *SQAH:* AAABB-AABBB.

M1RX LLB Law with Contemporary European Studies
Duration: 3FT Hon

Entry Requirements: *GCE:* AAB-ABB. *SQAH:* AAABB-AABBB.

M1L2 LLB Law with International Relations
Duration: 3FT Hon

Entry Requirements: *GCE:* AAB-ABB. *SQAH:* AAABB-AABBB.

M1L1 LLB Law with Politics
Duration: 3FT Hon

Entry Requirements: *GCE:* AAB-ABB. *SQAH:* AAABB-AABBB.

S93 SWANSEA UNIVERSITY

SINGLETON PARK
SWANSEA SA2 8PP
t: 01792 295111 f: 01792 295110
e: admissions@swansea.ac.uk
// www.swansea.ac.uk

MT17 LLB Law and American Studies

Duration: 3FT Hon

Entry Requirements: *GCE:* 240-300.

MT1R LLB Law and American Studies (with an Intercalary Year) (4 years)

Duration: 4FT Hon

Entry Requirements: *GCE:* 240-300.

MVC1 LLB Law and History

Duration: 3FT Hon

Entry Requirements: *GCE:* 260-300.

LM21 LLB Law and Politics

Duration: 3FT Hon

Entry Requirements: *GCE:* 260-340.

CM8C BSc Psychology and Law

Duration: 3FT Hon

Entry Requirements: *GCE:* 300-320.

T20 UNIVERSITY OF TEESSIDE

MIDDLESBROUGH TS1 3BA
t: 01642 218121 f: 01642 384201
e: registry@tees.ac.uk
// www.tees.ac.uk

M1L2 LLB Law with Politics

Duration: 3FT Hon

Entry Requirements: Contact the institution for details.

ML93 BSc Death Investigation

Duration: 3FT Hon

Entry Requirements: *GCE:* 240.

U20 UNIVERSITY OF ULSTER

COLERAINE
CO. LONDONDERRY
NORTHERN IRELAND BT52 1SA
t: 028 7032 4221 f: 028 7032 4908
e: online@ulster.ac.uk
// www.ulster.ac.uk

M1N6 LLB Law with Human Resource Management

Duration: 3FT Hon

Entry Requirements: *GCE:* ABB. *SQAH:* AAABC. *SQAAH:* ABB. *IB:* 26. *BTEC ND:* DDM.

M1LF LLB Law with International Politics

Duration: 3FT Hon

Entry Requirements: *GCE:* ABB. *SQAH:* AAABC. *SQAAH:* ABB. *IB:* 26. *BTEC ND:* DDM.

M1N5 LLB Law with Marketing

Duration: 3FT Hon

Entry Requirements: *GCE:* ABB. *SQAH:* AAABC. *SQAAH:* ABB. *IB:* 26. *BTEC ND:* DDM.

M1LG LLB Law with Politics

Duration: 3FT Hon

Entry Requirements: *GCE:* ABB. *SQAH:* AAABC. *SQAAH:* ABB. *IB:* 26. *BTEC ND:* DDM.

W75 UNIVERSITY OF WOLVERHAMPTON

ADMISSIONS UNIT
MX207, CAMP STREET
WOLVERHAMPTON
WEST MIDLANDS WV1 1AD
t: 01902 321000 f: 01902 321896
e: admissions@wlv.ac.uk
// www.wlv.ac.uk

M290 LLB Advice Work

Duration: 3FT Hon

Entry Requirements: HND required.

MT17 BA American Studies and Law

Duration: 3FT Hon

Entry Requirements: *GCE:* 160-220. *IB:* 28.

BM61 BA Deaf Studies and Law

Duration: 3FT Hon

Entry Requirements: *GCE:* 160-220.

QM31 BA English and Law

Duration: 3FT Hon

Entry Requirements: *GCE:* 160-220.

NM61 BA Human Resource Management and Law

Duration: 3FT Hon

Entry Requirements: *GCE:* 160-220. *IB:* 28.

CM81 BA Psychology and Law

Duration: 3FT Hon

Entry Requirements: *GCE:* 220-240. *IB:* 28.

NM81 BA Tourism Management and Law

Duration: 3FT Hon

Entry Requirements: *GCE:* 160-220. *IB:* 28.

GM4D BA/BSc Multimedia Applications Development and Law

Duration: 3FT Hon

Entry Requirements: *GCE:* 160-220.

FM41 BSc Forensic Science and Law

Duration: 3FT Hon

Entry Requirements: *GCE:* 160-220.

W76 UNIVERSITY OF WINCHESTER

WINCHESTER
HANTS SO22 4NR
t: 01962 827234 f: 01962 827288
e: course.enquiries@winchester.ac.uk
// www.winchester.ac.uk

NM41 BA Accounting and Law

Duration: 3FT Hon

Entry Requirements: *Foundation:* Distinction. *GCE:* 260-300. *IB:* 26. *BTEC NC:* DD. *BTEC ND:* MMM. *OCR ND:* Distinction.

LM51 BA Childhood, Youth & Community Studies and Law

Duration: 3FT Hon

Entry Requirements: *Foundation:* Pass. *GCE:* 220-260. *IB:* 26. *BTEC NC:* DD. *BTEC ND:* MMP. *OCR ND:* Distinction.

NM81 BA Event Management and Law

Duration: 3FT Hon

Entry Requirements: *GCE:* 240-280. *IB:* 24.

WM61 BA Film & Cinema Technologies and Law

Duration: 3FT Hon

Entry Requirements: *GCE:* 240-280. *IB:* 24.

MV14 BA Law and Archaeology

Duration: 3FT Hon

Entry Requirements: *Foundation:* Pass. *GCE:* 220-260. *IB:* 26. *BTEC NC:* DD. *BTEC ND:* MMP. *OCR ND:* Distinction.

MX13 BA Law and Education Studies

Duration: 3FT Hon

Entry Requirements: *Foundation:* Pass. *GCE:* 220-260. *IB:* 26. *BTEC NC:* DD. *BTEC ND:* MMP. *OCR ND:* Distinction.

MX1H BA Law and Education Studies (Early Childhood)

Duration: 3FT Hon

Entry Requirements: *Foundation:* Merit. *GCE:* 220-260. *IB:* 24. *BTEC NC:* DM. *BTEC ND:* MMP.

MQ13 BA Law and English

Duration: 3FT Hon

Entry Requirements: *Foundation:* Pass. *GCE:* 220-260. *IB:* 26. *BTEC NC:* DD. *BTEC ND:* MMP. *OCR ND:* Distinction.

MV16 BA Law and Ethics & Spirituality

Duration: 3FT Hon

Entry Requirements: *Foundation:* Pass. *GCE:* 220-260. *IB:* 26. *BTEC NC:* DD. *BTEC ND:* MMP. *OCR ND:* Distinction.

MP13 BA Law and Film Studies

Duration: 3FT Hon

Entry Requirements: *Foundation:* Pass. *GCE:* 220-260. *IB:* 26. *BTEC NC:* DD. *BTEC ND:* MMP. *OCR ND:* Distinction.

MV11 BA Law and History

Duration: 3FT Hon

Entry Requirements: *Foundation:* Pass. *GCE:* 220-260. *IB:* 26. *BTEC NC:* DD. *BTEC ND:* MMP. *OCR ND:* Distinction.

MP15 BA Law and Journalism

Duration: 3FT Hon

Entry Requirements: *Foundation:* Pass. *GCE:* 220-260. *IB:* 26. *BTEC NC:* DD. *BTEC ND:* MMP. *OCR ND:* Distinction.

MP1H BA Law and Media Production

Duration: 3FT Hon

Entry Requirements: *Foundation:* Pass. *GCE:* 220-260. *IB:* 26. *BTEC NC:* DD. *BTEC ND:* MMP. *OCR ND:* Distinction.

MPC3 BA Law and Media Studies

Duration: 3FT Hon

Entry Requirements: *Foundation:* Pass. *GCE:* 220-260. *IB:* 26. *BTEC NC:* DD. *BTEC ND:* MMP. *OCR ND:* Distinction.

MW1X BA Law and Modern Liberal Arts

Duration: 3FT Hon

Entry Requirements: *Foundation:* Distinction. *GCE:* 260-300. *IB:* 26. *BTEC NC:* DD. *BTEC ND:* MMM. *OCR ND:* Distinction.

MW1K BA Law and Performing Arts
Duration: 3FT Hon

Entry Requirements: *Foundation:* Pass. *GCE:* 220-260. *IB:* 26. *BTEC NC:* DD. *BTEC ND:* MMP. *OCR ND:* Distinction.

ML12 BA Law and Politics & Global Studies
Duration: 3FT Hon

Entry Requirements: *Foundation:* Pass. *GCE:* 220-260. *IB:* 26. *BTEC NC:* DD. *BTEC ND:* MMP. *OCR ND:* Distinction.

MC18 BA Law and Psychology
Duration: 3FT Hon

Entry Requirements: *Foundation:* Pass. *GCE:* 220-260. *IB:* 26. *BTEC NC:* DD. *BTEC ND:* MMP. *OCR ND:* Distinction.

MN1V BA Law and Sports Management
Duration: 3FT Hon

Entry Requirements: *GCE:* 240-280. *IB:* 24.

XM3C DipHE Education Studies (Early Childhood) and Law
Duration: 2FT Dip

Entry Requirements: *Foundation:* Pass. *GCE:* 120. *IB:* 20. *BTEC NC:* MP. *BTEC ND:* PPP.

XM31 DipHE Education Studies and Law
Duration: 2FT Dip

Entry Requirements: *Foundation:* Pass. *GCE:* 120. *IB:* 20. *BTEC NC:* MP. *BTEC ND:* PPP.

QM31 DipHE English and Law
Duration: 2FT Dip

Entry Requirements: *Foundation:* Pass. *GCE:* 120. *IB:* 20. *BTEC NC:* MP. *BTEC ND:* PPP.

NM8C DipHE Event Management and Law
Duration: 2FT Dip

Entry Requirements: *Foundation:* Pass. *GCE:* 120. *IB:* 20. *BTEC NC:* MP. *BTEC ND:* PPP.

PM3C DipHE Film & Cinema Technologies and Law
Duration: 2FT Dip

Entry Requirements: *Foundation:* Pass. *GCE:* 120. *IB:* 20. *BTEC NC:* MP. *BTEC ND:* PPP.

VM11 DipHE History and Law
Duration: 2FT Dip

Entry Requirements: *Foundation:* Pass. *GCE:* 120. *IB:* 20. *BTEC NC:* MP. *BTEC ND:* PPP.

PM51 DipHE Journalism and Law
Duration: 2FT Dip

Entry Requirements: *Foundation:* Pass. *GCE:* 120. *IB:* 20. *BTEC NC:* MP. *BTEC ND:* PPP.

MV1K DipHE Law and Archaeology
Duration: 2FT Dip

Entry Requirements: *Foundation:* Pass. *GCE:* 120. *IB:* 20. *BTEC NC:* MP. *BTEC ND:* PPP.

MPD3 DipHE Law and Media Studies
Duration: 2FT Dip

Entry Requirements: *Foundation:* Pass. *GCE:* 120. *IB:* 20. *BTEC NC:* MP. *BTEC ND:* PPP.

MW19 DipHE Law and Modern Liberal Arts
Duration: 2FT Dip

Entry Requirements: *Foundation:* Pass. *GCE:* 120. *IB:* 20. *BTEC NC:* MP. *BTEC ND:* PPP.

MW1L DipHE Law and Performing Arts
Duration: 3FT Hon

Entry Requirements: *GCE:* 240-280. *IB:* 24.

ML1F DipHE Law and Politics & Global Studies
Duration: 2FT Dip

Entry Requirements: *Foundation:* Pass. *GCE:* 120. *IB:* 20. *BTEC NC:* MP. *BTEC ND:* PPP.

MC1V DipHE Law and Psychology
Duration: 2FT Dip

Entry Requirements: *Foundation:* Pass. *GCE:* 120. *IB:* 20. *BTEC NC:* MP. *BTEC ND:* PPP.

ML1M DipHE Law and Social Care Studies
Duration: 2FT Dip

Entry Requirements: *Foundation:* Pass. *GCE:* 120. *IB:* 20. *BTEC NC:* MP. *BTEC ND:* PPP.

MN18 DipHE Law and Sports Management
Duration: 2FT Dip

Entry Requirements: *Foundation:* Pass. *GCE:* 120. *IB:* 20. *BTEC NC:* MP. *BTEC ND:* PPP.

MC1Q DipHE Law and Sports Studies
Duration: 2FT Dip

Entry Requirements: *Foundation:* Pass. *GCE:* 120. *IB:* 20. *BTEC NC:* MP. *BTEC ND:* PPP.

PATENT LAW

M20 THE UNIVERSITY OF MANCHESTER
OXFORD ROAD
MANCHESTER M13 9PL
t: 0161 275 2077 f: 0161 275 2106
e: ug-admissions@manchester.ac.uk
// www.manchester.ac.uk

F1M2 MChem Chemistry with Patent Law
Duration: 4FT Hon

Entry Requirements: *GCE:* ABB. *SQAH:* AAAAB. *SQAAH:* ABB. *IB:* 35.
BTEC ND: DDD. Interview required.

SCOTTISH LAW

D65 UNIVERSITY OF DUNDEE
DUNDEE DD1 4HN
t: 01382 383838 f: 01382 388150
e: srs@dundee.ac.uk
// www.dundee.ac.uk/admissions/undergraduate

M114 LLB Law (Scots)
Duration: 4FT Hon

Entry Requirements: *GCE:* BBB. *SQAH:* AABB-ABBBB. *IB:* 33.

M114 LLB Law (Scots)
Duration: 4FT Hon

Entry Requirements: *GCE:* BBB. *SQAH:* AABB-ABBBB. *IB:* 33.

M114 LLB Law (Scots)
Duration: 4FT Hon

Entry Requirements: *GCE:* BBB. *SQAH:* AABB-ABBBB. *IB:* 33.

M114 LLB Law (Scots)
Duration: 4FT Hon

Entry Requirements: *GCE:* BBB. *SQAH:* AABB-ABBBB. *IB:* 33.

M114 LLB Law (Scots)
Duration: 4FT Hon

Entry Requirements: *GCE:* BBB. *SQAH:* AABB-ABBBB. *IB:* 33.

M104 LLB Law (Scots) - Accelerated
Duration: 2FT Ord

Entry Requirements: Contact the institution for details.

S78 THE UNIVERSITY OF STRATHCLYDE
GLASGOW G1 1XQ
t: 0141 552 4400 f: 0141 552 0775
// www.strath.ac.uk

M1R1 LLB Law (Scots) with French
Duration: 5FT Hon

Entry Requirements: *GCE:* AAB. *SQAH:* AAAAB. *IB:* 38.

M114 LLB Law(Scots)
Duration: 3FT Deg

Entry Requirements: *GCE:* AAB. *SQAH:* AAAAB. *IB:* 38.

SOCIOLOGY & ANTHROPOLOGY COMBINATIONS

A20 THE UNIVERSITY OF ABERDEEN
UNIVERSITY OFFICE
KING'S COLLEGE
ABERDEEN AB24 3FX
t: +44 (0) 1224 273504 f: +44 (0) 1224 272034
e: sras@abdn.ac.uk
// www.abdn.ac.uk/sras

LM69 MA Anthropology and Legal Studies
Duration: 4FT Hon

Entry Requirements: *GCE:* CCC. *SQAH:* BBBB. *SQAAH:* BCC. *IB:* 28.
BTEC ND: MMM.

A60 ANGLIA RUSKIN UNIVERSITY
BISHOP HALL LANE
CHELMSFORD
ESSEX CM1 1SQ
t: 0845 271 3333 f: 01245 251789
e: answers@anglia.ac.uk
// www.anglia.ac.uk

LM41 BA Social Policy and Law
Duration: 3FT Hon

Entry Requirements: *GCE:* 220-260. *SQAH:* AABC. *SQAAH:* AB. *IB:* 30.

B06 BANGOR UNIVERSITY
BANGOR
GWYNEDD LL57 2DG
t: 01248 382016/2017 f: 01248 370451
e: admissions@bangor.ac.uk
// www.bangor.ac.uk

M1L4 LLB Law with Social Policy
Duration: 3FT Hon

Entry Requirements: *GCE:* 280. *IB:* 28.

B80 UNIVERSITY OF THE WEST OF ENGLAND, BRISTOL

FRENCHAY CAMPUS
COLDHARBOUR LANE
BRISTOL BS16 1QY

t: +44 (0)117 32 83333 f: +44 (0)117 32 82810
e: admissions@uwe.ac.uk
// www.uwe.ac.uk

LM31 BA Law and Sociology

Duration: 3FT Hon

Entry Requirements: *GCE:* 240-300.

C15 CARDIFF UNIVERSITY

PO BOX 927
30-36 NEWPORT ROAD
CARDIFF CF24 0DE

t: 029 2087 9999 f: 029 2087 6138
e: admissions@cardiff.ac.uk
// www.cardiff.ac.uk

ML13 LLB Law and Sociology

Duration: 3FT Hon

Entry Requirements: *GCE:* AAB. *SQAAH:* AAB. *IB:* 35. Interview required.

C30 UNIVERSITY OF CENTRAL LANCASHIRE

PRESTON
LANCS PR1 2HE

t: 01772 201201 f: 01772 894954
e: uadmissions@uclan.ac.uk
// www.uclan.ac.uk

ML13 BA Sociology and Law

Duration: 3FT Hon

Entry Requirements: *GCE:* 220. *IB:* 26. *BTEC NC:* DM. *BTEC ND:* MMP.

C55 UNIVERSITY OF CHESTER

PARKGATE ROAD
CHESTER CH1 4BJ

t: 01244 511000 f: 01244 511300
e: enquiries@chester.ac.uk
// www.chester.ac.uk

ML13 BA Law and Sociology

Duration: 3FT Hon

Entry Requirements: *GCE:* 240. *SQAH:* BBBB. *IB:* 24. *BTEC NC:* DM. *BTEC ND:* MMM.

M1L3 BA Law with Sociology

Duration: 3FT Hon

Entry Requirements: *GCE:* 240. *SQAH:* BBBB. *IB:* 24. *BTEC NC:* DM. *BTEC ND:* MMM.

L3M1 BA Sociology with Law

Duration: 3FT Hon

Entry Requirements: *GCE:* 240. *SQAH:* BBBB. *IB:* 24. *BTEC NC:* DM. *BTEC ND:* MMM.

D39 UNIVERSITY OF DERBY

KEDLESTON ROAD
DERBY DE22 1GB

t: 08701 202330 f: 01332 597724
e: askadmissions@derby.ac.uk
// www.derby.ac.uk

LM31 BA Law and Sociology

Duration: 3FT Hon

Entry Requirements: *Foundation:* Merit. *GCE:* 180-240. *IB:* 26. *BTEC NC:* DM. *BTEC ND:* MMP.

D86 DURHAM UNIVERSITY

DURHAM UNIVERSITY
UNIVERSITY OFFICE
DURHAM DH1 3HP

t: 0191 334 2000 f: 0191 334 6055
e: admissions@durham.ac.uk
// www.durham.ac.uk

L3M1 BA Sociology with Law

Duration: 3FT Hon

Entry Requirements: *GCE:* ABB. *SQAH:* AAABB. *SQAAH:* ABB. *IB:* 34.

E28 UNIVERSITY OF EAST LONDON

DOCKLANDS CAMPUS
UNIVERSITY WAY
LONDON E16 2RD

t: 020 8223 2835 f: 020 8223 2978
e: admiss@uel.ac.uk
// www.uel.ac.uk

LM31 BA Law/Sociology

Duration: 3FT Hon

Entry Requirements: *GCE:* 240. *IB:* 28. *BTEC NC:* DD. *BTEC ND:* MMM.

L3M1 BSc Sociology (Professional Development) with Law

Duration: 3FT Hon

Entry Requirements: *GCE:* 200. *IB:* 24.

E56 THE UNIVERSITY OF EDINBURGH
STUDENT RECRUITMENT & ADMISSIONS
57 GEORGE SQUARE
EDINBURGH EH8 9JU
t: 0131 650 4360 f: 0131 651 1236
e: sra.enquiries@ed.ac.uk
// www.ed.ac.uk/studying/undergraduate/

ML14 LLB Law and Social Policy
Duration: 4FT Hon
Entry Requirements: *GCE:* BBB. *SQAH:* BBBB. *IB:* 34.

ML13 LLB Law and Sociology
Duration: 4FT Hon
Entry Requirements: *GCE:* BBB. *SQAH:* BBBB. *IB:* 34.

M1L6 LLB Law with Social Anthropology
Duration: 4FT Hon
Entry Requirements: *GCE:* BBB. *SQAH:* BBBB. *IB:* 34.

LM41 MA Social Policy and Law
Duration: 4FT Hon
Entry Requirements: *GCE:* BBB. *SQAH:* BBBB. *IB:* 34.

G14 UNIVERSITY OF GLAMORGAN, CARDIFF AND PONTYPRIDD
ENQUIRIES AND ADMISSIONS UNIT
PONTYPRIDD CF37 1DL
t: 0800 716925 f: 01443 654050
e: enquiries@glam.ac.uk
// www.glam.ac.uk

M1L3 BA Law with Sociology
Duration: 3FT Hon
Entry Requirements: HND required.

LM31 BSc Sociology and Law
Duration: 3FT Hon
Entry Requirements: *GCE:* 220-260.

L3M1 BSc Sociology with Law
Duration: 3FT Hon
Entry Requirements: *GCE:* 220-260.

G70 UNIVERSITY OF GREENWICH
GREENWICH CAMPUS
OLD ROYAL NAVAL COLLEGE
PARK ROW
LONDON SE10 9LS
t: 0800 005 006 f: 020 8331 8145
e: courseinfo@gre.ac.uk
// www.gre.ac.uk

ML13 BA Law and Sociology
Duration: 3FT Hon
Entry Requirements: *GCE:* 180. *IB:* 24.

K12 KEELE UNIVERSITY
STAFFS ST5 5BG
t: 01782 734005 f: 01782 632343
e: undergraduate@keele.ac.uk
// www.keele.ac.uk

LM31 BA Law and Sociology
Duration: 3FT Hon
Entry Requirements: *GCE:* 300-320.

M1L3 BA Law with Social Science Foundation Year
Duration: 4FT Hon
Entry Requirements: *GCE:* 160. Interview required.

K24 THE UNIVERSITY OF KENT
INFORMATION, RECRUITMENT & ADMISSIONS
REGISTRY
UNIVERSITY OF KENT
CANTERBURY. KENT CT2 7NZ
t: 01227 827272 f: 01227 827077
e: information@kent.ac.uk
// www.kent.ac.uk

LM31 BA Law and Sociology
Duration: 3FT Hon
Entry Requirements: *GCE:* 320. *SQAH:* AAAAA. *IB:* 34. *BTEC NC:* DD. *BTEC ND:* DDM.

K84 KINGSTON UNIVERSITY
STUDENT INFORMATION & ADVICE CENTRE
COOPER HOUSE
40-46 SURBITON ROAD
KINGSTON UPON THAMES KT1 2HX
t: 020 8547 7053 f: 020 8547 7080
e: aps@kingston.ac.uk
// www.kingston.ac.uk

MLC3 BSc Law and Sociology
Duration: 3FT Hon
Entry Requirements: *GCE:* 280-320.

L3MC BSc Sociology with Law

Duration: 3FT Hon

Entry Requirements: *GCE:* 220-320.

L68 LONDON METROPOLITAN UNIVERSITY

166-220 HOLLOWAY ROAD
LONDON N7 8DB
t: 020 7133 4200
e: admissions@londonmet.ac.uk
// www.londonmet.ac.uk

ML14 BA/BSc Law and Social Policy

Duration: 3FT Hon

Entry Requirements: *GCE:* 240. *IB:* 28.

MLC3 BA/BSc Law and Sociology

Duration: 3FT Hon

Entry Requirements: *GCE:* 240. *IB:* 28.

L72 LONDON SCHOOL OF ECONOMICS AND POLITICAL SCIENCE (UNIVERSITY OF LONDON)

HOUGHTON STREET
LONDON WC2A 2AE
t: 020 7955 7125/7769 f: 020 7955 6001
e: ug-admissions@lse.ac.uk
// www.lse.ac.uk

ML16 BA Anthropology and Law

Duration: 3FT Hon

Entry Requirements: *GCE:* ABB. *SQAH:* AAABB-AABBB. *SQAAH:* ABB. *IB:* 37.

L75 LONDON SOUTH BANK UNIVERSITY

103 BOROUGH ROAD
LONDON SE1 0AA
t: 020 7815 7815 f: 020 7815 8273
e: enquiry@lsbu.ac.uk
// www.lsbu.ac.uk

M1L3 LLB Law with Sociology

Duration: 3FT Hon

Entry Requirements: *GCE:* 240. *IB:* 24.

L4M1 BSc Social Policy with Law

Duration: 3FT Hon

Entry Requirements: *GCE:* 240. *IB:* 24.

L3M1 BSc Sociology with Law

Duration: 3FT Hon

Entry Requirements: *GCE:* 240. *IB:* 24.

N37 UNIVERSITY OF WALES, NEWPORT

CAERLEON CAMPUS
PO BOX 101
NEWPORT
SOUTH WALES NP18 3YH
t: 01633 432030 f: 01633 432850
e: admissions@newport.ac.uk
// www.newport.ac.uk

LM32 BA Sociology and Youth Justice

Duration: 3FT Hon

Entry Requirements: *GCE:* 240. *IB:* 24. Interview required.

N38 UNIVERSITY OF NORTHAMPTON

PARK CAMPUS
BOUGHTON GREEN ROAD
NORTHAMPTON NN2 7AL
t: 0800 358 2232 f: 01604 722083
e: admissions@northampton.ac.uk
// www.northampton.ac.uk

M1L3 BA Law/Sociology

Duration: 3FT Hon

Entry Requirements: *GCE:* 220-260. *SQAH:* AAB-BBBB. *IB:* 24.

L3M1 BA Sociology/Law

Duration: 3FT Hon

Entry Requirements: *GCE:* 220-260. *SQAH:* AAB-BBBB. *IB:* 24.

O66 OXFORD BROOKES UNIVERSITY

ADMISSIONS OFFICE
HEADINGTON CAMPUS
GIPSY LANE
OXFORD OX3 0BP
t: 01865 483040 f: 01865 483983
e: admissions@brookes.ac.uk
// www.brookes.ac.uk

LM61 BA/BSc Anthropology/Law

Duration: 3FT Hon

Entry Requirements: *GCE:* BBB.

LM31 BA/BSc Law/Sociology

Duration: 3FT Hon

Entry Requirements: *GCE:* AAB.

P55 PETERBOROUGH REGIONAL COLLEGE
PARK CRESCENT
PETERBOROUGH PE1 4DZ

t: 0845 8728722 **f:** 01733 767986
e: info@peterborough.ac.uk
// www.peterborough.ac.uk

ML13 BA Law and Sociology
Duration: 3FT Hon

Entry Requirements: Interview required.

P60 UNIVERSITY OF PLYMOUTH
DRAKE CIRCUS
PLYMOUTH PL4 8AA

t: 01752 588037 **f:** 01752 588050
e: admissions@plymouth.ac.uk
// www.plymouth.ac.uk

M2L3 BSc Law with Sociology
Duration: 3FT Hon

Entry Requirements: *GCE:* 300. *IB:* 32.

L3MF BSc Sociology with Law
Duration: 3FT Hon

Entry Requirements: *GCE:* 260-300. *IB:* 28.

S09 SCHOOL OF ORIENTAL AND AFRICAN STUDIES (UNIVERSITY OF LONDON)
THORNHAUGH STREET
RUSSELL SQUARE
LONDON WC1H 0XG

t: 020 7074 5106 **f:** 020 7898 4039
e: undergradadmissions@soas.ac.uk
// www.soas.ac.uk

LM61 BA Social Anthropology and Law
Duration: 3FT Hon

Entry Requirements: *GCE:* AAA. *SQAH:* AAAAA. *SQAAH:* AAA. *IB:* 38. *BTEC ND:* DDD.

S72 STAFFORDSHIRE UNIVERSITY
COLLEGE ROAD
STOKE ON TRENT ST4 2DE

t: 01782 292753 **f:** 01782 292740
e: admissions@staffs.ac.uk
// www.staffs.ac.uk

LM31 LLB LLB with Sociology
Duration: 3FT Hon

Entry Requirements: *GCE:* BB-ABB. *SQAAH:* BB-ABB. *IB:* 26. *BTEC NC:* DM. *BTEC ND:* DDM. *OCR ND:* Distinction.

S75 THE UNIVERSITY OF STIRLING
STIRLING FK9 4LA

t: 01786 467044 **f:** 01786 466800
e: admissions@stir.ac.uk
// www.stir.ac.uk

ML14 BA Law and Social Policy
Duration: 4FT Hon

Entry Requirements: *GCE:* CCC. *SQAH:* BBBB. *SQAAH:* AAA-CCC. *BTEC ND:* DMM.

ML13 BA Law and Sociology
Duration: 4FT Hon

Entry Requirements: *GCE:* CCC. *SQAH:* BBBB. *SQAAH:* AAA-CCC. *BTEC ND:* DMM.

S78 THE UNIVERSITY OF STRATHCLYDE
GLASGOW G1 1XQ

t: 0141 552 4400 **f:** 0141 552 0775
// www.strath.ac.uk

ML13 BA Law and Sociology
Duration: 4FT Hon

Entry Requirements: *GCE:* BBC. *SQAH:* ABBB-BBBBC. *IB:* 30.

S84 UNIVERSITY OF SUNDERLAND
STUDENT HELPLINE
THE STUDENT GATEWAY
CHESTER ROAD
SUNDERLAND SR1 3SD

t: 0191 515 3000 **f:** 0191 515 3805
e: student-helpline@sunderland.ac.uk
// www.sunderland.ac.uk

LM31 BA Law and Sociology
Duration: 3FT Hon

Entry Requirements: *GCE:* 220-360. *BTEC NC:* DM. *BTEC ND:* MMM. *OCR ND:* Distinction. *OCR NED:* Merit.

M1L3 BA Law with Sociology
Duration: 3FT Hon

Entry Requirements: *GCE:* 220-360. *BTEC NC:* DM. *BTEC ND:* MMM. *OCR ND:* Distinction. *OCR NED:* Merit.

S90 UNIVERSITY OF SUSSEX

UNDERGRADUATE ADMISSIONS
SUSSEX HOUSE
UNIVERSITY OF SUSSEX
BRIGHTON BN1 9RH

t: 01273 678416 f: 01273 678545
e: ug.applicants@sussex.ac.uk

// www.sussex.ac.uk

M1L6 LLB Law with Anthropology

Duration: 3FT Hon

Entry Requirements: *GCE:* AAB-ABB. *SQAH:* AAABB-AABBB.

W20 THE UNIVERSITY OF WARWICK

COVENTRY CV4 8UW

t: 024 7652 3723 f: 024 7652 4649
e: ugadmissions@warwick.ac.uk

// www.warwick.ac.uk

ML13 BA Law and Sociology (4 years)

Duration: 4FT Hon

Entry Requirements: *GCE:* ABBc. *SQAAH:* ABB. *IB:* 36. *OCR ND:* Distinction.

W75 UNIVERSITY OF WOLVERHAMPTON

ADMISSIONS UNIT
MX207, CAMP STREET
WOLVERHAMPTON
WEST MIDLANDS WV1 1AD

t: 01902 321000 f: 01902 321896
e: admissions@wlv.ac.uk

// www.wlv.ac.uk

LM41 BA Social Policy and Law

Duration: 3FT Hon

Entry Requirements: *GCE:* 160-220. *IB:* 28.

LM42 BA Social Policy and Social Welfare Law

Duration: 3FT Hon

Entry Requirements: *GCE:* 160-220. *IB:* 28.

ML23 BA Social Welfare Law and Sociology

Duration: 3FT Hon

Entry Requirements: *GCE:* 160-220.

LM31 BA Sociology and Law

Duration: 3FT Hon

Entry Requirements: *GCE:* 160-220. *IB:* 24.

W76 UNIVERSITY OF WINCHESTER

WINCHESTER
HANTS SO22 4NR

t: 01962 827234 f: 01962 827288
e: course.enquiries@winchester.ac.uk

// www.winchester.ac.uk

ML13 BA Law and Sociology

Duration: 3FT Hon

Entry Requirements: *GCE:* 240-280. *IB:* 24.

ML1H DipHE Law and Sociology

Duration: 2FT Dip

Entry Requirements: *Foundation:* Pass. *GCE:* 120. *IB:* 20. *BTEC NC:* MP. *BTEC ND:* PPP.

PS